Writing on the Edge

Writing on the Edge

Paul's Use of Hyperbole in Galatians

by
CHARLES E. CRUISE

◥PICKWICK *Publications* • Eugene, Oregon

WRITING ON THE EDGE
Paul's Use of Hyperbole in Galatians

Copyright © 2019 Charles E. Cruise All rights reserved. Except for brief quotations in critical publications or reviews, no part of this book may be reproduced in any manner without prior written permission from the publisher. Write: Permissions, Wipf and Stock Publishers, 199 W. 8th Ave., Suite 3, Eugene, OR 97401.

Pickwick Publications
An Imprint of Wipf and Stock Publishers
199 W. 8th Ave., Suite 3
Eugene, OR 97401

www.wipfandstock.com

PAPERBACK ISBN: 978-1-5326-4732-1
HARDCOVER ISBN: 978-1-5326-4733-8
EBOOK ISBN: 978-1-5326-4734-5

Cataloguing-in-Publication data:

Names: Cruise, Charles E., author.

Title: Writing on the edge : Paul's use of hyperbole in Galatians / by Charles E. Cruise.

Description: Eugene, OR : Pickwick Publications, 2019 | Includes bibliographical references and indexes.

Identifiers: ISBN 978-1-5326-4732-1 (paperback) | ISBN 978-1-5326-4733-8 (hardcover) | ISBN 978-1-5326-4734-5 (ebook)

Subjects: LCSH: Bible. Galatians—Criticism, interpretation, etc. | Paul, the Apostle, Saint. | Hyperbole.

Classification: LCC BS2685.5 C78 2019 (print) | LCC BS2685.5 (ebook)

Manufactured in the U.S.A. 01/28/19

Scripture quotations are from the ESV® Bible (The Holy Bible, English Standard Version®), copyright © 2001 by Crossway, a publishing ministry of Good News Publishers. Used by permission. All rights reserved.

To Laura

Contents

Abbreviations | ix
Introduction | xi

Part I: Paul's Seeming Ambivalence toward the Law
1. Paul as Dead to the Law (Galatians) | 3
2. Paul as a Torah-Observant Jew (Romans, Acts) | 18
3. Toward a Solution | 35

Part II: Hyperbole: Definitions and Rhetoric
4. The Nature of Hyperbole | 69
5. The Rhetoric of Hyperbole | 91

Part III: Biblical Hyperbole
6. A Method for Detecting Biblical Hyperbole | 121
7. Hyperbole in the Old Testament | 130
8. Hyperbole in the New Testament | 144

Part IV: Hyperbole in Galatians
9. Paul's Vilification of His Opponents | 175
10. Paul's Denigration of the Law | 210
11. Paul's Magnification of the Consequences of Circumcision | 232
12. A Fresh Perspective on Galatians | 248

Bibliography | 251
Scripture Index | 265
Subject Index | 277

Abbreviations

AB	Anchor Bible
ANF	*Ante-Nicene Fathers*
BDAG	Baur, Danker, Arndt, and Gingrich. *Greek-English Lexicon of the New Testament and Other Early Christian Literature*
BECNT	Baker Evangelical Commentary on the New Testament
BJRL	*Bulletin of the John Rylands University Library of Manchester*
CBQ	*Catholic Biblical Quarterly*
De or.	Cicero, *De oratore*
Eloc.	Demetrius, *De elocutione*
Gorg.	Plato, *Gorgias*
ICC	International Critical Commentary
Inst.	Quintilian, *Institutio oratoria*
Inv.	Cicero, *De inventione rhetorica*
JBL	*Journal of Biblical Literature*
JSNT	*Journal for the Study of the New Testament*
JSNTSup	Journal for the Study of the New Testament: Supplement Series
JSOTSup	Journal for the Study of the Old Testament: Supplement Series
KD	*Kerygma and Dogma*

LCL	Loeb Classical Library
LNTS	Library of New Testament Studies
LW	*Luther's Works*
NAC	New American Commentary
Neot	*Neotestamentica*
NICNT	New International Commentary on the New Testament
NIDNTTE	*New International Dictionary of New Testament Theology and Exegesis*
NIGTC	New International Greek Testament Commentary
NovT	*Novum Testamentum*
NTL	New Testament Library
NTS	*New Testament Studies*
OCD	*Oxford Classical Dictionary*
Part. or.	Cicero, *Partitiones oratoriae*
Pis.	Cicero, *In Pisonem*
Rhet.	Aristotle, *Rhetorica*
Rhet. Her.	*Rhetorica ad Herennium*
SNTSMS	Society for New Testament Studies Monograph Series
[Subl.]	Longinus, *De sublimitate*
TDNT	*Theological Dictionary of the New Testament*
TPINTC	TPI New Testament Commentaries
TynBul	Tyndale Bulletin
TZ	*Theologische Zeitschrift*
Vit. poes. Hom.	Plutarch. *De vita et poesi Homeri*
WBC	Word Biblical Commentary
WTJ	*Westminster Theological Journal*
WUNT	Wissenschaftliche Untersuchungen zum Neuen Testament
ZAW	*Zeitschrift für die alttestamentliche Wissenschaft*

Introduction

"Well now, one winter it was so cold that all the geese flew backward and all the fish moved south and even the snow turned blue. Late at night, it got so frigid that all spoken words froze solid afore they could be heard. People had to wait until sunup to find out what folks were talking about the night before."[1] Hyperbole is commonplace in human discourse. Even in the pages of Scripture it is manifest, as in the lyric poetry of the OT ("my tears have been my food day and night," Ps 42:3), the teachings of Jesus ("if your right hand causes you to sin, cut it off," Matt 5:30), and the letters of Paul ("I die every day!" 1 Cor 15:31).[2] There is a place, then, for "an appropriate exaggeration of the truth" (as the ancient rhetorician Quintilian defined hyperbole) in proper communication.[3] Sometimes the phenomenon may be obvious, as with the opening quote above, while at other times it may be difficult to detect due to an apparent lack of textual cues or audience presuppositions. In such cases, a literal treatment of a passage laden with emotional/rhetorical undertones is at risk of yielding distortions and inconsistencies.

The present study is an investigation of hyperbole in the Letter to the Galatians. It seeks to mine the letter for occurrences of hyperbole and to examine what effect hyperbole has on the theology of the letter. A "corrected" theology will be proposed at the end.

The work is divided into four main parts. In part 1, "Paul's Seeming Ambivalence to the Law," I look at the differences between the Paul of Galatians (chapter 1) and the Paul of Romans and Acts (chapter 2). It is a classic problem that has occupied many a theologian (chapter 3 is a discussion of

---

1 Schlosser, "Babe the Blue Ox," para. 1. Used by permission.
2 Quoting the ESV.
3 Quintilian, *Inst.*, 8.6.68.

proposed solutions). The Paul of Galatians writes with such consistent negativity about the law. How do we harmonize such harshness with the more sober depiction of the law in Romans? What's more, how do we square it with Paul's own Torah-observant behavior (and that of the earliest Christian church)?

I will argue throughout the course of the study that Paul's ambivalence was only *seeming*. In fact, his true view toward the law is that of Romans and Acts. Galatians, I will contend, is an outlier, written in the style of hyperbole.

What is hyperbole, and how does it work? That is the subject of part 2, "Hyperbole: Definitions and Rhetoric." I will look at modern linguistic and ancient evidence. Logically, the chapters are structured so as to begin with a definition of hyperbole (chapter 4) and then proceed to its use in rhetoric (chapter 5).

In part 3, "Biblical Hyperbole," I apply the findings of part 2 to the biblical corpus. I first construct a methodology (chapter 6) whereby hyperbole can be identified through various logical, literary, and rhetorical aspects. Then I survey the OT (chapter 7) and the NT (chapter 8) for examples of hyperbole, showing the form and function of hyperbole in each. In those chapters I also practice the study's methodology on OT and NT case studies, moving closer to Galatians with each analysis.

Finally, in part 4, "Hyperbole in Galatians," I apply the methodology to Paul's letter. I examine the letter through three different lenses. First, how does Paul vilify his opponents (chapter 9)? Second, how does he denigrate the law (chapter 10)? And third, how does he magnify the consequences of circumcision (chapter 11)? At the end of each chapter I include a "reimagining" section, where a literal reading of Paul's letter is corrected to one that takes into account his use of hyperbole. Chapter 12 summarizes the investigation with a fresh perspective on Galatians.

All in all, the present study seeks to begin a conversation on Paul's use of hyperbole and how it impacts Pauline theology. A few works have already probed into this area.[4] However, none is as ambitious with regard to hyperbole as this study, which constructs a methodology for detecting hyperbole and applies it to multiple passages within a single letter to construct a theology of that letter.

I have tried, to the extent possible, to construct such theology organically, from the careful application of methodology to selected scriptural passages. In this endeavor, however, personal bias has no doubt crept in. The letter grade for each passage on the Hyperbole Scorecard, for example,

---

4 Schlueter, *Filling Up the Measure*; Livesey, *Galatians*; Schoeni, "Hyperbolic Sublime," 171–92; and, to some extent, Thurén, "Was Paul Angry?," 302–21; Cosby, "Galatians," 296–309.

which I will introduce in chapter 6, is somewhat subjective, based on both the number and strength of the various aspects detected in the passage. I have tried, however, to establish each of these grades with sufficiently nuanced discussion and not to dismiss as "mere rhetoric" things with which I simply do not agree. I hope that my judgment calls will seem reasonable to the reader.

Finally, the reader will no doubt perceive that this project has theological affinities with the New Perspective on Paul and Paul within Judaism. Many books have been written establishing a biblical and theoretical basis for these movements. I have, where needed, simply cited the best and most relevant materials. I could not seek to duplicate their foundations here. However, I do believe that they are right in proposing that Second Temple Judaism was based on grace and that Paul, though a messianic believer, remained within this gracious system. Perhaps the present investigation can remove some of the blocks hindering the internal consistency of these theological models.

PART I

Paul's Seeming Ambivalence toward the Law

1

Paul as Dead to the Law (Galatians)

> ### In this chapter…
>
> *Question(s) to be answered:*
> - What was Paul's attitude toward the law in Galatians?
>
> *Trajectory:*
> - In Chapter 2, we will look at Paul's more positive attitude toward the law as expressed in Romans and Acts
> - In Chapter 3, we will attempt to come to terms with Paul's seemingly ambivalent attitude toward the law

WERE THE APOSTLE PAUL to be brought before the Sanhedrin to answer for his negative statements on the law of Moses, it is likely that the Letter to the Galatians would be presented as Exhibit A.[1] Galatians could be described, in the words of one early Christian-Gentile author, as the "most decisive against Judaism" among Paul's epistles.[2] Imbued with obvious pathos which gives it an urgent, at times even hostile, tone, Galatians surely would have provided grist for anyone wishing to accuse Paul of treachery against the traditions of his ancestors.

In Galatians we encounter the thought world of an apostle who appears to have made a clean break with the law: "For through the law I died to the law" (ἐγὼ γὰρ διὰ νόμου νόμῳ ἀπέθανον, 2:19).[3] His argument for this apparent break is wide-ranging and encompasses the law's origins, purpose,

---

1. A hypothetical hearing is proposed in contrast to Paul's actual defense before the Sanhedrin in Acts 23. Also, when *law, Torah,* or νόμος are used, unless otherwise specified, they refer to the Sinaitic legislation and are used interchangeably.

2. Tertullian, *Marc.* 5.2.

3. English translations are my own unless otherwise specified.

consequences, and duration. This chapter will explore each of these areas in turn to demonstrate that Paul's view of the law in Galatians was uniformly and comprehensively negative.[4]

THE LAW'S TAINTED ORIGINS

According to Gal 3:19d the law was "put in place through angels, by the hand of a mediator" (διαταγεὶς δι' ἀγγέλων ἐν χειρὶ μεσίτου). The two prepositional phrases therein have been variously interpreted and denote either that the angels authored the law or that they merely took part in an auxiliary role in its origination. Evidence for angelic authorship will be dealt with first.

Beginning with the textual tradition, the LXX of Deut 33:2 places the angels on Mount Sinai at God's right hand: ἐκ δεξιῶν αὐτοῦ ἄγγελοι μετ' αὐτοῦ. Here ἄγγελοι is a rendering of the difficult Hebrew term אֵשְׁדָּת which modern versions translate variously as "host" (NRSV), "flaming fire" (ESV), or "flashing lightning" (NAS). There is also a rich tradition in Jewish and Christian literature (including Josephus, Philo, Acts 7:38, 53, and Heb 2:2) in which the angels are viewed as having participated in the origin of the law.[5] It is even possible, as J. Louis Martyn suggests, that Paul's opponents cited some of these traditions to the Galatians as proof of the heavenly origin of the law, which would help to explain Paul's remark in 1:8 about the opponents' gospel originating from an "angel from heaven."[6]

Second, there are linguistic signals that Paul may be referring to angelic authorship of the law in 3:19. The prepositional phrase δι' ἀγγέλων can be understood causally if διά is given the force of ὑπό (i.e., the law as instituted *by* angels).[7] Moreover, as Martyn points out, Paul's word choice in this section in describing the genesis of the law is telling. Instead of using the traditional phrase "God gave (δίδωμι) the law," Paul uses more passive verbiage: "the law *happened*" (γίνομαι; v. 17), "the law *was added*" (τίθημι; v. 19), and "the law was *put in place*" (διατάσσω; v. 19).[8] By contrast, the

---

4. With the possible exception of 5:14, on which see chapter 6.

5. See De Boer, *Galatians*, 228, and Bruce, *Galatians*, 177, for a discussion of the pertinent texts.

6. Martyn, *Galatians*, 357. Several terms have been offered for Paul's opponents, among them "agitators," "teachers," and "Judaizers." I will use "opponents" throughout.

7. Hübner, *Law in Paul's Thought*, 27; so also Martyn, *Galatians*, 357n209, "The evidence both from the papyri and from early Christian literature shows that in the Hellenistic period *dia* with the genitive and with a passive verb can mean either 'through' (mediating agent) or 'by' (originating actor). The analysis . . . strongly suggests that Paul thinks of the angels as the originating actors."

8. Martyn, *Galatians*, 364.

Abrahamic promises were "spoken" (λέγω; v. 16), "ratified" (προκυρόω; v. 17) and "given" (χαρίζομαι; v. 18) by God. As Martyn summarizes, "Using strong 'speaking' and 'giving' verbs to attribute the Abrahamic promise directly and clearly to God, Paul refers to the Law's genesis either by employing colorless verbs or by referring to the genesis of the Law as the act of angels."[9]

Third, the notoriously difficult verse 20 (ὁ δὲ μεσίτης ἑνὸς οὐκ ἔστιν, ὁ δὲ θεὸς εἷς ἐστιν) could refer to a mediator standing between the angels and Israel (Figure 1.1, left side). Here the oneness of God (likely an echo of the Shema) is contrasted with the non-oneness of the person or work of ὁ μεσίτης. If the Greek article is taken as anaphoric, μεσίτης refers back to the mediator of the previous verse, widely assumed to be Moses. Taking the mediator to be, by definition, the mediator of a plurality, Moses mediates on behalf of the *many*, that is, the angels.[10] If God were the originator, he would have dealt with Israel directly, without the need for a mediator.[11]

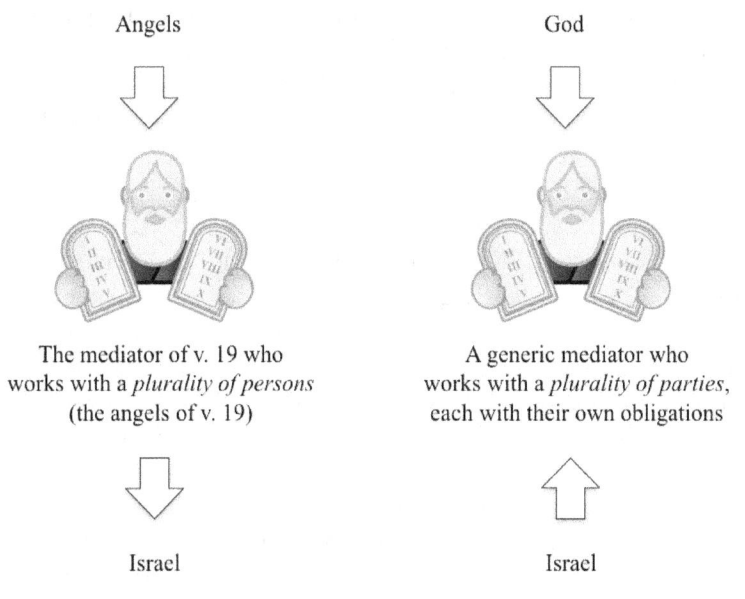

Figure 1.1. **Two Popular Interpretations of** ὁ μεσίτης ἑνὸς οὐκ ἔστιν **in Gal 3:20.**

Other scholars reject the idea of angelic authorship of the law, concerned that it goes too far in distancing the law from God. Moo, for instance, believes that the διά of v. 19 should be interpreted instrumentally (the law

9. Martyn, *Galatians*, 365.
10. Hübner, *Law in Paul's Thought*, 27.
11. Martyn, *Galatians*, 366; Schlier, *Der Brief an die Galater*, 161.

was ordained *through* angels) rather than causally.¹² He also asserts that the connection between angels and authorship of the law has been overplayed:

> The idea that angels were involved in the giving of the law is not taught anywhere in the OT (though see Deut. 33:2 LXX), but it is a common Jewish tradition (Jub. 1.27—2.1; Philo, *Somn.* 1.143; Josephus, *Ant.* 15.136) that has left its mark on the NT elsewhere (Acts 7:38, 53; Heb. 2.2). In none of these texts does the mention of angels suggest any question about its divine origin; on the contrary, the emphasis, if anything, is on the holiness and majesty of the law.¹³

Regarding the μεσίτης of verse 20, then, Moo and others take it to refer to a mediator in general, meaning that such a person by definition is involved between two parties (Figure 1.1, right side).¹⁴ The plurality here is not an inherent quality of either party to the mediation but rather an inherent aspect of mediation itself; the giving of the law requires the bilateral cooperation of the recipients, so it needs a mediator. The bestowal of the promises, conversely, is unilateral, involving God's initiative alone (with faith being simply the acceptance of the promises), so it does not require a mediator.¹⁵

How does one adjudicate the evidence on this tendentious issue? Admittedly, the Jewish textual tradition is inconclusive regarding the notion that angels actually authored the law; Moo is correct in pointing this out. The grammatical evidence is compelling on both sides. Martyn's analysis of Paul's colorless word choice in describing the giving of the law is somewhat suggestive in favor of angelic authorship. Moo's explanation of verse 20 seems strained in that it presumes too much on the reader to take into account the bilaterality versus unilaterality of the covenants. That angels are in view as originators, then, is slightly preferred.

Of the two most common interpretations, angelic authorship is the more extreme position relative to traditional Judeo-Christian doctrine. However, as the case will be made in later chapters, Galatians is full of extremes. Paul is not calmly crafting a systematic theology but rather "writing on the edge," executing an angry defense against his opponents who have challenged both his doctrine and his honor.¹⁶ If his language intentionally

---

12. Moo, *Galatians*, 235.

13. Moo, *Galatians*, 235.

14. This is the view of Moo, *Galatians*, 237; Fung, *Galatians*, 162; Betz, *Galatians*, 171; Lightfoot, *Galatians*, 147; Longenecker, *Galatians*, 142.

15. Moo, *Galatians*, 236.

16. Räisänen, *Paul and the Law*, 132–33, calls Paul's statements "radical" and "steeped in emotion," adding that "the verses in question seem to express a latent

leaves open the possibility that God had little if anything to do with the origin of the law, it is likely a bit of rhetorical wordplay meant to forcefully refute his opponents' arguments which have begun to infect the Galatian churches.

Of course, the issue of angelic authorship is subordinate to the main point here, that in 3:19–20 Paul paints the origin of the law in a negative light, especially vis-à-vis the Abrahamic promises. He seeks, as Ronald Fung suggests, to "show the inferiority of the law as that which was given not directly by God but only through angelic mediation."[17] Might also Paul's question in verse 21 ("Is the law against the promises of God?") signal that he is self-consciously aware of his negativity and needing to contain its implications?

THE LAW'S INSIDIOUS PURPOSE

The term "insidious" denotes something that seems harmless but upon developing over time comes to be seen as dangerous. It is derived from the Latin noun *insidiae*, ambush.[18] It is an apt term indeed to characterize the purpose of the law as described by Paul in Galatians.

I begin with Gal 3:19b, where Paul writes that the law was τῶν παραβάσεων χάριν προσετέθη. The fact that it was "added" (προστίθημι), as though to the covenantal promises, rather than being the basis for God's plan, is the first sign of Paul's disparagement of the law.[19] Then there is the difficulty with translating χάριν, which traditionally has been taken in one of three ways, (1) causal (*because of* transgressions, i.e., to deal with them), (2) cognitive (*to bring knowledge of* transgressions), or (3) telic (*in order to provoke* transgressions). James Dunn argues for the first interpretation, viewing the law as an interim measure in the form of a sacrificial system

---

resentment towards the law of which Paul was normally not conscious."

17. Fung, *Galatians*, 161; similarly, Hübner, *Law in Paul's Thought*, 26, "It is practically uncontested that the intention of this pronouncement is to emphasize the inferiority of the Law." The principle that indirectness in transmission implies inferiority is also emphasized by several scholars: Betz, *Galatians*, 169–70, "The Torah of Moses was not given by the one God directly but only through subaltern divine beings"; Longenecker, *Galatians*, 142, "God's true redemptive activity is always direct and unilateral in nature. To desire the [law], therefore, is to desire the inferior, whereas God wants to deal with his people directly"; Burton, *Galatians*, 189, "The intent of the whole phrase [v. 19c] is to depreciate the law as not given by God."

18. *Merriam-Webster's Collegiate Dictionary*, 11th ed., s.v. "insidious."

19. Longenecker, *Galatians*, 138; Burton, *Galatians*, 188, "προσετέθη marks the law as supplementary, and hence subordinate to the covenant."

with which to deal with sins prior to the coming of Jesus.[20] Richard Longenecker opts for the second reading because he feels that it accords better with the subsequent imagery of the supervisory custodian.[21] Reading χάριν as telic, however, is preferred. Most significantly, there is Paul's decision to use παράβασις rather than ἁμαρτία here. Παράβασις is a deviation from an established norm. Thus, by definition, the law as norm must be instituted before transgressions can be counted.[22] Compare this with Paul's statement in Rom 4:15 that "where there is no law, there is no transgression" or the similar statement in Rom 5:13 that "sin is not reckoned where there is no law." But could one go further and say that the law does not just *relabel* sin as transgression, but actually *provokes* transgressions to occur? That seems to be what Martyn is getting at when he says, "Paul surely thinks of the Law as antedating these transgressions and, indeed, very probably as producing them. If the gospel is now eliciting faith (3:2, 5), the Law entered the picture, in its own time, in order to elicit transgressions (so also Rom 5:20)."[23]

The telic reading of χάριν carries with it a couple of difficulties. For one, it imagines a malicious lawgiver: "For an interim measure which went on provoking transgressions for more than a millennium, without providing remedy for all that time, would imply a remarkably heartless picture of the God who so failed to provide."[24] Of course, this objection is negated if Paul is speaking in terms of angelic authorship. Then there is Longenecker's concern with how to reconcile verse 19a with the temporal clause ἄχρις οὗ ἔλθῃ τὸ σπέρμα ᾧ ἐπήγγελται: "For why should God want an increase of sin building up to the coming of Christ?"[25] However, the same could be said for an increase in the knowledge of sin, which is Longenecker's preferred

---

20. Dunn, *Galatians*, 190.

21. Longenecker, *Galatians*, 138. Longenecker's view of the παιδαγωγός is that of one who "taught by the supervision he gave and the discipline he administered" (148).

22. Moo, *Galatians*, 234, views the law as setting the context for sin to be called transgressions, i.e., conscious violation of God's norms (rather than the law actually provoking additional sin).

23. Martyn, *Galatians*, 354–55. So also De Boer, *Galatians*, 231, "It can be said that the law was 'added' to the promise in order to produce the transgressions of it that are now taking place, whether by Jews or by Gentiles"; Lightfoot, *Galatians*, 144; Burton, *Galatians*, 188; Bruce, *Galatians*, 175; Ridderbos, *Epistle of Paul*, 138; Schreiner, *Law and Its Fulfillment*, 75. Schlier, *Der Brief an die Galater*, 153, posits that the law was put in place for the sake of exacerbating sin: "Das Gesetz ist gegeben, um den Fall zur Fülle zu bringen (Röm 5:20), um die Sünde aktuell und intensiv werden zu lassen (Röm 7:7ff.), um sie zu einem empirischen 'Phänomen' zu machen (Röm 7:13) und sie in ihrer Sündigkeit auszuschöpfen."

24. Dunn, *Galatians*, 190.

25. Longenecker, *Galatians*, 138.

reading. Both are speculative questions. In either case, concerns about a malicious lawgiver or the senseless building up of sin are not dooming to the telic interpretation because they unnecessarily presume a rational precision and emotional sensitivity on the part of Paul, who shows no inclination for such accoutrements in the present context.

Elaborating on the topic in 3:22–23, Paul writes that the law (ἡ γραφή and ὁ νόμος appear to be used interchangeably) was meant to confine (συγκλείω; BDAG: confine, imprison) all things under sin until the time of Christ. Thus, it could be said that while sin acted as the prison, the law served as the warden.[26] To a first-century Jew, though, these words would have sounded seditious. In our imaginary courtroom scene, one can visualize the incredulous expressions of the council members as they hear this evidence against Paul: the law was not designed to give life (ζωοποιέω) to Israel after all; its purpose was not to free God's people from the shackles of sin but rather to maintain, even tighten, sin's grip until a new, post-law age could dawn; in all of this the process was "rigged" from the start—righteousness could never have been found from obeying the law. Paul's stalwart disregard for the traditions of his fathers is eclipsed only by his temerity.

The imagery of the παιδαγωγός furthers the dismissive tone of the section. There is a time for righteousness, and it is not during the law's tenure but rather the age of faith in Jesus Christ.[27] Before the age of faith, the law is meant to serve simply as a slave assistant, whose duty it is to supervise chores and administer (often harsh) discipline.[28] He is a "distinctly unfriendly and confining custodian, different in no significant way from an imprisoning jailer."[29] Εἰς Χριστόν (v. 24) has simply a temporal sense, then. The law functions in its role as a παιδαγωγός *during the time until* Christ. There is no sense here that the law somehow *prepares* a person for Christ (the telic sense of εἰς), as with the ancient concept of παιδεία (education)

---

26. Martyn, *Galatians*, 362.

27. The genitive in πίστεως Ἰησοῦ Χριστοῦ is taken objectively, given the antithesis between human faith and human works of the law, on which see Matlock, "Saving Faith," 81–83.

28. The negative connotation bound up with the παιδαγωγός is in keeping with the tone of vv. 22–23 and with Martyn, *Galatians*, 363; Moo, *Galatians*, 243; De Boer, *Galatians*, 240; Schlier, *Der Brief an die Galater*, 168; Lightfoot, *Galatians*, 148; Dunn, *Galatians*, 198; and Betz, *Galatians*, 177; who argue against the outdated view that the παιδαγωγός is a teacher. According to Betz, "These pedagogues had the bad image of being rude, rough, and good for no other business" (*Galatians*, 177). See also Martyn's discussion of the negative connation of ὑπο (*under the power of*) in verse 25 (Martyn, *Galatians*, 370–71).

29. Martyn, *Galatians*, 363.

leading to virtue.³⁰ Rather, Paul's anthropological pessimism as witnessed in 3:10 reinforces the improbability of this interpretation.

One objection must be considered at this point: If the purpose of the law is presented as uniformly negative, then how can Paul, in v. 21, deny that the law is *against* the promises of God? Phrased differently, in what way is the law *not* against the promises? Hans Hübner helpfully distinguishes between three intentions of the law: the intention of the angelic law-givers (to provoke people to sin), the immanent intention (to bring life if the stipulations are carried out), and the intention of God. These three intentions work at cross purposes but do so under the sovereignty and foreknowledge of God. According to Hübner:

> The angels' intention of bringing men to perdition is of course directed in the first instance against God's saving intention, but this intention of the angels which is at cross purposes with God's saving intention is nevertheless taken up into God's intention.... The evil intent of the angels is overcome and taken up into God's good intention.... Gal 3:19ff. is thus a development of what we find in Job: Satan, with his capacity to cause disaster, working in the service of the saving activity of Yahweh! ... God's good intention consisted in taking up the evil intention of the angels and turning it to the purposes of salvation.³¹

While Hübner's discussion helps to defuse the obvious tension between the deadly law and God's life-giving promises, he does not go quite far enough. For instance, *how* exactly is the evil intention of the angels taken up into God's intention? In other words, what positive purpose may be described for the institution of the law? Here neither Hübner nor Paul speaks as unambiguously as we might like. Yes, God foreknew the devastating effects of the law—and within that theology of superintendence there may be found a convergence of intentions between God and the angels—but did the law *have* to come prior to Christ? Galatians is silent on the answer.³²

---

30. Fung, *Galatians*, 169, "Paul does not mean that the law exerts a gradual, educative influence on people, either by inclining them toward good until they receive Christ or by enabling them to realize their own sin, turn their backs on trusting in their own merits, and desire the grace of Christ.... Paul's primary concern in these verses (22–25) is not to describe the genesis of individual faith in terms of psychological development, but to sketch the progress of salvation history." See also the discussion in Betz, *Galatians*, 177–78.

31. Hübner, *Law in Paul's Thought*, 29–30.

32. Moo, *Galatians*, 240, begs the question when he attempts to reconcile law and promise by writing, "Behind 'the Scripture' in verse 22a stands God himself, who has worked through the imprisoning and condemning effect of Scripture to accomplish his ultimate purpose." But *how* did the imprisoning and condemning effect accomplish

THE LAW'S TRAGIC CONSEQUENCES

According to traditional interpretations of Galatians, the law was designed to bring blessings upon those who kept it and to curse those who failed to observe it. The only problem, according to Paul's anthropological pessimism, is that no one fully keeps the law. Therefore, everyone is under a curse. Such is the thought behind Gal 3:10, where Paul states that "all those who are of works of the law are under a curse" (Ὅσοι γὰρ ἐξ ἔργων νόμου εἰσίν, ὑπὸ κατάραν εἰσίν). Paul cites the curse of LXX Deut 27:26, the last verse of the so-called Shechemite Dodecalogue, which he expands to include "all the things written in the book of the law" (πᾶσιν τοῖς γεγραμμένοις ἐν τῷ βιβλίῳ τοῦ νόμου).³³ Thus, Paul is expressing the criteria for obedience in as stringent and as comprehensive a manner as possible (cf. Gal 5:3). Redemption from the curse took place when Christ *became a curse for us* (γενόμενος ὑπὲρ ἡμῶν κατάρα) by being hung on a "tree" (Gal 3:13). This redemption applies only to those who believe in Christ, however. Since Paul is attempting to dissuade the Galatians from being circumcised and thus entering the realm of curse, those remaining in non-Christian Judaism are still under the curse of the law.

As detailed in the previous section, the law is also pictured as an imprisoning force. In Gal 3:22–23 Paul uses the verbs συγκλείω and φρουρέω to graphically illustrate his point. As with the curse, this state of affairs remains in effect for those who do not believe in Christ.

A third tragic consequence of the law is enslavement. According to 4:3, Paul and his fellow Jews (ἡμεῖς), when they were under the law, "were enslaved to the elemental principles of the cosmos" (ὑπὸ τὰ στοιχεῖα τοῦ κόσμου ἤμεθα δεδουλωμένοι). The mention of τὰ στοιχεῖα has occasioned a variety of interpretations.³⁴ What is clear from the context, however, is that

---

God's ultimate purpose? What is the functional or causal relation between the two ages? Fung, *Galatians*, 166, is guilty of begging the question as well: "There is no essential contradiction of the promise by the law, because, simply, the law is intended to serve the purposes of the promise, which has to do with justification by faith." How does the law serve the purposes of the promise other than by not stepping on them, as it were? It is not satisfying to simply conclude that their spheres of activity are mutually exclusive. Bruce, *Galatians*, 180, comes closer to postulating the role of the law in positive terms—"as driving men and women to flee from its condemnation and seek refuge in the promises"—but imports Lutheran theology into this passage. In the end we must content ourselves to the fact that in Galatians Paul explicates the purpose of the law solely in negative terms: the law is not against the promise because the law does not provide justification by faith.

33. The Shechemite Dodecalogue consists of twelve specific curses pronounced from Mt. Ebal.

34. Among them are (1) elemental substances (earth, water, air, fire), (2) essential

τὰ στοιχεῖα and the law are "functionally parallel entities: both enslaved, and God's sending of Christ has effected liberation from both."[35]

The Jews were not the only ones in this enslavement. The Galatians, prior to their conversion to Christ, had worshiped and been enslaved to the στοιχεῖα.[36] In 4:9 Paul pictures acquiescence to Judaism as equivalent to a return to such elemental principles for the Galatians. Their observance of the Jewish calendar was already a step in that direction.

Beginning in 5:2 Paul embarks on a "litany of dire consequences of accepting the Judaizers' message" of circumcision.[37] They occur in rapid order, introduced in the first instance by "Behold, I, Paul say to you" (Ἴδε ἐγὼ Παῦλος λέγω ὑμῖν) and in the second instance by "I testify again" (μαρτύρομαι δὲ πάλιν) for emphasis. Roughly paraphrased, they are:

> Christ will be of no benefit to you (5:2)
> You will be obligated to follow the whole law (5:3)
> You will be severed from Christ . . . You will be fallen
> away from grace (5:4)

The first is structured as a third-class conditional clause and views circumcision as a gateway into the law.[38] For anyone being circumcised, then, Christ ὑμᾶς οὐδὲν ὠφελήσει (will be of no advantage to you, ESV; will be no benefit to you, NRSV). The benefit of Christ here is likely a salvific one.[39] Therefore, Paul is saying that the Galatians could not consider themselves saved by Christ if they accept circumcision.

---

principles of an area of study (as in Heb 5:12), (3) elementary spirits, and (4) heavenly bodies. The first meaning is preferred as it "was by far the dominant meaning of the word στοιχεῖα in Paul's day" (Moo, *Galatians*, 262; see also Martyn, *Galatians*, 394–95; De Boer, *Galatians*, 252–56, [here 256] "The phrase . . . [is] a *summary designation* for a complex of religious beliefs and practices centered around the four elements of the physical cosmos, to which the phrase concretely refers. In Paul's usage, the phrase is an instance of *metonymy*," emphasis original). In light of the fact that both Judaism (4:3) and paganism (4:9) are subsumed under στοιχεῖα, it may be best to speak more generally about τὰ στοιχεῖα τοῦ κόσμου: "'The elements of the world' may be said to cover anything in which sinners place their trust apart from the living God revealed in Christ; any such object turns into a god, and the sinner becomes its slave" (*NIDNTTE* 4:380).

35. Martyn, *Galatians*, 394–95.

36. As Longenecker, *Galatians*, 181, notes, "Beyond question, Paul's lumping of Judaism and paganism together in this manner is radical in the extreme."

37. Longenecker, *Galatians*, 228.

38. The nature of the conditional clause with the subjunctive might imply that "the Galatians' circumcision was a fact still pending" (Longenecker, *Galatians*, 226; see also Dunn, *Galatians*, 264; Burton, *Galatians*, 273; Schlier, *Der Brief an die Galater*, 231).

39. So Dunn, *Galatians*, 264, and Betz, *Galatians*, 259; contra Longenecker, *Galatians*, 226, who interprets it as "direction and aid in their lives."

In 5:3 we meet a theme implicit from 3:10, namely, that the law is an all-or-nothing proposition; one may not simply pick and choose what prescriptions and tenets one wants to follow. Rather, one who chooses to be obedient to a single commandment is obliged to follow the fullness of the law code. Apparently, Paul's opponents had already made some inroads in getting the Galatians to observe the Jewish festivals (4:10). Did the Galatians realize they would have to obey the whole law? Probably not, as Paul seems to be presenting new information to them here.[40] Perhaps the opponents had planned to gradually introduce more and more laws.[41]

A further consequence of the law is that it causes one to be "severed" (ESV) from Christ (5:4 κατηργήθητε ἀπὸ Χριστοῦ). For καταργέω BDAG glosses "be estranged from Christ" under the meaning for the passive "to cause the release of someone from an obligation (one has nothing more to do with it), *be discharged, be released.*"[42] Noting the verb's elusiveness in translation, NIDNTTE states that "the sense of rendering something inoperative is clear and constant."[43] Judging from the parallel phrase τῆς χάριτος ἐξεπέσατε, Paul here certainly speaks of an end to one's fellowship with Christ. To be precise, however, he refers only to those who attempt to (conative force) be justified by the law (οἵτινες ἐν νόμῳ δικαιοῦσθε). However, Paul's argument in Galatians is constructed as representing a slippery slope: if you are circumcised, you are entering into the law; having entered into the law, you must take on all of its obligations or suffer a curse; having taken on the law's obligations, you have become as those who seek righteousness from the law. Moo concurs with this viewpoint: "Paul makes clear why circumcision is so decisive a step by making clear that it involves 'seeking to be justified by the law.' . . . Circumcision signifies the intention to put oneself under the law of Moses and therefore . . . to seek to secure one's status with God in terms of that law."[44] Burton echoes this sentiment:

---

40. Burton, *Galatians*, 274, "It is certain . . . that the judaisers had not proposed to [the Galatians] to undertake to keep the whole law."

41. Sanders, *Paul, the Law*, 29, "Paul's opponents may have adopted a policy of gradualism, requiring first some of the major commandments (circumcision, food, days), a policy which was probably not unique among Jewish missionaries."

42. The other instance of the passive of καταργέω with the preposition ἀπό is Rom 7:2, 6, where Paul talks about the release of a woman from her marriage vows upon the death of her husband.

43. *NIDNTTE* 2:641.

44. Moo, *Galatians*, 325. Cf. De Boer, *Galatians*, 314, "The sense matches that of 4:21, where Paul addresses the Galatians as 'you who are *wanting* [*hoi thelontes*] to be under the law'" (emphasis original).

> The acceptance of circumcision is, under the circumstances then existing in the Galatian churches, the acceptance of the principle of legalism, the committal of the Galatians to a relation to God wholly determined by conformity to statutes and leaving no place for Christ or the development of spiritual life through faith in him and spiritual fellowship with him.... The possibility of any compromise between the two conceptions of religion he does not consider, but points out the logical outcome of the adoption of the principle of legalism, which he conceives to be involved in the acceptance of circumcision.[45]

As Burton notices, nowhere in Galatians does Paul leave open the possibility that the Galatians could undertake circumcision and still have a proper heart for Christ. Rather, form and function go hand in hand as Paul sees it; that is, circumcision necessarily entails the seeking of justification through works of the law.

THE LAW'S LIMITED DURATION

Paul's language leaves no room for doubt that the usefulness of the law was restricted to a specific time period, one that terminated with the dawning of the age of faith in Christ:

> If I rebuild what I destroyed (2:18)
>
> Until the seed could come to whom the promise was made (3:19)
>
> Until the coming faith was revealed (3:23)
>
> No longer under a custodian (3:25)
>
> When the fullness of time came, God sent forth his son ... to redeem those under the law (4:4–5)
>
> Now that you have come to know God ... how is it that you are turning again to the weak and worthless principles ...? (4:9)

Thus, the "law" chapter in the story of salvation history has been closed and a new one is being written. The law is obsolete and is not to be returned to. An autobiographical note on Paul's behalf implicitly sums up what he recommends for others: νόμῳ ἀπέθανον, "I have died to the law" (2:19). The implication is that there is no sense remaining in what has been made obsolete. Moreover, one needs to make a clean break with the law in order to pass into the age of faith in Christ (νόμῳ ἀπέθανον, ἵνα θεῷ ζήσω).[46]

45. Burton, *Galatians*, 272.

46. Galatians 5:14 has puzzled commentators in that it can be interpreted as

To demonstrate the degree to which Paul's perspective is overly negative, even scandalous, in the face of traditional Jewish teaching, which held that the law was eternal and unchanging, a few traditions may be cited.[47] Josephus, for instance, writes, "For though we be deprived of our wealth, of our cities, or of other advantages we have, our law continues immortal."[48] Similarly, Philo writes:

> But the enactments of this lawgiver are firm, not shaken by commotions, not liable to alteration, but stamped as it were with the seal of nature herself, and they remain firm and lasting from the day on which they were first promulgated to the present one, and there may well be a hope that they will remain to all future

implying the continued need to fulfill the law, which raises tension with Paul's teachings regarding freedom from the law for the Christian (Longenecker, *Galatians*, 241, "Is it that having made such a great show of throwing out the law through the front door, Paul now unobtrusively readmits it through the back door?"). Hübner, *Law in Paul's Thought*, 37, seeks to alleviate the tension by arguing that Paul is not speaking about the law at all in 5:14. He believes that Paul modifies the phrase ὅλον τὸν νόμον of 5:3 to ὁ πᾶς νόμος in 5:14 to signal that he is speaking critically and ironically in the latter verse, as if referring to the "so-called" whole law: "By means of the linguistic strangeness of using πᾶς in a seemingly meaningless way ... Paul succeeds in reducing to absurdity the Jewish ideal of keeping the whole Law." Most other commentators demur (e.g., Sanders, *Paul, the Law*, 96–97, shows that Paul, who "quotes a passage on which was based a standard Jewish summary of the law," is indeed speaking of the Mosaic law). Westerholm, *Israel's Law*, 203–5, believes that Paul's switch from ποιέω (5:3) to πληρόω (5:14) is telling. Rather than "doing" the law, believers satisfy the law's true intention by loving each other: "*Plēroun* is specially suited, whereas *poiein* is not, for use by an author who claims to have superior insight into what is required to satisfy the 'true' intention of the lawgiver or the 'real' demand of the law" (204; similarly, Betz, *Galatians*, 275; Bruce, *Galatians*, 241–42; Dunn, *Galatians*, 291). Sanders and Westerholm, however, still do not adequately eliminate the tension of freedom from the law versus the need to satisfy a requirement of the law. The attempt by Moo, *Galatians*, 348, and Martyn, *Galatians*, 489–90, to solve this tension is more ambitious in that they identify Christ as the subject of the perfect passive πεπλήρωται. Thus, Jesus fulfills the whole law in his teaching about love and in his sacrificial death (cf. Matt 5:17). But this interpretation seems strained in the absence of any supporting verbiage (Martyn himself refers to it as "rather wild" at first glance [490]). At the risk of proposing yet another interpretation, it seems best to see the continued accountability to the law in this verse as hypothetical and Paul's comment as born out of the concern of the Galatians to fulfill the law. He temporarily enters the thought world of his audience, saying, "Let's imagine for the sake of argument that the law is still in effect. You want to fulfill it? Then simply love one another." Two additional considerations are worthy of note. First, Paul employs the rabbinical technique of reducing the law to a single command or group of commands (cf. Matt 22:40). Second, "fulfill" is being used in the sense of rendering one's obligations complete (cf. Burton, *Galatians*, 294–95).

47. Longenecker, *Galatians*, 139, "Paul's view here, of course, deviates widely from that of Judaism."

48. *Ag. Ap.* 2.277.

time, as being immortal, as long as the sun and the moon, and the whole heaven and the whole world shall endure.[49]

The eternality of the law is also expressed in Jub. 1.27; 3.31; 6.17; Wis 18:4; Sir 24:9; Bar 4:1; 2 Bar. 48:47; 77:15; 4 Ezra 9:37; 1 En. 99:2. Compare also the teachings of Jesus in Matt 5:18 and Luke 16:17. Davies devotes an entire monograph to the question of the eternity of Torah in *Torah in the Messianic Age and/or the Age to Come*. Examining the evidence from the OT, apocrypha, pseudepigrapha, and rabbinic sources, he concludes that there is "no evidence for the expectation of a New Torah in the Messianic Age. Changes in details and an increase in understanding there would be, but no substitution of the old Torah by a new one was envisaged."[50] In his comprehensive study of Judaism, Moore concurs:

> Inasmuch as the days of the Messiah are the religious as well as the political consummation of the national history, and, however idealized, belong to the world we live in, it is natural that the law should not only be in force in the messianic age, but should be better studied and better observed than ever before; and this was indubitably the common belief.[51]

SUMMARY

Paul's statements in Galatians cast a long shadow of negativity over the law. He hints at the possibility that God was not even involved in the origin of the law. Then he proposes that the law contributed to, perhaps even caused, the sins of Israel. The tragic consequences of the law are three, according to Paul: a nationwide curse which fell upon Israel, an imprisonment to sin, and an enslavement to the elemental principles of the cosmos. These three comprise a sociohistorically relevant triad of negativity with regard to the Galatians; curses, imprisonment, and slavery—all were dreaded aspects of everyday life in the first-century Roman empire and thus constituted

---

49. *Mos.* 2.14.

50. Davies, *Torah in the Messianic Age*, 70. Perhaps the most suggestive evidence against Davies's conclusion is a tradition in the Talmud that divides history into three epochs, each lasting two thousand years and followed by an eternal sabbath rest: "For six thousand years the world will exist. For two thousand it will be desolate, two thousand years [will be the time of] Torah, and two thousand years will be the days of the Messiah" (b. Sanh. 97A, quoted from Neusner, *Babylonian Talmud*, 16:520; on the eternal sabbath see m. Tamid 7:4). By implication one could take that to mean that the law would cease in the messianic age.

51. Moore, *Judaism*, 271.

a powerful rhetorical device for Paul. And lastly, Paul asserts that the law which was thought to be eternal is in actuality abolished at the coming of the messiah Jesus. Paul proclaims himself dead to this seemingly miserable and outdated phenomenon.

2

Paul as a Torah-Observant Jew (Romans, Acts)

In this chapter...

Question(s) to be answered:
- How was Paul more positive toward the law, as can be seen in Romans & Acts?

Trajectory:
- Chapter 1 and 2 stand in seeming contradiction. Chapter 3 will survey possible solutions.

IN THE WAKE OF reading Galatians, one might reasonably expect to find the Apostle Paul persisting in his criticism of the law and eschewing it in his personal conduct. But that is not the case. By the time Paul writes Romans his statements on the law are more measured, even occasionally complimentary, and at the time of his journey to Jerusalem in Acts 21 his life is characterized as being in accordance with the law.

PAUL'S MODERATED RHETORIC

The first half of this chapter will examine Paul's statements on the law in the Letter to the Romans for strands of positivity. It is by no means held that Paul's rhetoric in Romans is exclusively positive. Rather, it will be argued that his rhetoric is moderated, more balanced, in comparison with that of Galatians.[1] As will be seen in chapter 3, my purpose in this work

1. Weiss, *History of Primitive Christianity*, 549, "Paul not only does not repeat these

is ultimately not to establish Paul as an inconsistent thinker but to demonstrate how his negativity toward the law in Galatians is conditioned by rhetorical aims specific to that letter. For the moment the categories from chapter 1 will be evaluated in light of Romans.[2]

The Law's Divine Origin

In Romans, one does not find angelic involvement attached to the origination of the law. Rather, the law is proclaimed to be νόμος τοῦ θεοῦ, *God's* law in three separate places (7:22, 25; 8:7).[3] God's law is something to delight in and to serve (7:22, 25). It is something to which only those with Spirit-controlled minds can submit (8:7). Two additional verses are notable: (1) Paul's reference in 3:1 to the "oracles of God" (τὰ λόγια τοῦ θεοῦ), which contained the law and were entrusted to the Jewish people, and (2) his acknowledgement in 7:14 that the law is spiritual (πνευματικός).[4]

The Law's Noble Purpose

Far from the image of the law as a prison warden or slave assistant, in Rom 7:10 Paul is able to speak of ἡ ἐντολὴ ἡ εἰς ζωήν, "the commandment that leads to life" (ESV: "the very commandment that promised life"; NASB: "this commandment, which was to result in life"). The burden of blame for the death of humans, in this case, is placed squarely on sin itself (7:11–13) while in an extraordinary turn of phrase (7:12) the law is said to be "holy" and the commandment "holy, righteous, and good."[5]

Why, then, did God give the law? In Rom 3:20 the law is said to bring consciousness (ἐπίγνωσις) of sin. This is the cognitive, rather than causal or telic, relation of the law to sin. Moo's summary is apt:

---

sharpest antinomian statements [of Galatians] in the Epistle to the Romans, but in fact substitutes for them a considerably more positive estimate of the Law."

2. Although Paul has much to say concerning the law in his other letters, including the disputed ones, Romans and Galatians have historically proven to be the two major testbeds for explorations into Paul's thinking concerning the law. For the sake of simplicity and coherence, then, Romans will be the focus of the first part of this chapter.

3. Taking these occurrences to refer to the Mosaic law is the proper interpretation given Paul's argument in these passages. See Moo, *Romans*, 461; Longenecker, *Romans*, 375, 394.

4. Schreiner, *Romans*, 373, interprets this to mean that the law "has its origin from the Holy Spirit."

5. Rom 7:12, ὥστε ὁ μὲν νόμος ἅγιος καὶ ἡ ἐντολὴ ἁγία καὶ δικαία καὶ ἀγαθή.

> "Knowledge of sin" ... does not simply mean that the law defines sin; rather, what is meant is that the law gives to people an understanding of "sin" (singular) as a power that holds everyone in bondage and brings guilt and condemnation. The law presents people with the demand of God. In our constant failure to attain the goal of that demand, we recognize ourselves to be sinners and justly condemned for our failures.[6]

Next, Rom 5:20 says that "the law entered (παρεισῆλθεν) so that the trespass might increase." This section contains a contrast between death through sin and life/grace through Christ. As one increases, so does the other. The law is said to play an instrumental role in increasing (πλεονάσῃ) the trespass. Longenecker is too strong in his assertion that by using παρεισέρχομαι Paul means that the law slipped in illegitimately, as if not being a part of God's master plan.[7] Rather, Paul is "asserting that God's purpose (or one of his purposes) in giving the law of Moses to Israel was to 'intensify' the seriousness of sin."[8]

Does the law actually *provoke* sin, as with Gal 3:19? Romans 7:5 comes closest to this idea: "While we were living in the flesh, our sinful passions, aroused by the law, were at work (ἐνηργεῖτο) in our members to bear fruit for death" (ESV, NRSV; most modern translations are similar). There is a glaring problem with this translation, however, which is that the verb "arouse" does not occur in the Greek text unless ἐνεργέω is counted twice.[9] The phrase τὰ διὰ τοῦ νόμου is actually a verbless one and should be translated as such: "Our sinful passions were active (ἐνεργέω), *through the law*, in our members to bear fruit for death."[10] The focus, then, is not on the law but on τὰ παθήματα τῶν ἁμαρτιῶν and their work in the bodily members.

---

6. Moo, *Romans*, 210.

7. Longenecker, *Romans*, 599. Cf. Moo, *Romans*, 346, "It would be going too far to think that Paul pictures the God-given Mosaic law as 'slipping in' with an evil purpose."

8. Moo, *Romans*, 348.

9. Nevertheless, most contemporary commentators adopt some form of the translation with "arouse" and view the law in a causative role with relation to sin. Longenecker, *Romans*, 636: "Paul presents the law as playing an active part in actually 'arousing' people's 'sinful passions'"; Schreiner, *Romans*, 350: "Paul contends that [the law] aids and abets sin, that sin is provoked and stimulated"; cf. Moo, *Romans*, 410, 419; Dunn, *Romans 1–8*, 364.

10. Translation from Ziesler, *Paul's Letter to the Romans*, 177, who rejects the interpretation that the law arouses the sinful passions. Interestingly, Jewett, *Romans*, 436, also maintains the verbless phrase, stating that the sinful passions are *through the law* in the sense that they consist, not of sensual passions, but of the "yearning for honor in conforming to the law and in coercing compliance with its norms." BDAG 335 (ἐνεργέω) maintains the verbless phrase as well.

At the very least, circumspection is called for in interpreting a telic role for the law from this verse.

The final "purpose statement" concerning the law is in 7:13: "Did that which is good become death to me? By no means! But that sin might be shown to be sin, it worked death in me through what was good, so that sin might become exceedingly sinful through the commandment." As he has throughout the chapter, Paul appears to be protecting the reputation of the law—it is distinguished as "good"—while explaining how it indirectly results in an increase in sins. However, once more the role of the law is a cognitive one, not telic. The sinful nature takes advantage of the law. *It* is the driving force.

> Paul repudiates forcefully the notion that the law is the cause of death. Instead, sin used the law as its instrument . . . to effect death. The point being made is this: the law is not itself sinful nor did it cause death. Sin is the *ultimate* cause of death. The law is the *instrumental* cause, but it is not itself blameworthy, for it is inherently good. The state of affairs is that sin has taken a good thing—the law—and deployed it for its own evil purposes. Thereby sin has manifested itself as exceedingly sinful and wicked. The law has thereby been exculpated from blame inasmuch as it is inherently praiseworthy.[11]

The Law's Beneficial Consequences

The law in Romans is a two-edged sword. It can either bring good things (glory, honor, and peace, 2:10; eternal life, 2:7) or bad (wrath, fury, tribulation, distress; 2:8–9; wrath, 4:15; death, 7:9), depending on the behavior of the individual. However, given Paul's strong language in 3:9–20, it is safe to say that, outside of a few hints in chapter 2 (esp. 2:14–15), Romans does not picture a viable pathway to righteousness through the law. Even if we deem them as purely hypothetical, then, these beneficial consequences of the law are nonetheless expounded in Romans but absent in Galatians.

Another major benefit to being part of the law covenant is Israel's special status as God's chosen people. Paul asserts that the Jews have much profit from simply being Jews and being circumcised. For one, they are in possession of the very oracles of God (3:1–2), which include the entire revelation of the OT: the blessings, promises, rules of conduct, and prophetic

---

11. Moo, *Romans*, 372.

utterances.¹² For another, they lay claim to the adoption, the glory, the covenants, the giving of the law, the worship, the promises, the patriarchs, and Christ himself having been born of the Jewish race (9:4-5).

The Law's Indefinite Duration

In light of the fact that (a) righteousness through the law is impossible (3:20) and that (b) a new righteousness through faith has come into being (3:21), it is understandable that some commentators conclude that the law has been invalidated. However, Paul never explicitly says that. Whereas in Galatians we have abundant evidence that the law was temporary, there are no such indications in Romans.

If there is one place in Romans where the end of the law *appears to be* broached, it is in 10:4: "For Christ is the τέλος of the law unto righteousness for all who believe." The debate over the meaning of τέλος here largely concerns whether it is (1) temporal/terminal (Christ has abolished the law), (2) perfective/completive (Christ fulfilled the law), or (3) teleological (the law pointed to Christ).¹³ Whereas the first interpretation expresses discontinuity between the law and Christ and prevails among modern scholarship, the second and third express continuity and dominated during the early church and Reformation periods.¹⁴

In a comprehensive study Badenas sought to clarify the meaning of τέλος in Rom 10:4 by studying the term's use in Classical Greek literature, Greek philosophy, the LXX, the Pseudepigrapha, Aristeas, Philo, Josephus, and the NT. He concluded, "Semantics, grammar, and literature strongly favor a teleological interpretation of this phrase [τέλος νόμου]."¹⁵ Moo believes that Badenas's study is correct as far as extrabiblical literature but wrong on the use of τέλος in the LXX and NT: "In both the LXX and the NT the

---

12. See discussion of τὰ λόγια τοῦ θεοῦ in Fitzmyer, *Romans*, 326.

13. These are the categories used in Badenas, *Christ the End of the Law*, 3-4.

14. Badenas, *Christ the End of the Law*, 7-37. Among the scholars who read τέλος in Rom 10:4 as temporal/terminal are Longenecker, *Romans*, 848-52; Schreiner, *Romans*, 544-48; Schlier, *Der Römerbrief*, 311; Räisänen, *Paul and the Law*, 53-56; Westerholm, *Israel's Law*, 130; Sanders, *Paul, the Law*, 39; Morris, *Romans*, 379-81; Schmithals, *Der Römerbrief*, 369-70. Dunn, *Romans 9-16*, 596-98, here 598, qualifies his support for the temporal/terminal reading: "It is not the law as such which ceased with the new epoch brought in by Christ, but the law seen as a way of proving righteousness, of documenting God's special regard for Israel, of marking Israel out from the other nations, the law understood in terms of works." Those who interpret it teleologically include Fitzmyer, *Romans*, 584; Ziesler, *Paul's Letter to the Romans*, 257-58; Jewett, *Romans*, 619-20.

15. Badenas, *Christ the End of the Law*, 38-80, here 80.

temporal meaning ("closing part," "termination") of *telos* dominates."[16] As far as the LXX, Badenas acknowledges the occasional temporal use of τέλος as a "peculiar feature of biblical literature,"[17] but nonetheless concludes that:

> The predominant uses of τέλος in the LXX are indicative of fullness, totality and consummation. Τέλος is used in the LXX more often than in classical Greek literature in temporal expressions, frequently for designating the completion of a specific period of time, and in two instances for the consummation of the eschatological end, which is also a novelty.[18]

Within the NT Paul's use of τέλος can be readily investigated. He uses the term thirteen times in his extant letters outside of Rom 10:4. In Rom 13:7 it twice means "tax." In four occasions τέλος refers to the end of an era of history itself (1 Cor 1:8; 10:11; 15:24; 2 Cor 3:13). In four instances it refers to the result or outcome of something, as precipitated one's deeds (Rom 6:21, 22; 2 Cor 11:15; Phil 3:19). In two texts τέλος means fully or completely (2 Cor 1:13; 1 Thess 2:16). In one text it could best be translated as "aim" or "goal" (1 Tim 1:5). Thus, in only four out of thirteen occurrences does τέλος have a strictly temporal/terminal meaning.

Exegetically, τέλος makes better sense used teleologically in the immediate context, Rom 9:30–10:21. To begin with, Paul uses racing terminology (verbs διώκω, καταλαμβάνω, φθάνω, προσκόπτω) to express the idea that the Gentiles had reached the goal of righteousness whereas the Israelites had stumbled over the "stone" of Christ in their pursuit of righteousness. It would be natural to expect Paul to continue to talk from a forward-looking perspective in 10:1–4; the *outcome of the law*, then, is meant to be Christ and his righteousness for all.[19] It would not make sense to introduce here a disjunction in salvation history by saying that Christ abolished the law.

Moreover, in 10:5–21 Paul proceeds to demonstrate how, scripturally speaking, one can foresee the path to righteousness by faith in Christ: it is found in Deut 30:12–14 regarding the nearness of the word of faith within

---

16. Moo, *Romans*, 639. Moo (640n41) faults Badenas for including occurrences where τέλος means "result" or "outcome" in the teleological category. Moo claims that only a meaning of "purpose" is appropriately teleological. However, Badenas's labeling of Rom 6:21, 22; 2 Cor 3:13; and 1 Tim 1:5 as teleological seems fair in that these usages all point forward in time, whether in indicating purpose or the result of something.

17. Badenas, *Christ the End of the Law*, 57.

18. Badenas, *Christ the End of the Law*, 61.

19. Jewett, *Romans*, 619, "The words, 'For Christ is the goal of the law,' serve to explain the misunderstanding about the purpose of the law manifest in the phenomenon of competitive zeal, not to summarize Paul's doctrine of freedom from the law and justification by faith alone."

the choice of the path to life or death; it is found in Isa 28:16 regarding the confidence of choosing God's cornerstone; it is found in Joel 2:32 in the invitation to call on the name of Jesus; and it is found in Isa 52:17 regarding the splendor of the messengers of Christ. Scripture also foretells the acceptance of the gospel by the Gentiles and the rejection of the gospel message by some in Israel (Isa 53:1; Ps 19:4; Deut 32:21; Isa 65:1, 2). Scripture, then, *leads* us to Christ. It *points forward* to him. He is the goal and outcome of the law in its fuller, synecdochic, sense as the OT scriptures. Badenas likewise concludes:

> It is the contention of the present study that a teleological interpretation of Rom 10.4 is the only proper way to understand this verse, not only in harmony with its context, but as contributing to the explanation of such important elements in the context as "the word of God has not failed" (9.6), the "attainment of righteousness" by the Gentiles (9.30), Israel's "not attaining" to the law (9.31), its "ignoring God's righteousness" (10.2–3) and its "stumbling over the stone" (9.33).
>
> This verse becomes the key statement and the logical conclusion of the whole passage. It means that this righteousness that Christ has brought for all is the object and goal to which all along the law has been directed, its true intention and meaning.[20]

To summarize to this point, Paul's rhetoric concerning the law in Romans is a kinder, gentler one than in Galatians. Perhaps he deliberately tailors his language out of deference to the Jewish Christians living in Rome. Nonetheless, Romans presents a striking contrast to the negativity of the Galatian correspondence. In Romans the law is *God's* law. It has the potential to lead to life were it not for sin (the blame for the failure to attain righteousness, then, is placed squarely on sinful human beings, and the law is exculpated). The law is holy, righteous, and good, but it does serve as the measure against which sins and transgressions are judged; in that sense, sin increases where there is law. For the Jewish people the law is a treasure, and they are blessed to have it. Although some have attempted to find their own righteousness through the law, the law actually points forward to Christ. Now that he has come, the law continues as a state of affairs between Israel and God, though (1) its fulfillment is found in Christ and (2) it is clear that righteousness that is satisfactory before God cannot be found in obedience to it.

---

20. Badenas, *Christ the End of the Law*, 117.

PAUL'S TORAH-OBSERVANT CONDUCT

Having demonstrated Paul to be more moderate in his rhetoric concerning the law in Romans, I now turn to his personal conduct. In many ways Paul remained a Torah-observant Jew: "In his own life, Paul obviously remained consistently faithful to the Torah."[21] "Paul, also after his 'conversion,' talks and lives as a Jew, and is loyal to his people and his Jewish heritage."[22] While it may be difficult to discern these aspects of Paul in his letters to churches, several examples are evident when one turns to Luke's record of Paul's journeys.[23] I will examine these in an attempt to demonstrate that Paul's behavior is out of keeping with his thoughts concerning the law in Galatians.

The Circumcision of Timothy

Some time after the Jerusalem Council, Paul set off on his second missionary journey. It was in Lystra that he met Timothy, whose mother was Jewish and whose father was Greek (Luke's mention of this probably means that he wants us to think of Timothy as Jewish by matrilineal descent).[24] Luke writes in 16:3 that "Paul wanted to take [Timothy] with him, and, taking him, he circumcised him on account of the Jews that were in those places. For they all knew that Timothy's father was a Greek."

Paul's action in circumcising Timothy is shocking, but not because it occurred in the aftermath of the Jerusalem Council, the decree of which pertained only to Gentiles. It is shocking when held up to his statements to the Galatians.[25] Did Paul truly believe that the law was temporary, abrogated by the coming of Christ? Did he believe that it was an oppressive, enslaving force that should not be entered into by circumcision? If so, why would he have circumcised his young protégé?

It is not enough to say, as some commentators do and as the text implies (διὰ τοὺς Ἰουδαίους τοὺς ὄντας ἐν τοῖς τόποις ἐκείνοις [16:3]), that Timothy's

---

21. Schoeps, *Paul*, 199. See also Jervell, *Luke and the People of God*, 145; Jervell, *Theology of the Acts*, 53, "Paul is the prophetic charismatic, who has always kept the law and keeps it today, performing even more than the law requires."

22. Hvalvik, "Paul as a Jewish Believer," 122; see the entire chapter (121–53), as Hvalvik's methodology and conclusions are similar to my own in this section.

23. The historicity of Acts is assumed. See Keener's defense of Luke's accuracy in Keener, *Acts*, 1:166–220.

24. Cf. *b. Yebam.* 45b, "A Gentile or a slave who had sexual relations with an Israelite woman—the offspring is valid, whether it was a woman without marital ties or a married woman."

25. Cf. the refusal to circumcise Titus in Gal 2:1, 3.

circumcision was done *simply* for missionary expediency.[26] It is simply hard to believe that the same Paul who railed against the "foolish Galatians" and insisted that circumcision would sever them from Christ would take matters into his own hands here in favor of circumcision. Was Paul not willing to stand up for his principles? Furthermore, even if we grant that he gained ground among the Jews for ostensibly treating circumcision as a necessary rite, would these missionary targets not have been angry to later learn the truth?[27]

As Keener notes, many scholars take this difference to be a "serious incongruity: how could Paul battle circumcisionists in Acts 15:1–2 (on the Lukan literary level) and struggle with Barnabas and contend for Titus's freedom (Gal 2:3–5, 13, on the historical level), then circumcise Timothy afterward?"[28] Keener tries to solve the incongruity by bifurcating Paul's position on circumcision: "As Luke's Paul opposes only Gentile, not Jewish, circumcision, the same may be said for the epistolary Paul."[29] Unfortunately, as we will see in the next chapter, that solution does not work. "Epistolary Paul" (the Galatian version) is categorically opposed to circumcision for Gentiles *and* for the Jews who have been redeemed from the law's slavery. As Barrett observes:

> The epistles make it clear that the contention [against circumcision] had been sharper than Acts allows us to see. "If you are circumcised, Christ will do you no good at all" (Gal 5.2). "If anyone was called in a state of circumcision, let him not undo it; if anyone was called in a state of uncircumcision, let him not be circumcised" (1 Cor. 7.18). He had resisted attempts in Jerusalem to have Titus circumcised (Gal. 2.3–5). Is it likely that Paul would, apparently without pressure, circumcise his intended companion?[30]

---

26. E.g., Keener, *Acts*, 3:2320; Polhill, *Acts*, 343; Conzelmann, *Acts*, 125, argues that Paul needed to be accompanied by Jewish associates in order to enter synagogues, but Barrett, *Acts*, 2:761, holds that Gentiles favorable to Judaism could enter the synagogue.

27. Haenchen, *Acts*, 481, "Paul was convinced that [circumcision] did not lead to χάρις but to the ὀργὴ θεοῦ. Paul could not disregard the religious significance of circumcision. The idea that a man could allow himself to be circumcised in order to avoid any difficulties in the mission . . . would have been for him a lie and at the same time a blasphemy against God." Cf. Gal 5:11.

28. Keener, *Acts*, 3:2320–21. Cf. Becker, *Paul*, 127, "The idea that Paul should have [Timothy] circumcised (Acts 16:3) contradicts so blatantly the Pauline conception (Gal. 2:3; 1 Cor. 7:18–19) that this note deserves no credence."

29. Keener, *Acts*, 3:2322.

30. Barrett, *Acts*, 2:760–61.

Or is it only Gentiles who are obligated to obey the entire law if circumcised (Gal 5:3)? Is it only Gentiles who, being therefore "under the law," fall prey to its curses and enslaving power as well (Gal 3:10; 4:3)? And is it only Gentiles who, having trodden the treacherous path into slavery to the law, are severed from fellowship with the one who frees from the law? "Epistolary Paul" has dug a hole for himself which, if his words are taken at face value, seems impossible to escape from with his rhetorical consistency intact.

In the opinion of Paul and other Jewish Christians of that era, the law continued to be valid for the Jewish people. Thus, it was only natural that Jewish Christians continued to circumcise their male children.[31] And, it was only natural that, in the case of someone with mixed parentage, that they err on the side of caution and circumcise Timothy for the sake of the mission.[32] However, his circumcision was not *simply* for the sake of the mission. Paul was not being double-minded or hypocritical. He truly believed in the ways of the Torah for Jewish Christians and that they did not conflict with living in devotion to the messiah Jesus. His derogatory statements about the law in Galatians, as we will see later, are not to be taken at face value.

The Vow

In Acts 18:18 Luke writes that Paul, before he sailed from Corinth to Syria, had his hair cut off at Cenchrea because "he had taken a vow" (εἶχεν γὰρ εὐχήν). The term εὐχή is "a solemn promise with the understanding that one is subject to penalty for failure to discharge the obligation" (BDAG). The text is silent as to the reason for Paul's vow, but most scholars believe it was either a formal Nazirite vow or a private vow of thanksgiving for God's promise of protection in Corinth (Acts 16:9–10).[33] The fact that the vow

---

31. See Schnabel, *Acts*, 665; Johnson, *Acts*, 289: "Did Luke think circumcision appropriate for Jewish Christians? Once more, the answer is, emphatically, yes. The decision concerning the freedom of the Gentiles by the council did not affect the traditions of the Jewish people. Luke throughout his work considers the normativeness of Torah for the messianic community to consist primarily in its prophetic function. It is not the norm for righteousness or salvation. But as the *ethos* of the Jewish people, it is a legitimate expression of identity and their ancestral commitment to God."

32. Children of mixed Jewish-Gentile were still regarded as Jewish. Perhaps, as some suggest, Timothy's father had been opposed to his circumcision but was now deceased.

33. The opinion that it was a Nazirite vow is held by Johnson, *Acts*, 329; Haenchen, *Acts*, 543; Keener, *Acts*, 3:2781; Polhill, *Acts*, 390; Bock, *Acts*, 586; Marshall, *Acts*, 300; Bruce, *Acts*, 398; Munck, *Acts*, 180, in which case Paul may have been cutting his hair *before* the vow (since the cutting of hair to end the vow was supposed to take place in Jerusalem [Num 6:18], although there may have been exceptions allowed for those

involved the cutting of hair favors a Nazirite vow, but in either case Paul is acting based on established Jewish custom.

Once again we find Paul to be acting in strange relationship to the principles he enunciated in Galatians. Keener writes, "Some scholars find Paul's shaving of his head historically incredible in view of the stand they believe he takes against the law."[34] And so they should. Keener attempts to rehabilitate Paul in order to harmonize Acts and Galatians: "Paul was not against practicing the law (see, e.g., Rom 3:27–31; 7:12–16; 10:6–8 [with its basis in Deut 30:11–14]) but against abusing it as if it were a means to justify oneself before God by one's own obedience."[35] It is telling that Keener cites passages from Romans to back up his statement. It would be difficult, if not impossible, to do the same from Galatians. One wonders why, in light of Keener's reasoning, Paul could not have simply allowed the Galatians to be circumcised and still follow Christ, as long as they were not abusing the law. The so-called *status quo* principle is commonly cited as the counter argument (1 Cor 7:18–19; Gal 5:6; 6:15): "Just as Gentiles were not to become circumcised, Jews were not to become uncircumcised."[36] I will demonstrate the shortcomings of this attempted harmonization of Paul in chapter 3.

Keeping the Feasts

In Acts 19:21 we learn that Paul had decided to return to Jerusalem from Ephesus by way of Macedonia and Achaia. Paul's itinerary following the riot in Ephesus is recorded in chapter 20. In the midst of this travelogue Luke mentions two feasts, the observance of which causes modifications to Paul's travel plans. The first is when Paul remains in Philippi to celebrate the Feast of Unleavened Bread (20:6). The second, in 20:16, is when he decides to sail past Ephesus because "he was hurrying to be in Jerusalem, if possible, on the day of Pentecost."

Regarding the first instance, it may be assumed that Paul remained in Philippi for seven days to celebrate the Feast of Unleavened Bread.[37] Some commentators, however, see Luke's mention of the feast as merely a time

---

outside Jerusalem [Josephus, *J.W.* 2.309–14]). See Num 6:1–21 and *m. Nazir* for the many regulations concerning Nazirite vows.

34. Keener, *Acts*, 3:2784; Conzelmann, *Acts*, 155, argues that "one is not dealing with the historical Paul here at all."

35. Keener, *Acts*, 3:2784.

36. Keener, *Acts*, 3:2784.

37. So Schnabel, *Acts*, 834; Keener, *Acts*, 3:2959–60; Fitzmyer, *Romans*, 666; Bock, *Acts*, 619.

marker, arguing that Paul would not have celebrated a Jewish-style Passover in a majority Gentile community.[38] Marshall views the celebration as a Christianized Passover, that is, Easter.[39]

Acts 20:16 is a clearer sign that Paul remained Torah observant with regard to the feasts. It is a picture of "pious Paul."[40] As Johnson admits, "The mention of Passover and of Paul's desire to be in Jerusalem for the feast of Pentecost serve to demonstrate again the apostle's dedication to the *ethos* of Judaism."[41]

The Arrival in Jerusalem

Acts 21 delivers a remarkable account of Paul's Torah-observant behavior upon his arrival in Jerusalem at the close of his third missionary journey. First, the text indicates that he received a warm welcome (ἀσμένως ἀπεδέξαντο ἡμᾶς οἱ ἀδελφοί, "the brothers received us gladly," 21:17). There seemed to be no tension, then, between Paul and the Jerusalem apostles at this point. On the contrary, when Paul related the news of his ministry among the Gentiles, James and the elders gave glory to God (ἐδόξαζον τὸν θεόν, 21:20). It seems as if from Luke's standpoint that they were behind Paul's ministry.

Only there were some in Jerusalem who were questioning it. James and the elders told Paul about the thousands (μυριάδες) of Jewish Christian converts who were zealous for the law (21:20). These converts had been informed (κατηχέω) that Paul was teaching apostasy to Moses (ἀποστασίαν διδάσκεις ἀπὸ Μωϋσέως) among the Jews in the diaspora, telling them not to circumcise their children or to live according to Jewish customs (τοῖς ἔθεσιν περιπατεῖν, 21:21). No doubt concerned about hostility from this group, James and the elders devised a plan whereby Paul would join in the purification rites of, and pay the expenses for, four men who had taken a vow (21:23–24a).[42] A startling statement follows: καὶ γνώσονται πάντες ὅτι ὧν κατήχηνται περὶ σοῦ οὐδέν ἐστιν ἀλλὰ στοιχεῖς καὶ αὐτὸς φυλάσσων τὸν νόμον, "then all will know that there is no truth in what they have been informed about you but that you yourself live in observance to the law" (21:24b).

38. Pervo, *Acts*, 509n47; Haenchen, *Acts*, 583.
39. Marshall, *Acts*, 325.
40. Haenchen, *Acts*, 588.
41. Johnson, *Acts*, 355.
42. Paying the expenses of Nazirites was considered a pious act (see Josephus, *Ant.* 19.294, in which Herod Agrippa I commands a group of Nazirites to shave their heads upon his entry into Jerusalem and it is implied that he paid their expenses).

There is no indication here that James and the elders are attempting to pull the proverbial wool over the eyes of the zealous Jewish Christians. Rather, it is implied that this charge against Paul is false.[43] He was *not* teaching diaspora Jews to stop circumcising their children. He was *not* teaching them to stop following the law. And he *was* remaining Torah-observant himself. In order to confirm these truths, Paul purified himself along with the four men (21:26).[44]

This passage bears three important implications. (1) Paul distinguished between Jews and Gentiles in his teaching concerning the law. To the Gentiles the law was presented as temporary, but to Jews Paul regarded it as enduring (or at least he did not advocate forsaking it). (2) Jewish Christians, at least in Jerusalem, continued to circumcise their children and observe the law.[45] (3) Paul acted as though the law remained an enduring force for him as well.[46] It is not clear from the context whether Paul actually *believed* that the law was still valid or simply acted thusly as a missionary strategy (1 Cor 9:20).[47] One could surmise, in any case, that Paul's Torah observance was apparent, and thus well-known, to others (such an all-encompassing lifestyle would have been hard to conceal).[48]

As we have seen to this point, it is difficult to reconcile the Paul of Acts with the Paul of Galatians. Paul's actions upon entering Jerusalem represent yet another incident which appears to strain credulity. Either Luke has misrepresented Paul or scholars have misconstrued Paul's teachings in his letters. I argue the latter in chapter 3. Some scholars, however, prefer the former explanation, as with Hausrath, who asserted that it was more likely

---

43. Keener, *Acts*, 3:3127; Barrett, *Acts*, 1009.

44. It is difficult to determine the exact reason why Paul partook in purification. Had he taken a Nazirite vow himself (Munck, *Acts*, 211)? Was he engaging in some sort of ritual purification designed to cleanse Jews who had traveled abroad and thus been defiled (Haenchen, *Acts*, 612; Bruce, *Acts*, 447; Schnabel, *Acts*, 876). At the very least, Paul may have required purification in order to be active in the temple with the four men (Keener, *Acts*, 3:3138).

45. Apparently, however, the Jewish Christians in Antioch had relaxed their requirements for table fellowship with Gentiles (cf. Gal 2:12f.).

46. Polhill, *Acts*, 448, "There is no evidence that [Paul] urged Jewish Christians to abandon their ancestral law, and Acts would indicate that he himself remained true to the Torah in his own dealings with Jews (cf. 18:18; 20:6; 23:5)."

47. Bock, *Acts*, 648, epitomizes the attempt by some to harmonize this account with the Paul of the letters: "What we see here is Paul being asked to act with cultural sensitivity to the Jewish context he now finds himself in, without compromising the gospel. He is quite willing to do so for the sake of the unity it may create."

48. One wonders what Paul's Gentile converts would have thought of him for continuing to live according to a law that supposedly was abolished.

"that Calvin on his death-bed vowed a golden coat to the Holy Mother of God" than that Paul actually followed through on this ritual.[49]

The Defense Speeches

Much can be gleaned about how Paul saw himself in relation to the law by examining his own words as he defends his conduct in Acts. What one finds is that Paul's words are consistent with his actions described to this point. Jervell summarizes the defense speeches into three main points:

1. Paul was and is a Pharisee and a Jew who is faithful to the law (22:3; 23:1, 3, 5, 6; 24:14; 26:4-5)

2. He believes everything that is written in the law and the prophets, and he teaches only what Scripture says. Nothing in his preaching and teaching is un-Jewish (24:14f.; 26:22f).

3. He is charged because he preaches the resurrection, whereby it should be observed that the resurrection expresses God's promises to the people and the hope of Pharisaic Israel (23:6, 24:21, 26:6-8). Belief in the resurrection means fidelity to Scripture, law and people (24:14ff.; 26:22f).[50]

In 23:1, before the Sanhedrin, Paul says, "Brothers, I have lived before God in all good conscience to this day" (ἄνδρες ἀδελφοί, ἐγὼ πάσῃ συνειδήσει ἀγαθῇ πεπολίτευμαι τῷ θεῷ ἄχρι ταύτης τῆς ἡμέρας) The verb πολιτεύομαι is uncommon in the NT, occurring only here and in Phil 1:27. One might have expected the more common περιπατέω to describe his conduct.[51] Πολιτεύομαι, however, can also have the sense of being a citizen (BDAG; cf. Phil 1:27, where many commentators interpret it as having to do with civic duties of citizenship, partially due to the noun πολίτευμα in Phil 3:20).[52] In this case, τῷ θεῷ (the second part of the double dative) may picture God as the head of the community of Israel to whom its citizens are accountable (cf. NIV "I have fulfilled my duty before God").[53] In any event, Paul is certainly talking in terms of his obedience to the law.[54] The phrase

---

49. Hausrath, *History of New Testament Times*, 4:111-12.
50. Jervell, *Luke and the People of God*, 163.
51. According to Keener, *Acts*, 3:3266, Paul "almost certainly is speaking Greek here."
52. *NIDNTTE* 4:96.
53. Bock, *Acts*, 669, "He has lived as a good citizen before God."
54. Keener, *Acts*, 3:3268.

ἄχρι ταύτης τῆς ἡμέρας indicates that he has been law observant throughout his Christian life.

A little further on Paul proclaims, "I am a Pharisee," (ἐγὼ Φαρισαῖός εἰμι, 23:6), εἰμι being a customary present indicating an ongoing state.[55] His purpose here is to align himself with the Pharisaic members of the Sanhedrin, to express his continuity with their beliefs, especially with regard to the resurrection. Again, Paul makes no distinction between his pre- and post-conversion religious identity, between the salvation-by-works versus salvation-by-grace program. He is simply "a Pharisee," a Torah-observant Jew belonging to a strict sect. A larger point here is that Paul appears to be reducing his differences with the Sanhedrin to the matter of the resurrection. While this may be a divide-and-conquer strategy, designed to get the Pharisees on his side, his sentiment is, "I am one of you. There is no difference between us." Paul thus expresses a marked continuity between Pharisaism and Christianity as if there were little if any difference.[56] He stands as a living example of this continuity.

Two statements stand out in Paul's speech before Felix (24:11–21). The first is Paul's declaration in verse 14, "I worship the God of our fathers, believing all that is written according to the law and the prophets" (κατὰ τὸν νόμον καὶ τοῖς ἐν τοῖς προφήταις γεγραμμένοις, referring to the two parts of the Hebrew Scriptures). A clearer statement could not be found of Paul's allegiance to the law.[57] However, it presents a Pauline theologian with difficulties: "Could he have claimed to believe all the things according to the Law? Only if he were allowed to give some of them a new interpretation, to understand circumcision, for example, as circumcision of the heart, in spirit not letter."[58] The second statement that stands out is verse 16, "So I always do my best to have a clear conscience before God and man." This verse implies

---

55. The full proclamation, emphasizing Paul's Torah-observant lineage, is, "I am a Pharisee, a son of Pharisees." Since Paul is from Tarsus, the implication is that Pharisaism had reached the diaspora. Keener, *Acts*, 3:3289, however, believes it more likely that Paul's family moved to Jerusalem early in his life and that his father became a Pharisee there.

56. Haenchen, *Acts*, 643, "What Paul was now claiming was that one could be a Christian, while accepting the Pharisaic point of view"; Marshall, *Acts*, 364, "Paul's statements about his teaching, when on trial, are apologetically formed and reduce his teaching to the Jewish 'hope' of the resurrection of the dead. . . . These statements obscure the essential difference from Judaism, its law and its hope, which went with belief in Jesus as the Messiah. . . . In Acts . . . there is an uninterrupted continuity of redemptive history and the simple identification of the Jewish and Christian hope."

57. Paul's appeal is an appeal to ethos, to undermine the charge of *seditio* and reframe the case around an intra-religious dispute (Vielhauer, "On the 'Paulinism' in Acts," 41).

58. Keener, *Acts*, 4:3398–99.

that there is some behavioral standard of Jewish piety that Paul has met based on his own effort: "Paul is 'guilty' only of being religiously faithful, a good Jew."[59]

Paul mounts a similar defense before Festus, insisting that he has "committed no offense (ἥμαρτον) toward the Jewish law (τὸν νόμον τῶν Ἰουδαίων) or against the temple or against Caesar" (25:8). By using ἁμαρτάνω Paul may be indicating a legal wrong.[60] Here again, though, is a plain admission that "Paul had not abandoned Torah or encouraged other Jews to abandon the Torah."[61]

Finally, Paul's defense before Agrippa involves Paul rehearsing his history of adherence to strict nomistic norms: "I lived according to the strictest sect of our religion, the Pharisees" (κατὰ τὴν ἀκριβεστάτην αἵρεσιν τῆς ἡμετέρας θρησκείας ἔζησα Φαρισαῖος, 26:5). In saying this, Paul does not offer a *terminus ad quem* for his Pharisaic observance. A hearer would reasonably infer that Paul continued to follow the strictest regiments of Judaism: "Paul had been born a true Jew, reared a true Jew, trained in the strictest Pharisaic viewpoint of Judaism, and still remained a true Jew."[62] Keener adds, "Paul's claim . . . does not mean that he has since abandoned Pharisaism."[63]

SUMMARY

By his words in Romans and his actions detailed in Acts, Paul demonstrates his loyalty to, and affection for, the Jewish Torah. In Romans he expresses his belief that:

1. The law is from God.

2. The law is meant to bring life. As a side effect, however, it brings consciousness of sin, and sin takes advantage of the law.

3. The law promises rewards to those who keep it. As part of the oracles of God, it is a cherished part of Jewish life.

4. The law continues indefinitely.

---

59. Barrett, *Acts*, 1104.
60. Bock, *Acts*, 693.
61. Fitzmyer, *Romans*, 744.
62. Polhill, *Acts*, 500; Schnabel, *Acts*, 989, "Paul had not abandoned the Torah or encouraged other Jews to abandon the Torah."
63. Keener, *Acts*, 4:3498.

Paul's Torah observance is indicated by several of his actions as recorded in Acts:[64]

1. Paul's circumcision of Timothy (16:3)
2. Paul's Nazirite vow (18:18)
3. Paul's keeping of the Feast of Unleavened Break (20:6) and his desire to celebrate Pentecost (20:16)
4. Paul's joining in a Nazirite vow upon James's recommendation (21:17–26)
5. Paul's assertions that he is Torah-observant (23:1, 6; 24:14,16; 25:8; 26:5)

Taken together the evidence indicates that, as Vielhauer suggests, "Acts portrays the Gentile missionary Paul as a Jewish Christian who is utterly loyal to the law."[65] Thus, our picture of Paul and his relationship to the law advances in an antithetical trajectory from where we began in chapter 1. Which is the real Paul, the Paul of Galatians or the Paul of Romans/Acts? Strategies for solving this puzzle are the subject of chapter 3.

---

64. To this list Vielhauer, "On the 'Paulinism' in Acts," 38, adds (a) Paul's missionary method of beginning at the synagogue, (b) Paul's submission to the Jewish authorities, and (c) Paul's spreading of the apostolic decree (16:4).

65. Vielhauer, "On the 'Paulinism' in Acts," 38.

3

Toward a Solution

In this chapter…

Question(s) to be answered:
- How can Paul's negative attitude in Galatians be reconciled with his more positive one in Romans/Acts?

Trajectory:
- Chapter 3 establishes the rationale for the entire work. A new solution (hyperbole) is proposed.

IN THE FIRST TWO chapters I demonstrated the striking contrast between the Paul of Galatians and the Paul of Acts/Romans. From that discussion emerged the implication that Paul embodies a paradox. On the one hand, his statements in Galatians concerning the law are harsh. One might even say that they evince something approaching antinomianism. On the other hand, his writings in Romans and the biographical statements concerning him in Acts suggest an abiding loyalty to the law. Reconciling this tension has been the aim of many theologians throughout church history. Attempts at solutions generally fall along one of the following perspectives:

1. Acts as tendentious and unhistorical
2. Paul as accommodating to his audience
3. Paul as speaking differently to Jews and Gentiles
4. Paul as an inconsistent thinker
5. Paul as developing his thought over time
6. Paul as clarifying his thinking on the law

7. Galatians as anti-ethnocentric

In this chapter I would like to walk the reader through the above perspectives, considering the strengths and weaknesses of each. The list is not intended to be all-encompassing; there are likely to be angles I have overlooked. Nor is my aim necessarily to *disprove* the perspectives in this list. The viability of these perspectives, in other words, is not something upon which my overall thesis stands or falls. I will simply be laying the groundwork for presenting (in chapters 9 through 11) a new way of viewing Galatians, one which I feel offers a stronger explanation for the paradox than the perspectives included in this chapter.

ACTS AS TENDENTIOUS AND UNHISTORICAL

Does Acts exhibit a *Tendenz*? Let us assume for the sake of argument that it does. It would be difficult to imagine a completely bias-free history, after all, and Acts is no exception. Given the amount of space devoted to Paul and the positive construal of him, Acts appears to tilt in a favorable direction regarding this apostolic hero. Even a conservative scholar concedes as much:

> Some scholars think that Luke wrote partly to defend Paul or Pauline Christianity for his generation. Although I was for a time more skeptical of this approach, after working through especially the defense speeches (but also the rest of the Pauline part of Acts), I now concur that this is indeed part of Luke's apologetic objective (though not his only purpose). Ancients could certainly propagandize for or defend their heroes.[1]

But does admitting that Luke has a tendency to lionize Paul necessarily mean that he is *inaccurate* in his historiography? However selectively Luke might have presented the biographical details of Paul, there remains the more important (for our purposes) question of whether he was faithful in rendering those details.[2] In other words, is Luke's account historically trustworthy?

Let us take, as a starting point, the theory of F. C. Baur and the Tübingen school that the Christian church arose out of a tension between a

---

1. Keener, *Acts*, 1:222–23. Cf. Jervell's essay, "Paul: The Teacher of Israel: The Apologetic Speeches of Paul in Acts," in Jervell, *Luke and the People of God*, 153–83; Schneckenburger, *Ueber den Zweck der Apostelgeschichte*, cited in Tyson, "Wrestling with and for Paul," 16.

2. See Mattill, "Value of Acts," 76–98, for the different schools of thought among researchers concerning the historicity of Acts.

Jewish/Petrine version of Christianity, which held the law in high esteem, and Pauline Christianity, which emphasized grace over law. This early conflict may be suggested in the factionalism described by Paul within the Corinthian church: the Christ party and Peter party aligned against the Paul and Apollos parties.[3] Moreover, in Galatians one finds "the critical struggle which had begun between Judaism and Christianity, in the decision of the momentous question whether there should be a Christianity free from Judaism and essentially different from it, or whether Christianity should only exist as a form of Judaism, that is to say, as nothing else than a modified and extended Judaism."[4] In Acts, however, a more irenic tone appears between the apostles, as if the former battles of the church had given way to a unified front. Peter is pictured as acting in a Pauline way (being a missionary to the Gentile Cornelius), while Paul is depicted as behaving in a Petrine way (circumcising Timothy, taking a vow, declaring himself a Pharisee, etc.). For this reason Baur concluded that Acts is an early second century work composed some time after these internal tensions held sway in the early church.

The irenic tone of Acts also persuaded Baur that Acts was unreliable as a source for the life and work of Paul. "The unity of the work consists in this idea; its chief tendency is to represent the difference between Peter and Paul as unessential and trifling."[5] The account of the Jerusalem conference, which looks much different than the contentious debate envisioned by Gal 2, is not to be taken seriously: "The Acts of the Apostles represents the elder Apostles as agreeing with the Apostle Paul with regard to his views and principles in such a manner as never could have taken place according to the Epistle to the Galatians."[6] In all of this, Luke is guilty of throwing "a concealing veil" over the disputes in Jerusalem and Antioch.[7]

Baur also takes on Luke's portrayal of the Jewishness of Paul in Acts. For Paul to be cast as a Torah-abiding Jew is so different from his epistolary identity that it seems suspect. In fact, Baur believes that the accusation in Acts 21 that Paul apostatized from Judaism and taught Jews not to circumcise their newborns was true ("How could the Apostle maintain the necessity of circumcision for the Jews, if he ignored it for the Gentiles?").[8] Paul preached against circumcision to both Jews and Gentiles, Baur asserts,

---

3. Baur, "Die Christuspartei," 61–206; cf. Baur, *Church History*, 44–152.
4. Baur, *Paul the Apostle*, 1:263.
5. Baur, *Paul the Apostle*, 1:6.
6. Baur, *Paul the Apostle*, 1:123.
7. Baur, *Paul the Apostle*, 1:135.
8. Baur, *Paul the Apostle*, 1:209.

and no amount of missionary expediency would have deterred him.[9] The epistles, then, are the "only authentic documents for the history of [Paul's] apostolic labours."[10]

A further assault on Luke's historicity comes from the charge that Paul's speeches in Acts are different than the thinking he reveals in his letters. In his 1951 article, "On the 'Paulinism' of Acts," Philipp Vielhauer casts these differences along four theological constructs.[11] First, under the heading of natural theology, Paul condescends to the viewpoint of Hellenistic paganism in saying that humankind can have a knowledge of God:

> The basic difference from the Pauline view of Christian and pre-Christian existence cannot be ignored. When the Areopagus speaker refers to the unity of the human race in its natural kinship to God and to its natural knowledge of God, and when he refers to the altar inscription and to the statements of pagan poets to make this point, he thereby lays claim to pagan history, culture, and religion as the prehistory of Christianity.[12]

Paul's statements in Acts regarding "man's kinship to God" are markedly different, then, from his harsher rhetoric in Rom 1:19f. concerning God's wrath and human guilt.[13] Second, in Acts, Paul exhibited a favorable attitude toward Judaism as expressed in beginning his preaching at synagogues, submitting to the Jerusalem apostles, circumcising Timothy, spreading the apostolic decree, taking a vow(s), intending to participate in Jewish festivals, and stressing that he is a Pharisee when on trial.[14] It is unthinkable, according to Vielhauer, that the same Paul who wrote Galatians would have participated in such activities as Luke describes. Luke must have fundamentally misunderstood Paul: "Luke did know that Paul proclaimed justification by faith, but he did not know its central significance and absolute importance . . . the whole problem of the law—was entirely foreign to Luke."[15] Third, the Paul of Acts appears, in the eyes of some, to manifest an underdeveloped, pre-Pauline Christology, which Luke drew from the early kerygma of the church. This Christology shows up only in the speech to the synagogue at Antioch (13:13–43) and before Agrippa (26:22–23.). Vielhauer describes

---

9. Baur, *Paul the Apostle*, 1:136.

10. Baur, *Paul the Apostle*, 1:255.

11. Vielhauer, "On the 'Paulinism' in Acts," originally published as "Zum 'Paulinismus' der Apostelgeschichte," *EvT* X (1950–51) 1–15.

12. Vielhauer, "On the 'Paulinism' in Acts," 37.

13. Vielhauer, "On the 'Paulinism' in Acts," 37.

14. Vielhauer, "On the 'Paulinism' in Acts," 38.

15. Vielhauer, "On the 'Paulinism' in Acts," 42.

it as adoptionistic rather than a Christology of preexistence: "Nothing is said of the saving significance of the cross of Christ; and consequently also nothing of the reality of 'in Christ' and of the presence of the whole of salvation."[16] Fourth, the eschatology of the epistolary Paul seems missing from Acts. "Eschatology has been removed from the center of Pauline faith to the end and has become a 'section on the last things.'"[17] As with Baur, Vielhauer concludes from all of this that the author of Acts could not have been the traveling companion of Paul and probably wrote as part of the "nascent early catholic church."[18]

Yet another charge against the historical reliability of Acts derives from the observation that a number of facets of Luke's history do not seem to square with Paul's account. For example, Ernst Haenchen points out the incongruity in Luke's account of Paul's activity following his call (according to Acts 9:20, Paul remained in Damascus for several days and then went to Jerusalem and met with the disciples; in Paul's own account in Gal 1:15–24 he first went to Arabia, then to Damascus, and only after three years to Jerusalem).[19] Haenchen calls the circumcision of Timothy "one of those slanderous rumors which were spread abroad about Paul" that Luke believed because it "corresponded to his ideal of a law-abiding Jew."[20] And, Haenchen considers the report that Paul, Silas, and Timothy remained in Berea after the Jewish uprising against Paul in Thessalonica (17:13–16) to be spurious, as 1 Thess 3:2 indicates that Timothy instead went to Athens with Paul.[21]

Lastly, the portrait of Paul in Acts seems, in many ways, "too good to be true."[22] John Lentz believes that Luke endows Paul with high social status for evangelistic purposes among his readers: "The Lucan Paul possesses high social credentials and personifies what would have been recognized, by the first reader/hearer of Acts, as the classical cardinal virtues."[23] It is difficult, Lentz believes, to imagine that Paul could simultaneously have been a Greek, Roman, and Pharisee due to the incompatibilities implicit among these identities.[24]

16. Vielhauer, "On the 'Paulinism' in Acts," 45.
17. Vielhauer, "On the 'Paulinism' in Acts," 45.
18. Vielhauer, "On the 'Paulinism' in Acts," 49.
19. Haenchen, "Book of Acts as Source Material," 268–69.
20. Haenchen, "Book of Acts as Source Material," 271.
21. Haenchen, "Book of Acts as Source Material," 273.
22. Lentz, *Luke's Portrait of Paul*, 171.
23. Lentz, *Luke's Portrait of Paul*, 171.
24. Lentz, *Luke's Portrait of Paul*, 24, Lentz finds it "highly improbable" that a strict

These challenges to the historicity of Acts have not gone unanswered, however. Modern scholars have repeatedly demonstrated that Luke was a historian who utilized trustworthy sources and whose narrative details corresponded well with the surrounding geopolitical landscape. Archaeologist Sir William Ramsay, for instance, once convinced of the Tübingen theory, extensively studied the topography of first century Asia Minor and thereafter found himself an advocate for the historicity of Acts:

> I may fairly claim to have entered on this investigation without any prejudice in favour of the conclusion which I shall now attempt to justify to the reader. On the contrary, I began with a mind unfavourable to it, for the ingenuity and apparent completeness of the Tübingen theory had at one time convinced me. It did not lie then in my line of life to investigate the subject minutely; but more recently I found myself often brought in contact with the book of *Acts* as an authority for the topography, antiquities, and society of Asia Minor. It was gradually borne in upon me that in various details the narrative showed marvellous truth.[25]

Additional undermining of the Tübingen theory resulted from J. B. Lightfoot's research into the Apostolic Fathers.[26] The letters of Clement and Ignatius were found to have referred to Peter and Paul together in a way without suggesting any enmity between them. This was a devastating blow to the Tübingen theory:

> If the theories were correct, certain phenomena should have been observable in these letters. In point of fact, not merely is none of these phenomena to be observed, but what is to be found is so contradictory of what is to be expected as to raise the question whether any of these phenomena were ever at any time anywhere to be found in the Christian world. . . . The whole mythology of the enmity between Peter and Paul, of the later reconciliation in the Church, and of the dating of New Testament

---

Pharisee would also have had Roman citizenship, especially in the diaspora. Also unlikely, in his view, was that there were Pharisees in the diaspora at all (55).

25. Ramsay, *St. Paul the Traveller*, 7–8. Also see Ramsay, *Cities of St. Paul*; Ramsay, *Bearing of Recent Discoveries*, 79–89 (here 85), "Further study of Acts XIII.–XXI. showed that the book could bear the most minute scrutiny as an authority for the facts of the Aegean world, and that it was written with such judgment, skill, art, and perception of truth as to be a model of historical statement."

26. On which see Neill and Wright, *Interpretation of the New Testament*, 53–60.

books in the middle of the second century, had collapsed like a house of cards.²⁷

The past hundred years have seen additional research in support of the historicity of Acts. Commentaries on Acts have been produced supporting Luke's trustworthiness.²⁸ Colin Hemer's 1989 *magnum opus* is also known for its comprehensiveness in establishing the historicity of Acts.²⁹ Hemer presents "a wealth of material suggesting an author or sources familiar with the particular locations and at the times in questions."³⁰ Craig Keener, for his part, devotes one hundred thirty pages to issues of historiography in his recent four-volume commentary.³¹

Several authors have attempted to support the historicity of Acts by demonstrating correspondences to Paul and his letters. F. F. Bruce does so in a 1976 article.³² In his commentary, Keener includes earlier lists of correspondences and then provides his own substantial contribution, including correspondences concerning:³³

- Paul's conversion (Acts versus Paul)
- Paul's escape from Damascus (Acts 9:23–25 versus 2 Cor 11:32–33)
- Paul's visit to Jerusalem (Acts 9:26–30 versus Gal 1:18–19)
- Paul's immediate circle (Acts versus Paul)
- Paul's missionary strategy of beginning with synagogues (Acts versus Paul)
- Paul's stoning in Lystra (Acts versus Paul)
- The Jerusalem Council (Acts 15:6–22 versus Gal 2:1–10)
- Paul's Thessalonian ministry (1 Thessalonians versus Acts 17:1–9)

27. Neill and Wright, *Interpretation of the New Testament*, 60.

28. See, e.g., Marshall, *Luke*, 53–76; Marshall, *Acts*; Bruce, *Acts*. Gasque, "Historical Value of the Book of Acts," 177–96, recounts the scholarly contributions of Lightfoot, Ramsay, and Bruce.

29. Hemer, *Book of Acts*, esp. 101–276. See the summary of Hemer's work in Gasque, "Historical Value of Acts," 136–57.

30. Hemer, *Book of Acts*, 412.

31. Keener, *Acts*, 1:90–220; also see Padilla, *Acts of the Apostles*, 107–20.

32. Bruce, "Is the Paul of Acts the Real Paul?," 282–305. Interestingly, Bruce points out a flaw in the logic of Baur and the Tübingen school. In Gal 2:11–14 Paul characterizes Peter's reaction as ὑπόκρισις, indicating his "awareness that Peter's conduct did not conform with his inner convictions." Therefore, Paul and Peter must have held the same convictions after all.

33. Keener, *Acts*, 1:238–49. The earlier lists of correspondences are from Adolf von Harnack, Thomas H. Campbell, and Michael D. Goulder.

- Paul's Corinthian ministry (Acts versus Paul)
- Paul's travel plans (Acts 19:21 versus Paul)
- Paul's traveling companions (Acts 20:4 versus Paul)

These correspondences are meant to show that Luke's information is historically reliable.

Scholars have also responded to the issue of supposed theological differences between Acts and Paul. Peder Borgen shows how several passages in Paul (Rom 9–11, Rom 15, and 1 Cor 15:1–11) actually illustrate the background for much of Luke's theology.[34] In Rom 11:7–8 Paul interprets Israel's rejection of the Messiah in terms of a hardness of heart; Luke echoes this in Acts 28:26ff. Also, in Rom 11:3 Paul accuses Israel of murdering the prophets; according to Luke, Israel murdered (Luke 13:34) and persecuted (Acts 7:52–53) the prophets. Statements about fulfillment of the promises to Israel, and the sharing of these promises by the Gentiles, are found in both Paul (Rom 15:7–13) and Luke (Acts 3:25–26). And, the chronology of Jesus's death, resurrection, appearances, ascension, and epiphany to Paul from 1 Cor 15 is paralleled in Luke-Acts (Luke 23:33–49, 50–56; 24:1–11, 12–53; Acts 1:1–11; 7:58—8:3; 9:1f.; 13f.; 18:1f.). Borgen concludes:

> Even though there are differences at some points between the Pauline and the Lucan theologies, the theology of Lk must to a great extent be considered a further development of elements occurring in Paul's letters. Lk hardly ever uses the letters, but he is partly dependent on traditions from and concerning Paul, and both Lk and Paul are partly dependent on the same early Christian traditions.[35]

As for Vielhauer and the apparent differences in theology between the Paul of Acts and the Paul of the epistles, Keener argues that Vielhauer is comparing "apples and oranges" in that Paul's letters and Acts "present not only different (yet not necessarily contradictory) emphases but even different genres."[36] Keener answers Vielhauer point for point. Regarding natural theology, Keener argues that Rom 1:19–23 and Acts 17:24–27, though different, are not incompatible. He sees Vielhauer as being "overstrict" in his

---

34. Borgen, "From Paul to Luke," 168–82.
35. Borgen, "From Paul to Luke," 181.
36. Keener, *Acts*, 1:250–51. See also the rebuttal of both Vielhauer and Haenchen in chapter 9 of Porter, *Paul in Acts*, 187–206; Porter concludes, "There are admittedly some differences between the two authors . . . but I would contend that these are merely the kinds of differences that one could expect to find between virtually any two different yet accomplished authors when writing about the same events" (206).

comparison, stating that the accounts "are no more different than one would expect for one writer summarizing another's views or . . . even for the same philosopher (e.g., Seneca) in different passages at different times addressing different concerns in the wide spectrum of natural theology."[37] Regarding Christology, Keener notes that Acts 13 is an evangelistic sermon and that Paul's letters do not tell us how much Christology he typically infused into such sermons.[38] As for the charge that Luke puts "adoptionistic" Christology (and a focus on the resurrection more than the cross) onto Paul's lips, that is an argument from silence, since we do not have an exhaustive account of Paul's preaching, according to Keener.[39] And, finally, Luke's removal of eschatology to the peripheral level is a matter of emphasis, not opposition (Acts 1:67; 3:19–21; 10:42; 17:31).[40]

In conclusion, one attempt to defuse the tension between the Paul of the epistles and the Paul of Acts has been to try to dislocate Acts from its historical setting in the first century and to view the author as someone other than Luke, Paul's traveling companion. I have reviewed the proposals of Baur, the Tübingen school, Vielhauer, Haenchen, and Lentz. The authentic Paul, these scholars say, can only be found in his epistles.

Apologists for Luke's historicity have effectively countered the major arguments lodged against it. Largely missing from their approach, however, is a satisfactory way of dealing with the contradictory perspectives concerning Judaism and the law in Acts and Galatians. Most commonly the response is to employ 1 Cor 9:19–23, as with Porter's attempt to explain Paul's behavior in Acts 21:17–26:

> Paul, maintaining his love for Israel and remembering that God is determined to bring Israel to salvation (Rom 11:11 ff.), clearly illustrates in the book of Acts what he articulates in his letters elsewhere: he made himself a "slave to all, that I might win more" (1 Cor 9:19). This means that "to the Jews I become as a Jew, in order to win Jews, to those under the law I become as one under the law" (1 Cor 9:20), without believing that he has compromised himself.[41]

The inadequacy of this approach will be discussed in the following section.

37. Keener, *Acts*, 1:251.
38. Keener, *Acts*, 1:251.
39. Keener, *Acts*, 1:252.
40. Keener, *Acts*, 1:252.

41. Porter, *Paul in Acts*, 185. Cf. Rudolph, *Jew to the Jews*, 9, "The vast majority of 1 Corinthians and Acts commentators identify Acts 16:3 and Acts 21:17–26 as instances of Paul applying his 1 Cor 9:20 principle of adaptation in a Jewish setting."

PAUL AS ACCOMMODATING TO HIS AUDIENCE

How far was the Apostle Paul willing to go to win converts for Christ? Did he adapt, chameleon-like, to his environment in order to become as similar to his target audience as he could be? Specifically, are Paul's pro-law behavior and rhetoric from Acts simply examples of accommodation to Jews? The prevailing viewpoint in scholarship is that this is precisely what they are.

Researchers lean heavily on 1 Cor 9:19–23 to advance this perspective. This passage begins with a statement concerning Paul's swapping of his freedom for slavery: "For though I am free from all I have made (ἐδούλωσα) myself a slave to all" (verse 19). Eyebrows were no doubt raised among the social status-conscious Corinthians at Paul's voluntary relinquishing of his freedom. As Robinson Butarbutar notes, "Paul's course of conduct runs counter to the standards of morality of these educated Greeks."[42] Paul follows the self-enslavement clause with a purpose clause: "so that I might win (κερδήσω) more of them." His use of the verb κερδαίνω is likely a specialized missionary term for winning converts.[43] Paul willingly enslaves himself to all people so that he might win them to Christ.

Four target groups are named: Jews (Ἰουδαίοις), those under the law (τοῖς ὑπὸ νόμον), those without the law (τοῖς ἀνόμοις), and those who are weak (τοῖς ἀσθενέσιν). The first two likely constitute an instance of synonymous parallelism.[44] Those without the law are Gentiles, while those who are weak are those who, as in Rom 14, are inside the church but who are especially scrupulous regarding some aspect of behavior.[45]

The passage is simple enough in the above respects. The *crux interpretum*, however, is what Paul means by "becoming as" (γίνομαι ... ὡς) a Jew or Gentile. The range of possibilities includes theological accommodation, epistemological/methodological accommodation, and ethical accommodation. Few if any accuse Paul of theological accommodation, especially given his distaste for distortions of the gospel, which amounts to pleasing people (Gal 1:10). Epistemological/methodological accommodation is put forth

---

42. Butarbutar, *Paul and Conflict Resolution*, 169.

43. Daube, *New Testament and Rabbinic Judaism*, 352–61.

44. So Thiselton, *1 Corinthians*, 702; Fee, *1 Corinthians*, 473; Fitzmyer, *First Corinthians*, 369; Conzelmann, *First Corinthians*, 160. Robertson and Plummer, *1 Corinthians*, 191, contend that with "Jews" Paul is speaking of ethnicity and that with "those under the law" he is speaking of religion: "There were some who were under the Mosaic Law who were not Jews by race." Rudolph, *Jew to the Jews*, 153–59, views the distinction in terms of Jews in general versus those who take a strict interpretation of the law.

45. Most commentators interpret "weak" similarly. Garland, *1 Corinthians*, 433–34, however, argues for the continued sense here of κερδαίνω as winning converts, thus, "The 'weak' in this verse represent non-Christians whom he seeks to win for the Lord."

for consideration by Longenecker, Henry Chadwick, and Mark Nanos. Longenecker writes concerning Paul's preaching:

> In every case he seeks to work from the one element of truth which they have grasped to a fuller understanding and expression of their liberty in Christ. . . . And by beginning with them at the point where there is common agreement and omitting such matters and arguments as will cause unnecessary offence, he is but manifesting his missionary and pastoral principle of being "all things to all men."[46]

Similarly, Chadwick emphasizes Paul's methodological flexibility: "Paul's genius as an apologist is his astonishing ability to reduce to an apparent vanishing point the gulf between himself and his converts and yet to 'gain' them for the Christian gospel."[47] The advantage of this approach, which Nanos calls rhetorical adaptability, is that "Paul's behaviour can be described as free of . . . duplicitous conduct."[48]

The bulk of interpreters, though, opt for seeing some kind of ethical accommodation. The verb γίνομαι lends itself to this interpretation, as does the context of 1 Cor 8:1—11:1 concerning participation in food offered to idols.[49] Passages where Paul is seen to be Torah-observant, such as Acts 16:3; 18:18; and 21:23-26, might then be viewed as "occasional accommodation to Jewish practice in order to open doors of evangelism."[50] Perhaps also Paul kept kosher among the Jews but not among the Gentiles.[51] In any event, this interpretation holds that Paul had abandoned important aspects of his Jewishness: "His Judaism was no longer of his very being, but a guise he could adopt or discard at will."[52]

46. Longenecker, *Paul*, 244.
47. Chadwick, "All Things to All Men," 275.
48. Nanos, "Paul's Relationship to Torah," 124.
49. Richardson and Gooch, "Accommodation Ethics," 97, "The passage clearly deals with Paul's behaviour and not simply his methodology in mission or instruction." Also see Rudolph, *Jew to the Jews*, 15-17, who lists a number of reasons for viewing 1 Cor 9:19-23 as lifestyle adaptability: (1) the expression ἐγενόμην . . . ὡς, (2) nomistic language in 9:20, (3) the remark in 9:27 about Paul punishing his body, (4) the fact that 10:32-33 recapitulates 9:19-23 and includes language about pleasing people, (5) the theme of food-related accommodation in the overall context, 1 Cor 8-10, (6) the parallel with "strong" versus "weak" in Rom 14-15, which emphasizes lifestyle adaptability, and (7) the possibility that Paul is speaking here about halakhic adaptability in different table-fellowship contexts.
50. Taylor, *1 Corinthians*, 219; also see Robertson and Plummer, *1 Corinthians*, 191; Fitzmyer, *First Corinthians*, 369.
51. Fee, *1 Corinthians*, 472.
52. Barrett, *1 Corinthians*, 211.

This perspective raises a number of troubling ethical issues, however. First, Paul would have been behaving deceptively, acting as if he valued obedience to the law as did the Jews around him. It would have been impossible for Paul to conceal his true views for very long as he moved between groups of Jews and Gentiles and often even in mixed company. When the Jews discovered Paul's inconsistencies, it would have been a stumbling block for them.[53] For Jews, the law was not something to be obeyed in such a whimsical fashion. As Francis Watson submits, "Occasional conformity to the law is entirely alien to the Jewish way of life, and could never have helped him to 'win those under the law.'"[54]

Second, Paul would have been evidencing a lack of theological integrity. Let us take the issue of circumcision as an example of the ethical adaptability that many think is called for by 1 Cor 9:20–23. How could Paul have felt that it was within his ethical flexibility to circumcise his young friend Timothy if at the same time he held the belief (as expressed in Galatians) that to circumcise a Gentile means putting them under the yoke of the law, which in turn means becoming enslaved and under a curse? He would have been, as Baur suggests, "denying essential principles."[55] One simply cannot use 1 Cor 9:19–23, then, to justify Timothy's circumcision:

> In my opinion it is wrong to cite I Cor. 9:19–23 to demonstrate the historicity of this episode. . . . Circumcision is never a matter of indifference, but rather is confession and acknowledgment of the saving significance of the law, is a denial of baptism, and therefore splits the church: "Now I, Paul, say to you that if you receive circumcision, Christ will be of no advantage to you." The

---

53. Knox, *St. Paul*, 122n54, "S. Paul could not both behave as a Jew when dealing with Jews and as free from the Law when dealing with Gentiles, since apart from the moral dishonesty of pretending to observe the Law when in Jewish society and neglecting it in Gentile society, it would be impossible for him to conceal from Jews whom he hoped to convert the fact that he disregarded the Law when not in Jewish company. Obviously no Jew would be in the smallest degree influenced by the fact that he observed the Law when it suited his purpose to do so; obedience to the Law was a lifelong matter." Also see Rudolph, *Jew to the Jews*, 12–13.

54. Watson, *Paul, Judaism and the Gentiles*, 29. Also see Bornkamm, "Missionary Stance," 197, 1 Cor 9:19ff. "cannot be taken to mean that the apostle played different roles in different places simply for the sake of the missionary effect. To follow such a course would have concealed from his listeners the true reason for his flexible stance. . . . To speak as if Paul Judaized it in one place and paganized it in another is wholly inaccurate"; Garland, *1 Corinthians*, 430, "Paul does not mean that he occasionally obeyed Jewish customs to decoy Jews into listening to his message."

55. Baur, *Paul the Apostle*, 136.

statement about the circumcision of Timothy stands in direct contradiction to the theology of Paul.[56]

And Bornkamm similarly adds:

> It is sometimes said that Paul's consideration for the Jews living in Cilicia reflects the freedom of which he speaks in I Cor. 9:20. . . . It must have been impossible for Paul, especially after the agreements made at the Apostolic Council, to consider circumcision as a ceremony irrelevant to faith and missionary activity. He could scarcely do such a thing for the sake of the Jews for whom circumcision meant more than that.[57]

One is forced, then, to consider a more restrictive application 1 Cor 9:19–23, one that does not run too far afield from its immediate context.

Third, Paul would have been in conflict with his own stance towards Peter at Antioch (Gal 2:11–14). If Paul were accommodating to Jews and Gentiles in some areas, why would he have so vehemently attacked Peter for his own efforts to accommodate the "men from James" with regard to table fellowship with Gentiles?[58]

Fourth, Paul would have undermined his ministry to Gentiles if they discovered him practicing a part-time Judaism. Could not the Galatians have argued, then, that they too were merely wanting to enter into such a lifestyle?[59] Paul would have been hard-pressed to mount an argument against them without appearing as a hypocrite.

To avoid the above difficulties some scholars attempt to limit the range of Jewish behavior on the part of Paul.[60] Garland, for instance, wonders

---

56. Vielhauer, "On the 'Paulinism' in Acts," 40–41.

57. Bornkamm, "Missionary Stance," 203. Bornkamm holds that Acts 21:17-26, although untrustworthy as a whole, is a better example of Paul's accommodation according to 1 Cor 9:20.

58. This question is the subject of Richardson, "Pauline Inconsistency," 347–62. Richardson asserts that Paul and Peter had similar views on accommodation but differed in their application. Paul was angry at Peter because Paul felt that in the situation among the weak at Antioch, accommodation was not the proper response. "Paul's concern for the weak in Antioch and his view that Peter, because he shared Paul's view, was strong in the good sense, pushed him to a statement of a 'no accommodation' principle" (362). See the rebuttal to Richardson in Carson, "Paul's Inconsistency," 7–45.

59. Nanos, *Irony of Galatians*, 3.

60. Two other "solutions" are worth noting at this point. The first is that of Sanders, *Paul, the Law*, 186, who labels 1 Cor 9:19–23 as hyperbolic: "I doubt that in each city where he worked he switched back and forth in the way that would have been required if 1 Cor. 9:19–23 were a literal description of his practice." The second is to view Paul as transcending Jewishness in his post-conversion state. He can now be classified as a third entity—neither Jew nor Gentile but as part of the church of God, according to the

whether becoming like a Jew to the Jews means simply submitting to the discipline of the synagogue (2 Cor 11:24): "He bowed to synagogue discipline to maintain his Jewish connections."[61] Or, reflecting upon the larger context of 1 Cor 8:1 to 11:1 is the theory that Paul is speaking mainly about avoiding food sacrificed to idols.[62] This theory takes into consideration the unity of 8:1–11:1 around the question of "Now concerning food offered to idols (τῶν εἰδωλοθύτων; 8:1)." Paul was likely freer when in Gentile settings to partake of such foods than when he was around fellow Jews.[63] It is to this solution that I now turn.

---

supposed formula of 1 Cor 10:32. In the concomitant freedom, he may act in Jewish or Gentile circles not as a member of those groups but as someone with an entirely unique identity. Sanders, *Paul, the Law,* develops this idea in pp. 173–75. Compare also the comment of Richardson and Gooch, "Accommodation Ethics," 111: "It is Paul's freedom which makes it possible for him to adapt his behaviour to a variety of situations. Someone who is tightly tied to a particular set of regulations defining his behaviour will find it difficult to alter the rules without thereby altering his identity. If he accommodates without wholeheartedly changing his beliefs about what he ought to do, then he may well be accused of hypocrisy. He will be pretending, wearing a disguise. Paul, however, would not look at it that way. His freedom from all people and systems opens up for him a new identity 'in Christ.' He is really a Jew no longer—but no more is he a Gentile; if he is not under law it is not that he is really lawless, and so on. So to adopt the behaviour of the Gentile is not play-acting on the part of someone who is underneath a Jew; to act as without law is not to be someone really under law putting on a disguise. Paul is free from all those identities and cannot be charged with 'dressing up.' As Christ's slave he may freely wear whatever clothing the situation hands him. Since there can be, and indeed are, some Christians who are Jews and some who follow law and some without law and some who are weak, Paul legitimately identifies himself with each group as the occasion warrants it." However, in their approach Richardson and Gooch overplay the distinctions implicit in 1 Cor 10:32. As Rudolph, *Jew to the Jews,* 34, notes, "The viability of the model is significantly weakened by Pauline references to Jesus-believing Jews as 'Jews' and Jesus-believing Gentiles as 'Gentiles' (1 Cor 1:22, 24; 12:13; Gal 2:3, 12, 14; Rom 11:13; Eph 2:11; Col 4:10–11; Acts 21:39; 22:3). He does not speak of them as 'former Jews' and 'former Gentiles.' Moreover, there is no direct evidence that the third entity in 1 Cor 10:32 is independent of Jews and Gentiles. It is just as possible . . . that Paul viewed the third entity as a body of Jews and Gentiles who believed in Jesus."

61. Garland, *1 Corinthians,* 430.

62. Fee, *1 Corinthians,* 472–73.

63. Although, as Zetterholm, "Question of Assumptions," 99–103, suggests, Paul was not necessarily violating or relaxing Jewish law in his teaching concerning meat offered to idols: "Paul seems to be saying that it is a person's religious orientation . . . that determines whether or not the food should be considered an idol offering, which determines whether the Jesus-believing Gentile can eat it or not. The power of idolatry, according to this way of reasoning, is not in the food, but in the attitude and intention of those who are devoted to Greco-Roman gods. . . . Far from declaring Jewish law null and void, Paul is engaged either in *establishing* a halakah concerning idol food for Jesus-oriented Gentiles, or *teaching them an existing* local Corinthian Jewish halakah" (99).

Toward a Solution

David Rudolph makes a compelling case that 1 Cor 9 is about food sacrificed to idols in his monograph, *A Jew to the Jews: Jewish Contours of Pauline Flexibility in 1 Corinthians 9:19–23*. Rudolph presents his evidence in three stages: intertextual issues, contextual issues, and textual issues.

With regard to *intertextual issues* Rudolph demonstrates how the traditional interpretation of 1 Cor 9 (i.e., ethical accommodation) falls short of adequately explaining Acts 16:3 and 21:17–26. Regarding Acts 16:3 (Timothy's circumcision), it is unthinkable, Rudolph says, that "Paul advocated surgical operations to facilitate cross-cultural evangelism.... Were they so lacking in common sense as to think that circumcision for the wrong reason would have impressed people?"[64] But Acts 16:3 says Paul did it διὰ τοὺς Ἰουδαίους τοὺς ὄντας ἐν τοῖς τόποις ἐκείνοις. Does this not sound like he was acting expediently? Rudolph responds that it was the *timing of the circumcision*, not the circumcision itself, that was expedient. "Paul thought that the optimum time for Timothy to be circumcised (in order to confirm his covenant identity as a Jew) was prior to visiting his home region. The covenant-keeping motive for circumcision would have been *well received* by the Lystra Jewish community and would have opened hearts to Paul's message."[65]

The ethical implications are similarly stacked against the accommodation interpretation of Acts 21, according to Rudolph:

> From an ethical standpoint ... using a reasonable person's standard, the accommodation argument presents a disturbing image of Paul.... The accommodation argument would seem to suggest that Paul alone fooled the naïve Jewish converts for their own good.
>
> Is it likely that Paul publicly set the record straight that he remained a Torah-observant Jew but that he gave no thought to the fact that his testimony would shortly thereafter be contradicted by his actions? Was Paul so facile? Was there a darker side to Paul?[66]

With regard to *contextual issues*, a better interpretation of 1 Cor 9 begins with viewing 1 Cor 8:1–11:1 as a compositional unity. Drawing from

---

64. Rudolph, *Jew to the Jews*, 25–26.

65. Rudolph, *Jew to the Jews*, 27, emphasis original.

66. Rudolph, *Jew to the Jews*, 68. Rudolph (28–34) also effectively refutes the traditional interpretation regarding the so-called "erasure language" (language that purportedly erases the Jew-Gentile distinction, as in 1 Cor 7:19; Gal 3:28; 5:6; 6:15) and "third entity language" ("the church" in 1 Cor 10:32 as a third entity beyond "Jew" and "Gentile").

numerous studies, Rudolph establishes this case early on by pointing to the following evidence:[67]

- The lack of textual support to support partitioning the section
- Paul's rhetorical skill in organizing the section
- Vocabulary similarities throughout the section
- The compositional unity of the section

Once 8:1–11:1 is taken as a whole, then, it becomes clear that 1 Cor 9 is in line with Paul's train of thought concerning food sacrificed to idols. Such idol-food was permissible if eaten unknowingly and outside of a pagan cultic context: "Paul did not consider idol-food to be intrinsically dangerous. It was not the essence of the food that was the problem. Rather, it was knowingly eating food offered to a false god that was the problem (1 Cor 10:19–20)."[68] Thus, 1 Cor 9 is an integral part of Paul's larger argument, urging the "strong" to avoid being a stumbling block to others in regards to table fellowship.

In his analysis of the *textual data*, Rudolph develops an argument based on 1 Cor 11:1 ("Become imitators of me, as I am of Christ") and the language of being "in Christ's law" (9:21) that there is an *imitatio Christi* ethic implicit in 9:19–23.[69] "As Jesus became all things to all people through eating with ordinary Jews, Pharisees and sinners, Paul became 'all things to all people' through eating with ordinary Jews, strict Jews (those 'under the law') and Gentile sinners."[70] Thus, a more narrow accommodation is in view in 1 Cor 9:19–23, one concerning food offered to idols rather than Torah regulations pertaining to circumcision, vows, or kosher regulations in general. By adhering to this more narrow accommodation Paul had not come to view the law itself as indifferent; rather, he had come to contest the strict Pharisaic halakhic interpretations and expansions of the Mosaic law.[71]

The traditional argument for 1 Cor 9 as widespread practical accommodation, then, cannot stand in the face of the ethical objections noted above. Rather, Rudolph's explanation, that 1 Cor 9 continues the thought of the unit 8:1–11:1 concerning idol-food, is preferred. This assessment supports the portrait of Paul as a Torah-observant Jew as was developed in

---

67. See the footnotes in Rudolph, *Jew to the Jews*, 91 for the citations.

68. Rudolph, *Jew to the Jews*, 94.

69. Rudolph, *Jew to the Jews*, 147–49. Rudolph also bases his assertion on the view that 10:32–33 is a recapitulation of 9:19–23 and that 11:1 continues the recapitulation of chapter 10 (174–76).

70. Rudolph, *Jew to the Jews*, 190.

71. Rudolph, *Jew to the Jews*, 209.

chapter 2.⁷² The tension between Galatians and Acts must be addressed in another way.

PAUL AS SPEAKING DIFFERENTLY TO JEWS AND GENTILES

We have thus far examined two perspectives that attempt to resolve the tension between the Torah-observant Paul and the dead-to-the-law Paul. Historically, these two solutions (Acts as unhistorical, Paul as accommodating to his audience) have been the "go to" solutions. Recently, however, a third perspective has been gaining traction in the academy.

This perspective concedes the fact that Paul is talking negatively regarding the law in Galatians but argues that Paul only does so in speaking to the Gentiles about the law's relationship concerning them:

> In short, Paul did not say nasty things about the law and Israel; he did not draw the inference that the law brought death to Israel; he did not ignore or deny the biblical doctrine of repentance and forgiveness for Israel.... *In all likelihood Paul, the apostle to the Gentiles, is not speaking about the law as it relates to Israel but only about the law and Gentile members of the Jesus-movement.*⁷³

Since Paul's Galatian readership may be assumed to be mostly Gentile (the primary exigency, after all, was Gentile circumcision), this is naturally an attractive position. At least one base is covered—Paul is undoubtedly speaking *to* Gentiles. But is he speaking exclusively *about* them? In other words, does Paul speak negatively only with regard to the Gentiles and the law?

The above perspective is advanced by the "Paul within Judaism" movement (also known as the Radical New Perspective on Paul). This movement has coalesced around the objective of rehabilitating Paul from his supposed

---

72. My own view is that Paul remained Torah-observant. I therefore concur with the assessment of Rudolph (Rudolph, *Jew to the Jews*, 75–88) regarding 1 Cor 7:17–24, which describes, as he puts it, "enduring *callings* and not merely temporary situations in life" (75, emphasis original). I read this passage as an exhortation for people to continue in their respective Jewishness or Gentileness and not to seek to undo their calling. Jews should continue to observe the Mosaic law, and Gentiles should follow the commandments that apply universally to all (1 Cor 7:19; possibly a reference to the Noachide laws). This view, in turn, reinforces the interpretation of 1 Cor 9 given above. As Rudolph writes, "How does 1 Cor 7:17–24 inform one's understanding of 1 Cor 9:19–23? Since Paul was circumcised (Phil 3:5), and his rule in all the churches was for Jews to remain Jews and not Gentilise themselves (1 Cor 7:17), one would reasonably assume that Paul observed his own rule and consistently lived as a Jew" (88).

73. Gager, *Reinventing Paul*, 44, emphasis original.

anti-Judaic tendencies (and, in the process, rehabilitating post-Holocaust interpretation of Judaism by NT scholars) and eliminating what is perceived to be an anachronistic divide between first century "Christianity" and Judaism. These scholars argue that we have fundamentally misunderstood Paul's comments in Galatians.[74] A major stimulus for the movement has been the work of Lloyd Gaston and John Gager over the past four decades. They conclude that in Galatians Paul is talking only to—and about—Gentiles.

Gaston and Gager arrive at their conclusions regarding Paul by taking a dual perspective of the relationship of humanity to God and distinguishing multiple forms of νόμος. On the one hand, the Jews relate to God through the νόμος as Torah, the covenant established on Mount Sinai. On the other hand, the Gentiles relate to God through the νόμος as law, a concept derived from the Jewish view of the law as preexistent wisdom.[75] In this latter sense, the law conveys God's will to Gentiles but does not empower them to perform it. Thus, it involves only a negative relationship; the law simply condemns Gentiles.[76]

By distinguishing between the senses of νόμος in this way, Gaston and Gager are able to overlay their interpretive schema onto difficult texts of Galatians such as 2:15-19 and 3:10-14. Where Paul talks about νόμος, then, it is the law that condemns the *Gentiles*—not the Jews—resulting in a curse. This is also what Paul means by being "under the law," that is, being enslaved to the principalities and powers that make up the law (cf. Col 1:15-20).[77]

---

74. Such misunderstanding purportedly extends to Romans as well—see esp. Stowers, *Rereading of Romans*; Rodriguez and Thiessen, *So-Called Jew*. For the current state of the research see Nanos and Zetterholm, *Paul within Judaism*.

75. Gaston, *Paul and the Torah*, 32, "Whether Gentile Christians keep one commandment or many . . . they exist in a covenant and commandment relationship to God which is different from but parallel to that of Sinai"; (79) "[Paul] can be understood, at least implicitly, as affirming something like the two-covenant concept of F. Rosenzweig. That is, Paul affirms the new expression of the righteousness of God in Christ for the Gentiles and for himself as Apostle to the Gentiles without in any sense denying the righteousness of God expressed in Torah for Israel."

76. Gaston, *Paul and the Torah*, 28, "For Gentiles, who do not have the Torah as covenant, Torah as law functions in an exclusively negative way, to condemn"; (86) "As a consequence of the identification of the law and wisdom (ben Sira), the whole of creation was seen by some early Jews (for example, 4 Ezra) to be under the law of God, but law without covenant, law which enslaves, law which works wrath." On the double meaning of νόμος in contemporary Jewish texts, see Gager, *Origins of Anti-Semitism*, 237, "In the first instance, *Torah* meant 'the revelation of God . . . in his knowability, in his presence, in his electing will, in his covenant for Israel.' In the second instance, *Torah* came to be seen as God's revealed wisdom for all the nations who by virtue of knowing God's will are obligated to fulfill the commandments even while not coming under the covenant with Israel."

77. Gager, *Origins of Anti-Semitism*, 236.

Toward a Solution

Gaston and Gager use rabbinical and apocalyptic literature to demonstrate that, historically, the Jewish view of Gentiles and salvation has been somewhat fluid. Under debate was whether the Gentiles needed to fully Judaize (through circumcision and accepting the yoke of the Torah) in order to be saved or whether some lesser regimen would be acceptable. Such ambiguity set the occasion for the development of so-called "works of the law" that the stricter sects (like the Pharisees, of which Paul was a former one) insisted upon imposing on the Gentiles.[78]

The Christ event is seen in two ways from the perspective of Gaston and Gager. For the Jews, Christ is the Messiah, the fulfillment of their Torah.[79] For the Gentiles, he is the fulfillment of the promise to Abraham that the blessings would one day be extended to the nations.[80] Paul awakened to this reality on the road to Damascus. Although he thereafter remained Torah-observant, he was commissioned to carry this message to the Gentiles.[81] Gaston writes, "For Paul [who writes from within the Gentile perspective], Jesus is neither a new Moses nor the Messiah, he is not the climax of the history of God's dealing with Israel, but he is the fulfilment of God's promises concerning the Gentiles."[82] The Jerusalem Conference reaffirmed Paul's commission to the Gentiles. Although Paul visited synagogues, he mainly, if not exclusively, dealt with Gentiles there, as the synagogues were popular among the Gentiles of various cities.[83]

Paul's gospel for the Gentiles, then, is that they are redeemed from the curse of the law through the faithfulness of Christ (subjective genitive). They do not have to perform works of the law in order to inherit the promise

---

78. Gaston, *Paul and the Torah*, 24–25.

79. Gaston, *Paul and the Torah*, 31; "Jewish Christians understood Christ as a confirmation of the covenant and as expiation for the forgiveness of sins. That is, for Jewish Christians Christ probably replaced the temple as the locus of atonement but not Sinai as the locus of election" (79).

80. Gaston, *Paul and the Torah*, 32.

81. Gaston, *Paul and the Torah*, 78, "Whether or not Paul continued to keep the commandments is probable but not sure." Gaston views Paul as an apostate only in the technical sense, "a shift from election at Sinai to election in Christ, a move which Christians praise and Jews should not hold against him" (76). See his appendix "Paul as Apostate" (76–79). Gager, *Who Made Early Christianity?*, 143, is more definitive: "Paul himself was a Jew who followed Christ and (nevertheless) still observed the Torah commandments."

82. Gaston, *Paul and the Torah*, 33.

83. Gaston, *Paul and the Torah*, 22, "Paul was not commissioned to preach among Jews, whether about Jesus Christ or the Torah or anything else." Also see Gager, *Who Made Early Christianity?*, 53–85, (here 61), "Why, then, was Paul the apostle to the Gentiles preaching his gospel in Jewish synagogues? . . . Because he knew that he would find significant numbers of Gentiles there."

of Abraham. They are "under the equivalent of the yoke of the Kingdom but not under the yoke of the commandments."[84]

The interpretive practices of Gaston and Gager are interesting. Gaston refers to their program as an "experiment which questions traditional assumptions."[85] Gager sets a rather paradigmatic hermeneutical rule: "When Paul appears to say something (e.g., about the law and Jews) that is unthinkable from a Jewish perspective, it is probably true that he is not talking about Jews at all. Instead we may assume that the apostle to the Gentiles is talking about the law and Gentiles."[86] In order to properly evaluate the relative success or failure of their experiment, I will now present their exegesis of some of the significant texts.

Beginning with 2:15–21, the traditional reading takes these verses to be a reprimand against Peter and a statement opposed to Jewish legalism (works of the law). Neither one of those is true, according to Gaston and Gager.[87] The passage is about Paul and the Gentiles. Verse 15 begins with ἡμεῖς (we) in the first (emphatic) position, and verse 16b starts with καὶ ἡμεῖς (we also). These first person plurals, along with the first person plural verb εὑρέθημεν in verse 17, could be taken as reflecting the same continuous speaker (Paul and those who are "by nature" Jews) in verses 15–17. Gaston, however, while acknowledging that Paul begins talking from the standpoint of "we" Jews, sees him as transitioning in verse 16 to speaking about "himself in relation to the Gentile Galatians."[88] As he puts it, "The pronoun referring to him (we) shifts in meaning as the story progresses."[89] Gaston then wonders, "Does that mean that Paul so identifies with the Gentiles to whom he is sent that he himself in a sense has become a Gentile?"[90]

What textual bases justify this interpretive maneuver? To reinforce the idea that Paul is talking about Gentiles, Gaston cites Paul's use of ἄνθρωπος in verse 16a, which he asserts to be a marker for speaking about Gentiles in the Pauline literature, yielding the translation: "knowing [therefore] that a [Gentile] human being is not justified from works of law. . . ."[91] However,

---

84. Gaston, *Paul and the Torah*, 31.
85. Gaston, *Paul and the Torah*, 69; also see 64.
86. Gager, *Reinventing Paul*, 58.
87. Gaston, *Paul and the Torah*, 68.
88. Gaston, *Paul and the Torah*, 70.
89. Gaston, *Paul and the Torah*, 70.
90. Gaston, *Paul and the Torah*, 70. See also "Paul can so identify with his readers that the first person plural can actually mean 'we Gentiles'" (29).
91. Gaston, *Paul and the Torah*, 66; Gaston's translation is given on p. 65. Also see Gager, *Reinventing Paul*, 86, "For Gaston (and others) *anthropos* is a typically Pauline term for Gentiles"; Gager, *Origins of Anti-Semitism*, 233, "That *anthropos* in v. 16 must

Toward a Solution 55

this translation lacks a lexical foundation, as Moo points out;[92] the term ἄνθρωπος typically refers to humanity in general. Gaston also refers to ἔργα νόμου, which he takes to be a subjective genitive—the works *done by* the law. What is the work done by the law? It is God's wrath (Rom 4:15). Therefore, "As God's or Christ's faithfulness is expressed in a work done for human blessing, so the law apart from covenant also does works for human cursing. It is then at least possible to understand 'the works of the law' in a way that does not refer to Jews keeping commandments but to God punishing Gentiles."[93] Gaston's interpretation here seems to be an instance of special pleading. The evidence from Jewish literature and from Paul's use of the phrase indicates that ἔργα νόμου refers to "actions performed in obedience to the law, works which are commanded by the law."[94] Overall, then, Gaston's experiment is not compelling enough to overturn the traditional interpretation. We should continue to see Paul's use of the first person plural as continuing the speech, or an expansion thereupon, to Peter from 2:10–14.[95] The "we" in verses 15 and 16 refers to Jewish Christians, not Gentiles.[96]

Gaston's argument that 2:18 refers to the church being torn down and rebuilt ("Paul began to build up the church he had previously persecuted") is likewise tenuous.[97] He lists other passages where Paul elsewhere uses οἰκοδομέω and καταλύω in relation to the church, as well as Gal 1:13, 23 where Paul seeks to destroy [πορθέω] the church.[98] However, the verses containing οἰκοδομέω or καταλύω have more of a sense of encouraging or discouraging fellow believers than they do of building up or destroying/persecuting the church as a whole, as Gaston takes it here. Furthermore, it better fits the surrounding context to view Paul as referring to tearing down and rebuilding the system of rules related to table fellowship with Gentiles, in continuity with 2:11–15.

When it comes to Gal 2:19 Gaston's case struggles for consistency. He confesses to developing in his thought concerning Paul, from the view that Paul remained Torah observant to the view that he was an apostate who may

---

refer to Gentiles in clear enough from the context, for Paul's sole concern here is the Gentile Judaizers."

92. Moo, *Galatians*, 157n3.
93. Gaston, *Paul and the Torah*, 69–70.
94. Moo, "'Law,' 'Works of the Law,'" 92; see also Moo, *Galatians*, 173–76.
95. Moo, *Galatians*, 156.
96. With the majority of interpreters, e.g., Fung, *Galatians*, 112; Longenecker, *Galatians*, 83; Betz, *Galatians*, 115–17; Bruce, *Galatians*, 137–39; Burton, *Galatians*, 123.
97. Gaston, *Paul and the Torah*, 71.
98. Gaston, *Paul and the Torah*, 71.

not have remained observant.[99] Gaston's thought development can perhaps be seen across his different translations and interpretations of 2:19 on pages 31 and 71 of his book, respectively (though in fairness these represent two essays written at different times). In the earlier section he employs the νόμος-as-Torah (Sinai covenant) and νόμος-as-law (the law that condemns the children of Adam) distinction and translates, "I through the Torah died to the law."[100] In the latter case, he translates "For through the law I have died to the law." For this rendering he takes the first νόμος to be faithfulness of Christ and the second to be the yoke of the covenant, which Paul has "deliberately cast off."[101] This makes Paul "an apostate" who "commends himself openly as such without apology, for his life is subordinate to his calling to proclaim the righteousness of God among the Gentiles."[102] In addition to the problem of inconsistency, Gaston's approach opens itself to the criticism of relying on a distinction between uses of νόμος that is absent from the text itself. As a reviewer notes, "Even if such a distinction were clear in Paul's mind, it would be precarious to assume that his readers were just as sophisticated and would have understood νόμος in these specific ways."[103]

Gaston and Gager also see Paul speaking exclusively to and about Gentiles in Gal 3:10–14, the curse in question being not the curses of Deuteronomy 27–28 but rather the condemnation of the sons of Adam under the νόμος as law.[104] Gaston justifies his exegesis in this way:

> Since the ones "Christ redeemed from the curse of the law" are explicitly called Gentiles in verse 14, the curse of verse 10 must also be one which lay upon Gentiles. Paul is able to find this in the LXX (not the MT) of Deut 27:26 which inserts the word *pas* twice: *everyone* is under a curse, including Gentiles, who do not do *all* the commandments, not just those incumbent on God-fearers.[105]

For Gaston to reason from Paul's use of πᾶς that he means to include *all* of humanity stretches the sense of the passage too far. Deuteronomy 27:26 is the end of the so-called Shechemite Dodecalogue, part of the curses to be

---

99. Gaston, *Paul and the Torah*, 77.
100. Gaston, *Paul and the Torah*, 31.
101. Gaston, *Paul and the Torah*, 71.
102. Gaston, *Paul and the Torah*, 72.
103. Stuckenbruck, "Theology, Exegesis and Paul's Thought," 144.
104. To assert, as Gaston does, that Paul refers to "we Gentiles" in verses 13 and 14 is, according to Longenecker, *Galatians*, 121, "impossible to maintain."
105. Gaston, *Paul and the Torah*, 74.

read from Mount Ebal to the Israelites. The *all* in view here is certainly *all* Israelites (who are required to do *all* the commandments).[106]

Gaston applies his paradigm throughout the rest of Gal 3 and into chapter 4. Against the vast majority of commentators he claims that it is the Gentiles who were under a παιδαγωγός (3:24), enslaved to the στοιχεῖα τοῦ κόσμου (4:3), and redeemed from being ὑπὸ νόμον (4:5).[107] Even ὑπὸ νόμον applied to Jesus's birth (4:4) does not signify that he was a Jew, according to Gaston and Gager; rather, "Like Gentiles, he lived 'under the law' in order to redeem those 'under the law. . . .' Jesus' sole function, so it would seem, is to bring to fulfillment the promise to Abraham regarding the Gentiles."[108] Lastly, Gaston leaves his own interpretive mark on the allegory of Sarah and Hagar in 4:21–31. In his view, Hagar is not to be associated with Israel and the law but rather with the Gentiles being "under the law but apart from the covenant of grace. The slavery from which the Galatians, as heirs of the promise to Sarah, have been liberated is slavery to the non-gods, 'the weak and impotent elements, whom again they wish to serve as slaves anew' (4:9)."[109] Thielman rightly rejects this interpretation:

> It is difficult to see how the Jews can be absent from Paul's statement that "Hagar is Mount Sinai in Arabia, and she corresponds to the present Jerusalem, for it is enslaved with her children" (4:25). Here is a place where Paul clearly describes non-Christian Judaism as "enslaved." He believes that if the Galatian Gentiles give in to the Judaizers in their midst they too will become enslaved to a law which, when elevated over the faith of Christ, can only bring condemnation.[110]

A more recent voice from the Paul within Judaism movement is that of Matthew Thiessen. In his book, *Paul and the Gentile Problem*, Thiessen, like Gaston and Gager before him, lays out the case for a "thoroughgoing consistency" with regard to Paul by viewing him as writing to Gentiles, not Jews.[111] Rather than being a mark of legalism, circumcision was one par-

---

106. Moreover, the commandments in view, according to the LXX, are "the words of *this* law" (τοῖς λόγοις τοῦ νόμου τούτου, emphasis mine), indicating the law that was being read to the Israelites at the time.

107. Gaston, *Paul and the Torah*, 29–30, 74–75.

108. Gager, *Origins of Anti-Semitism*, 240.

109. Gaston, *Paul and the Torah*, 86.

110. Thielman, *From Plight to Solution*, 130–31. Thielman devotes the appendix of his book to rebutting the claims of Gaston and Gager. Also see the counterarguments to Gaston in Seltzer, "Does Paul Need to Be Saved?," 289–97.

111. Thiessen, *Paul and the Gentile Problem*, 8.

ticular solution conceived among Jews to deal with the "Gentile problem" (how to incorporate Gentiles into the Jewish family). For Paul, Gentiles can only become children of Abraham by receiving the Spirit of Christ: "If Gentiles want to receive the promises and inheritance of Abraham, then they need to become genealogically related to him. They need to become his sons. . . . Gentiles who have received [the] *pneuma* become both Abraham's sons and his seed."[112]

Also like his predecessors within the movement, Thiessen's interpretive stance toward Galatians is to see the entire letter as written to and about Gentiles. However, his exegetical work in Galatians is more limited than that of Gaston and Gager. Regarding the promise to Abraham that "all the nations will be blessed in you" (Gal 3:8), Thiessen writes that this statement

> demonstrates that Paul's main concern in writing Galatians 3–4 is to give an account not of the justification of all people, but of the Gentiles specifically. Whatever the precise meaning of the various assertions that Paul makes in Galatians 3–4, they must be understood in relation to God's dealings with Gentiles, not Jews. Gal 3:8 demonstrates that what Paul says about the Jewish law in Gal 3:10–14 (which also ends with an explicit reference to Gentiles) relates not to all humanity, but to Gentiles alone. Thus, the curse of the law rests not upon Jews because they cannot or did not keep the entirety of the law, an ahistorical and derogatory understanding of the function of the Jewish law, but upon Gentiles who attempt to keep it. As Lloyd Gaston observes, "Since the ones 'Christ has redeemed from the curse of the law' are explicitly called Gentiles in verse 14, the curse of verse 10 must also be one which lay upon Gentiles."[113]

True enough, in Galatians Paul is writing mainly to Gentiles—and granted, the promises of Abraham are pictured in Gal 3:8 as extending to the Gentiles—but Thiessen fails to exegetically justify his assertions regarding 3:10–14 (other than with a quote from Gaston) and places too heavy of a load on 3:8 to bear as a determining statement for what follows.

A little later on Thiessen returns to 3:14:

> This verse highlights a real difficulty in reading Paul, especially here in Galatians 3–4: the sudden shifts between first- and second-person pronouns and verbs. To whom does Paul refer when he uses the first-person plural "we" or "us"? Most scholars

---

112. Thiessen, *Paul and the Gentile Problem*, 128.

113. Thiessen, *Paul and the Gentile Problem*, 106. The quote from Gaston is from Gaston, *Paul and the Torah*, 74.

> take these first-person plurals to refer to all of those who are in Christ.... Yet another solution is to read the first-person plurals as referring to Gentiles-in-Christ. Lloyd Gaston, for instance, claims that "Paul can so identify with his readers that the first person plural can actually mean 'we Gentiles,' as in 3:14, 'that in Christ the blessing of Abraham might come upon the Gentiles, that we might receive the promise of the Spirit through faith.'"[114]

Thiessen here simply points out the possibility of taking the "we" clauses as Paul identifying with Gentiles (far from being an obvious interpretation) without presenting an argument for doing so other than a supporting quote from Gaston (whose theory regarding the dual-νόμος has not been widely accepted). More compelling, though, is Thiessen's case concerning the two purpose clauses of verse 14:

> Although few scholars find such a use of "we" likely, the two purpose clauses of Gal 3:14 confirm that Paul identifies the Gentiles in the first purpose clause with the "we" in the second purpose clause. Since the second purpose clause of v. 14 is in apposition to the first, those Gentiles who receive the blessing of Abraham in 14a are the "we" who receive the *pneuma* through faith in 14b.[115]

Scholars acknowledge that the pronouns of 3:13–14 are difficult to translate, but the discussions typically concern whether "we" refers to Jewish Christians or all Christians.[116] It is difficult to find an exegetical discussion outside of the aforementioned Gaston study that supports translating "we" as "we Gentiles." Thiessen's point about the two purposes clauses being in appositional relation is interesting; however it must be seen as speculative until the entire passage can be dealt with more fully (specifically, explaining how Gentiles are redeemed from being under a curse, one that is actually foretold in Deut 27:26).

Thiessen also attempts to reframe Gal 4:21–31. The traditional interpretation follows Paul's own statement that Hagar is a picture of "the present Jerusalem, in slavery with her children" (4:25). Thiessen, however, asserts that "Paul neither attacks Judaism or Jews in this allegory, nor denigrates circumcision or the Jewish law."[117] Hagar symbolizes Paul's opponents, not Jews under the law in general. In other words, Paul is attacking Gentile judaizing under the principle that "no amount of law observance can transform

---

114. Thiessen, *Paul and the Gentile Problem*, 130.
115. Thiessen, *Paul and the Gentile Problem*, 130.
116. See, e.g., Moo, *Galatians*, 211.
117. Thiessen, *Paul and the Gentile Problem*, 87.

a Gentile into a Jew."[118] Once again, though, these conclusions appear to be based less on the grammatical features of the text than they are Thiessen's assumption that all of Paul's statements must be about the relationship of the law to Gentiles.[119]

To summarize this section, it is an intriguing possibility that, because Paul is writing *to* Gentiles in Galatians, he is only writing *about* them. On this basis Gaston, Gager, and Thiessen present proposals for reshaping the interpretation of such texts as 2:15–21; 3:10–14; and 4:21–31 in radical ways. While these proposals offer the potential of a thoroughgoing consistency in Paul, they are nevertheless plagued by three difficulties: (1) the understanding that Gentiles are under the law (and under the curse of the law) is predicated upon Gaston's dual-νόμος theory, which is based on rabbinical and apocalyptic literature and requires more substantiation to prove that it would have likely been in the minds of Paul and his audience;[120] (2) a more robust grammatical exegesis of the relevant passages in their context is needed; and (3) Paul's statements in Galatians have such a categorical quality to them (the law results in a curse; it is an enslaving force; it is temporary; Paul has died to it, etc.), that it is difficult to imagine that these assertions are being made only in relation to one ethnic group and not another. While it may be a noble undertaking to rescue Paul from anti-Semitism (Gaston

---

118. Thiessen, *Paul and the Gentile Problem*, 101. See the similar treatment of this passage in Gaston, *Paul and the Torah*, 80–91, and Gager, *Reinventing Paul*, 92–97.

119. Thiessen, *Paul and the Gentile Problem*, 77–99, highlights the issue that Ishmael was not circumcised on the eighth day, as was Isaac. In Thiessen's view, this is why Ishmael is not part of the covenant and is the reason why one cannot read Gen 17, as Paul's opponents did, as evidence that circumcision functioned for Gentiles as a valid rite of conversion. "Paul believes that the circumcision of the Galatians models the circumcision of Ishmael, not that of Isaac, since if they undergo circumcision it will not be done at the age of eight days. And, as the law makes clear, one not circumcised on the eighth day after birth cannot be part of the covenant of Genesis 17" (91). Thiessen also goes on to conclude that 5:3 pertains to the necessity of having to perform the entire law *of circumcision* (93) and that 6:13 means that Paul's opponents do not themselves keep the law *of circumcision* by forcing the Galatians to Judaize. Thiessen's overarching argument is not convincing. If Paul's main issue concerning circumcision were about its timing, he could have easily made this point more explicitly rather than couch it in the vague terminology of 4:21–31. However, this argument is nowhere to be found in Paul's letters.

120. Seltzer, "Does Paul Need to Be Saved?," 294, "Gaston's evidence is problematic. Many of his rabbinic examples are from late sources, which cannot be applied to Paul's time. *Exodus Rabbah*, which Gager also cites as an example, is redacted in the early medieval period. In the rabbinic citations, the people the Torah turns against in these examples are not usually Gentiles, but those who misuse the Torah, do not perform its commandments, or do not follow it for its own sake. Many of the apocalyptic sources, though early enough to use for understanding Paul, are about the election of Israel, not the condemnation of Gentiles."

and Gager), such revisionism of Galatians collapses under the sheer weight of the plain sense of Paul's own statements.

PAUL AS AN INCONSISTENT THINKER

Even for those who hold to the inerrancy or infallibility of Scripture, there is no necessary reason why diversity among the biblical authors, or even tensions among the writings of a single author, should be a cause for concern. However, when the scope of those tensions reaches a certain threshold—qualitative or quantitative—then the trustworthiness and usefulness of those writings begin to be called into question. What defines an inconsistency? The threshold is up to the individual reader, providing that the author is being interpreted accurately. I do not wish to enter into a discussion on hermeneutics at this point, only to lay the groundwork for determining whether Paul may be labeled as inconsistent. The issue at hand is Paul's view of the law. I propose that interpreters may reasonably apply the label of "inconsistent" to Paul if he asserts at roughly the same time and without qualification that the law both is good and bad or that the law has both ended and it is still continuing—again, provided that he is being interpreted accurately. In this section I will take up the view of Heikki Räisänen that Paul is inconsistent in his approach to the law. It is differentiated from the development view, which is presented in the next section, in that Räisänen's view envisions a short time interval between Galatians and Romans, and he "[does] not detect any straightforward development from any one *extant* letter to another."[121]

Räisänen holds that "both Galatians and Romans are beset with internal tensions and contradictions."[122] Sometimes the law seems just for the Jews, and at other times it seems to extend to the Gentiles.[123] Sometimes the law appears to be abolished, while at other times it retains a normative character.[124] Regarding Paul, he "is thoroughly radical in his missionary practice and in many of his theological conclusions. Yet, on the other hand, he has a need to pass for a loyal Jew, faithful to the Torah. This can hardly be just missionary strategy."[125] Regarding the law, sometimes it seems impossible to fulfill, while at other times Gentiles are said to fulfill the law and Christians

---

121. Räisänen, *Paul and the Law*, 8–9, emphasis original. In addition to inconsistencies *between* Galatians and Romans, Räisänen also holds that there are inconsistencies *within* each letter.
122. Räisänen, *Paul and the Law*, 9.
123. Räisänen, *Paul and the Law*, 18–23.
124. Räisänen, *Paul and the Law*, 42–72.
125. Räisänen, *Paul and the Law*, 71.

are exhorted to fulfill it.[126] Paul also vacillates between a negative origin/purpose for the law and a positive one.[127]

Why was Paul so seemingly inconsistent? According to Räisänen, it was because of internal psychological pressure brought about by living as a conservative Jew on the cusp between two ages:

> We find Paul struggling with the problem that a *divine* institution has been *abolished* through what God has done in Christ. Most of Paul's troubles can be reduced to this simple formula. Paul tries to hush up the abolition; he never admits that he has actually rejected large parts of the law. Instead, he has recourse to the arbitrary assertion that it is *his* teaching that really fulfils or "upholds" the law.
>
> The problem of an abolition of a divine institution is clearly reflected in Paul's inability to give a satisfactory answer to the question "Why then did God give this weak and imperfect law in the first place?"
>
> Paul did (at times even passionately) cling to the traditional idea that the law was all divine; this is why he was caught up in so many inconsistencies in trying to relate the new experience to the authoritative tradition. While his life was totally oriented to the new powerful experience of Christ, he was bound to pay lip service (surely never realized as such by himself) to the tradition in order not to undercut the unity of the divine purpose and will.[128]

What are we to do with Räisänen's picture of an inconsistent Paul? Admittedly, the issue strikes a nerve, as Räisänen concedes in the preface to the second edition, with laymen and scholars alike.[129] That aside, to accept that Paul was inconsistent should be done only after investigating all of the reasonable attempts to harmonize him. In the end, if a compelling explanation can be mounted based on historical and grammatical features of the text (rather than an appeal to psychological states), then it should at least be considered. I will attempt to do so in the following chapters by arguing that Paul is actually consistent—the problem is that we have misinterpreted him.

---

126. Räisänen, *Paul and the Law*, 94–127.
127. Räisänen, *Paul and the Law*, 128–61.
128. Räisänen, *Paul and the Law*, 264–66, emphasis original.
129. Räisänen, *Paul and the Law*, xi.

PAUL AS DEVELOPING HIS THOUGHT OVER TIME

What if Paul, after having denigrated circumcision and disparaged the law as an enslaving force, reflected further on the situation of Jewish Christians in Jerusalem with whom he wanted to maintain fellowship, who continued to circumcise their newborn males and live according to the law? What if those Jewish Christians, having read Galatians, asked Paul to clarify his theological stance? Hans Hübner believes that Paul was prompted in this way to further develop his line of thinking between the writing of Galatians and the writing of Romans: "It was perhaps the very fact of Galatians becoming known in Jerusalem that occasioned the posing of critical questions to the author—which the latter then also, contrary to all expectations, began to ask himself!"[130]

Hübner expounds Paul's theological development from Gal 3 to Rom 4 as follows:[131]

Elements in Gal 3 not present in Rom 4

- The law needing to be obeyed in full (and the resultant curse for failure)
- Christ taking the curse of the law upon himself
- Covenant (διαθήκη) and the chronological relationship of the Mosaic law to the Abrahamic promises
- The connection between Abraham and the reception of the Holy Spirit

New elements in Rom 4 not found in Gal 3

- The theme of God as creator (Rom 4:17)
- Faith as hoping against hope (Rom 4:18)
- The Sarah theme (Rom 4:19–22)
- Circumcision as a σημεῖον; Abraham as the father of circumcision to Jewish Christians (4:12)

Elements modified from Gal 3 to Rom 4

- Abraham is "the epitome of a justification by faith . . . but nevertheless with here the specific purpose of upholding the law. . . . Paul upholds the Law by using Abraham to show that justification before God is the very thing which does not come from the *nomos*."

---

130. Hübner, *Law in Paul's Thought*, 55.
131. The following points are from Hübner, *Law in Paul's Thought*, 52–53.

- The seed of Abraham is more directly linked with spiritual descendants

While Hübner's model has explanatory power, there are two problems intrinsic to his proposal of a Paul who engages upon further reflection after encountering objections from the Jerusalem apostles. The first is that Paul asserts his independence against these same individuals in Galatians (1:1) and calls down a curse on anyone who would change his gospel message (1:8–9). It is unlikely that Paul would have so drastically modified his presentation in reaction to their concerns. Second, Paul's statements concerning the law in Galatians, if taken at face value (which Hübner does), are so unequivocal, so expressive of strongly held core convictions, that it is hard to imagine these convictions undergoing significant evolution between Galatians and Romans or allowing Paul to perform the kinds of Torah-observant actions he does in Acts (an aspect of Paul's thought development that Hübner does not address).

PAUL AS CLARIFYING HIS THINKING ON THE LAW

This perspective starts from the same assumption as the previous one—that Jewish Christians, both in Galatia and Jerusalem, had been offended by the letter to the Galatians—but ends up in a different place. In this perspective, Paul does not *develop* in his thinking in some substantial way; rather, he simply *clarifies* it for his Roman audience. What was written about the law in Galatians is true. The problem was that it had not been sufficiently nuanced, as Louis Martyn writes:

> From Galatians to Romans, therefore, Paul is fundamentally consistent in drawing a connection between the Law and tyranny, but in Romans he clarifies—to some extent modifies—what he had said in Galatians. The Law is connected with tyranny, but only by way of Sin. For the tyrant itself is Sin, whereas the holy and spiritual Law is only an instrument in Sin's hands, and, in that sense, Sin's effective power.[132]

This position is attractive in that it sustains the view of a theologically consistent Paul across his letters. Unfortunately, Martyn only interacts in this regard with the two letters—Galatians and Romans—and does not take into account Paul's Torah observant behavior in Acts, which accentuates the apparent inconsistency with Galatians and begs for a different solution.

---

132. Martyn, *Theological Issues*, 43.

GALATIANS AS ANTI-ETHNOCENTRIC

Before the Paul within Judaism (Radical New Perspective) movement, the New Perspective on Paul (NPP) was arguing that Judaism was a religion of grace and that, rather than tackling legalism in his main letters, Paul was reacting against ethnocentrism. Scholars such as Stendahl, Sanders, Dunn, and Wright have helped to shape the overall effort.[133] Although the NPP does not focus on the disjunction between the Paul of the letters and the Paul of Acts, or between Galatians and Romans, it is worth briefly mentioning their contribution in that it has occupied a large amount of attention in Pauline scholarship over the past few decades.

Like the Paul within Judaism movement, the NPP seeks to rehabilitate Paul in his expressed attitude toward the law in Galatians. For instance, Paul did not see the law as "negative" except in the way in which it was used to exclude Gentiles from the covenant. As Dunn writes, "It was the law, then, which prevented the blessing of Abraham reaching out to the Gentiles, by functioning as a mark which distinguished Jew from Gentile, as a barrier between Jew and Gentile."[134] The curse falls upon Israel, not because Israel failed to do all the works of the law (it had a ceremonial system in place for forgiveness), but because it impeded the working out of the covenant, which was to result in a blessing to all the nations: "Since the 'works of the law' attitude thus prevented the fulfilment of a central feature of the covenant promise it was in fact being false to the covenant, it put itself outside the terms of the covenant, and consequently under a curse."[135] Wright takes a more or less traditional stance on Gal 3 ("God's final purpose of constituting a covenant people would never be accomplished through Torah") while insisting on an overall positive view of Torah that worked within God's salvation plan for Israel and the world:[136]

> [A] negative view of Torah is utterly mistaken. Torah, in Paul's vision, had a specific job to perform within the deeply and necessarily ambiguous vocation of Israel. Israel was called to bear the solution to the larger human problem, but was itself part of, enmeshed within that same problem.... The whole point of

---

133. Among some of the key writings on the NPP are Stendahl's article "The Apostle Paul and the Introspective Conscience of the West," in Stendahl, *Paul Among Jews and Gentiles*; Sanders, *Paul and Palestinian Judaism*; Dunn, *New Perspective on Paul*; Wright, *Paul and the Faithfulness of God*.

134. Dunn, *Galatians*, 169.

135. Dunn, *Galatians*, 173.

136. Wright, *Paul and the Faithfulness of God*, 2:864 (preceding quote), 2:866 (subsequent quote).

Galatians 3 is that Torah belongs at the key intermediate stage in the divine purpose. It was shaped to perform the task that was necessary if Abraham's children, carrying the worldwide promise, were themselves to be narrowed down to a single point, that of their representative Messiah.

The NPP, therefore, does not make Paul into a Torah-observant Jew—nor does it purport to, as with the Paul within Judaism movement—although it leaves him "stubbornly and intentionally a deeply Jewish thinker."[137] In stressing the continuity of Judaism and Christianity, Dunn and Wright go a little ways but do not entirely iron out the wrinkles between the dead-to-the-law-Paul and the Torah-observant Paul. For the purposes of this investigation, then, I do not consider the NPP to be an attempted "solution" to this problem. If there is one weakness, it is that they have not gone as far as their more "radical" colleagues in seeking to arrive at a more consistent view of Paul.

A PROPOSED SOLUTION

In this chapter I have reviewed several possible efforts at reconciling the Paul of Galatians with the Paul of Romans and Acts. Some, such as the historical critical case against the historicity of Acts, have long since been discredited from several angles, while others (Paul within Judaism) are still being worked out. Admitting that there even exists an inconsistency is, in my view (following Räisänen), the best conclusion from the data I have presented in chapters 1 and 2. But might that inconsistency be only at the verbal level? In other words, might the thoughts behind the words be different from the *prima facie* reading of the words themselves?

I propose that we have misread Paul's letter to the Galatians and that the "true" Paul is, in fact, loyal to Torah and optimistic about its continued use. These two assertions I share with the Paul within Judaism camp. Where Paul appears to be speaking negatively with regard to the law, I propose that he is actually speaking hyperbolically, exaggerating his statements for the sake of effect. Over the next several chapters I will lay out the evidence to back up this claim. I will seek to demonstrate that not only was hyperbole recognized by the ancients as a valuable rhetorical technique but that it is *a*, if not *the*, method of choice among the biblical writers when seeking to add force to their assertions.

---

137. Wright, *Paul and the Faithfulness of God*, 1408.

PART II

Hyperbole: Definitions and Rhetoric

4

The Nature of Hyperbole

In this chapter...

Question(s) to be answered:
- What is hyperbole?
- How does it work?

Trajectory:
- In Chapter 5, the rhetoric (use in persuasion) of hyperbole will be examined.
- Chapters 6–8 look at hyperbole in the Bible.

IN THIS CHAPTER I will examine the nature of hyperbole: What is it? How is it used in human conversation? What are the cues for recognizing it? Answers to such questions will take advantage of the abundance of research literature on linguistics and figurative language that has been developed over the past fifty years. Insights from this literature will then be leveraged into developing the methodology for the present study of Paul's use of hyperbole in Galatians (chapter 6).

I wish to tread carefully as the risk of anachronism is ever present when applying modern linguistic principles to an ancient work such as the Bible. My view, however, is that the journey will be well worth it. At some point in later chapters I will need to provide justification for selecting some passages as hyperbolic. Some kind of mutual understanding of the "ground rules" between the reader and me is essential in preparation for that exercise. These ground rules should be well thought out and explicated as clearly as possible to avoid accusations of bias or subjectivity. And, I believe, they should be informed by as wide a knowledge base as possible. With that said, I present several assumptions which will guide my work in this chapter:

Part II: Hyperbole: Definitions and Rhetoric

1. A conversation on biblical hyperbole will benefit from having a terminological basis that is clearly and thoroughly developed.

2. This terminological basis may be informed by modern research, which has shed significant light on the nature and use of figurative language, including hyperbole, among human beings.

3. Though the form and content of figurative tropes such as hyperbole is undoubtedly culturally determined, the use of hyperbole has been shown to be cross-cultural and present at early stages in human psychological development.[1]

4. Judging from the sheer volume of what we recognize to be hyperbole in the Bible (see chapters 7 and 8), it seems that the biblical authors conceived of, and practiced, a form of linguistic expression that corresponds very closely to what we consider, from a modern vantage point, hyperbole.

5. Analyzing hyperbole in biblical literature is no different than recognizing and discussing other aspects of figurative language such as simile, metaphor, irony, or personification. Commentators frequently talk about such figurative language in the Bible while importing modern terminology and understanding.[2]

6. Due caution should be exercised when crossing the so-called hermeneutical bridge. Modern understandings of a phenomenon such as hyperbole may not entirely comport with ancient forms or usage. There may be differences that are worthy of recognizing and bearing in mind. These will be duly noted in the ensuing chapters.

I also wish to prepare the reader for the fact that the theoretical literature I will be reviewing in this chapter may at times be technical or cumbersome, especially for those without a background in linguistics. I will do my

---

1. Kennedy, *Comparative Rhetoric*, 165, 188, for instance, finds hyperbole to be basic to both Chinese and Indian literary theory. McFadden, "Hyperbole," 648, claims that hyperbole is common across all literatures. Colston, *Using Figurative Language*, 95, discusses his research showing that by the age of seven, children's production of hyperbole is indistinguishable from that of adults. Also see Gibbs, *Poetics of Mind*, 80–119, who argues that the human mind is innately wired to use and understand figurative language such as hyperbole. Like Gibbs, Claridge, *Hyperbole in English*, 1, believes that hyperbole "may be wired in the cognitive structuring of our experience: the concept of size, to which exaggeration must primarily be connected, is a very basic and salient one."

2. See, e.g., Ryken, *How to Read*, in its entirety. Also consider the significant works in the field of narrative criticism, such as Rhoads, Dewey, and Michie, *Mark as Story*, and Kingsbury, *Matthew as Story*.

The Nature of Hyperbole

best, however, to explain things as clearly as possible and to avoid unnecessary rabbit trails. I will also work from examples in order to provide concise demonstrations of my outworking of theory into practice.

DEFINITION OF HYPERBOLE

Hyperbole is a deliberate exaggeration for the sake of effect. The term derives from the Greek ὑπερβολή (verb form ὑπερβάλλω, originally meaning "to cast beyond," as in a spear contest [BDAG]). In Latin it is known as *superlatio*. According to Neal Norrick, "Hyperbole is an *amplificatio*, a vertical-scalar metaphor.... An *amplificatio* says more than necessary or justified ... either through repetition ... or through lexical substitution."[3]

Attempts have been made in the research literature to distinguish hyperbole from exaggeration or overstatement.[4] Raymond Gibbs, for instance, believes that hyperbole should be viewed as an intentionally used device whereas simple overstatement can be unconscious or unintentional.[5] Javier Ruiz argues that overstatement is the superordinate category, encompassing hyperbole and other terms related to amplification.[6] Stein makes the distinction that, while overstatement describes something literally possible, hyperbole is something literally impossible.[7] In this and the following chapters I will side with Claudia Claridge in viewing and using the terms rather synonymously, with the preference for hyperbole as the main term:

> *Hyperbole* is the traditional term taken originally from classical rhetoric and thus is associated with formal and persuasive speech, later with stylistics and literature. It is the term listed in dictionaries of rhetorical and literary terminology, while *overstatement* and even more so *exaggeration* are everyday terms with no clear affiliation to any domain or use.[8]

---

3. Norrick, "On the Semantics of Overstatement," 168. Lausberg, *Handbook of Literary Rhetoric*, §579, calls it "a metaphor with vertical gradations."

4. While hyperbole usually involves exaggerating along an increasing scale (*auxesis*, or augmentation), it can also work in the opposite direction (*meiosis*, or diminution). These two uses are colloquially called *overstatement* and *understatement*, respectively. Understatement is also referred to as *litotes*.

5. Gibbs, *Poetics of Mind*, 391. No others that I know of have followed this distinction.

6. Ruiz, *Understanding Tropes*, 48.

7. Stein, *Basic Guide*, 175.

8. Claridge, *Hyperbole in English*, 6.

I would also like to clarify the use of the expression "literal meaning" before proceeding further. It may be interpreted as a term bound up in the belief that there is a one-to-one correspondence between a lexical term and some aspect of reality. But, as Ruiz states with regard to the contemporary understanding, "meaning is characterised by an encyclopaedic nature and, so, it is not simply perceived as related to truth conditions or objective correspondences (denotative aspects), but it is inseparable from both our world-knowledge (connotative aspects), and the cognitive structures related to conceptualisation processes."[9] In her study of hyperbole, Claridge also acknowledges the problem of the word "literal," yet she nonetheless adopts it in her explanations and graphics (at times, though, in quotation marks).[10] In fact, it is challenging to conceptualize hyperbole without using the term or something like it, as Claridge exemplifies: "The existence of the literal meaning of a hyperbolic expression is nevertheless very important. It is the anchor for the contrast to the corresponding non-hyperbolic literal expression."[11] For my purposes, while it may be necessary to use the term "literal" in discussing the literature on hyperbole (other published linguists besides Claridge still use it), I will be sparing in employing it when dealing with my own conceptual formulations and applications, especially in the coming chapters.

CHARACTERISTICS OF HYPERBOLE

In this section I will discuss some of the characteristics of hyperbole. This list is not meant to be exhaustive, and there is no doubt some overlap between items.

Nonveridicality

Hyperbole is the art of honest deception. It involves, at its core, asserting something that is not true. For example, imagine two students, Amy and Josh, walking in the halls of a school, books under their arms. Amy turns to Josh and says, "These books weigh a ton!" That statement is nonveridical, or untrue. The books may weigh a great deal, but Josh would not reasonably infer that Amy's books really do weigh two thousand pounds.

9. Ruiz, *Understanding Tropes*, 68.
10. Claridge, *Hyperbole in English*, 5, explains that "'literal' is a shorthand for the expression that agrees as closely as possible with the state of affairs and that is, thus, factually appropriate."
11. Claridge, *Hyperbole in English*, 27.

The Nature of Hyperbole

However, Amy is not mistaken. Even she does not really believe that her books weigh a ton. Nor does she intend for Josh to believe that they do. She is engaged in what Herbert Clark calls "a kind of joint pretense in which speakers and addressees create a new layer of joint activity."[12] This aspect of purposeful nonveridicality in hyperbole has been recognized since the ancient Greco-Roman handbooks: "Hyperbole is a liar, but does not lie to deceive."[13]

Intentionality

Every hyperbole is, according to Claridge, "an intentional linguistic act."[14] Inherent is an intention to "[transport] an attitude of the speaker to the facts, without misrepresenting the facts themselves."[15] As Claridge herself acknowledges, however, only speakers can know their own intention, so it is up to the addressee to infer an intention in the speaker to exaggerate.[16]

Subjectivity

Hyperbole communicates things about the speaker. It acts as a conveyance mechanism for the speaker's perspective in discourse (also known as the "speaker's imprint"). Claridge explains, "Subjectivity thus comprises the expression of various aspects, such as the colouring of the message by/through the speaker's perspective or viewpoint, affect and attitude, epistemic modality and metalinguistic comments on the style of speaking."[17] In the example of the students, Amy is communicating several possible aspects of subjectivity through her statement that the books weigh a ton: not only that her books are experienced as heavy but that she feels exhausted, her arms hurt,

---

12. Clark, *Using Language*, 143. See also McCarthy and Carter, "'There's Millions of Them,'" 152.

13. Quintilian, *Inst.* 8.6.74. Also see Fontanier, *Les Figures du Discours*, 123, "L'Hyperbole augmente ou diminue les choses avec excès, et les présente bien au-dessus ou bien au-dessous de ce qu'elle sont, dans la vue, non de tromper, mais d'amener à la vérité même."

14. Claridge, *Hyperbole in English*, 7.

15. Claridge, *Hyperbole in English*, 18.

16. Cf. Perrin, "La Vérité dans l'Exagération," 25, "L'interprète doit avant tout reconnaître l'intention du locuteur d'exagérer ouvertement, ostensiblement—c'est-à-dire non seulement d'exagérer à dessein mais de faire savoir qu'il exagère."

17. Claridge, *Hyperbole in English*, 74.

she is in an irritable mood, she wants help carrying the books, and that she feels comfortable complaining to Josh.

Gradability

As Claridge asserts, "the notion of degree is basic to hyperbole."[18] There are three types of scales which hyperbole utilizes: semantic, pragmatic, and argumentative. Semantic scales have to do with the properties inherent in the words themselves. They depend on linguistic contrast and can be expressed as series, such as <all, most, many, some> or <freezing, cold, cool>, in descending order along a scale.[19]

Pragmatic scales depend not on linguistic structure but on extralinguistic information, "in speaker assumptions and expectations about the world leading to the (nonce) creation of a partially ordered set in a given context."[20] Such a scale, for Amy, could be <Calculus, Physics, Economics, English>, representing her courses from hardest to easiest. Since extralinguistic facts (in this case, Amy's abilities, interests) inform these scales, they tend to be more subjective (i.e., dependent on the speaker) and to rely on both quantitative and qualitative contrasts.

The third type of scale is the argumentative scale. There the items in the series are arranged according to argumentative strength. For Amy, saying "These books weigh a ton!" is likely a more convincing way of asking for help than simply saying "These books weigh a lot" or "These books are heavy."

Modulation

Hyperbole is often accompanied by certain key words that serve to intensify or downtone (reduce the intensity of) the meaning of an utterance. Claridge lists several intensifiers (*hate, nothing, absolutely, really, incredible, brilliant,*

---

18. Claridge, *Hyperbole in English*, 7.

19. Claridge, *Hyperbole in English*, 7. The technical term for these scales is a Horn scale (named after the researcher Laurence Horn). A Horn scale is a lexicalized scale of items from the same word class and register. It is an entailment scale, where each item in the series "entails" the semantically weaker item to its right. For example, a sentence that uses the word "all" entails the idea of a sentence that uses the word "most," but not vice versa. See Horn, "On the Semantic Properties"; Huang, *Pragmatics*, 44–48.

20. Claridge, *Hyperbole in English*, 8. These scales are termed Hirschberg scales. For more information see Levinson, *Presumptive Meanings*, 104–8; Huang, *Pragmatics*, 49–54.

massive, terrified, literally) and downtoners (*probably, just about, virtually*).[21] Downtoners are also known as hedges.[22] In our example above, Amy could have intensified her message by stating, "These books *absolutely* weigh a ton!" To downtone her message she could have added the hedge *just about*, as in "These books *just about* weigh a ton!"

Discrepancy

Hyperbole reflects a discrepancy between a person's actual experience and their wishes or expectations. This aspect is highlighted by Herbert Colston:

> According to the inflation account of hyperbole ... a speaker encounters some event or situation that fails to meet his or her expectations. Something about the event/situation is of greater or lesser magnitude than is normal or that is somehow different relative to explicit expectations in the current context. A speaker wishes to point out this discrepancy to hearers, so an attempt is made to render the violation more prominent. A basic psychological principle holds that, all else being equal, things that are larger, physically or semantically, are more noticeable relative to smaller things. Thus the speaker inflates the magnitude of the discrepancy between expectations and reality by speaking as if it is bigger that [sic] it is—by stating the target magnitude in terms that exceed its actual levels—and typically in a direction consistent with the violation (e.g., uttered magnitudes are increased if violations are more than expectations but decreased if violations are less than expectations).[23]

In our example, Amy encounters a situation (having to carry an armload of books) that violates her expectations (the books are heavier than usual). She expresses this by inflating this discrepancy (bigger = more important) in a way that directs Josh's attention to it.

CATEGORIES OF HYPERBOLE

There are many different ways that hyperbole may be manifested in an utterance. This section deals with the nomenclature of hyperbole in an attempt to distinguish one kind of hyperbole from another.

21. Claridge, *Hyperbole in English*, 102–11.
22. Norrick, "Hyperbole," 201.
23. Colston, *Using Figurative Language*, 196.

Basic and Composite Hyperbole

Hyperbole can be classified according to how many semantic domains are involved. If one domain is involved, it is called *basic* hyperbole. If more than one, it is *composite* hyperbole. In our example of the students and textbooks, the hyperbole is *basic* because both the hyperbolic meaning (ton) and the non-hyperbolic meaning (heavy) are in the same domain (descriptions of weight). If, however, Amy says, "These books are a beast," then the hyperbolic meaning switches domains (Figure 4.1). "Beast" conjures associations with large, threatening animals. The domain switching nature of composite hyperbole is why it is also called *metaphorical hyperbole*. Metaphorical hyperbole can have powerful effects: "The advantage of metaphorical hyperbole can be found in the fact that such examples can also have a greater effect on the audience, often because more than one semantic attribute plays a role, a fully rounded picture/concept is evoked and/or the surprise value is greater. Thus, the hyperbolic effect is achieved in a more striking way."[24]

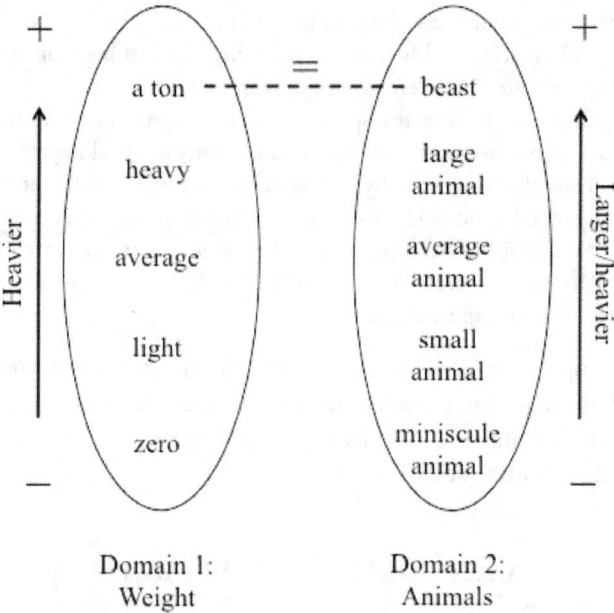

Figure 4.1. The Vertical (Scalar) and Horizontal (Domain Switching) Dimensions of Metaphorical Hyperbole. The domains *weight* and *animals* each have gradations that can be arranged along a vertical scale. When combined they form a metaphor.

24. Claridge, *Hyperbole in English*, 42. Claridge adds that composite hyperbole may also be metonymic in nature (43). See also Lausberg, *Handbook of Literary Rhetoric*, §579, "The intended vertical shift can be expressed and made concrete by means of a horizontal (thus metaphorical) shift ('hyperbolic metaphor')."

The Nature of Hyperbole

Extreme Case Formulations

In some cases hyperbole is constructed with the use of adjective modifiers such as *all, none, every,* and *any*. These hyperbolic expressions have been given the designation *extreme case formulations* (ECFs) in the research literature. Some examples are:

- Brand new
- Completely innocent
- He was driving perfectly
- He didn't say a word
- I really don't know who he is
- No time
- Forever
- Every time
- Everyone[25]

ECFs are a sub-category of hyperbole and are distinguished by their use of the endpoints of a scale.[26] They are commonly found in proverbs, which are known for their apodictic nature.[27] Because of their obvious falseness, of course, they are easily defeasible.[28]

ECFs are also frequently used in complaining (e.g., "You never let me finish what I'm saying!"):

> Part of the business of complaining involves portraying a situation as a legitimate complainable [sic]. This may take the form of portraying the offense committed and/or the suffering endured in a way such that it would not be dismissed as minor. So as to legitimize a complaint and portray the complainable situation as worthy of the complaint, a speaker may portray the offense and/ or the suffering with Extreme Case formulations. In both accusing and defending, participants often present their strongest cases, including specifying Extreme Cases of their claims.[29]

25. From Pomerantz, "Extreme Case Formulations," 219.
26. Norrick, "Hyperbole," 201, "Overstatement occurs any time a speaker makes a claim higher (or lower) on some scale than warranted, while ECFs make claims involving the end points on such scales."
27. Norrick, "Hyperbole, Extreme Case Formulation," 1730.
28. Norrick, "Hyperbole, Extreme Case Formulation," 1733.
29. Pomerantz, "Extreme Case Formulations," 227–28. See Norrick, "Hyperbole,

Naturally, speakers who use ECFs demonstrate their investment in the point they are attempting to make.[30]

Taxonomies

Most hyperboles can be classified according to a handful of discrete categories. In a 1963 article Spitzbardt proffered the following taxonomy:[31]

1. Numerical hyperbole ("I told you more than a hundred times")
2. Words of a hyperbolic nature
    a. Nouns ("ages")
    b. Adjectives ("colossal")
    c. Adverbs ("endlessly")
    d. Verbs ("dying to know")
3. Simile and metaphor ("as cross as the devil")
4. Comparative and superlative degrees ("in less than no time")
5. Emphatic genitive ("the finest of fine watches")
6. Emphatic plural ("the sands of the desert")
7. Whole sentences ("He is nothing if not deliberate")

To Spitzbardt's classification system Claridge adds the distinction between single-word, phrasal, and clausal hyperbole, as well as repetition ("he's just *really really really* strange").[32]

McCarthy and Carter studied a five-million word corpus called the Cambridge and Nottingham Corpus of Discourse in English, or CANCODE, for instances of hyperbole. They categorized their results as follows:[33]

1. Expressions of number: plural forms ("dozens of")
2. Expressions of number: singular forms ("a million")
3. Words referring to large amounts/quantities ("loads of")

Extreme Case Formulation," 1727–39, on the differences between ECF and non-extreme hyperbole.

30. Edwards, "Extreme Case Formulations," 364.

31. Spitzbardt, "Overstatement and Understatement," 278–80, with one representative example included for each category.

32. Claridge, *Hyperbole in English*, 49–70.

33. McCarthy and Carter, "'There's Millions of Them,'" 179–80.

4. Adjective modification of *amount(s)* and *number(s)* ([adj] "numbers of")
5. Time expressions ("years")
6. Size, degree and intensity ("huge")

Only one nomenclature (to my knowledge) has been suggested for classifying hyperbole in the Bible. The one below covers the OT only.[34] There are many hundreds of instances of hyperbole in the OT (see chapter 7); however, here only one representative example is given for each class of hyperbole.

1. Quantifiable
    a. Lifetime (1 Kgs 1:31)
    b. Numerical (Gen 4:24)
        i. Factor of 10 (Lev 26:26)
        ii. Factor of 7 (Ruth 4:15)
        iii. Factor of 2 (Isa 40:2)
        iv. 100/1000/10,000 (Deut 1:11)
    c. All-nothing (1 Kgs 14:23)
    d. Size/mass (2 Sam 17:11–13)
    e. Dimensional (Gen 11:4)
2. Qualitative
    a. Idealizations (Num 11:29)
    b. Fertility (Exod 3:8)
    c. Irresistibility (2 Sam 1:23)
    d. Love (Song 2:2)
    e. Self-deprecation (Gen 18:3)
    f. Contempt/disdain/scorn (1 Sam 17:43)
    g. Boasting (2 Kings 19:23–24)
    h. Emotions (Exod 16:3)
    i. Crying (Isa 40:6)
    j. Accusations (Isa 1:21)
    k. Mockery/ridicule (Prov 19:24)

34. Jenni, "Sprachliche Übertreibungen," 76–83.

l. Apparent exaggerations (Hos 2:5)

HOW HYPERBOLE "WORKS"

The study of hyperbole transports us into the realm of pragmatics, the subfield of linguistics concerned with how language is used. When a speaker chooses to use figurative language like hyperbole, there is additional meaning conveyed beyond the conventional meaning of the words. As in our example, Amy's utterance that "These books weigh a ton!" carries with it certain tentative implications: Amy feels exhausted, her arms hurt, she is in an irritable mood, she wants help carrying the books, and so on. There are a few different approaches to discussing how humans deal with this extra information. Each approach has spawned several books and its own technical language. Nevertheless, I will attempt a rudimentary presentation of each approach in the space that follows. This background will enrich our analysis of the passages in Galatians in chapters 9 through 11.

Speech Act Theory

Speech act theory, shaped by British philosopher J. L. Austin and refined by his pupil, American philosopher John R. Searle, holds that "the uttering of a sentence is, or is part of, an action within the framework of social institutions and conventions.... Saying is (part of) doing, or words are (part of) deeds."[35] According to the theory, there are three acts performed by each utterance. One is the *locutionary act*, or what is literally said. The second is the *illocutionary act*, the type of function the speaker intends to be fulfilled by the locution.[36] The third is the *perlocutionary act*, or what effect the utterance produces.[37] In our example, Amy's locution consists of the sentence "These books weigh a ton!" By performing this utterance Amy also commits

---

35. Huang, *Pragmatics*, 119.

36. Austin, *How to Do Things with Words*, 98–99, offers examples of illocutionary acts: "asking or answering a question, giving some information or an assurance or a warning, announcing a verdict or an intention, pronouncing sentence, making an appointment or an appeal or a criticism, making an identification or giving a description, and the numerous like."

37. Austin, *How to Do Things with Words*, 101, "Saying something will often, or even normally, produce certain consequential effects upon the feelings, thought, or actions of the audience, or of the speaker, or of other persons: and it may be done with the design, intention, or purpose of producing them.... We shall call the performance of an act of this kind the performance of a 'perlocutionary' act, and the act performed, where suitable ... a 'perlocution.'"

an illocutionary act, attempting to inform Josh that her books are heavy.[38] But there is also a perlocutionary value to Amy's utterance, which is the effect her information has on Josh; for instance, he might feel sorry for her and offer to help in carrying the books.

Searle's work on metaphor is also applicable. He represents metaphor as follows: the speaker says "S is P" (the *sentence meaning*) but really means (figuratively) that "S is R" (the *speaker's utterance meaning*).[39] Searle conceives of comprehension of figurative language as a multistep process. First, the addressee recognizes the defectiveness (untruthfulness) of the sentence meaning. Consequently, the addressee looks for an utterance meaning that is different from the sentence meaning. An indefinite number of possible values present themselves. Thus, a third step is needed: the addressee must somehow restrict the range of possible utterance meanings.[40]

Gricean Theory

Another way of conceptualizing the effects of hyperbole is from philosopher Paul Grice, who in his 1967 *William James Lectures* put forth the theory that human conversation typically takes place within certain parameters of cooperation. Grice's *cooperative principle* specifies four maxims which need to be mutually recognized by speaker and addressee for effective communication to take place. They are the (1) *quantity maxim* (give as much information as required but no more), (2) *quality maxim* (be truthful), (3) *maxim of relation* (be relevant), and the (4) *maxim of manner* (be perspicuous).[41] Speakers can choose to go along with or violate these norms in conversation. In our example with Amy and Josh, Amy is said to be *flouting* (bla-

---

38. Mac Cormac, *Cognitive Theory of Metaphor*, 160–62, suggests that metaphors (and, for our purposes, metaphorical hyperbole) carry three illocutionary forces: "stimulating emotion, producing perplexity, and creating a sense of intimacy in shared language" (162).

39. Searle, *Expression and Meaning*, 77, 83. I believe it is fair to generalize from Searle's statements concerning metaphor to hyperbole, at least to metaphorical hyperbole. Even some of Searle's own examples are metaphorical hyperbole (e.g., "Sally is a block of ice," "Sam is a giant," "Sam is a pig").

40. Searle, *Expression and Meaning*, 106, "Here again the hearer may employ various strategies for doing that but the one that is most commonly used is this. *Go back to the S term and see which of the many candidates for the values of R are likely or even possible properties of S.*" Unsatisfied with this explanation is Colston, *Using Figurative Language*, 24–25, who considers the lack of precision in explaining how meaning is inferred from an illocution to be a major drawback to speech act theory's ability to deal with pragmatic effects.

41. Grice, *Studies in the Way of Words*, 26–28.

tantly violating) the quality maxim by her statements that her books weigh a ton. This is where the Gricean concept of *implicatures* comes into play.[42] Implicatures are the range of assumptions implicitly suggested by Amy's utterance minus the words themselves (i.e., things not strictly *entailed* by her speech). By flouting the maxim of quality she is *implicating* that there are additional assumptions (e.g., "help me!") behind her literal utterance. Josh, on the other hand, may choose to believe that Amy has abandoned the cooperative principle altogether, but more likely he will recognize that she intends the infringement as a signal for hyperbole.

There are a few shortcomings, however, to Gricean theory in regard to its applicability to hyperbole. First, though Grice conceives of hyperbole as a flout of the maxim of quality, there may be other maxims that apply.[43] Second, Grice supplies only a single example of hyperbole ("Every nice girl loves a sailor") and does not give a conceptual explanation for it.[44] Third, he treats irony, metaphor, and hyperbole similarly even though they are different tropes.[45] Fourth, because classical Gricean theory is primarily speaker-oriented, it does not adequately address what happens in the addressee during the cognitive processing of hyperbole.[46]

Relevance Theory

Relevance theory, developed by Dan Sperber and Dierdre Wilson, views the aim of human communication, from both the speaker and addressee perspectives, as achieving *optimal relevance*: "human cognitive processes . . . are geared to achieving the greatest possible cognitive effect for the smallest possible processing effort. To achieve this, individuals must focus their attention on what seems to them to be the most relevant information available."[47] This theory purports to be better than Gricean theory at explaining how humans choose among a variety of hypotheses that arise based

---

42. Grice, *Studies in the Way of Words*, 24–26.

43. Claridge, *Hyperbole in English*, 133, 136, proposes the maxims of relation and quantity as also governing hyperbole.

44. Grice, *Studies in the Way of Words*, 34.

45. Claridge, *Hyperbole in English*, 133.

46. Claridge, *Hyperbole in English*, 133, "Noticing a quality flout does not indicate at all to the addressee the direction the intended interpretation should take, i.e., the 'downgrading' . . . is by no means a necessary next step, nor is the interpretation of the attitudinal force." Although the neo-Gricean approaches of Horn and Levinson have "moved more towards a hearer perspective," (133) Claridge notes, "(most) hyperbole will presumably still fall under Quality flouts in the neo-Gricean view" (134).

47. Sperber and Wilson, *Relevance*, vii.

on implicatures.[48] The hypothesis chosen is the one that is most relevant. Colston explains:

> Optimal relevance means in the simplest sense that speakers normally will produce utterances that fit with or are relevant to the currently shared background knowledge of the interlocutors. This background knowledge is made up of specific bits of shared info called *contextual assumptions*. Comprehenders then will use those contextual assumptions, along with the utterances, to compute *positive cognitive effects*. . . . Positive cognitive effects involve such things as confirmations or disconfirmations of contextual assumptions, as well as computations of additional meaning.[49]

What happens, then, in hyperbole from the standpoint of relevance theory? "A hyperbolic utterance is an ostensive stimulus."[50] As such, it may be presumed that it has been chosen by the speaker as the most relevant form of speech. In addition, the addressee can expect the utterance to be relevant (the addressee, again, is aiming toward maximizing cognitive effects at the lowest possible expense of cognitive processing effort). Let us return to our example. When Amy expresses the assumption "These books weigh a ton!" she simultaneously implicates the assumptions "These books are heavy," "I would like help carrying them," and so on. These assumptions share logical and contextual implications with the hyperbolic utterance.[51] The utterance "These books weigh a ton!," however, also has many other implications which Amy does not wish to communicate. Amy must rely on Josh to choose among them—to accept some and ignore/discard others—based on how relevant they are to him.

The advantage of understanding hyperbole through the lens of relevance theory is that relevance theory treats figurative and literal language processing the same (with the exception that figurative language produces a

---

48. According to Sperber and Wilson, *Relevance*, 37, what Gricean theory fails to show "is that on the same basis, an equally convincing justification could not have been given for some other interpretation that was not in fact chosen. There may be a whole variety of interpretations that would meet whatever standards of truthfulness, informativeness, relevance and clarity have been proposed or envisaged so far."

49. Colston, *Using Figurative Language*, 28.

50. Claridge, *Hyperbole in English*, 134. An ostensive stimulus, according to Sperber and Wilson, *Relevance*, 49, is a stimulus "which makes manifest an intention to make something manifest." In other words, it is not just the intention to inform the audience of something; it is also the intention to have that intention recognized by the audience.

51. Relevance-theoretic implicatures, or r-implicatures, are distinguished from Gricean (conversational) implicatures in the research literature.

set of weak implicatures). There is no multistep process needed for handling indirect utterances, as with speech act theory and Gricean theory. This is seen by several theorists as an advantage to relevance theory.[52]

Pragmatic Effects

In contrast to maxims/implicatures (Grice) and positive cognitive effects (Sperber and Wilson), Colston proposes viewing figurative language from the superordinate category of *pragmatic effects*, which are simply "additional complex meaning" conveyed by an expression.[53] Pragmatic effects go beyond the cognitive and linguistic dimensions of the above approaches to encompass effects that are *structural* (e.g., arising from the structural elements involved with similes and metaphors such as the juxtaposition of domains), *embodied* (e.g., having to do with physical aspects of pronunciation), *psychological* (e.g., mental states such as cognitive dissonance), and *sociocultural* (e.g., the degree of familiarity and shared knowledge between interlocutors). One pragmatic effect at which hyperbole excels, according to Colston, is its ability to highlight discrepancy between a person's wants and expectations versus actual events.[54] Thus, many people use hyperbole to express negativity when the world does not match up to their wishes.[55] Of course, hyperbole could also be used to express positivity when reality surpasses expectations. In Colston's words,

> Hyperbole, in typically inflating a discrepancy between expectation/desires and reality, also focuses a hearer's attention on that discrepancy so that he or she notices it. A straightforward characteristic of human attention is that, all else held equal, the bigger something is, the more likely it is that it will be noticed. The inflation draws attention. The very structure of hyperbole

---

52. Claridge, *Hyperbole in English*, 134; Colston, *Using Figurative Language*, 29; Gibbs, *Poetics of Mind*, 232, "Although there may be instances when listeners or readers spend considerable mental effort teasing out the weak contextual implications of a metaphor, the psychological research . . . clearly shows that listeners do not ordinarily devote extra processing resources to understanding metaphors compared with more literal utterances."

53. Colston, *Using Figurative Language*, 5.

54. Colston, *Using Figurative Language*, 72–74.

55. Which is also why, according to Colston, *Using Figurative Language*, 95, 111, children develop a knack for hyperbole early in life: "Children do not like that reality frequently differs from expectations/preferences/desires in their everyday experiences . . . and children are emotionally unable to contain that frustration" (95).

thus can produce one of its pragmatic effects—highlighting a discrepancy between expectations and reality.[56]

Primary Metaphors

Certain *primary metaphors* may play a basic role in the inferential processing of hyperbole. Primary metaphors are those acquired in early childhood through the sensorimotor system and which "universally form part of the cognitive unconscious."[57] Claridge proposes that two such metaphors are important in learning to understand hyperbole: (a) *important is big* (which describes the world of big things/people, especially from a young child's viewpoint), and (b) *more is up* (which links quantity with vertical orientation).[58]

Strengthening and Mitigating

Hyperbole is part of human language at its most creative. The use of it establishes a space wherein verbal play happens. The "rules" of this game are mutually understood between speaker and addressee. In overstatement, the speaker strengthens an utterance, while the addressee mitigates it to arrive at the intended (non-hyperbolic) meaning. In understatement, the opposite of hyperbole occurs: the speaker mitigates the meaning, while the addressee strengthens it (Figure 4.2). For example, imagine Amy saying to Josh, "These books are a tad heavy today." In this instance, the understatement needs to be corrected *toward*, rather than away from, the polar extreme. Or, as an example of an ironic utterance, imagine that Josh sees Amy struggling to carry her books. He asks her, "Do you need any help?" to which Amy replies with a tone of sarcasm, "Nah, these books are light as a feather." In this case, Amy's simile appears to express a positive sentiment, but she really means it negatively. The correction is made to the opposite extreme and the polarity of the statement (negative versus positive) is actually reversed.

---

56. Colston, *Using Figurative Language*, 89.
57. Claridge, *Hyperbole in English*, 137.
58. Claridge, *Hyperbole in English*, 137.

86   Part II: Hyperbole: Definitions and Rhetoric

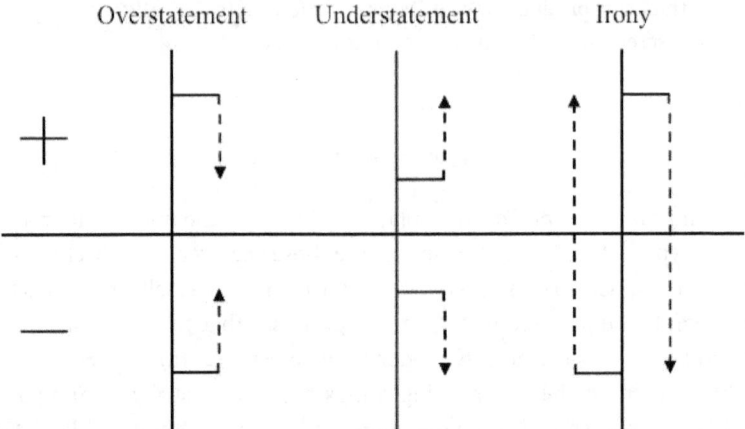

Figure 4.2. A Comparison of Overstatement, Understatement, and Irony. In overstatement, the correction is made away from the extreme. In understatement, the correction is made toward it. In irony, meanwhile, the correction is made away from the extreme and the polarity of the utterance is reversed.[59]

How far do corrections typically extend in hyperbole? Mitigation operations tend to reduce the intensity of an utterance to the point along the scale just below the exaggeration.[60] For example, an addressee hearing, "That was the best dinner in my life" would not interpret it to mean that the dinner was *good* or even *very good*, but that it was *excellent* (Figure 4.3).

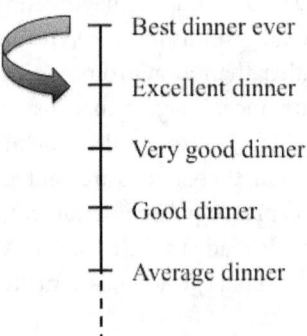

Figure 4.3. Scalar Corrections. In comprehending hyperbole, they are typically made to one point toward the midline.

---

59. Adapted from Fogelin, *Figuratively Speaking*, 15, by permission of Oxford University Press. I have changed "hyperbole," to "overstatement," since I define hyperbole as encompassing both overstatement and understatement.

60. Bach and Harnis, *Linguistic Communication*, 68; Ruiz, *Understanding Tropes*, 216.

RECOGNIZING HYPERBOLE

How do addressees (whether hearers or readers) go about deciding whether a speaker is participating in the "game" of hyperbole and flouting the truthfulness maxim? Two proposals will be presented in this section. The first was developed for an analysis of a written corpus of spoken English language. The second was initially developed for the biblical Gospels.

McCarthy and Carter (2004)

As previously noted, McCarthy and Carter studied a five-million word corpus (CANCODE) for instances of hyperbole. Of primary interest here is their methodology. Below are the criteria they used for identifying hyperbole:[61]

- *Disjunction with context:* Is the utterance "at odds with the general context"?
- *Shifts in footing:* Has the speaker's attitude shifted "to a conversational frame where impossible worlds or plainly counterfactual claims may appropriately occur"?
- *Counterfactuality not perceived as a lie:* Is the speaker perceived as not attempting to deceive?
- *Impossible worlds:* Does the counterfactuality invite the listener into the creation of a fictitious world, one in which exaggerated events happen?
- *Listener take-up:* Does the listener respond with supportive behavior such as laughter?
- *Extreme case formulations and intensification:* Does the utterance contain ECFs and intensifiers such as *endless, massive, literally, nearly,* or *totally*?
- *Syntactic support:* Are syntactic devices used (e.g., polysyndeton or complex modification) "to underline the amplification of the expression"?
- *Relevant interpretability:* Is the hyperbole "interpretable as relevant to the speech act being performed"?

---

61. McCarthy and Carter, "'There's Millions of Them,'" 162–63.

Stein (2011)

In his biblical hermeneutics textbook, Stein develops the idea that hyperbole is present throughout the Bible as part of the "game" of exaggeration. What Stein means by this is that, as I have discussed above, exaggeration depends on both the writer and audience being participants in (i.e., having knowledge of the rules of) the game: "The acceptability of this literary form of communication depends on its being shared."[62] He suggests ten "rules" by which hyperbole may be recognized in Scripture:

1. The statement is literally impossible
2. The statement conflicts with what the speaker teaches elsewhere
3. The statement conflicts with the actions of the speaker elsewhere
4. The statement conflicts with the teachings of the Old Testament
5. The statement conflicts with the teachings of the New Testament
6. The statement is interpreted by another biblical writer in a nonliteral way
7. The statement has not been literally fulfilled
8. The statement would not achieve its desired goal
9. The statement uses a literary form prone to exaggeration
10. The statement uses universal language (e.g., "all," "everyone," "no one")[63]

As can be seen from the list above, Stein's rules rely heavily on flouts of the maxim of quality. How does one decide when the quality maxim is being flouted? Stein spells out certain assumptions. Since Stein's rules will be influential in the methodology of this study (see chapter 6), it would be judicious to explore his rules in greater detail by examining their underlying assumptions.[64]

1. The statement is literally impossible

    Assumption: "Even in a world-view that accepts the supernatural, certain teachings of Jesus are clearly impossible."[65]

---

62. Stein, *Basic Guide*, 175.

63. Stein, *Basic Guide*, 177–87. These rules initially appeared, in slightly different form, as thirteen "canons" applied to the Gospels in Stein, *Difficult Sayings*, 33–56.

64. Most of the assumptions given here are taken from Stein's earlier (1985) text because in my opinion he did a better job of explaining the justification for his rules in that text.

65. Stein, *Difficult Sayings*, 34.

2. The statement conflicts with what the speaker teaches elsewhere
   Assumption: "A reasonably intelligent person is logically consistent."[66]
3. The statement conflicts with the actions of the speaker elsewhere
   Assumption: Jesus practiced what he preached.[67]
4. The statement conflicts with the teachings of the Old Testament
   Assumption: Jesus viewed his teachings as being in continuity with (and a fulfillment of) the Old Testament.[68]
5. The statement conflicts with the teachings of the New Testament
   Assumption: The other New Testament writers understood Jesus's teachings accurately.[69] They are understood to be "divinely inspired interpreters of Jesus's teaching," so inconsistency is unlikely.[70]
6. The statement is interpreted by another biblical writer in a nonliteral way
   Assumption: A biblical writer's redaction—or presentation within a certain context—of a saying of Jesus may indicate how that saying was meant to be understood.[71]
7. The statement has not been literally fulfilled
   Assumption: Jesus "expected his listeners to assume certain qualifications" regarding predictions and gnomic sayings.[72]
8. The statement would not achieve its desired goal
   Assumption: Jesus spoke certain commands which, if carried out literally, would not achieve what he intended.[73]
9. The statement uses a literary form prone to exaggeration
   Assumption: The Bible contains genres, such as proverbs, prophecy, poetry, metaphor, and parable, which by their nature are inclined toward hyperbole.[74]

66. Stein, *Difficult Sayings*, 36.
67. Stein, *Difficult Sayings*, 41.
68. Stein, *Difficult Sayings*, 44.
69. Stein, *Difficult Sayings*, 45.
70. Stein, *Basic Guide*, 180.
71. Stein, *Difficult Sayings*, 51. In the original (1985) presentation of the rules Stein's argument here was limited to the Evangelists, not the entire New Testament.
72. Stein, *Difficult Sayings*, 54.
73. Stein, *Difficult Sayings*, 55–56.
74. Stein, *Difficult Sayings*, 56–75.

10. The statement uses universal language (e.g., "all," "everyone," "no one")
    Assumption: "The presence of universal language in a statement is also an indication that the saying may be an exaggeration.... It is more often true than not that unqualified general propositions found in the Bible are exaggerated statements."[75]

CONCLUSION

In this chapter we have examined what hyperbole is and how it works in communication. The discussion has been detailed and technical but necessary to produce a framework for what is to follow. In the subsequent chapters this conceptual framework will be overlaid onto the Bible (OT in chapter 7, NT in chapter 8, and finally Galatians in chapters 9–11) to tease apart the hyperbolic sayings and examine them. At the same time, however, the methodology of this project will be refined (chapter 6) as we encounter the historical and biblical data.

---

75. Stein, *Difficult Sayings*, 80–81. As noted above, linguists refer to these types of statements as extreme case formulations (ECFs).

5

The Rhetoric of Hyperbole

In this chapter…

Question(s) to be answered:
- How has hyperbole been a part of persuasive speech since at least the classical age of Greece?
- How does invective make use of hyperbole?
- Was Paul a rhetorician?

Trajectory:
- Chapters 6–8 narrow the focus to hyperbole in the Bible.

RHETORIC IS, SUCCINCTLY, THE art of persuasion. The systematic study of rhetoric apparently originated in the fifth century BC in Sicily, where a rhetorician named Corax offered to train citizens to effectively plead their land claims in court.[1] From there the art form was carried to the Greek city-states, where, in the midst of democratization, professional teachers of rhetoric known as Sophists found a ready market in which to ply their skills: "As a large number of men entered the political arena, the key factor in personal success and public influence was no longer class but skill in persuasive speaking."[2] In Athenian trials, moreover, there were no lawyers—citizens

---

1. According to Kennedy's introduction to Aristotle, *On Rhetoric*, 8, features of rhetorical style, argument, and arrangement could already be seen in Homer's *Odyssey* and *Iliad*. These two works achieved their present form around 550 BC. Plutarch mentioned Homer's use of hyperbole (Plutarch, *Vit. poes. Hom.*, 71, "He often uses hyperbole as well, which goes beyond the truth and exaggerates, to give force to the discourse, as 'Whiter than snow and as fast as the winds [Il. 10.437].' Since he used such tropes and figures and passed them on to those who followed, Homer rightly receives the credit for them before all others").

2. Herrick, *History and Theory of Rhetoric*, 32.

had to represent themselves—so being equipped to effectively persuade an audience of one's peers through oratory gave a defendant an advantage.[3]

The Sophists recognized the power of words to move people's emotions, even to shape people's perception of reality. Reality itself came to be viewed as simply a "linguistic construction rather than an objective fact. If truth and reality depend on who can speak the most persuasively, what becomes of justice, virtue, and social order? Truth became a completely subjective notion, with the individual capable of creating a private view of morality and even of existence."[4] Against such excesses Plato wrote the dialogue *Gorgias*, in which he argued that rhetoric must have its foundation in justice. His well-known quote, "As cookery is to medicine, so is rhetoric to justice" reveals Plato's disdain for rhetoric, which, like cookery, was a pretender to a true art.[5] Plato's argument is nicely summed up as follows:

> Sophistic rhetoric deceives audiences into thinking they are dealing with truth when they are dabbling in opinions, that they are rendering justice when they are committing injustice, and that they are completely healthy when they are desperately sick. Moreover, rhetoric dupes even its practitioners into thinking they wield real power when they are, in fact, slaves to public opinion.[6]

Despite Plato's suspicions, though not ignorant of them, the study of rhetoric flourished and became an important component of Greek culture, forming the core of the curriculum for schoolchildren. Young boys learned grammar until the age of twelve, at which point they transitioned to formal learning in rhetoric. Their education consisted of formal lectures combined with practical exercises in declamation.[7] When the entire region was hellenized in the late fourth century, rhetoric was exported from Greece to the Near East and Mediterranean, and schools of rhetoric were established in every major urban center.[8] This cultural dominance of the field of rhetoric continued throughout the Roman period.

---

3. Herrick, *History and Theory of Rhetoric*, 34.
4. Herrick, *History and Theory of Rhetoric*, 40.
5. Plato, *Gorg.*, 465c.
6. Herrick, *History and Theory of Rhetoric*, 63.
7. Kennedy, "Historical Survey of Rhetoric," 18–19.
8. Kennedy, "Historical Survey of Rhetoric," 18.

HYPERBOLE AND THE RHETORICAL HANDBOOKS

Along with the rapidly increasing importance of rhetoric came handbooks (τέχναι) that could be used to teach rhetoric.[9] This section will survey several of these handbooks, both ancient and modern, to determine what can be gleaned with regard to hyperbole as an element of rhetorical style.

Aristotle

While still a student at Plato's Academy, Aristotle (384–322 BC) began teaching rhetoric in the afternoons during the mid-350s BC. He wanted to counteract the influence of Isocrates, the leader of a rival school who taught a version of sophistic rhetoric.[10] Thus was born Aristotle's *On Rhetoric*, much of which came from his notes from those afternoon teaching sessions. *On Rhetoric* blends the theoretical and the practical and serves as a corrective to what he saw as Plato's unduly critical and overly moralizing *Gorgias*.[11]

According to Aristotle, rhetoric is "the faculty of discovering the possible means of persuasion in reference to any subject whatever."[12] These means of persuasion, or "proofs," may be *non-artistic* (provided by something other than the speaker; e.g., an ancient witness) or *artistic* (provided by the speaker). The latter category consists of appeals by the speaker based on logic (*logos*), the emotions of the audience (*pathos*), or the speaker's character (*ethos*).

Aristotle mentions hyperbole in the course of discussing metaphor and other devices of style:

---

9. While there were many rhetorical handbooks written, few have survived. Kennedy, "Historical Survey of Rhetoric," 9, notes, referring to the list of handbooks mentioned in Plato's *Phaedrus*, that there were several handbooks in circulation even during the early fifth century BC. On a broader scale, "Literally hundreds of rhetorical handbooks, plus monographs on specific aspects of rhetoric, were written by rhetoricians, orators, grammarians, philosophers, and enthusiastic amateurs throughout antiquity. Most were ephemeral and are known, if at all, only from incidental references by other writers" (19).

10. See Kennedy's introduction to Aristotle, *On Rhetoric*, 4: "The most evident difference between Aristotelian and Isocratean teaching is the great emphasis put on truth, knowledge of a subject, and logical argument by Aristotle in contrast to Isocrates' inclination to gloss over historical facts and his obsession with techniques of amplification and smoothness of style. Aristotle doubtless thought that Isocrates was at heart a sophist, that his philosophy was shallow, and that as a teacher of rhetoric he failed to give his students an adequate understanding of logical argument—which many at the time regarded as tiresome verbal pedantry" (13).

11. Herrick, *History and Theory of Rhetoric*, 74.

12. Aristotle, *Rhet.*, 1.2.1.

> Approved hyperboles are also metaphors. For instance, one may say of a man whose eye is all black and blue, "you would have thought he was a basket of mulberries," because the black eye is something purple, but the great quantity constitutes the hyperbole. Again, when one says "like this or that" there is a hyperbole differing only in the wording:
>
> Like Philammon punching the leather sack...
>
> Carrying his legs twisted like parsley....
>
> There is something youthful about hyperboles; for they show vehemence. Wherefore those who are in a passion most frequently make use of them.... Wherefore it is unbecoming for elderly people to make use of them.[13]

In the above quote, Aristotle describes the heart of hyperbole as being an exaggerated comparison. He gives a few examples. His evaluation seems overall to be negative—hyperbole is juvenile, used by people in a passion (ὀργιζόμενοι).

Ad Herennium

Mention of hyperbole shows up a few centuries later in a Latin handbook, one that was attributed to Cicero until the Renaissance but which is now considered anonymous. *Rhetorica ad Herennium*, composed circa 85 BC, was one of the leading texts on rhetoric used during the Middle Ages:[14]

> Hyperbole is a manner of speech exaggerating the truth, whether for the sake of magnifying or minifying something. This is used independently, or with comparison. Independently, as follows: "But if we maintain Concorde in the state, we shall measure the empires vastness by the rising and the setting of the sun." Hyperbole with comparison is formed from either equivalence or superiority. From equivalence, as follows: "His body was as white as snow, his face burns like fire." From superiority, as follows: "From his mouth flowed speech sweeter than honey." Of the same type is the following: "So great was his splendor in arms that the sun's brilliance seem to dim by comparison."[15]

The definition here is a more full fledged one. Hyperbole can magnify or "minify." It can be used independently or as part of a comparison (cf.

---

13. Aristotle, *Rhet.*, 3.11.15.
14. Kennedy, "Historical Survey of Rhetoric," 24.
15. *Rhet. Her.*, 4.44.

Aristotle's metaphorical examples). *Ad Herennium* does not, however, comment on the appropriateness of hyperbole as did Aristotle.

Cicero

A third mention of hyperbole occurs in Cicero's *On the Orator (De Oratore)*. Completed circa 55 BC, the book is written as a philosophical dialogue between four main characters. According to Kennedy, "It is the earliest Latin work to show direct knowledge of Aristotle's *Rhetoric* and to adapt some of Aristotle's concepts to Roman conditions."[16] Cicero's teaching concerning hyperbole (specifically *minuendi aut augendi*, "understatements or overstatements") occurs in the course of discussing wit:

> Then again there are those intentional understatements or overstatements which are exaggerated to a degree of the astonishing that passes belief, such as your own assertion, Crassus, made in a speech before a public assembly, that Memmius thought himself so exalted an individual that, on his way down into the Market Place, he lowered his head in order to pass under the Arch of Fabius. To this category also belongs the taunt said to have been uttered by Scipio at Numantia, when he was in a rage with Gaius Metellus, that "if the mother of Metellus should bear a fifth time, she would be found to have borne an ass."[17]

Positioned as this comment is in a lengthy section on jesting, it appears that Cicero saw hyperbole as a means of getting a laugh out of the audience. Both of his examples, it should be noted, have to do with invective directed against individuals. We will return to this topic later in this chapter.

Quintilian

A fourth source for hyperbole is the orator Quintilian. *The Orator's Education (Institutio Oratoria)*, written in the latter half of the first century AD, is "the fullest account of classical rhetoric, based on his twenty years of teaching the subject and over two years of research in earlier sources."[18] Quintilian's treatment of hyperbole is quite extensive, so I will need to abridge his comments somewhat.

---

16. Kennedy, "Historical Survey of Rhetoric," 25.
17. Cicero, *De or.*, 2.66.267.
18. Kennedy, "Historical Survey of Rhetoric," 31.

Part II: Hyperbole: Definitions and Rhetoric

Quintilian states that hyperbole is a species of amplification and attenuation (8.4.29; 8.6.68; 9.1.29), so it is necessary to understand what he means by amplification (*amplificandi* or *augendi*) and attenuation (*minuendi*). Amplification and attenuation essentially involve the use of words or things to enhance or diminish the effect of an elocution, respectively. Words can *amplify* the effect of oratory on an audience, such as by saying "that a man who was beaten was 'murdered,' or that a dishonest man is a 'brigand.'"[19] Or, words can *attenuate* an effect, as in saying "that a man who struck someone 'touched' him or one who wounded a man 'hurt' him."[20]

Quintilian considers four ways in which amplification takes place:[21]

1. *Increment*—This is advancing an argument step by step in an attempt to make a comparatively insignificant thing seem important. "The process not only goes to the top, it sometimes in a sense goes beyond it."[22]

    a. *Choosing a stronger word*—as in the above example, "We may say that a man who was *beaten* was *murdered*"[23]

    b. *Building words upon words*—"It is wrong to bind a Roman citizen, a crime to flog him, little short of parricide to put him to death: what shall I say about putting him on the cross?"[24]

    c. *Reiterating that which cannot be surpassed*—"You beat your mother. What more can I say? You beat your mother"[25]

---

19. Quintilian, *Inst.*, 8.4.1. The persuasive power of amplification may be seen in modern psychological research. In Loftus and Palmer, "Reconstruction of Automobile Destruction," 585–89, subjects viewed films of car crashes and then answered a series of questions about what they saw. Those who were asked, "About how fast were the cars going when they smashed into each other?" rated the speed of the cars as higher than those who were asked the same question but with the word *smashed* replaced by *collided*, *bumped*, *contacted*, or *hit*. A week later, subjects who received the verb *smashed* were more likely to respond *yes* when asked if they had seen broken glass at the scene (even though there was no broken glass in the film).

20. Quintilian, *Inst.*, 8.4.1.

21. Schlueter, *Filling Up the Measure*, 82, "Quintilian did not list all the possible methods of amplification, omitting the most frequent and obvious ones, but including the most general ones."

22. Quintilian, *Inst.*, 8.4.3.

23. Quintilian, *Inst.*, 8.4.1. This tripartite summary of increment is adapted from Schlueter, *Filling Up the Measure*, 83–84.

24. Quintilian, *Inst.*, 8.4.4. In this example and most others Quintilian quotes material from Cicero.

25. Quintilian, *Inst.*, 8.4.7.

2. *Comparison*—This involves exaggerating the lower stage to raise the level of the higher one. A parallel example may be employed as follows: "If my slaves feared me as all your fellow-citizens fear you, I should think I ought to leave my house."[26]

3. *Inference*—"This Amplification is made in a certain place, but has its effect in another. One thing is magnified to augment another."[27] For instance, speaking about the violence by which the wine burst out of Antony's mouth augments the other facets of the account, such as the fact that he vomited in an inappropriate place or that there was likely to be more vomiting the next day.[28]

4. *Accumulation*—In this method "the facts are raised by being piled up."[29] Often it "shows a rising pattern, when every word marks a step in an ascending series: 'There stood the doorkeeper of the prison, the praetor's executioner, the death and terror of the allies and citizens of Rome, lictor Sextius.'"[30]

As for attenuation, Quintilian's treatment is brief. He gives a single example, talking about the speech of a man named Rullus: "A few, who stood nearest to him, suspected that he meant to say something about the agrarian law."[31] Apparently the attenuation involved here is that Rullus was relatively obscure and unskilled at oration, so his speech amounted to little more than "saying something."

In his section on tropes, Quintilian discusses hyperbole in its own right:

> I have left Hyperbole, which belongs to a bolder kind of Ornament, to the last. It is an appropriate exaggeration of the truth. It has an equal value in the opposite functions of Amplification and Attenuation. There are various forms.
>
> (1) We may say more than the facts: "As he vomited, he filled his lap and the whole platform with gobbets of food," or
>
> Twin rocks that threaten skywards.
>
> (2) We may exaggerate by means of a Simile:
>
> You would think they were the Cyclades uprooted and afloat.

26. Quintilian, *Inst.*, 8.4.10.
27. Quintilian, *Inst.*, 8.4.15.
28. Quintilian, *Inst.*, 8.4.17.
29. Quintilian, *Inst.*, 8.4.26.
30. Quintilian, *Inst.*, 8.4.27.
31. Quintilian, *Inst.*, 8.4.28.

(3) Or by Comparison:

Swifter even than the lightning's wings.

(4) Or by some kind of Sign:

Over the top shoots of the untouched corn she flew and, running, never bruised the ears.

(5) Or by a Metaphor, as in "flew" in the last example....[32]
The types of Attenuation by Hyperbole are just as numerous: "they [starved sheep] scarcely stick to their bones."[33]

Quintilian's material to this point is mainly descriptive. Next, he offers some evaluative comments on hyperbole:

> I feel it distasteful to report the many faults arising from this Trope, especially as they are by no means unfamiliar or obscure. It is enough to remind the reader that Hyperbole is a liar, but does not lie to deceive. We must therefore consider all the more carefully how far it is appropriate to exaggerate a thing which is not believed. The attempt very often raises a laugh. If that is what was aimed at, it comes to be called wit; if not, folly.
>
> It is in ordinary use, too, among the uneducated and with country people, no doubt because everybody has a natural desire to exaggerate or to minimize things, and no one is satisfied with the truth. It is pardoned, however, because we do not vouch for what we say.[34]

Quintilian thus strongly cautions against the indiscriminate use of hyperbole, lest the speaker be perceived as a fool or "uneducated." But it would be incorrect to say that Quintilian frowns upon the use entirely. For one, he goes to great length to describe its forms. Also, he lists hyperbole in a later section as one of the devices used by ideal orators:

> Here is how our ideal orator will speak.... He will also pursue the other "virtues" of oratory: brevity when required, often making the facts seem to be present to our eyes, often using hyperbole, often hinting at more than he says, often employing humour, and often imitating life and nature. In all this—you see what a mass of material he has—the greatness of his eloquence should shine through.[35]

---

32. Quintilian, *Inst.*, 8.6.67–72.
33. Quintilian, *Inst.*, 8.6.73.
34. Quintilian, *Inst.*, 8.6.74–75.
35. Quintilian, *Inst.*, 9.1.45.

Longinus

There are two other Greek writings worth mentioning which comment on the subject of hyperbole. They are not exactly handbooks on rhetoric but rather treatises on literary style. One of them is Longinus's *On the Sublime*, the authorship and date (the first or third century AD has been suggested) of which is a matter of controversy. Longinus's purpose is to expound on the grand style of writing, "to identify the characteristics that mark out the emotionally intense and elevated from the merely pleasing and soothing."[36] In commenting on hyperbole, Longinus writes:

> One must know, then, where to draw the line in each case. The hyperbole is sometimes ruined by overshooting the mark. Overdo the strain and the thing sags, and often produces the opposite effect to that intended. For instance, Isocrates fell into unaccountable puerility through his ambition to amplify everything [e.g., in *Panegyric*].... For his praise of the power of words has all but issued a prefatory warning to the audience that he himself is not to be believed. Perhaps then, as we said above of figures, the best hyperbole is the one which conceals the very fact of its being a hyperbole. And this happens when it is uttered under stress of emotion to suit the circumstances of a great crisis.... As I am never tired of saying, to atone for a daring phrase the universal specific is found in actions and feelings that almost make one beside oneself. Thus, too, comic expressions, even if they result in the incredible, yet sound convincing because they are laughable:
> His field was shorter than a Spartan letter.
> Laughter indeed is an emotion based on pleasure. Hyperbole may tend to belittle as well as to magnify: the common element in both is a strain on the facts. In a sense too vilification is an amplification of the low and trivial.[37]

Like Quintilian, then, Longinus cautions against overindulging in front of an audience with regard to hyperbole. A more restrained, concealed approach is better. Otherwise, the hyperbole may end up seeming juvenile, as with Isocrates. Notable also are the mentions of hyperbole's use in humor and vilification, the latter of which I will take up later in this chapter.

---

36. Translator's introduction to Longinus, *[Subl.]*, 153.
37. Longinus, *[Subl.]*, 38.

Demetrius

The other Greek treatise is Demetrius's *On Style*. The authorship and date of this work is uncertain as well (suggestions for dating range from the second century BC to the first century AD).[38]

> The most frigid of all devices is hyperbole, which is of three kinds.[39] It is expressed either in the form of a likeness, for example "like the winds in speed"; or of superiority, for example "whiter than snow"; or of impossibility, for example "with her head she reached the sky."
>
> Admittedly every hyperbole is an impossibility. There could be nothing "whiter than snow," nothing "like the winds in speed." But this last kind is especially called impossible. And so the reason why every hyperbole seems particularly frigid is that it suggests something impossible.
>
> This is also the chief reason why the comic poets use it, since out of the impossible they create laughter, for example when someone said hyperbolically of the voracity of the Persians that "they excreted entire plains" and that "they carried oxen in their jaws."
>
> Of the same type are the expressions "balder than a cloudless sky" and "healthier than a pumpkin." Sappho's phrase, "more golden than gold" is also in form a hyperbole and impossible, but by its very impossibility it is charming, not frigid. Indeed, it is a most marvelous achievement of the divine Sappho that she handled an intrinsically risky and intractable device to create charm. This concludes my account of frigidity and hyperbole.[40]

Demetrius is highly negative toward hyperbole. It is a *frigid* (defective) style of speaking characterized by inordinate excess. Not only is it frigid, it is the *most frigid* of all devices. It is the domain of the comic poets looking for a laugh (or the exceptionally skilled Sappho).

Lausberg

Three modern day handbooks also deserve mention. I begin with Heinrich Lausberg's *Handbook of Literary Rhetoric*, which defines hyperbole as "an extreme, literally implausible onomastic surpassing of the *verbum proprium*.

38. Translator's introduction to Demetrius, *Eloc.*, 310–11.

39. Frigidity is a faulty style, "that which exceeds its appropriate form of expression" (Demetrius, *On Style*, 114).

40. Demetrius, *On Style*, 124–27.

The Rhetoric of Hyperbole

It is a metaphor with vertical gradations and so (like the horizontal metaphor) has evocoative [sic], poetical effect, which is used in rhetoric in the interests of one's party (*augere/minuere*). . ."[41] Once again, the vertical and horizontal dimensions of hyperbole are stressed. Then, in a later section, Lausberg expands on hyperbole's rhetorical effects:

> It is a means of gradual *amplificatio* and is, as a thought figure, also a heightening of *evidentia*. Its purpose and limits do not go beyond the creation of a momentary poetical *evidentia*. Credibility is relegated to the backgrond [sic] for a moment in favor of a [sic] impressive *evidentia*. It is difficult to keep to the limits.[42]

Lausberg here pictures hyperbole as a rhetorical device adding to the *evidentia* of some object. There is a momentary suspension of believability as the hyperbole produces its effect. However, in keeping with Quintilian and others, Lausberg cautions that excess is associated with this device.

Lastly, Lausberg lists the forms that hyperbole can take:

1. Gradual intensification
2. Similitude
3. Comparison
4. Sign
5. Metaphor

This list is identical to Quintilian's own (8.6.68–69).[43]

Martin

Josef Martin's *Antike Rhetorik* defines hyperbole as follows:

> Die ὑπερβολή wird von Quintilian zum *ornatus audacior* gerechnet. Das tut er einmal ihres Zieles wegen, der *delectatio* des Hörers, der von der Schönheit der Rede ergriffen und fortgerissen werden soll, was sich auch auf die Glaubwürdigkeit der Rede auswirkt. Sie ist aber auch deshalb glaubwürdig, weil sie,

---

41. Lausberg, *Handbook of Literary Rhetoric*, §579.

42. Lausberg, *Handbook of Literary Rhetoric*, §909. Evidentia is defined in §810 as "the vividly detailed depiction of a broadly conceived whole object through the enumeration of (real or invented) observable details."

43. Lausberg also cites Tryphonis, "Περὶ Τρόπων," 198, on hyperbole (Ὑπερβολή ἐστι φράσις ὑπεραίρουσα τὴν ἀλήθειαν αὐξήσεως ἢ μειώσεως χάριν) as well as an anonymous source and Cocondriou (pp. 211 and 237 in von Spengel, respectively).

was alle Rhetoren betonen, *augendi minuendique causa* sich weit über die Wahrheit erhebt. Ihre *virtus* ist eben das *augere* oder *minuere*, und sie wird dadurch wirksam, daß man entweder mehr sagt als wirklich geschehen kann, oder man hebt die Dinge durch ein Gleichnis, einen Vergleich, durch gewisse Zeicehn oder durch eine Metapher hervor. Es gilt aber, in der Verwendung der Hyperbel Maß zu halten, da sie an sich schon gegen alle Glaubwürdigkeit geht. Sie weicht von der Wahrheit ab, allerdings nicht, um zu täuschen, was ja nur zum Lächerlichen fürchen würde. Sie lebt auch in der gewöhnlichen Sprache Ungebildeter, weil die Lust zu übertreiben angeboren ist und sich niemand mit der Wahrheit zufrieden geben will. Aristoteles sagt, die Hyperbel habe eine jugendliche Art, sie deute eine Heftigkeit an, und deshalb würden Zornige am meisten in Hyperbeln reden. Attische Redner bedienten sich ihrer am meisten.[44]

In Martin's view, then, hyperbole accomplishes its goals through stimulating the *delectatio* (delight) of the hearer, who is carried away by the beauty of the speech. Martin also lists Quintilian's five forms of hyperbole. Credibility is a concern, however. Hyperbole must be measured so that it does not disaffect the listener. Martin ends his comment by reviewing Aristotle's concern that hyperbole has a youthful way to it.

Porter et al.

Our survey of the rhetorical handbooks concludes with the *Handbook of Classical Rhetoric in the Hellenistic Period 330 B.C.—A.D. 400*, published about twenty years ago and edited by Stanley Porter. The book is divided into three parts: (1) Rhetoric Defined, (2) Rhetoric in Practice, and (3) Individual Writers and the Rhetorical Tradition. In a chapter on style, Galen Rowe defines hyperbole as "a fitting exaggeration of the truth in order to make something appear greater or smaller than it is."[45] Rowe provides one example each from Cicero and Demosthenes. However, hyperbole is not treated in any depth in this volume.

---

44. Martin, *Antike Rhetorik*, 264.
45. Rowe, "Style," 128.

Conclusion

Having surveyed the rhetorical literature for viewpoints on hyperbole, a few conclusions may be rendered regarding the mechanisms and overall evaluation of the use of hyperbole in rhetoric:

1. Hyperbole works on both vertical (amplification/augmentation, diminution) and horizontal (metaphorical) dimensions to surprise and delight an audience.
2. Hyperbole can take different forms.
3. Commonly, hyperbole is regarded as humorous and can evoke laughter. If taken too far, however, the speaker will seem juvenile and foolish.
4. Hyperbole may be used effectively in speaking passionately about a topic.
5. Hyperbole may be used in invective (vilification).

HYPERBOLE AND INVECTIVE

> What need for me to publish abroad the banqueting that filled those days, your gleeful self-congratulation, and your unbridled potations with your crew of infamous associates? Who in those days ever saw you sober, or engaged in any activity befitting a free man? Who indeed ever saw you in public at all? When the house of your colleague rang with song and cymbals, and when he himself danced naked at a feast at which, when executing those whirling gyrations of his, even then he felt no fear of Fortune and her wheel. Piso meanwhile, neither so elegant nor so artistic a debauchee, lolled amid his tipsy and malodorous Greeks, while, amidst all the miseries of his country, his colleague's feast was proclaimed a sort of banquet of Lapiths and Centaurs; and in it none can say whether that wretch spent more time in drinking or in vomiting or in excreting his potations.[46]

One of the main uses for hyperbole in the Hellenistic period was in the art of praising and blaming (epideictic speech).[47] Imagine a rhetorical "game" of sorts, with mutually understood rules, between the speaker and addressees. A person's character is lauded in a manner that seems too good

---

46. Cicero, *Pis.*, 22.
47. Schlueter, *Filling Up the Measure*, 87, "Although pervasive in all oratory, exaggeration was used most in speeches of vituperation and eulogy."

to be true, whereupon the addressees know to scale down the meaning. By the same token, certain individuals are vilified in such a profoundly negative way (see quote above) that the hearers understand that they need to make a mental correction and to not take the sayings literally. All the participants laugh and enjoy the game (except perhaps the vilified individuals, but grace in receiving criticism was expected).

In this section I will focus on the second part of this game—blame, or more precisely, its tool, *invective*—in preparation for analyzing the highly contentious Letter to the Galatians in chapter 9. Before seeking to identify or characterize Paul's own invective as hyperbolic, it is important to understand what invective is and how it functioned in the world of Paul's day. I will attempt to demonstrate that Roman invective during the Hellenistic period was quite similar to that found in the NT and that it was/is universally considered to be hyperbolic.

Invective: Definition

Invective (Latin: *vituperatio*) is the public denigration of another individual with "regard to the *mores* and ethical preconceptions of a given society."[48] The goal of invective is not just to humiliate the speaker's opponent but to simultaneously build the speaker up in the eyes of the audience.[49] "Such self-commendation may be direct or, as is more often the case, implied by the unfavourable comparison made with the enemy."[50]

The Practice of Invective

Invective was practiced according to certain conventional loci, or points of comparison, the most popular being:

1. Embarrassing family origins
2. Being unworthy of one's family

---

48. Watson, "Invective," 740. I will expand on the latter half of the definition in the section on Invective and Audience.

49. Arena, "Roman Oratorical Invective," 153, "Invective had a twofold aim: labeling his opponent as deviant while simultaneously asserting his own superiority in prestige and influence. It was not enough just to parry an adversary's blows; the orator had to assert his own dominance." Tatum, "Invective Identities in *Pro Caelio*," 167, "Invective does not merely dishonor its victim and reassure its audience, it also constructs the identity of the calumniator."

50. Marshall, *Enmity in Corinth*, 52; see Marshall's discussion of σύγκρισις on pp. 53–55.

3. Physical appearance
4. Eccentricity of dress
5. Gluttony and drunkenness
6. Hypocrisy in appearing virtuous
7. Avarice
8. Taking bribes
9. Pretentiousness
10. Sexual conduct
11. Hostility to one's family
12. Cowardice in war
13. Squandering one's patrimony, or financial embarrassment in general
14. Aspiring to regnum or tyranny
15. Cruelty to citizens and allies
16. Plunder of private and public property
17. Oratorical ineptitude[51]

The rhetorical handbooks had much to say about the art of invective. Aristotle, for instance, conceived of blameworthy attributes as being the opposite of the qualities of virtue (ἀρετή).[52] Cicero, considered the master of invective, followed suit:

> Praise and censure will be derived from the topics that are employed with respect to the attributes of persons.... The virtue of the mind is that whose parts we discussed only recently. The virtues of the body are health, beauty, strength, speed. Extraneous virtues are public office, money, connexions by marriage, high birth, friends, country, power, and all other things that are understood to belong to this class. And the principle ought to apply to these which applies everywhere; the opposites of these qualities and their nature will be apparent.[53]

Ad Herennium is particularly detailed in regard to invective and demonstrates several of the above loci in its treatment:

---

51. Craig, "Audience Expectations," 190–91; cf. the similar lists in Corbeill, "Ciceronian Invective," 200–201; Süss, *Ethos*, 247–54; Nisbet, *M. Tulli Ciceronis*, 192–97.

52. Aristotle, *Rhet.*, 1.9.5; cf. 3.19.1.

53. Cicero, *Inv.*, 2.177; cf. Cicero, *De or.*, 2.43.182, 2.11.46; Cicero, *Part. or.* 82. Prime examples of Ciceronian invective are *In Vatinium*, *In Pisonem*, and *Second Philippic*.

> From the discussion of the person of our adversaries we shall secure goodwill by bringing them into hatred, unpopularity, or contempt. We shall force hatred upon them by adducing some base, high-handed, treacherous, cruel, impudent, malicious, or shameful act of theirs. We shall make our adversaries unpopular by setting forth their violent behaviour, their dominance, factiousness, wealth, lack of self-restraint, high birth, clients, hospitality, club allegiance, or marriage alliances, and by making clear that they rely more upon these supports than upon the truth. We shall bring our adversaries into contempt by presenting their idleness, cowardice, sloth, and luxurious habits.[54]

Invective and the Audience

Invective plays upon the emotions of the audience (pathos).[55] As Cicero writes:

> Now nothing in oratory, Catulus, is more important than to win for the orator the favour of his hearer, and to have the latter so affected as to be swayed by something resembling a mental impulse or emotion, rather than by judgement or deliberation. For men decide far more problems by hate, or love, or lust, or rage, or sorrow, or joy, or hope, or fear, or illusion, or some other inward emotion, than by reality, or authority, or any legal standard, or judicial precedent, or statute.[56]

In stirring audience emotions, orators were bound only by the limits of their imagination. Cicero, for instance, brands Antony as an arch-pirate, an assassin, a savage beast, a brigand, a drunkard and glutton, an embezzler and forger, a gladiator, Hannibal, a monster, and Spartacus.[57] His opponent Piso suffered much the same treatment, being portrayed as a monster, funeral pyre of the commonwealth, butcher, scoundrel, gelded pig, and a most foul

---

54. *Rhet. Her.* 1.5.8; cf. 3.10.

55. Arena, "Roman Oratorical Invective," 150, "The highlighting of an individual's faults in an abusive or humorous manner provided a powerful means of manipulating the audience's emotions. Rather than supplying logical proofs, invective adds *pathos* to *logos* and turns the audience against the orator's opponent and toward his own cause." Also see Corbeill, "Ciceronian Invective," 200, "The narration of faults . . . aims at influencing an audience's emotions rather than at providing logical proof."

56. Cicero, *De or.*, 2.178.

57. Stevenson, "Tyrants, Kings and Fathers," 98n13.

and inhuman monster.[58] In addition, "Cicero mocks Piso's distinctive forehead and eyebrows ... and makes disparaging comments about his complexion, hairy cheeks, and discolored teeth."[59] Often such abuses provoked laughter. In fact, Cicero prided himself on his ability to amuse his audience: "Persuasion of the onlookers in his favour he saw as the true end of wit rather than the pain inflicted on an opponent or the cleverness per se."[60]

Of course, invective aimed at a deeper and more protracted endgame than just momentary laughter or disgust. Indeed, there were powerful group dynamics at play. Recall that our working definition of invective is the "public denigration of another individual with regard to the *mores* and ethical preconceptions of a given society." The speaker's goal, then, was to have the audience come to view the opponent with such moral and ethical disfavor that they would be willing to cast the opponent out of the community; at the same time the speaker reinforces, or even enhances, his own social status.[61] This could be accomplished if three conditions were satisfied:

1. The designated victim has to be an established part of the community, so as to be exposed to its assault and marginalized.
2. The orator must possess the skill to manipulate the audience's emotions.
3. The audience must be won over to his side and conspire with him against the victim. In order to achieve this, the orator has to be able to exploit biases already present in his audience.[62]

Invective and Truth

While it would be too strong to say that speakers did not care about facts, communicating objective truth was not the primary purpose of invective.

---

58. Arena, "Roman Oratorical Invective," 152 lists these qualities from the first third of Cicero's *In Pisonem* while noting, "The rules of engagement also permitted a degree of direct abuse that we would not countenance today."

59. Arena, "Roman Oratorical Invective," 152.

60. Marshall, *Enmity in Corinth*, 56.

61. Arena, "Roman Oratorical Invective," 153, "The speaker's aim in this contest of words was to cast out his target from the community, or at least brand him as deviant." Cf. Corbeill, "Ciceronian Invective," 198, "It is notable that [Cicero] employs his most angry invective at those key points in his career at which he needs to shape new aspects of his public identity: as a righteous young prosecutor (*Against Verres*), as an elected head of state (*Against Catiline*; *On the Agrarian Law*), as a former exile reestablishing authority (*Against Vatinius*; *Against Piso*), and as an elder statesman exercising that authority for the last time (*Philippics*)."

62. Arena, "Roman Oratorical Invective," 155.

Returning to our game analogy, honesty was not even listed in the rulebook: "Aristotle, and those who followed him, considered that the establishing of facts, either by witnesses or documented evidence, did not belong to the art of rhetoric."[63] The secondary literature is also replete with comments on the hyperbolic nature of Roman invective.[64] In the language of pragmatics (see my chapter 4), Javier Uría writes:

> What is the point of using this exaggeration? The traditional answer to this question is: hyperbole is a means of creating *páthos*. I think we can be more accurate. In certain genres, as in certain social contexts, expectations arise of either attenuation or exaggeration: panegyrics, love-letters, thanksgiving speeches, letters of introduction raise an expectation of exaggeration, while in self-presentations modesty and attenuation are expected. Accordingly listeners know when they must diminish and when they must magnify. The skilful orator, in turn, is aware of his listeners' expectations, and, knowing that they will certainly diminish what he says, has recourse to hyperbole. By means of hyperbole Cicero not only forestalls an eventual diminishing of his attacks, but also (and mainly) gets his audience actively involved in the evaluation of Cloelius and, secondarily, of Clodius himself. By exploiting the maxim of quality, the orator calls

---

63. Marshall, *Enmity in Corinth*, 56.

64. Watson, "Invective," 740, "The primary object of invective is to persuade the audience that one's accusations were true. Plausibility was thus more important than veracity"; Syme, *Roman Revolution*, 149, "Crime, vice and corruption in the last age of the republic are embodied in types as perfect of their kind as are the civic and moral paragons of early days; which is fitting, for the evil and the good are both the fabrication of skilled literary artists"; Arena, "Roman Oratorical Invective," 157, "Our extant examples of Roman invective show that the same individual could be attacked in very different and sometimes contradictory ways.... This fact ... has led many scholars to question the veracity of such accusations"; Nisbet, *M. Tulli Ciceronis*, 193, invective "often shows more regard for literary convention than for historical truth"; Craig, "Audience Expectations," 194, the speaker and audience outside the courts were "not concerned with the plausibility, much less the actual validity, of specific assertions"; Stevenson, "Tyrants, Kings and Fathers," 98, regarding invective in the *Philippics*, "Certainly, a huge amount seems unreliable to the modern historian, and a huge amount seems conventional rhetorical exaggeration or simply ridiculous.... [T]he basis is ideological rather than factual. In other words, the resonance is in the moral power of the ideas and values to which the orator appeals, not their basis in fact"; Manuwald, "Function of Praise and Blame," 199, "[P]raise and blame in the *Philippics* fulfil a tactical function in political deliberative speeches and are not ... true reflections of the orator's beliefs"; on Roman invective, Marshall, *Enmity in Corinth*, 57–58, "While invective might contain elements of truth, much of it was exaggerated or invented. It was not necessary for it to be truthful at all.... The use of generalizations or defamatory conjecture was as good as historical fact if it would sharpen the point of invective."

once more for the listeners' complicity. Putting it baldly, Cicero's thinking in using the hyperbole would be: "if I say he is the filthiest of four-legged animals, they will be inclined to believe at least that he is the filthiest of two-legged animals."[65]

That is not to say that hearers did not care about the truth. Indeed, "an appearance of artificiality had to be avoided" in the manner of the speaker, "as did an appearance of excessive frivolity or cruelty."[66] But the truth was secondary. What mattered most was persuasion. The goal was to "shape community morality":

> Invective would have been effective only when the audience (whether senate, popular assembly or judicial court) embraced the picture as described for it by the speaker. The moral description of specific acts constituted an essential element in winning the audience's approval. . . If the speaker succeeds in convincing his audience of this new moral description, he has to some extent also succeeded in modifying the social perceptions of that behavior.[67]

Invective and the New Testament

Is there a connection between Roman invective and the NT? Andrie du Toit argues in the affirmative, suggesting that invective in the NT "should be understood against the background of the widespread convention of vilifying opponents which obtained throughout the Mediterranean world."[68] He has identified several loci around which NT invective clusters:

1. Hypocrisy and falseness
2. Obscure, shadowy characters
3. Sorcery
4. Inflated self-esteem
5. Moral depravity
6. A perversive influence
7. Associated with dubious historical characters

---

65. Uría, "Semantics and Pragmatics," 59.
66. Tatum, "Invective Identities in *Pro Caelio*," 168.
67. Arena, "Roman Oratorical Invective," 158–59.
68. Du Toit, "Vilification," 404.

8. Prone to judgment
9. Ludicrous characters[69]

Du Toit's examples will be taken up in chapter 8. For now I wish to simply explore some points of connection between the literature on Roman invective and that of the NT. For instance, like classical scholars, du Toit represents the primary aim of invective as being community building: "The perlocutionary aim of the relevant early Christian passages was intended primarily not to characterize the adversaries, but to put pressure on the readers/audience to dissociate themselves from them and reaffirm their allegiance to the author's position."[70] Also, du Toit recognizes the hyperbolic quality of NT invective:

> The hyperbolical and often stereotyped character of vilificatory utterances belonged to the rules of the polemical 'game' in general, and was accepted and understood as such by both speaker and audience. Everyone knew that these utterances were basically intended to convey the thrust of the author's negative feeling and convictions regarding his adversaries, and to induce his addressees to share them; in short, he wanted, by means of the vilificatory process, primarily to influence.[71]

Luke Timothy Johnson also establishes a connection between NT invective and the larger culture. In a 1989 essay he writes, "I suggest that the slander of the NT is typical of that found among rival claimants to a philosophical tradition. . . . I further suggest that the way the NT talks about Jews is just about the way all opponents talked about each other back then." Johnson identifies four loci for NT invective:

1. Their teaching was self-contradictory, trivial, led to bad morals
2. They were hypocrites (preached but did not practice)
3. They lived corrupted lives
4. They were lovers of pleasure, money, glory

As with du Toit, Johnson sees a sociological purpose to NT invective. Messianists were in a struggle for survival and for maintaining the identity of their group. Invective was used to solidify group cohesion by marginalizing

---

69. Du Toit, "Vilification," 406–10.
70. Du Toit, "Vilification," 412.
71. Du Toit, "Vilification," 411.

The Rhetoric of Hyperbole

threats to the messianic movement: "Because of these pressures, NT polemic is mostly turned inward against fellow members of the movement."[72]

Paul's use of invective has roots in the larger culture as well:

> By using invectives, Paul employed a typical polemical tool of his time. In his letters, particularly in 2 Corinthians 10–13 and Galatians, he participated in a general culture of quarreling and disputing. This polemical culture culminated in invectives, as exemplified in Cicero's speeches against Catilina, in Sallust's writings against Cicero, in some poems by Archilochos and Catullus, in Ovid's *Ibis* and in many other documents.[73]

Five features from Roman invective can also be found in Pauline writings:[74]

- The adversaries often do not attempt sensitively to explore the motivations and reasons of their opponents. They frequently quote the enemies' views in biased, emotional and—even more important—highly selective ways, so that it is difficult for historians to reconstruct the positions of the opponents.

- Often no differentiation between persons and views is made. Therefore, the polemics can be personally insulting and hurtful.

- Adversaries, especially in court, often do not look for balanced compromises. Frequently, there is only winning or losing; the polemic aims at running the opponents into the ground.

- The corresponding debating pattern, therefore, often is based on binary logic, on exclusive either-ors, on black and white, on axes of evil and sons of light, on a Satan-Christ opposition.[75]

---

72. Johnson, "New Testament's Anti-Jewish Slander," 426; also see Freyne, "Vilifying the Other," 132, who focuses on invective in Matthew and John: "Two complementary motifs occur which are simply the reverse sides of the same concern, namely, that of community building. These are as follows: 1) discrediting the opponents at the points where particular and exclusive claims for one's own community need to be established, and 2) using the opponents' failures and inadequacies as a means of warning one's own community."

73. Lampe, "Can Words Be Violent," 225.

74. This list is quoted from Lampe, "Can Words Be Violent," 226–27.

75. According to Schlueter, *Filling Up the Measure*, 164–85, those who employ invective often use language to draw boundaries between themselves and their opponents, creating an us versus them mentality, heightened by the deployment of bipolar categories which eliminate a middle ground.

- The rhetorical means include *suggestive questions* and direct and indirect *accusations*. Other instruments are *irony . . . parody* (e.g., ψευδαπόστολος, ψευδάδελφος, and εὐαγγέλιον ἕτερον) . . . *sarcasms*.

CONCLUSION

In this chapter I have attempted to show that hyperbole as a known rhetorical device has a long history in the ancient handbooks. Hyperbole was used in the business of persuasion—joking to evoke a laugh, adding pathos to an argument, or vilifying an opponent to marginalize that person in the eyes of those in the community. The truth was not as important as was the force of the hyperbole, which should be carefully calibrated as to not seem puerile.

Invective as a common application of hyperbole was also explored in this chapter. In the hands of one skilled in rhetoric, it could be devastating to an opponent. Winning and losing was everything. When we enter the world of the NT writers and their community, the ἐκκλησία of God they attempted to shape and manage, we find that they were neither unique nor innovative in their use of invective; rather, they shared loci and objectives (community building) with other writers of the Greco-Roman world.

Excursus: Was Paul a Rhetorician?

An important and oft-debated question is whether Paul was consciously aware of the Greco-Roman rhetorical standards when he wrote his epistles. This question is germane to the present discussion, as I have worked to elucidate Greco-Roman thinking on hyperbole as portrayed in the ancient handbooks. If Paul had little or no exposure to the handbooks—if his style of writing, in other words, originates solely from Jewish influences—then the handbooks are of no value to us in investigating hyperbole in Galatians. In this section I will argue that Paul did, in fact, have at least a rudimentary knowledge of the handbooks, gained through his early schooling as a young man and his wider exposure to the Hellenistic culture as a tradesman and missionary. I offer three benchmarks on which to base my conclusions. The first concerns Paul's letters and what features of rhetoric they manifest.[76] The

---

76. Paul's speeches in Acts could be put forward as evidence for rhetorical training as well. Porter, "Paul as Epistolographer *and* Rhetorician?," 248, however, cautions against this: "It is highly debatable whether we have direct access to the historical Paul as speechmaker, and this for two reasons. The first is that there is a highly debatable relationship in ancient historiography between the delivery of speeches and their record in later literary works. The second is that what is found in Acts is for various reasons not

second concerns Paul's life and what education and cultural exposure could be expected of a person of his origin and upbringing. The third concerns Paul's mission, most notably the rhetorical exigencies he had to confront and the means (written letters) with which it was necessary to address them.

Benchmark 1: Paul's Letters

Though Hans Dieter Betz was not the first to subject Paul's letters to rhetorical analysis (he was preceded by, among others, Chrysostom, Augustine, and Philip Melanchthon), he certainly stimulated modern interest in the rhetorical analysis with the publication of his *Commentary on Galatians*.[77] Betz argued that Galatians is an apologetic letter in the judicial (forensic) genre and in keeping with the structure prescribed by the ancient handbooks. He outlined the letter as follows:

- 1:1–5   Epistolary prescript
- 1:6–11   Exordium
- 1:12–2:14   Narratio
- 2:15–21   Propositio
- 3:1–4:31   Probatio
- 5:1–6:10   Exhortatio
- 6:11–18   Epistolary postscript[78]

Betz's conclusions have been subject to much scrutiny.[79] Scholars have debated whether Galatians might better be classified as deliberative or epideictic (or a mixture of genres). Another contentious issue has been whether Betz's rhetorical outline is a valid description of the structure and flow of Galatians.[80] Of course, the sheer number of competing outlines that have

---

complete Pauline speeches but at best later summaries or even prematurely curtailed speeches possibly designed to give the gist of the original speech. These cannot provide an adequate basis for rhetorical analysis of the speeches of the historical Paul."

77. Betz, *Galatians*.

78. Betz, *Galatians*, 16–23.

79. For instance, Porter, "Paul of Tarsus," 542, lists several faults: (1) the handbooks have no place for probatio (chapters 3–4) in a judicial speech; (2) the exhortations of chapters 5–6 are also out of place in a judicial speech; (3) a rhetorical structure is overlaid onto an epistolary form; (4) the Galatian situation was not a judicial proceeding; and (5) Roman rhetorical theory is favored over Greek theory.

80. The issues are numerous and cannot be detailed here. I refer the reader to Kern, *Rhetoric and Galatians*, 90–119, for a discussion of the difficulties.

been offered since Betz's commentary speaks to the highly subjective nature of the enterprise.

Then there is the larger debate of whether the rhetorical handbooks should be applied at all to Paul's letters, as George Kennedy did in his 1984 book, *New Testament Interpretation through Rhetorical Criticism*, in which he attempted to classify the NT writings according to rhetorical genre.[81] After all, the rhetorical handbooks were written for speechmaking.[82] Would not the epistolary handbooks be a more suitable place from which to launch an analysis?[83] The flip side of the argument is that Paul's letters were written to be read aloud as speeches.

> No documents in antiquity were intended for "silent" reading, and only a few were intended for private individuals to read. They were always meant to be read out loud and usually read out loud to a group of people. For the most part they were simply necessary surrogates for oral communication. This was particularly true of ancient letters.[84]

As for the appropriateness of using the epistolary handbooks to analyze NT documents:

> Analyzing the majority of the NT on the basis of epistolary conventions—many of which did not become *de rigeur* nor put into a handbook until *after* NT times—while a helpful exercise to some degree, has no business being the dominant literary paradigm by which we examine the Pauline, Petrine, Johannine, and other discourses in the NT. The dominant paradigm when it came to words and the conveying of ideas, meaning, and persuasion in the NT era was rhetoric, not epistolary conventions.[85]

81. See also the more recent attempt by Watson, "Three Species of Rhetoric," 28–39.

82. See Porter, "Theoretical Justification," 100–122; Porter, "Hellenistic Oratory and Paul of Tarsus," 319–60; cf. Lampe, "Rhetorical Analysis," 13–17, who recommends building an integrative bridge between the two approaches of epistolography and rhetorical analysis.

83. Thurén, "Epistolography and Rhetoric," 141–59, is pessimistic about using epistolography to study Paul's letters. "The resemblances with real ancient letters remain indistinct and sporadic. . . . Compared to ancient private letters, Paul's letters are excessively long and theoretical; compared to official ones they are too personal."

84. Witherington, *New Testament Rhetoric*, 1. Also see Forbes, "Ancient Rhetoric and Ancient Letters," 159, "Paul's letters were not written to be read, but to be *performed*. As such they function as speeches, as rhetoric, every bit as much as they function as conventional letters. They are thoroughly atypical letters, in size, in content, and in style, precisely because they are letters designed to be delivered orally to (thoroughly atypical) groups"; Botha, "Verbal Art of the Pauline Letters," 409–28.

85. Witherington, *New Testament Rhetoric*, 5. Witherington calls Galatians "pure

The Rhetoric of Hyperbole

Paul's letters evidence certain technical terms that suggest that he at least indirectly knew the handbooks. For instance: ἀνακεφαλαιοῦσθαι (Rom 13:9) is a rare word "used almost exclusively in works of rhetoric. Both verb and noun always refer to the recapitulation of the most essential elements of a speech."[86] Likewise suggestive is Paul's use of ἀλληγορεῖν (Gal 4:24), βεβαίωσις (Phil 1:7), ἐν πειθοῖ ... ἐν ἀποδείξει (1 Cor 2:4), μετασχηματίζειν (1 Cor 4:6), the juxtaposition of παράκλησις and παραμυθία (and their respective verbs; see 1 Cor 14:3; Phil 2:1; 1 Thess 2:12), μακαρισμός (Rom 4:6, 9; Gal 4:15), the combination of δυσφημία and εὐφεμία (2 Cor 6:8), and συντέμνειν (Rom 9:28).[87] These findings lead Classen to admit,

> Paul was familiar with a number of technical terms of Greek rhetoric. Where he knew them from I do not venture to decide; their use, however, together with that of technical terms of philosophy signify a standard of education which warrants the assumption that Paul was familiar through theory (handbooks) or practice (actual application) with the rules and precepts of ancient rhetoric (and epistolography).[88]

In addition to technical terms, Paul's letters evidence a variety of "forms of argumentation and many stylistic devices that are recommended in rhetorical theory ... [and] that are very common in the practice of classical orators."[89] These may be called *microrhetoric*, as opposed to *macrorhetoric*, which encompasses structure and arrangement.[90] Under the category of microrhetoric would fall "rhetorical questions, dramatic hyperbole, personification, amplification, irony, enthymemes (i.e., incomplete syllogisms), and the like."[91]

Conclusion: the matter of whether Paul based the arrangement of his letters (macrorhetoric) on the ancient rhetorical handbooks is still up for debate. However, Paul seems to exhibit knowledge of the technical

---

speech material" (124). Watson, "Influence of George Kennedy," 50–52, takes a moderate stance on the issue.

86. Classen, *Rhetorical Criticism*, 30–31.

87. Classen, *Rhetorical Criticism*, 30–39.

88. Classen, *Rhetorical Criticism*, 44.

89. Classen, "Can the Theory of Rhetoric," 23; Porter and Dyer, "Paul and Ancient Rhetoric," 4: "That Paul made use of rhetorical techniques—even some of those techniques or categories, especially of style, described in the ancient handbooks and *progymnasmata*—is not in serious doubt." Kremmydas, "Hellenistic Rhetorical Education," 82: "Echoes of such preliminary rhetorical exercises can be found in his epistles."

90. Witherington, *New Testament Rhetoric*, 7.

91. Witherington, *New Testament Rhetoric*, 7.

terminology and proficiency with the rhetorical devices (microrhetoric) described in the handbooks.[92]

Benchmark 2: Paul's Life

According to Acts 22:3 Paul was born in Tarsus of Cilicia and at some point moved to Jerusalem to receive a traditional Jewish education from Gamaliel. At issue is how much time he spent in Tarsus before moving to Jerusalem. Keener, based on the work of Van Unnik, argues for an early departure: "Luke's text offers no indication of a youth in Tarsus."[93]

Other scholars, however, argue that Paul obtained at least a primary education in Tarsus. Andrew Pitts, citing Strabo's *Geographica*, notes that it was customary for natives of Tarsus, a center for Greco-Roman education, to complete the first phase of their education in their homeland and then to study abroad for advanced education.[94] Such education would take place under a *grammaticus* who would teach a student Greek literacy skills, the poets, and the *progymnasmata* (preliminary exercises, which included basic rhetorical concepts).[95] Pitts believes that Paul spent his early school years in Tarsus before moving to Jerusalem to study with Gamaliel, considering (a) Paul's fluency in Greek literary forms and literature, (b) his preference for the LXX, and (c) Gamaliel's descent from the diaspora rabbi Hillel, who displayed a fondness for the Greek *paideia* and hellenistic rhetoric.[96] Pitts also proposes that Paul's parents, as likely members of the artisan class, would have had sufficient resources to fund a Greek education for their son in Tarsus. Such an education "would have been an important asset to Paul's trade as he sought to establish business relationships and travel for business purposes."[97] However, Pitts does not think that Paul obtained a formal rhetorical education in Tarsus, as such education was typically vocational (i.e., only for those wishing to pursue a career in politics or law) and would have

---

92. Cf. Classen, "St. Paul's Epistles," 269, "Anyone who could write Greek as effectively as St. Paul did, must have read a good deal of works written in Greek and thus imbibed applied rhetoric from others, even if he never heard of any rules of rhetorical theory; thus, even if one could prove that St. Paul was not familiar with the rhetorical theory of the Greeks, it can hardly be denied that he knew it in its applied form."

93. Keener, *Acts*, 3:3207–08; Van Unnik, *Tarsus or Jerusalem*, 52, "The use of the word ἀνατεθραμμένος necessitates the supposition that this removal [to Jerusalem] took place quite early in Paul's life."

94. Strabo, *Geogr.* 14.5.13, cited in Pitts, "Paul in Tarsus," 44.

95. On the *progymnasmata* see Kennedy, *Progymnasmata*.

96. Pitts, "Paul in Tarsus," 46.

97. Pitts, "Paul in Tarsus," 55.

had to have taken place during the same years (twelve to fifteen) Paul was said to have been studying Torah under Gamaliel.[98]

Conclusion: if Paul was raised in Tarsus, then he received the first phase of Greco-Roman education there. This education, paid for by his artisan class family, would have equipped him with the literacy skills (including elementary rhetorical concepts) to prosper in business in the wider region. He likely did not, however, receive formal rhetorical training as an adolescent.

Benchmark 3: Paul's Mission

By all accounts—including his epistles and his recorded speeches in Acts—Paul was an intelligent, skilled communicator capable of crafting complex arguments and taking full advantage of logos, pathos, and ethos. As a world traveler, missionary to the Gentile world, he was in the business of persuading people to change their minds and behavior. It would have been in his interest to have and to exercise a level of rhetorical competence that was expected in the culture of that day.[99] As Watson writes:

> If Paul's epistles were to be read in the churches, a logical assumption is that they were fashioned in a way closely akin to a speech. Since the body of the ancient letter was dictated by the needs of the author, we should expect his use of rhetorical theory in his letters. Needing to communicate over vast distances, Paul has a rhetorical need to be persuasive and would be expected to have used rhetorical theory.[100]

Although Paul seems at times to disclaim rhetorical eloquence (1 Cor 1:17; 2:1–5; cf. 2 Cor 10:10; 11:17; see esp. 11:6 where he admits that he is ἰδιώτης τῷ λόγῳ), it is likely that he was actually *using* rhetoric in these cases, projecting ethos as a way of differentiating himself from professional rhetoricians who sometimes had a reputation for lacking a foundation of truth behind their rhetoric.[101] And, while 2 Cor 11:6 seems to slight Paul's speaking abilities in comparison to others at Corinth, it could also be taken as "evidence for the comparative forcefulness of his letters."[102]

98. Pitts, "Paul in Tarsus," 66.
99. Forbes, "Ancient Rhetoric," 148, "[Paul] may or may not have had formal rhetorical training, but he certainly knew from observation and experience which styles of argument would, and would not, hold the attention of his 'target audience.'"
100. Watson, "Influence of George Kennedy," 53.
101. Kremmydas, "Hellenistic Rhetorical Education," 69.
102. Porter, "Paul of Tarsus," 537.

For an intelligent and culturally savvy person like Paul, it would have been harder to *avoid* rhetorical theory than to have imbibed it. As Longenecker states, "the forms of classical rhetoric were 'in the air,' and Paul seems to have used them almost unconsciously for his own purposes."[103] As Kennedy states:

> Paul . . . would, indeed, have been hard put to escape an awareness of rhetoric as practiced in the culture around [him], for the rhetorical theory of the schools found its immediate application in almost every form of oral and written communication: in official documents and public letters, in private correspondence, in the lawcourts and assemblies, in speeches at festivals and commemorations, and in literary composition in both prose and verse.[104]

Conclusion: Paul knew the rhetorical handbooks, if only informally through his exposure to the wider region and culture. His intelligence and concern for the church would have motivated him to have and to exercise a level of rhetorical competence appropriate to his task. In short, "Paul was a man of his times . . . he knew what would and would not work with the audiences he addressed in the Greco-Roman world."[105]

---

103. Longenecker, *Galatians*, cxiii.

104. Kennedy, *New Testament Interpretation*, 10. See also Hughes, "Paul and Traditions," 95, "I believe that Paul consciously used various elements of rhetoric that he likely picked up from the wider cultures of cities, if not from actual instruction in rhetoric, in order to do the persuasion he believed he needed to do, using the difficult mode of doing persuasion by letter."

105. Witherington, *New Testament Rhetoric*, 153.

PART III

Biblical Hyperbole

6

A Method for Detecting Biblical Hyperbole

In this chapter...

Question(s) to be answered:
- How do we decide whether a biblical passage is hyperbolic?

Trajectory:
- Chapters 7–8 survey the Old and New Testaments for hyperbole and apply the methodology constructed in this chapter to a few sample passages

BEFORE LAUNCHING INTO AN analysis of Galatians (chapters 9–11), it is necessary to first examine our decision-making apparatus: On what basis shall it be decided that a statement is hyperbolic? I desire to cast a net that is neither too wide nor too narrow. Some sort of methodology, therefore, is needed. Otherwise, the process could devolve into something subjective and highly disputable.

We have the benefit of the previous chapters' worth of information. Those chapters have illuminated what hyperbole is from the standpoint of modern linguistic (chapter 4) and classical rhetorical theory (chapter 5).

What constitutes a hyperbole, then? In Figure 6.1 below, I have consolidated the decision making process developed over the past couple of chapters into a checklist. This "scorecard" will be used in chapters 9–11 in adjudicating hyperbole in Galatians (and on a trial basis in the next two chapters). It is based on three types of aspects—logical, literary, and rhetorical—and includes a summary "grade" of A–D. In this chapter I will detail each element of the scorecard and why it was chosen.

Hyperbole Scorecard

Logical aspects
- ☐ Flouting of the quality maxim
- ☐ Comparisons (A=B, A<>B, A is like B)

Literary aspects
- ☐ Universal language (ECFs), intensifiers, or generalizations
- ☐ Extreme or extravagant language
- ☐ Figurative language
- ☐ Economy of expression
- ☐ Amplification or attenuation

Rhetorical aspects
- ☐ Rhetorical situation
- ☐ Pathos
- ☐ Shock
- ☐ Invective

Likelihood
A: high
B: moderate
C: somewhat
D: none

Figure 6.1. Scorecard for Grading Instances of Suspected Hyperbole.

LOGICAL ASPECTS

Logical aspects of hyperbole include (a) flouting of the quality maxim and (b) comparisons. These aspects represent logical operations rather than purely literary or rhetorical aspects of the text.

Flouting of the Quality Maxim

Hyperbole is an exaggeration of the truth. In Gricean terms (see chapter 4), the speaker *flouts the quality* (truthfulness) *maxim*. That is not to say that an intentional deception is occurring, however. Rather, there will typically be signals for hyperbole present in the communication, which is why we talk about flouting rather than violating the quality maxim.

Stein's criteria (see chapter 4) will be helpful in this regard. We can tell that a speaker is not telling the truth if *the statement is literally impossible* (Stein's criterion 1). A camel passing through the eye of a needle, for instance, is plainly hyperbolic. Also, if *the statement conflicts with the actions or teachings of the speaker elsewhere* (criteria 2 and 3), hyperbole may be indicated. Hating one's parents to become a disciple of Jesus, then, is likely hyperbolic because it conflicts with Jesus's other commands regarding love and honoring one's parents. Furthermore, if *the statement conflicts with other teachings of the Old or New Testament* (criteria 4 and 5), we may have reason to interpret it hyperbolically.[1] For instance, Jesus's prohibition against judging (Matt 7:1) may be deemed to be overly general when put up against Paul's judging in 1 Cor 5:3 and his rebuke of the church for not judging in a particular instance in 1 Cor 6:1–6. And finally, if *the statement has not been literally fulfilled* (criterion 7) then it may be hyperbolic (see, for instance, the prophecy of no stone being left upon another regarding the temple destruction in Matt 24:2).

Stein's criteria only get us so far, however. They presume the judgments of a modern reader who has the benefit of a completed canon. But as I have argued before (in chapters 4 and 5), hyperbole does not intend to deceive. A flout of the quality maxim, then, must be understood as such by the original audience. How shall we determine whether Paul's Galatian readers understood his language in terms of quality flouts when they did not have the benefit of Romans or Acts at the time they received the letter? What can we presume that they already knew about Paul and his attitude toward the law? First, it is a reasonable assumption that Paul's Torah-observant behavior was relatively consistent (chapter 3 clarifies that Paul did not accommodate his Torah keeping based on which group he found himself among, a common misunderstanding of 1 Cor 9:19–23). The Galatians would have known Paul to be an observant Jew, valuing circumcision (for Jewish Christians) and keeping the feasts. Second, we may also assume that Paul's genuine attitude toward the Torah was at least occasionally present in his teaching of the Galatians. In his cooler moments, a less angry Paul no doubt taught that the principles by which the Christian life is to be lived descend from the Torah itself. We have Gal 5:14, and possibly 6:2, as prime examples of such teaching.[2] Moreover, the fact that Paul uses the OT so much in his theological argumentation likely indicates that he had bathed the Galatians in the Scriptures as neophytes to the Christian community, so they had a baseline from which to judge his later, more provocative comments.

1. This project assumes, not that the scriptural canon must be internally consistent, but that inconsistency in the canon simply *makes it more likely that a rhetorical device such as hyperbole is being used.* That is not to say, though, that any and all apparent contradictions will be labeled as hyperbolic. There will be other criteria imposed besides flouting of the quality maxim.

2. Jipp, *Christ Is King*, 62, "The similarities between Gal. 5:14 and 6:2 are readily discernible and establish that the referent of τὸν νόμον τοῦ Χριστοῦ cannot entirely exclude the Torah, even if Christ reconfigures Torah and the love-commandment through his cruciform death."

Comparisons

Many biblical hyperboles involve comparisons (unlike flouting of the quality maxim, however, this is not a *necessary* component of hyperbole). Comparisons can take the form of a simile, *A is like B*, or a metaphor, *A is B*. Or, as is common in the OT, *A is stronger/faster/higher than B*, which I have designated as A<>B, that is, any comparison where A is less than or greater than B.

It is important to distinguish metaphorical hyperbole from plain metaphor. The difference is simply put: non-hyperbolic metaphors do not flout the quality maxim. So, for instance, "The Lord is my shepherd" (Ps 23:1) is an A=B metaphor in the plain (truthful) sense. It does not flout the quality maxim, but rather compares God to a shepherd and, by implication, the writer to a sheep. God's shepherding qualities include his guidance and protection. However, "Saul and Jonathan . . . were swifter than eagles; they were stronger than lions" (2 Sam 1:23) is a metaphorical hyperbole of the A>B variety. The statement strains believability in its literal sense.

LITERARY ASPECTS

Literary aspects are those which are embedded in the words and phraseology. They include universal language or generalizations, extreme or extravagant language, figurative language, economy of expression, and amplification or attenuation. These aspects are not necessary for a judgment of hyperbole to be made, but they collectively increase the likelihood that a statement is hyperbolic.

Universal Language, Intensifiers, and Generalizations

One sign of hyperbole is the use of universal language (all, every, none, always, never, etc.).[3] Universal language hyperbole is also called extreme case formulation (ECF; see chapter 4). Because it utilizes certain keywords, universal language is easy to recognize.

Intensifiers are words like *absolutely, really, incredible, brilliant, massive, literally, endless, nearly,* or *totally* that serve to intensify the strength of an utterance and often accompany hyperbole. See chapter 4 for more details.

Generalizations are also a common aspect of hyperbole. Generalizations may also use universal language, but they are typically worded in the

---

3. Stein has universal language as his tenth criterion.

form of a maxim or proverbial saying that requires qualification to be understood properly. For example, Paul's statement that "all things work together for good . . ." (Rom 8:28) uses universal language but is also a generalization in that it can easily be taken too far by itself, without requisite qualification. Jesus's admonition to "Give to the one who begs from you" (Matt 5:42) likewise requires a limitation to be inferred in order to be properly understood (although it does not use universal language).

Extreme or Extravagant Language

Jesus's remedy for some types of sin is to gouge out one's eye or cut off one's hand. Obviously Jesus is flouting the quality maxim, but there is also an extreme quality to the words and the images they convey. Amputation and eye gouging are drastic and exceedingly painful measures. Thus, the hyperbole is signaled by both the flouting of the quality maxim and the extreme language.

Hyperbole is also signaled by extravagant language, as when Paul slips into a sublime or poetic way of speaking. First Corinthians 13:1–3 comes to mind, as does 1 Cor 4:8–13, because of their unique wording and style.

Figurative Language

Several forms of figurative language are found in the Bible, including metaphor (see above under the heading Comparisons), idioms, metonymy, and irony, among others. Figurative language can be extreme, so there is some overlap between these two aspects. For instance, when Jesus says to eat his flesh and to drink his blood, the language is both figurative and extreme. Non-extreme figurative language is, of course, more common. Figurative language sets the stage for hyperbole and makes its occurrence more likely (cf. Stein's criterion 9: *The statement uses a literary form prone to exaggeration*). Take, for instance, Paul's comment, "So I was rescued from the lion's mouth" (2 Tim 4:17). The use of a lion to metaphorically represent the threat of death signals the likelihood that Paul is speaking hyperbolically.[4]

---

4. Towner, *Letters to Timothy and Titus*, 644, points out that Paul may be echoing LXX Ps 21:22, which itself is poetic language.

Economy of Expression

Hyperbole allows for much to be said in a few words. Consider, for instance, "Blessed are you who are poor, for yours is the kingdom of God" (Luke 6:20). This is, on the one hand, a generalization; certainly the true Israel is not defined strictly along socioeconomic lines. But it is also a figure evidencing economy of expression. The word "poor" (πτωχοί) is a powerful one-word designation for those who have been oppressed by the rich of this world and yet have maintained their humility and trust in God. In its unexpanded form, however, "poor" represents a hyperbole.

Amplification or Attenuation

"Amplification is fundamental to the art of persuasion, and hyperbole is the servant of amplification."[5] Amplification and attenuation designate the enhancement or diminution, respectively, of the force of words. Below is a summary of the ways in which amplification takes place. See chapter 5 for more details.

1. Increment
    a. Choosing a stronger word
    b. Building words upon words
    c. Reiterating that which cannot be surpassed
2. Comparison
3. Inference
4. Accumulation

RHETORICAL ASPECTS

Rhetorical aspects include the rhetorical situation, pathos, shock, and invective. As with literary aspects, these are not necessary for hyperbole to occur, but they do increase the likelihood of it.

Rhetorical Situation

Hyperbole can function not just as a literary trope but as a rhetorical device, used in the service of persuasion. It can be geared, in other words, toward

---

5. Schlueter, *Filling Up the Measure*, 85.

addressing a *rhetorical situation*, "a complex of persons, events, objects, and relations presenting an actual or potential exigence which can be completely or partially removed if discourse, introduced into the situation, can so constrain human decision of action as to bring about the significant modification of the exigence."[6] It will be important, then, to identify the rhetorical situation(s) of texts under study in order to see how words and phrases that might be hyperbolic are functioning.

Pathos

Hyperbole finds itself at home amidst passionate speech. Aristotle, the reader may recall from chapter 5, wrote, "There is something youthful about hyperboles; for they show vehemence. Wherefore those who are in a passion most frequently make use of them."[7] It would not surprise us to find hyperbole in a letter such as Galatians, then, given that it is laden with pathos.

Shock

Hyperbolic language can shock an audience in a way that normal-toned words simply cannot. It may be necessary, from the standpoint of a speaker, to shock an audience in order to dislodge thinking that has become cemented into erroneous foundations. Or, a speaker can use shock in order to increase memorability.

Jesus expertly used hyperbole in the Sermon on the Mount to shock his audience. The beatitudes, for instance, turned the reigning thinking upside down regarding who was blessed by God. The warning that one's righteousness needed to exceed that of the scribes and Pharisees undoubtedly puzzled and disquieted his listeners. The antitheses, with their incommensurate punishments for anger and lust, was a salvo of biting wordplay to obliterate the distorted logic and misapplication of the oral law.

Paul uses shock effectively as well (see the upcoming case study in chapter 8 on his use of "dogs, evildoers, and mutilators" in Phil 3:2). As we delve into Galatians, we will be alert for words and phrases that seem designed to shock the audience of the letter.

---

6. Bitzer, "Rhetorical Situation," 6.
7. Aristotle, *Rhet.*, 3.11.15.

Invective

As discussed in chapter 5, hyperbole was commonly used in vilifying one's opponent. In ancient times the purpose of invective was not so much to tell the truth about an enemy; it was to shame the enemy in the eyes of the community while reinforcing one's own social position. One would expect that in Galatians, which is heavy with invective, hyperbole would occur often.

WHAT'S NEXT AFTER IDENTIFYING HYPERBOLE?

Once an instance of hyperbole is identified, then the surrounding passage can be read with new eyes. This is the process known as *mitigation* (see chapter 4). In essence, the passage is reread with the hyperbolic meaning scaled down. More generally, this kind of rereading is what Laurie Thurén calls *derhetorization*: "This means in short, that we must identify the persuasive devices in the text and . . . filter out their effect on the ideas expressed."[8] What we end up with is a meaning and a theology more accurate to what the original authors intended to convey and the means they used to convey it (Figure 6.2).

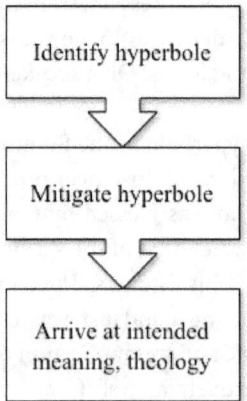

Figure 6.2. Process Flow for the Study of Galatians.

---

8. Thurén, *Derhetorizing Paul*, 28.

CONCLUSION

In this chapter I have laid out a detailed methodology for determining whether biblical texts contain hyperbole. The methodology essentially involves detection of certain aspects known to be associated with hyperbolic discourse, culminating in a Hyperbole Scorecard. This checklist is both quantitative and qualitative. The probability for hyperbole increases as the number of checked boxes increase, but it also depends on the strength of each individual item (especially the flouting of the quality maxim). In the coming chapters, this methodology will be put to the test in analyzing several biblical passages.

7

Hyperbole in the Old Testament

In this chapter…

Question(s) to be answered:
- What form does hyperbole take in the Old Testament?
- What function does it fulfill?

Trajectory:
- In this chapter and the next we will test the methodology from Chapter 6 with various Old and New Testament texts.

THE WRITINGS OF THE ancient Israelites reveal a penchant for extravagant discourse. Not only is a city imposing, but it reaches up to heaven. Tears coalesce into rivers. Brave warriors run swifter than eagles and are stronger than lions. These are all, of course, examples of hyperbole.

My goal in this chapter is to explore this ancient linguistic convention, as best as I can from the written evidence, so as to complement our understanding of Greco-Roman influence on Paul's use of hyperbole (chapter 5) with Jewish influence. While one could find instances of hyperbole in virtually all of the ancient Jewish texts, including deuterocanonical ones, I will limit my focus in this chapter to Paul's favorite quotation source: the OT.[1] Two questions will be asked regarding the use of hyperbole:

- What form does it take?
- What function does it fulfill?

---

1. Hyperbole is also found in ancient Ugaritic and Akkadian texts. See Watson, *Traditional Techniques*, 459; Watson, *Classical Hebrew Poetry*, 317. For an example of hyperbole in an apocryphal text, see Hilbert, "185,000 Slain Maccabean Enemies," 102–6.

THE FORM OF HYPERBOLE IN THE OT

While OT hyperbole does not depend on a particular syntactical structure, it is particularly at home in comparisons. For instance, "[t]he hyperbolic *simile* is very frequent in Hebrew."[2] Similes are comparative constructions using "like" or "as." When Isaiah writes that "your offspring would have been like the sand, and your descendants like its grains" (Isa 48:19), he is using a common hyperbolic simile.[3] (Since they involve more than one semantic domain, comparisons are also *composite hyperbole*—see chapter 4.) Other examples of hyperbolic similes include "Tyre has built herself a rampart and heaped up silver like dust, and fine gold like the mud of the streets" (Zech 9:3; cf. Job 27:16) and "The dead bodies of men shall fall like dung upon the open field, like sheaves after the reaper" (Jer 9:22).

Hyperbolic metaphors are also common, as in "Their throat is an open grave" (Ps 5:10) or "my heart . . . leaps out of its place" (Job 37:1). A simile and metaphor can also be combined in one hyperbolic expression: "As when one plows and breaks up the earth, so shall our bones be scattered at the mouth of Sheol" (Ps 141:7).

Comparisons do not necessarily have to be similes or metaphors. They can follow the construction "*x* was more numerous than *y*" or "*x* was more wicked than *y*." See Table 7.1 for examples from the Latter Prophets.

Table 7.1. Hyperbolic Comparisons in the Latter Prophets[4]

General category	Reference	Subject	Intensified Quality	Comparative Object
Abundance	Jer. 15.8	Jerusalem's widows	more numerous than	the sand of the seas
	Jer. 46.23	Babylonians	more numerous than	locusts
	Nah. 3.16	Nineveh's merchants	increased more than	the stars of the heavens
Hardness	Jer. 5.3	The faces of Jerusalem's inhabitants	harder than	rock

2. Watson, *Classical Hebrew Poetry*, 318. See Watson, 318–19, for more examples than those supplied here.

3. Scripture citations in this chapter and the next are from the ESV unless otherwise noted.

4. From Eric A. Seibert, "Harder than Flint, 289. Used by permission. Seibert admits, "One might argue that the intensified comparatives used to demonstrate the depth of Judah's/Jerusalem's wickedness are 'accurate' and thus not hyperbolic, though I suppose this would be a matter of perspective" (297n52).

	Ezek. 3.9	Ezekiel's forehead	harder than	flint
Scarcity	Isa. 13.12	human beings	rarer than	fine gold/the gold of Ophir
Speed (and destructiveness)	Jer. 4.13	an invading army's horses	swifter than	eagles
	Hab. 1.8	Babylon's horses	swifter than/more menacing than	leopards/wolves at dusk
Wickedness	Jer. 7.26; 16.12	Jeremiah's generation	did worse than	their ancestors
	Ezek. 5:6–7	Jerusalem	more wicked than/more turbulent than	the nations and the countries all around/the nations . . . all around
	Ezek. 16.47, 51–52	Jerusalem	more corrupt than and abominable than	Samaria and Sodom
	Ezek. 23.11	Oholibah (Jerusalem)/her lusting and whorings	more corrupt than/worse than	her sister = Oholah (Samaria)
Wisdom	Ezek. 28.3	prince (king) of Tyre	wiser than	Daniel
Worth	Isa. 56.5	a monument and a name better than	better than	sons and daughters

Hyperbole can occur in simple ("The king made silver as common in Jerusalem as stone" [1 Kgs 10:27]) or extended form:

> God gives me up to the ungodly
>   and casts me into the hands of the wicked.
> I was at ease, and he broke me apart;
>   he seized me by the neck and dashed me to pieces;
> he set me up as his target;
>   his archers surround me.
> He slashes open my kidneys and does not spare;
>   he pours out my gall on the ground.
> He breaks me with breach upon breach;
>   he runs upon me like a warrior.
> I have sewed sackcloth upon my skin

and have laid my strength in the dust.
My face is red with weeping,
and on my eyelids is deep darkness. (Job 16:11-16)

Additional examples of extended hyperbole are Jer 5:16-17; 15:7-9; Nah 3:15b-17; Job 3:4-9; Ps 22:16-18; 69:2-3, 14-15; Joel 2; Amos 9:2-4; Mic 6:6-7.[5]

Hyperbole in the OT can also be classified according to content, as it tends to cluster around certain stock categories. Below I have collected instances of OT hyperbole from a variety of sources into a slightly modified version of Jenni's outline from chapter 4.[6]

- Quantitative hyperbole

  - *Lifetime/forever*—"May my lord King David live forever!" (1 Kgs 1:31; cf. Neh 2:3; Ps 21:4; 61:7; 72:5; 74:1, 3; Eccl 6:3, 6; Dan 2:4; 3:9; 5:10; 6:6, 21; Isa 34:10; Jer 15:14; 17:27; 18:16; Jon 2:6)

  - *Numerical*

    - *Factor of 2*—". . . she has received from the LORD's hand double for all her sins" (Isa 40:2)

    - *Factor of 7*—"The barren has borne seven, but she who has many children is forlorn" (1 Sam 2:5; cf. Gen 4:24; Ruth 4:15; Ps 119:164; Prov 24:16; Isa 4:1; Mic 5:5)

    - *Factor of 10*—"When I break your supply of bread, ten women shall bake your bread in a single oven and shall dole out your bread again by weight, and you shall eat and not be satisfied" (Lev 26:26; cf. Gen 31:7, 41; Num 14:22; 1 Sam 1:8; Neh 4:12; Job 19:3; Eccl 7:19; Isa 5:10; Dan 1:20; Amos 5:3; 6:9; Hag 2:16)

---

5. According to Watson, *Classical Hebrew Poetry*, 319, extended form hyperbole is also attested in Ugaritic and Akkadian literature.

6. The following outline is adapted from Jenni, "Sprachliche Übertreibungen," 76-83, and is not meant to be exhaustive. I have added a few categories and removed a few citations that I did not feel were appropriate. I have also modified the wording of the categories a bit to make for a smoother translation from German to English. Other sources were consulted in constructing the outline, including Eybers, "Some Examples of Hyperbole," 38-49; Anthony, "Hebrew Hyperbole," 742-44; Bullinger, *Figures of Speech*, 423-28; Watson, "Hebrew Poetry," 277; Watson, *Classical Hebrew Poetry*, 318-19; Sandy, *Plowshares and Pruning Hooks*, 43-44; Douglas, *Overstatement*, 3-36; Lavoie, "Ironie et ambiguïtés," 200; Whitekettle, "When More Leads to Less," 446; Kissling, "Self-Defense," 113; Mariaselvam, *Song of Songs*, 66; Schökel, *Manual of Hebrew Poetics*, 168; Zuck, *Basic Bible Interpretation*, 154-55.

Part III: Biblical Hyperbole

- *Factor of 100/1,000/10,000*—"May the LORD, the God of your fathers, make you a thousand times as many as you are and bless you, as he has promised you!" (Deut 1:11; cf. 1 Sam 18:7; 21:11; 29:5; 2 Sam 24:3; Ps 3:6; Prov 17:10; Eccl 6:6; 8:12; Song 5:10; Mic 6:7)

- *Universal language (all, every, none)*—"For they also built for themselves high places and pillars and Asherim on every high hill and under every green tree" (1 Kgs 14:23; cf. Gen 6:5; Josh 11:23; 21:44–45; Judg 4:16; 19:10; 2 Kgs 16:4; 17:10; 2 Chr 28:4; 36:23; Ezek 6:13)

Size (extent)

- *Full of, filled*—"For all tables are full of filthy vomit, with no space left" (Isa 28:8; cf. 1 Kgs 20:27; 2 Kgs 6:17; 21:16; Job 3:15; Jer 13:13; Ezek 11:6; 30:11; 37:1; Zech 8:5)

- *Infinite magnitude*—"Their land is filled with silver and gold, and there is no end to their treasures; their land is filled with horses, and there is no end to their chariots" (Isa 2:7)

- *Sand*—". . . all Israel be gathered to you . . . as the sand by the sea for multitude" (2 Sam 17:11; cf. Gen 22:17; 32:12; 41:49; Josh 11:4; Judg 7:12; 1 Sam 13:5; 1 Kgs 4:20, 29; Job 6:3; 29:18; Ps 78:27; 139:18; Isa 10:22; 48:19; Jer 15:8; 33:22; Hos 1:10; Hab 1:9)

- *Dust*—"I will make your offspring as the dust of the earth" (Gen 13:16; cf. 28:14; Num 23:10; 1 Kgs 20:10; Job 27:16; 2 Chr 1:9; Ps 78:27; Jer 9:21; Zech 9:3)

- *Stones*—"The king made silver as common in Jerusalem as stone" (1 Kgs 10:27)

- *Water*—"They have poured out their blood like water" (Ps 79:3; cf. 22:14; Lam 2:13)

- *Dew*—". . . we shall light upon him as the dew falls on the ground" (2 Sam 17:12; cf. Mic 5:7)

- *Hairs*—"More in number than the hairs of my head are those who hate me without cause" (Ps 69:4)

- *Stars*—"I will surely bless you, and I will surely multiply your offspring as the stars of heaven" (Gen 22:17; cf. 15:5; 26:4; Exod 32:13; Deut 1:10; 10:22; 28:62; 1 Chr 27:23; Neh 9:23; Jer 33:22; Nah 3:16)

- *Size (dimensions)*—"The cities are great and fortified up to heaven" (Deut 1:28; cf. Gen. 11:4; Num 13:33; Deut 9:1; 1 Kgs 1:40; 12:10; Job 14:13; Amos 2:9; Isa 40:22; Jer 51:9; Obad 4)

- *Time (night and day)*—"Night and day [Edom] shall not be quenched; its smoke shall go up forever. From generation to generation it shall lie waste; none shall pass through it forever and ever." (Isa 34:10)

- Qualitative hyperbole[7]

  - *Universal statements* (made without qualification)—"The LORD does not let the righteous go hungry" (Prov 10:3; cf. 3:9–10; 13:21; 15:1)

  - *Idealizations*—"Would that all the LORD's people were prophets" (Num 11:29; cf. 1 Sam 25:28; 29:6, 9; 2 Sam 14:17–20)

  - *Fertility*—". . . a land flowing with milk and honey" (Exod 3:8; cf. Deut 7:14; 8:7–9; 2 Kgs 18:32; Job 20:17; Joel 4:18)

  - *Prowess in battle*—"Saul and Jonathan . . . were swifter than eagles; they were stronger than lions" (2 Sam 1:23; cf. Isa 5:27; 41:15; Jer 8:16)

  - *Righteousness, perfection*—"Job . . . was blameless and upright" (Job 1:1; cf. Gen 6:9; 17:1)

  - *Love*—". . . love is strong as death" (Song 8:6; cf. 2:2, 5; 5:8; 6:4, 5; 8:7)

  - *Hate*—"When the LORD saw that Leah was hated, he opened her womb, but Rachel was barren" (Gen 29:31; cf. 29:33; Exod 18:21; 20:5; Deut 21:15–17; 24:3; Judg 15:2; Prov 1:22; Mal 1:3)

  - *Self-deprecation*—"O Lord, if I have found favor in your sight, do not pass by your servant" (Gen 18:3; cf. 18:5, 27; 42:10, 11, 13; Ruth 2:13; 1 Sam 1:11; 24:15; 26:20; 2 Sam 9:8)

  - *Dead man*—"Behold, you are a dead man because of the woman whom you have taken" (Gen 20:3; cf. 25:32; Exod 12:33; Num 11:6; 2 Sam 9:8; 19:28)

  - *Contempt/disdain/scorn*—"Why should this dead dog curse my lord the king?" (2 Sam 16:9; cf. 1 Sam 17:43; 2 Sam 3:8; 22:43; Ps 18:42)

---

7. Qualitative hyperboles are those that are not quantifiable.

- *Boasting*—"By your messengers you have mocked the Lord, and you have said, 'With my many chariots I have gone up the heights of the mountains, to the far recesses of Lebanon; I felled its tallest cedars, its choicest cypresses; I entered its farthest lodging place, its most fruitful forest'" (2 Kgs 19:23–24; cf. Isa 10:14; 14:13–14; 37:24–25; 47:8; Ezek 28:2, 9; Dan 11:36)
- *Skill*—"Among all these were 700 chosen men who were left-handed; every one could sling a stone at a hair and not miss" (Josh 20:16; cf. Song 2:8)
- *Emotions*—"Would that we had died by the hand of the LORD in the land of Egypt" (Exod 16:3; cf. Gen 42:28; Deut 28:67; Josh 2:11; 5:1; 7:5; 2 Sam 19:1; 1 Kgs 10:5; 19:4; Ps 22:14; 32:3; Hos 2:11)
- *Impermanence*—"All flesh is grass, and all its beauty is like the flower of the field" (Isa 40:6; cf. 1 Chr 29:15; Job 14:2; 30:19; Ps 102:11; 103:15; 109:23; 144:4; Eccl 6:12)
- *Crying*—"Every night I flood my bed with tears; I drench my couch with my weeping" (Ps 6:6; cf. 119:136; Jer 9:1)
- *Accusations*—"How the faithful city has become a whore, she who was full of justice! Righteousness lodged in her, but now murderers" (Isa 1:21; cf. 5:11, 22; Amos 4:1; Zeph 3:3)
- *Judgment*—". . . For the stars of the heavens and their constellations will not give their light; the sun will be dark at its rising, and the moon will not shed its light" (Isa 13:10; cf. Jer 4:23–26)
- *Mockery/ridicule*—"The sluggard buries his hand in the dish and will not even bring it back to his mouth" (Prov 19:24; cf. 26:15; 2 Sam 5:6; Neh 4:3)
- *Nakedness*[8]—"For you have exacted pledges of your brothers for nothing and stripped the naked of their clothing" (Job 22:6; cf. 24:7, 10; Isa 20:2–4; 58:7; Ezek 18:7, 16; Amos 2:16)
- *Other*:
  - "And all the people went up after him, playing on pipes, and rejoicing with great joy, so that the earth was split by their noise" (1 Kgs 1:40)
  - "He drew me up from the pit of destruction" (Ps 40:2)

---

8. These verses refer to the deficiently clothed rather than literal nakedness.

- "Even in your thoughts, do not curse the king . . . for a bird of the air will carry your voice, or some winged creature tell the matter" (Eccl 10:20)
- "Shall mortal man be more just than God?" (Job 4:17 ASV)
- "From heaven the stars fought, from their courses they fought against Sisera" (Judg 5:20)
- "The fathers have eaten sour grapes, and the children's teeth are set on edge" (Jer 31:29; cf. Ezek 18:2)

What does this list reveal to us? First, it shows the multiplicity of forms that hyperbole took in ancient Hebrew writing. Second, it exposes the wide variety of genres in which OT hyperbole occurs—not just in poetic verse but in narrative and legal texts as well. Every major division of the Hebrew canon is represented—the law, the prophets, and the writings. Third, it provides a basis for comparison for when we come to the subject of NT hyperbole (chapter 8), especially that of Paul.

THE FUNCTION OF HYPERBOLE IN THE OT

In the previous section I addressed the question, "How did the OT authors use hyperbole?" In this section I will answer the question, "*Why* did the OT authors use hyperbole?" In other words, why not say, instead of that Saul and Jonathan were "swifter than eagles," that they were "very fast"? What is gained when hyperbole is employed? I will examine these questions through complementary lenses: literary effects and rhetorical effects.

Literary Function of OT Hyperbole

In the example above, writing that Saul and Jonathan were "swifter than eagles" does a few things from the perspective of figurative language. For one, a phrase is used to substitute for the adjective, "fast." Why not just use the adjective? Such adjectives could then become overused in a language and thus appear dull and uninteresting. "The main function of hyperbole is to replace overworked adjectives with a word or phrase which conveys the same meaning more effectively. The languages which are not rich in adjectives tend to be rich in hyperbolic expressions."[9]

---

9. Mariaselvam, *Song of Songs*, 66; cf. Watson, *Classical Hebrew Poetry*, 319, "The main function of hyperbole, in fact, is to replace over-worked adjectives (such as 'marvellous,' 'enormous,' 'colossal') with a word or phrase which conveys the same meaning

Also, the phrase "swifter than eagles" combines common terms and transforms them into a powerful figure of speech. "It seems to me that the function of hyperbole (or at least one of its functions) is to denote extravagance of size, numbers, proportions, quality and so on without having to resort to extravagant language. Hence its appeal."[10] A few carefully chosen words can say much—therefore OT hyperbole also tends to exhibit economy of expression.[11]

There is a certain amount of basic wordplay that happens in OT hyperbole as well. Using the words "hate" instead of "disfavored," or "dead man" to express the idea of "under threat," appears to be a conventional way of pushing the semantic scalar level of a term to the extreme (see Figure 7.1). The writers expected a mitigation process to occur; no Israelite reader, for instance, would really think that Jacob hated his wife Leah or that God hated Esau.

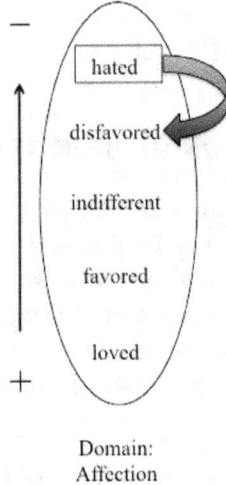

Figure 7.1. The Semantic Scale for Affection.
The term "hated" is mitigated to "disfavored" by the audience.

---

more effectively."

10. Watson, *Traditional Techniques*, 460.

11. Watson, *Classical Hebrew Poetry*, 317, "In essence, hyperbole belongs to economy of expression, which is the hallmark of good poetry and can therefore be related to the principle of thrift operative in oral composition."

Rhetorical Function of OT Hyperbole

Not all OT hyperbole had a clear rhetorical function. As with "hated" above, certain instances of hyperbole had become conventional, almost proverbial, through overuse, diminishing their rhetorical function significantly. Take for instance, the comparison of some amount to the "sands of the seashore." Wilfred Watson calls this a "jaded simile," reflecting on the tendency of hyperbole to become banal through overuse: "Hyperbole is common to the poetry of almost every language, eventually becoming part of normal speech, so that there is always the danger of over-used hyperboles turning into meaningless clichés."[12] Another overused OT hyperbole is "For they also built for themselves high places and pillars and Asherim on every high hill and under every green tree." Note that this is an extreme case formulation (ECF; see chapter 4) because it uses the word "every." The phrase expresses widespread culpability for idolatry throughout Israel. Despite its obvious hyperbolic nature, though, the phrase כָּל־עֵץ רַעֲנָן ("every green tree") occurs a full eleven times in the OT in connection with idolatry and so had likely lost much of its rhetorical impact.

Many of the OT hyperboles that did have an obvious rhetorical function were built upon the primary metaphors (see chapter 4) that *important is big* and *more is up*. Recall that these metaphors are learned as part of childhood, where one must negotiate environments where big things can be dangerous (animals) or vital (parents). These metaphors especially underlie quantitative hyperbole. When a city is said to have its top reaching into the heavens, or when its residents are imagined as giants (and the implied readers as grasshoppers), the language taps into a childlike sense of wonder and awe. I would submit that these same primary metaphors are at work in the tendency to lionize individuals or to exaggerate military prowess. In sum, attention is drawn to things that are big.

Another application of the rule that inflation draws attention may be seen in the many OT hyperbolic references to suffering. The statement that one's bed is flooded with tears is an obvious flouting of the quality maxim, designed to trigger a mitigation response on the part of the audience. Recall from chapter 4, however, that the hyperbole has a subjective dimension, revealing important information about the speaker: the speaker is sad and oppressed by circumstances. More significantly, these circumstances are more oppressive than what is typical (Colston's discrepancy theory of hyperbole: people use hyperbole to express negativity when the world does

---

12. Watson, *Classical Hebrew Poetry*, 319.

not match their wishes or expectations). The speaker, in turn, expresses this discrepancy through magnified language.

Of course, language about suffering and divine deliverance does not just convey informational content, or *logos*—it is saturated with *pathos* as well. It is an *illocutionary act* intended to affect the audience emotionally—to drive readers to the depths of despair, to elevate them to the heights of hope and joy, and to finally deliver them to the serenity of trust in God:

> The question is whether emotional language is necessarily exact language.... Of course sometimes an emotional statement can be exact, but the pattern is that the stronger the emotion, the more likelihood of inexactness. Hyperboles, in effect, stretch the truth in order to increase the impact of the words. "The prophets' statements [may be] grossly inaccurate. Yet their concern is not with the facts, but with the meaning of the fact.... What seems to be exaggeration is often only deeper penetration."[13]

To conclude, one of the main rhetorical functions of the OT is to produce repentance and trust in God's people. The Deuteronomic history chronicles the lessons learned by the Israelites in their covenant relationship with Yahweh. The Latter Prophets then graphically elucidate the resulting judgments for sin and the hope of restoration. In all of this, hyperbole serves to emphasize both the severity of judgment and the gloriousness of life lived in obedience to the covenant.

> Lift up your eyes all around, and see;
>   they all gather together, they come to you;
> your sons shall come from afar,
>   and your daughters shall be carried on the hip.
> Then you shall see and be radiant;
>   your heart shall thrill and exult,
> because the abundance of the sea shall be turned to you,
>   the wealth of the nations shall come to you.
> A multitude of camels shall cover you,
>   the young camels of Midian and Ephah;
>   all those from Sheba shall come.
> They shall bring gold and frankincense,
>   and shall bring good news, the praises of the LORD.
> All the flocks of Kedar shall be gathered to you;
>   the rams of Nebaioth shall minister to you;
> they shall come up with acceptance on my altar,
>   and I will beautify my beautiful house. (Isa 60:4–7)

---

13. Sandy, *Plowshares and Pruning Hooks*, 41, quoting Abraham J. Heschel, *The Prophets*, 2 vols. in 1 (New York: Harper Collins, 1962), p. 14.

CASE STUDY: CITIES FORTIFIED UP TO HEAVEN (DEUT 1:28)

When Moses sent the twelve men to reconnoiter the land of Canaan, they came back with a report (Num 13:28) that the cities were fortified (בְּצֻרוֹת) and very great (גְּדֹלֹת מְאֹד). This report is recounted by Moses in Deut 1:28: עָרִים גְּדֹלֹת וּבְצוּרֹת בַּשָּׁמָיִם (the cities are great and *fortified up to heaven*). In order to kick the tires (so to speak) of the hyperbole detection process, let us apply the methodology from chapter 6 to this phrase.

Logical Aspects

The first question to ask is: Does Deut 1:28 violate the quality (truthfulness) maxim? According to Stein's first criterion—*the statement is literally impossible*—it does. It is inconceivable that city walls could be built as high as the sky.

The phrase is also in the form of a comparison: the city walls are as high as the sky (A=B). Comparisons in the Bible, as noted earlier, are particularly prone to hyperbole.

Literary Aspects

Extreme language is detected in the phrase בַּשָּׁמָיִם, *up to heaven* (so most English translations; LXX ἕως τοῦ οὐρανοῦ). Such language is an extreme degree of height, especially for any non-naturally occurring phenomenon.

There is also amplification in this verse. The recounting of the spies' message involves three clauses, which build to a crescendo when at last the Anakim (traditionally feared to be giants) are mentioned:[14]

> The people are greater and taller than we
> The cities are great and fortified up to heaven[15]
> We have seen the sons of Anakim there

This kind of amplification is what Quintilian referred to as "building words upon words" (see chapter 5).

---

14. Christensen, *Deuteronomy 1:1—21:9*, 31.

15. The *waw*-conj. introducing this clause is absent in the MT but included in the SP, LXX, and the Syr.

Rhetorical Aspects

As for the rhetorical situation, in Deut 1:28 Moses is summarizing the rebellion of the Israelites while he reiterates God's covenantal activity among them. The exigency is the need for them to be strengthened and encouraged prior to entering the promised land.

There is strong pathos evident in the larger context: "Where are we going up? Our brothers have made our hearts melt, saying, 'The people are greater and taller than we. The cities are great and fortified up to heaven. And besides, we have seen the sons of the Anakim there.'" The expression "they made our hearts melt" (הֵמַסּוּ אֶת־לְבָבֵנוּ; cf. Deut 20:8; Josh 2:11; 5:1; 7:5; Isa 13:7; 19:1) is a particularly pathos-heavy phrase, also used in Josh 2:11 on the lips of Rahab to describe the feeling of intimidation of the Canaanites at the prospect of an Israelite invasion. The mention of the size of the people recalls the original report in Num 13:33 that "we seemed to ourselves like grasshoppers, and so we seemed to them."

The original words of the spies were designed to shock the Israelites, to dissuade them from attempting to conquer the land of Canaan. As repeated by Moses, here, the words may have lost some, but not all, of their shock value. The Israelites have still not entered the land. They are seemingly still very much afraid in the fact of what lies ahead.

Conclusion

The scorecard for Deut 1:28 is shown in Figure 7.2. As can be seen, the evidence is plentiful that Deut 1:28 is hyperbolic. I will return to the hyperbole detection methodology for three more case studies in the next chapter before moving into the heart of my study in chapter 9.

Hyperbole Scorecard: *Deut 1:28*

Logical aspects
- ☑ Flouting of the quality maxim
- ☑ Comparisons (A=B, A<>B, A is like B)

Literary aspects
- ☐ Universal language (ECFs), intensifiers, or generalizations
- ☑ Extreme or extravagant language
- ☐ Figurative language
- ☐ Economy of expression
- ☑ Amplification or attenuation

Rhetorical aspects
- ☑ Rhetorical situation
- ☑ Pathos
- ☑ Shock
- ☐ Invective

Figure 7.2. Hyperbole Scorecard for Deut 1:28.

8

Hyperbole in the New Testament

In this chapter...

Question(s) to be answered:
- What form does hyperbole take in the New Testament?
- What function does it fulfill?

Trajectory:
- In Chapters 9–11 the methodology from chapter 6 will be applied to Galatians.

The New Testament is more than history or biography or didactic discourse. It contains all of these; but it has also that without which it could not strictly be classed literature, namely, that emotional element which grew out of the dramatic and thrilling experiences of men who were not only interested in themselves but also in others, and not only in temporal and material things and values, but also in spiritual and eternal values. Everything they have to say bears the impress of this major interest, and it is this that motivated the telling of their story and the propagation of their message.[1]

ONE CAN SEE STRAIGHTAWAY in perusing the NT that it is not the cold, sterile counterpart to the OT. Rather, it continues the warm (at times blazing hot), passionate, vibrant, and extravagant language of its older companion. From the prescription to amputate one's sinful hand to the exhortation to pray without ceasing, from Jesus's railing against whitewashed tombs to Paul's alliterative invective directed toward the κύνας... κακοὺς ἐργάτας...

1. Douglas, *Overstatement*, xxii–xxiii.

κατατομήν, the NT is a treasury of hyperbolic language intended to interest, excite, and even overwhelm its reader (witness the gripping passion narrative and Jesus's "sweat like great drops of blood," Luke 22:44). Try as we might to find one, there is no such thing as home for Western intellects in the NT, even in the "cerebral" discourse of Paul (more to come on that later in this chapter): "Para los lectores occidentales, habituados al sentido de la medida y la claridad greco-romana, las hipérboles bíblicas resultan irracionales, pero no para los orientales que buscan ante todo el choque imaginativo más que la precisión discursiva lógica."[2]

In this chapter we will continue our exploration of the ancient Israelite linguistic conventions begun in the last chapter. Form and function of hyperbole will once again be analyzed. However, Paul's writings will be looked at separately from the other NT writings in order to make a comparison between Paul and the other writers. Ultimately, of course, Paul is our interest in the coming chapters.

THE FORM OF HYPERBOLE IN THE NON-PAULINE WRITINGS

As with the OT, simile and metaphor are common vehicles for hyperbole in the NT. Jesus's "face shone like the sun" (Matt 17:2), his voice is "like a trumpet" (Rev 1:10), and the "devil prowls around like a roaring lion" (1 Pet 5:8), are rich examples of similes. Metaphors include comparing death to sleep (Matt 9:24; John 11:11; 1 Thess 4:13–15; 2 Pet 3:4) and spiritual obtuseness to blindness (John 9:39–41; 2 Pet 1:9; 1 John 2:11; Rev 3:17), among many others.

Below is an outline (similar to the one in chapter 7 but with a few additional categories) for the hyperbole in the non-Pauline writings:[3]

- Quantitative hyperbole

---

2. García Cordero, "Hipérboles," 105.

3. Once again, ESV citations are used in this chapter. Also, like the outline in chapter 7, this one is assembled from a variety of sources, including Douglas, *Overstatement*, 37–226; Sheets, *When Jesus Exaggerated*, 9–83; Culy, "Would Jesus Exaggerate?," 105–9; Bonilla, "Jesus, What an Exaggerator"; García Cordero, "Hipérboles . . . (Ia Parte)," 106; García Cordero, "Hipérboles . . . (IIa Parte)," 246–47; Theobald, "Wie die Bergpredigt gelesen werden will," 268–69; Bullinger, *Figures of Speech*, 423; Thurén, *Derhetorizing Paul*, 33–34; Thurén, "'By Means of Hyperbole,'" 105; Schlueter, *Filling Up the Measure*, 88–92, 124–63; Stein, *Difficult Sayings*, 19–85; Stein, *Basic Guide*, 175–87; Zuck, *Basic Bible Interpretation*, 155.

- *Lifetime*—"[Melchizedek] is without father or mother or genealogy, having neither beginning of days nor end of life" (Heb 7:3)

Numerical

  - *Factor of 2*—"You make him twice as much a child of hell as yourselves" (Matt 23:15)
  - *Factor of 100*—"There is no one who has left house or brothers or sisters or mother or father or children or lands . . . who will not receive a hundredfold now in this time" (Mark 10:30)

- *Universal language (all, every, whole, always, none)*—"The whole city was gathered together at the door" (Mark 1:33; cf. Matt 2:3; 3:5; 4:23, 24; 8:34; 9:35; 12:15, 25; 14:35; 21:10; 27:25; Mark 1:28, 37, 45; 5:20; 6:33; 8:36; 9:15; 14:53; Luke 1:65; 2:47; 3:3, 15, 21; 4:15, 22, 28, 37, 40; 5:17; 6:19; 7:17, 29; 8:37; 9:25; 10:4; 13:17; 18:43; 19:7; 21:38; 22:70; 23:5, 48, 49; John 2:10; 3:26, 32; 8:33; 9:33; 11:49; 12:19; 14:26; Acts 2:5, 47; 7:51; 10:22; 17:6, 21; 21:28, 31; 28:22; Heb 2:17; 4:15; Jas 1:8; 2:10; 3:7, 16; 1 John 3:15)

Size (extent)

  - *Full of, filled*—". . . full of greed and self-indulgence. . . . full of dead people's bones and all uncleanness. . . . full of hypocrisy and lawlessness" (Matt 23:25, 27–28; cf. Luke 2:40; John 16:6; Acts 5:3, 28; Jas 3:8)
  - *Sand, stars*—"Therefore from one man . . . were born descendants as many as the stars of heaven and as many as the innumerable grains of sand by the seashore" (Heb 11:12)
  - *Hairs*—"But even the hairs of your head are all numbered" (Matt 10:30)
  - *Books*—". . . I suppose that the world itself could not contain the books that would be written" (John 21:25)

- *Size (dimensions)*—"Her sins are heaped high as heaven" (Rev 18:5)
- *Time (night and day)*—"She did not depart from the temple, worshiping with fasting and prayer night and day" (Luke 2:37; cf. Mark 5:5; Acts 20:31)

- Qualitative hyperbole

  - *Similes*—"His face shone like the sun, and his clothes became white as light" (Matt 17:2; cf. Luke 22:44; Acts 6:15; 1 Pet 5:8; Rev 1:10; 6:1; 9:7–10)

- *Parables*—". . . the master of that servant . . . will cut him in pieces" (Luke 12:46; cf. Matt 20:1–16; Luke 14:16–24; 15:1–7)
- *General statements* (made without qualification)—"Give to the one who begs from you, and do not refuse the one who would borrow from you" (Matt 5:42; cf. Matt 5:3–10; 5:22, 28–30, 32, 34, 39–41, 48; 6:24; 7:7; 26:52; Mark 4:34; 6:4; Luke 4:24; 5:39; 6:37; 16:10; Acts 7:51; Jas 1:5; 1 Pet 2:13–14; 1 John 3:8, 22; 2:15; 5:15)
- *Dichotomies*—"He who is not with me is against me" (Matt 12:30; cf. Mark 9:40; Luke 11:23)
- *Impossibilities*—"But when you give to the needy, do not let your left hand know what your right hand is doing" (Matt 6:3; cf. 7:3; 19:24; 23:24; Luke 19:40; John 7:38; Heb 6:6b)
- *Apparent contradictions*—". . . that your giving may be in secret" (Matt 6:4) versus "let your light shine before others, so that they may see your good works and give glory to your Father who is in heaven" (Matt 5:16; cf. Matt 5:33–37 versus Matt 26:63b; Rom 1:9; 2 Cor 1:23; Gal 1:20; Phil 1:8)
- *Extreme measures*—"If your right eye causes you to sin, tear it out and throw it away. . . . And if your right hand causes you to sin, cut it off and throw it away" (Matt 5:29–30; cf. John 6:53)
- *Righteousness, perfection*—"For I tell you, unless your righteousness exceeds that of the scribes and Pharisees, you will never enter the kingdom of heaven" (Matt 5:20; cf. 5:19, 48; 11:11; Luke 1:6; 2:25; Jas 3:2)
- *Hate*—"If anyone comes to me and does not hate his own father and mother and wife and children and brothers and sisters, yes, and even his own life, he cannot be my disciple" (Luke 14:26; cf. 16:13; John 7:7; 12:25)
- *Self-deprecation*—"So you also, when you have done all that you were commanded, say, 'We are unworthy servants; we have only done what was our duty'" (Luke 17:10; cf. Matt 3:11; 8:8; Mark 1:7)
- *Faith*—"If you have faith like a grain of mustard seed, you will say to this mountain, 'Move from here to there,' and it will move, and nothing will be impossible for you" (Matt 17:20; cf. 21:22; Mark 9:23; Luke 17:6; Heb 11:4)
- *Protection, success*—"I have given you authority to tread on serpents and scorpions, and over all the power of the enemy, and

nothing shall hurt you" (Luke 10:19; cf. Matt 16:19; 18:19; Mark 16:18)

- *Death*
  - *As sleep*—"Go away, for the girl is not dead but sleeping" (Matt 9:24; cf. John 11:11; 2 Pet 3:4)
  - *Figurative*—". . . your brother was dead, and is alive; he was lost, and is found" (Luke 15:32)
- *Poverty*—"The Son of Man has nowhere to lay his head" (Matt 8:20; cf. Mark 5:26; 12:44; Luke 9:58)
- *Blindness*—"For whoever lacks these qualities is so nearsighted that he is blind" (2 Pet 1:9; cf. John 9:39–41; 1 John 2:11; Rev 3:17)
- *Slavery*—". . . and deliver all those who through fear of death were subject to lifelong slavery" (Heb 2:15)
- *Milk*—"You need milk, not solid food" (Heb 5:12; cf. 1 Pet 2:2)
- *Fire*—"The tongue is a fire" (Jas 3:6; cf. Jude 23)
- *Emotions*—"They were astonished beyond measure" (Mark 7:37; cf. Matt 2:10; 17:23; 26:22, 38; 27:54; Mark 5:42; 9:15; 10:26; 11:18; 14:33–34; Luke 5:26; 8:37; 22:44; Acts 21:13)
- *Impermanence*—"What is your life? For you are a mist that appears for a little time and then vanishes" (Jas 4:14; cf. 1 Pet 1:24)
- *Accusations*—"Come now, you rich, weep and howl . . . Your riches have rotted and your garments are moth-eaten. Your gold and silver have corroded, and their corrosion . . . will eat your flesh like fire. . . . Behold, the wages of the laborers . . . are crying out against you. . . . You have lived on the earth in luxury and in self-indulgence. You have fattened your hearts in a day of slaughter. You have condemned and murdered the righteous person" (Jas 5:1–6; cf. Matt 23:13–35)
- *Judgment*—"There will not be left here one stone upon another that will not be thrown down" (Mark 13:1–2; cf. 13:24–25)
- *Mockery/ridicule*—"What does this babbler wish to say?" (Acts 17:18; cf. 24:5)
- *Invective*—"Go and tell that fox . . ." (Luke 13:32; cf. Matt 16:23; 23:13–35; John 6:70; 8:44; Acts 7:51; 13:10; 2 Pet 2:15; Jude 11)
- *Nakedness*—". . . not realizing that you are wretched, pitiable, poor, blind, and naked" (Rev 3:17)

When compared to the outline in chapter 7, a few commonalities may be noted. First, the conventional use of "hate" to mean disfavored is continued in the NT. Second, accusations and judgment are present as a part of the continuation of the prophetic tradition. Third, hyperbolic statements regarding emotional responses are quite common in both the OT and NT. Claude Douglas's comments regarding this category are worth a brief discussion. After listing thirty-one synoptic passages (e.g., "they rejoiced exceedingly with great joy," Matt 2:10; "all the crowd, when they saw him, were greatly amazed," Mark 9:15; "amazement seized them all, and they glorified God and were filled with awe," Luke 5:26), he writes:

> Here the words "exceeding" and "exceedingly" are found eight times. The words "amazed," "amazement," and "astonished," occur sixteen times in the list; once "amazed with a great amazement," once "astonished exceedingly," and once, "beyond measure astonished." This shows that the tendency to use such expressions has become a habit.... No better evidence is needed to show that these are stock expressions.[4]

These passages, then, may or may not exaggerate the facts regarding people's emotions. The important point is that they are cast in a hyperbolic style that had become a stock way of expressing oneself (compare the modern tendency to overuse the word "amazed/amazing": "I'm amazed that you said that," "That movie was amazing," and "You look amazing.")

Several interesting distinctions between the OT and NT lists can be seen as well. I will concentrate on the main ones here. First, the NT non-Pauline authors (hereafter in this section, "the NT authors") show less of a tendency to use numerical hyperbole. Aside from an allusion to the OT in Heb 11:12, gone are the comparisons of populations to the sands on the seashore, the stars in the sky, or the dust of the earth (although compare Revelation's "from every tribe and language and people and nation," which may be hyperbolic).

Second, the NT authors use far more universal language (extreme case formulations; see chapter 4) than their OT counterparts. People from "every town" come to see Jesus (Mark 6:33), he heals them "all" (Luke 6:19), and his fame spreads "everywhere" (Mark 1:28). The "whole city" becomes stirred up about him (Matt 21:10). Outside of the gospel writers, James displays a penchant for universal language as well. The person who doubts is unstable in "all" his ways (1:8). The one who fails in just one point of the law is guilty of "all" of it (2:10). "Every" kind of animal has been tamed by humanity

---

4. Douglas, *Overstatement*, 54–55.

(3:7). And, those who are jealous and selfish commit "every" vile practice (3:16).

Third, the NT authors describe people and places more realistically. No longer do cities reach into the heavens, nor do the natives seem like giants against grasshoppers. There is understandably far less wonder and amazement regarding frontier areas since by the first century the Jews inhabited a world that was settled and far less mysterious than it had been over a millennium ago. The land they formerly idealized as flowing with milk and honey is now occupied by Gentiles.

Fourth, there are more general statements (i.e., those made without qualification) in the NT. These utterances (e.g., "Give to the one who begs from you") are commonly on the lips of Jesus, the master teacher for whom hyperbole was a favored device. Because they are unqualified, many of Jesus's statements, if not taken hyperbolically, raise far more questions than they answer. For example:

- Re: Matt 5:21–26, is it not incommensurate for an insult to result in divine judgment? How could enough law courts be established to hear every case of anger? Is not righteous anger appropriate in some cases, as Jesus himself demonstrated? How many in Jesus's audience lived close enough to the temple to literally fulfill his command to leave a gift there and return later?
- Re: Matt 5:27–30, is it not incommensurate for lust to result in death by stoning (the penalty for adultery)? Would removal of a hand or eye prevent future lusting?
- Re: Matt 5:31–32, should every wife dismissed by her husband for reasons other than sexual immorality receive death by stoning as an adulteress?
- Re: Matt 5:33–37, if Jesus was against oaths, why did he allow himself to be placed under an oath (Matt 26:63–64)? Was Paul breaking Jesus's command when he invoked God as his witness multiple times in his letters (Rom 1:9; Gal 1:20; 2 Cor 1:23)?
- Re: Matt 5:42, is unlimited generosity to beggars really good for them (or society)? It the principle not contradicted by 2 Thess 3:10?

Such examples could be multiplied. These general statements require that sensitivity to hyperbole be part of the reader's interpretive grid; otherwise, difficulties abound.

Fifth, Jesus's vivid use of impossibilities goes far beyond the apodictic style of much of the OT law in creativity. It is easy to see the hyperbole in these types of statements, which concern a left hand not knowing what the right hand is doing, a log in one's eye, a camel passing through the eye of a needle, swallowing a camel, and stones crying out. The audacity of these utterances is continued in statements involving extreme measures such as self-mutilation as a remedy for lust or eating Jesus's flesh and drinking his blood.

Sixth, Jesus makes use of invective in a way that the OT writers did not (though they certainly depicted their enemies, even fellow Israelites, in colorful ways in the prophetic literature). He links his opponents to satanic (Matt 23:15; John 8:44) or serpentine parentage (Matt 23:33)—and at times even Satan himself (Matt 16:23; John 6:70). They are blind guides/fools (Matt 23:16, 17, 24), hypocrites (Matt 23:13, 15, 23, 25, 27, 29), and "whitewashed tombs, which outwardly appear beautiful, but within are full of dead people's bones and all uncleanness" (Matt 23:27).

THE FUNCTION OF HYPERBOLE IN THE NON-PAULINE WRITINGS

Hyperbole serves the larger goal of defining and instructing the Christian community. Questions of whether one is a child of God or a child of Satan and whether one will inherit eternal life or damnation are worked out using extravagant speech. Moral and theological precepts are expounded in colorful terminology. In pursuit of this agenda, hyperbole functions in several ways.

First, hyperbole makes the teachings of Jesus more arousing and penetrating: "Jesús, como oriental era imaginativo, y le gustaba utilizar la hipérbole y la paradoja con una intención provocativa para despertar ilusiones en el auditorio demasiado ocupado en los problemas de subsistencia cotidiana, siempre dependiendo de necesidades urgentes materiales."[5] Flouting the quality maxim (as with the image of swallowing a camel) adds to the entertainment value of the discourse. Also, as with the OT, hyperbole in

---

5. García Cordero, "Hipérboles," 102; cf. Stein, *Method and Message*, 8, "One means by which Jesus sought to capture the attention of his listeners was that of overstating a truth in such a way that the resulting exaggeration forcefully brought home the point he was attempting to make"; Zuck, *Teaching as Jesus Taught*, 196, "Jesus' use of hyperboles [are] exaggerations that, like daggers, deeply penetrated the consciences of his hearers." Theobald, "Wie die Bergpredigt gelesen werden will," 270, "Um Jesus zu charakterisieren, könnten wir mit guten Gründen sagen: Auch er war ein Übertreibungskünstler, manche hielten ihn vielleicht sogar für einen Narren. Übertrieben hat er des Öfteren, er liebte hyperbolische Rede und setzte sie ein, um aufzuschrecken und zur Beginnung zu bringen."

the NT takes advantage of the *pathos*-saturated culture to add an arresting emotional component to the teaching. Which is more memorable, "Be careful not to lust, because God takes sin seriously," or "If your eye causes you to sin, pluck it out"?

> The overstatement of fact or of abstract truth has great mnemonic value. It is safe to say that some fine things in the New Testament would never have found their way there had they not been expressed in extravagant style; doubtless many good things said by Jesus were not preserved because stated in a merely matter-of-fact style; and some parts of the New Testament would be dry reading had they been limited to mere statement of facts or truth in precise and uncolored language. Extravagance of speech challenges the attention and compels appraisement of the fact or truth thus misrepresented. And the more a fact or truth is exaggeration the more likely are we to seek for its true evaluation.[6]

Second, hyperbole is used for economy of expression. As noted above, one of the distinctive qualities of NT hyperbole is its use in general sayings without qualification. Is everyone who is poor (or poor in spirit) a child of God? Certainly not. One would need to qualify that statement in several different ways, and perhaps even then a satisfactory definition of a "child of God" would not be reached. Hyperbole allows Jesus the freedom to speak in simple and direct terms without endlessly parsing the meaning of his sayings.

Third, hyperbole serves as coloring for invective toward those outside the Christian community. In chapter 5, I introduced the subject of invective and established the connection between Hellenistic invective and that of the NT. Below are some of the basic categories (based on du Toit's loci) around which NT invective clusters:

- *Hypocrisy and falseness*—"Woe to you, scribes and Pharisees, hypocrites!" (Matt 23:15)

- *Obscure, shadowy characters*—". . . there will be false teachers among you, who will secretly bring in destructive heresies" (2 Pet 2:1)

- *Inflated self-esteem*—"they love the place of honor at feasts and the best seats in the synagogues and greetings in the marketplaces and being called rabbi by others" (Matt 23:6–7)

---

6. Douglas, *Overstatement*, xiv–xv.

- *Moral depravity*—"For you tithe mint and dill and cumin, and have neglected the weightier matters of the law: justice and mercy and faithfulness" (Matt 23:23)

- *A perversive influence*—"For you travel across sea and land to make a single proselyte, and when he becomes a proselyte, you make him twice as much a child of hell as yourselves" (Matt 23:15)

- *Associated with dubious historical characters*—"They have followed the way of Balaam, the son of Beor, who loved gain from wrongdoing" (2 Pet 2:15)

- *Prone to judgment*—"You serpents, you brood of vipers, how are you to escape being sentenced to hell?" (Matt 23:33)

To summarize the function of hyperbole in the non-Pauline NT:

1. Hyperbole makes the teachings of Jesus more arousing and penetrating
2. Hyperbole is used for economy of expression
3. Hyperbole serves as a coloring for warning and invective toward those outside the Christian community

CASE STUDY: TURNING THE OTHER CHEEK (MATT 5:38-41)

Six antitheses ("You have heard it said ... but I say to you") occur in the Sermon on the Mount immediately following Matt 5:17–20. The first four are widely recognized as being hyperbolic, and even the sixth one has obvious hyperbolic elements ("be perfect"). The fifth antithesis, however, has long resisted being interpreted in a hyperbolic sense.[7] The implications are enormous: is self-defense permitted? Is any form of aggression, even state-sponsored, allowed? Let us apply the criteria from the hyperbole scorecard.

Logical Aspects

Besides the hyperbolic nature of the entire passage around it, there are a few "reasonableness" tests that clue the audience that Jesus is violating the quality (truthfulness) maxim, and, hence, that Matt 5:38–41 is hyperbolic as

---

7. Weaver, "Transforming Nonresistance," 36, "As the evidence indicates, Matt. 5:38–42 has over time been the object of intense scrutiny. Study of this text has led to significant controversy and virtually no consensus. The passage has clearly earned its reputation as one of 'the hard sayings of Jesus.'"

well. First, the command to not resist evil seems unconscionable. Commentators agree: "Ethically, there can be no question that total nonresistance to evil constitutes an irrational and unjustifiable position incompatible with the rest of early Christian teaching and its numerous admonitions to combat, avoid, or escape from evil."[8] And France writes, "Jesus's position is shockingly radical: not only no retaliation, but even no *resistance* to one who is admittedly 'bad.'"[9]

Second, the counsel to turn the other cheek following a slap (most commentators regard this as an insult—a strike with the back of the hand—rather than a close-fisted punch) defies attempts to justify it. Perhaps the victim gains some sense of dignity or control in turning the cheek in front of an abuser, but such ends are never commanded in the NT; on the contrary, Jesus calls people to *lose* control of their lives and to *risk* humiliation for him. There is a chance, perhaps, that the abuser would be led to feel shame when the victim turns the other cheek, but this too is speculation: "It is by no means certain that by offering the other cheek in a fight one can intimidate one's enemy so that he really feels the 'coals of fire' on his head (Rom 12:20). . . . The passion narrative in particular showed the Christians that this does not work."[10]

Third, in the next verse Jesus seems to require giving up both one's tunic and cloak. "Here the hyperbolic formulation is clear, since a man whose shirt and cloak were also taken in a trial would be naked,"[11] which was an extreme dishonor in Palestinian society. Furthermore, a person was prohibited by OT law (Exod 22:26–27; Deut 24:12–13) from taking another person's cloak since, as the outer garment, it served as a bed for the night, especially for the poor.

Fourth, it is difficult to justify the statement concerning going a second mile after being compelled (presumably by a Roman soldier) to carry a load for one mile. What spiritual benefit would the soldier incur? More likely, carrying something for a Roman soldier would be a fruitless endeavor.[12]

---

8. Betz, *Sermon on the Mount*, 280.

9. France, *Matthew*, 217, emphasis mine.

10. Luz, *Matthew*, 273; cf. Davies and Allison, *Matthew 1–7*, 541, "Jesus often resorted to extreme exaggeration in order to drive home his points. . . . The command to turn the other cheek cannot be understood prosaically." Also, by their own example Jesus and Paul contradict this sort of passive nonresistance in the way they themselves respond to being struck by adversaries (John 18:22–23; Acts 23:2–5).

11. Luz, *Matthew*, 272.

12. Luz, *Matthew*, 273, "Eager collaboration with an occupying power is neither a way of escaping without harm—it is better to remain unnoticed and to do only what one must—nor a way of converting a political enemy, nor even a means of passive resistance."

Literary Aspects

There are a few literary aspects associated with hyperbole which are to be found in Matt 5:38–41. First, to speak of nonresistance to evil is to make a rather sweeping generalization. The ensuing examples are general as well. For instance, no one would reasonably think that because the right cheek is spoken of that a strike to the left cheek does not also fall under Jesus's rule. The same may be said for the other two examples. Each qualifying statement retains the general, proverbial style of teaching.

Second, there is amplification in this passage. Jesus uses increment (in this case, building words upon words; see chapter 5) to enhance the force of his elocution. After stating his topic sentence ("Do not resist the one who is evil"), he follows it with three case examples, each shocking in its own right.

Rhetorical Aspects

Jesus focuses in this passage on the legal principle of *lex talionis*. It stands to reason that people had been abusing this principle, and Jesus was attempting to set them straight. This is the rhetorical situation.

Jesus prosecutes his argument through the use of pathos and shock. As Kennedy writes, "The proof of 5:17–48 is largely based on ethos and pathos, not on logical argument."[13] We have in this passage what Stein calls *commissive language*, perlocutionary utterances which have as their "main goal evoking decisions, conveying emotions, eliciting feelings, arousing sentiment, and affecting change."[14]

Conclusion

There are several aspects of this passage that suggest hyperbole is present (see Figure 8.1). Especially strong are the indications that the speaker (Jesus) is flouting the quality maxim. There are also generalizations, amplification, rhetorical situation, pathos, and shock. It is highly likely that Jesus is speaking hyperbolically.

---

13. Kennedy, *New Testament Interpretation*, 56.
14. Stein, *Basic Guide*, 68.

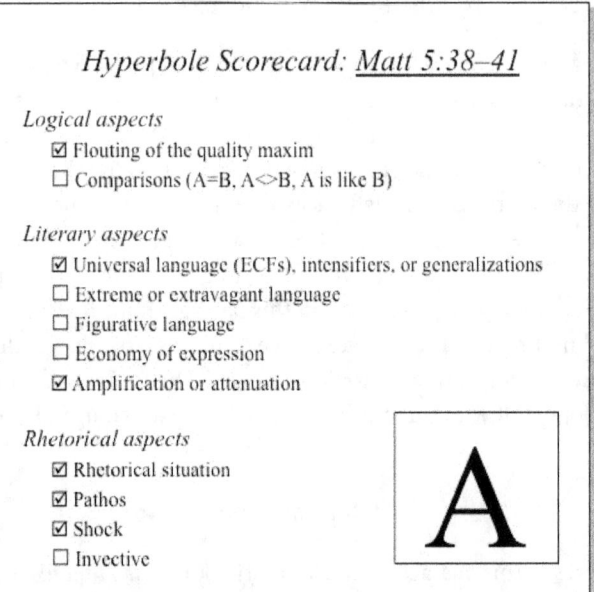

Figure 8.1. Hyperbole Scorecard for Matt 5:38–41.

What is Jesus *actually* saying, then? The key to piecing together this three-pronged hyperbolic puzzle into one coherent unity is to dimensionalize it along a vertical scalar axis. This can be done if we conceptualize Jesus's three sayings in terms of *an economy of giving and taking*. On the one hand, we have an offender who, in each case, takes something from a victim: in the first case, dignity; in the second, property; in the third, freedom. On the other hand, we have three potential victim responses in view: (1) take what is rightfully yours according to the *lex talionis*, (2) forgive the debt, or (3) not only forgive the debt but give additionally to the offender. These three responses can be placed along a vertical axis (Figure 8.2). The third response is the hyperbolic one. When the hyperbole is mitigated, the hearer lands on the intended meaning, forgiveness, for which there is plenty of corroborating evidence in the NT.

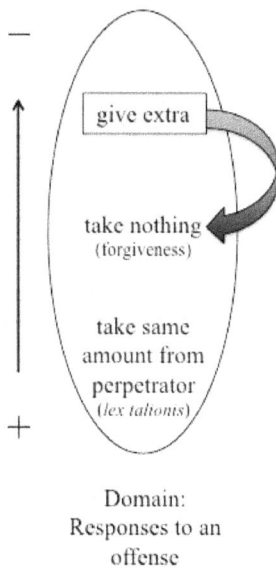

Figure 8.2. Three Responses to Being "Robbed" of Dignity, Property, or Freedom (Matt 5:39–41): (1) the victim may take an equal amount from the perpetrator; (2) the victim may forgive the offense altogether; or (3) the victim may give additional to the offender (the hyperbolic level). The vertical axis is scaled according to acquisition (+ = more possessions, — = less possessions).

To wrap up this case study, in Matt 5:38–41 Jesus is not commanding something irrational or extreme. He is addressing an overly litigious society which had developed the principle of *lex talionis* into a variety of oral traditions (the Mishnah details the elaborate system of compensation in Second Temple Judaism that included financial restitution for damage, pain, healing, loss of time, and disgrace).[15] Forgiveness, then, is a way of insuring that *lex talionis* is not abused: when you are wronged, simply forgive instead of exacting retribution. This meaning is arrived at when the hyperbole of Matt 5:38–41 is mitigated as it should be.

Why does Jesus not express it in simpler terms? Why not just say "forgive your offender" rather than "turn to him the other cheek also"? There are a few reasons. First, as I have already discussed, hyperbole makes the teaching more shocking and memorable. Second, hyperbole in this case accentuates the seriousness of sin. By exaggerating the lengths to which people should go to avoid sin (cf. "do not let your left hand know what your right hand is doing"), Jesus in effect *builds a fence around the Torah* (to use

15. *m. B. Qam.* 8:1.

a rabbinical phrase) to insure that God's people do not even come close to trespassing.

THE FORM OF HYPERBOLE IN THE PAULINE WRITINGS

We now turn to the Pauline correspondence, for which hyperbole "is one of the most obvious oratorical features."[16] Utilizing the sources from the NT non-Pauline hyperbole outline, I will construct one just for Paul (minus, of course, Galatians, which I will save for chapters 9–11).[17] This outline will help us to answer the question, How does Paul use hyperbole in ways that are unique to him as a NT author?

- Quantitative hyperbole
  - *Universal language (all, every, whole, always, none)*—"Your faith is proclaimed in all the world" (Rom 1:8; cf. 1:9–10; 16:19; 1 Cor 1:4–5, 7; 2:2; 3:7, 21; 7:19; 9:22; 10:33; 11:2; 13:2, 7; 15:30–31; 2 Cor 4:8; 8:7; Eph 6:18; Phil 1:3, 13; 2:21; 4:4, 13; Col 1:9; 1 Thess 1:2, 8; 5:16–17; 2 Thess 1:3; 1 Tim 4:4; 6:4, 10; 2 Tim 1:15; 2:7; 3:12; Titus 1:12, 15; 3:2; Phlm 4)
  - *Size (extent)*
    - *Full of, filled*—". . . that you yourselves are full of goodness, filled with all knowledge" (Rom 15:14; cf. 1:29; 2 Cor 7:4; Eph 3:19; 5:18; Phil 1:11; 2 Tim 1:4)
    - *Time (night and day)*—". . . we pray most earnestly night and day that we may see you face to face" (1 Thess 3:10; cf. 2:9; 2 Tim 1:3)
- Qualitative hyperbole
  - *Similes*—". . . their talk will spread like gangrene" (2 Tim 2:17; cf. 1 Thess 2:7)
  - *General statements (made without qualification)*—"And we know that for those who love God all things work together for good" (Rom 8:28; cf. 12:20; 13:1; 1 Cor 6:12; 7:29–31; 10:23)
  - *Impossibilities*—"For they gave according to their means, as I can testify, and beyond their means" (2 Cor 8:3)

---

16. Thurén, "'By Means of Hyperbole,'" 105.
17. For the purposes of this exercise I will treat the Pauline disputed and undisputed letters together.

Hyperbole in the New Testament

- *Extreme or extravagant language*—"... you are to deliver this man to Satan for the destruction of the flesh" (1 Cor 5:5; cf. 4:8–13; 6:15; 13:1–3; Eph 5:8; 1 Tim 1:20)
- *Hate*—"As it is written, 'Jacob I loved, but Esau I hated'" (Rom 9:13)
- *Self-deprecation*—"... even though I am nothing" (2 Cor 12:11; cf. 1 Cor 4:13; 15:9; Eph 3:8; 1 Tim 1:15)
- *Protection, success*—"So I was rescued from the lion's mouth" (2 Tim 4:17)
- *Poverty*—"as having nothing, yet possessing everything" (2 Cor 6:10; cf. 1 Cor 4:11)
- *Milk*—"I fed you with milk, not solid food, for you were not ready for it" (1 Cor 3:2)
- *Blindness*—"... the god of this world has blinded the minds of the unbelievers" (2 Cor 4:4)
- *Slavery*—"I am of the flesh, sold under sin" (Rom 7:14; cf. 2 Tim 2:26; Titus 3:3)
- *Death as sleep*—"But we do not want you to be uninformed, brothers, about those who are asleep" (1 Thess 4:13–15)
- *Life and death*—"... but when the commandment came, sin came alive and I died" (Rom 7:9–11; cf. 6:2–4; 8:13; 2 Cor 3:6; Eph 2:1; Col 2:13; 3:3, 5; 1 Tim 5:6)
- *Invective*—"Look out for the dogs, look out for the evildoers, look out for those who mutilate the flesh" (Phil 3:2; cf. 2 Cor 11:13; Phil 3:19; 1 Thess 2:14–16; 1 Tim 4:2; Titus 1:10
- *Other*:
  - "For the foolishness of God is wiser than men, and the weakness of God is stronger than men" (1 Cor 1:25)

As can be seen from the outline, one of the most common ways in which Paul uses hyperbole is with universal language (extreme case formulations). Were one to interpret Paul literally it would seem as if Paul spends every minute of his time praying and thanking God for his converts (Rom 1:9–10; Phil 1:3; Col 1:9; 1 Thess 1:2; 2 Thess 1:3; Phlm 4; cf. under the Time [night and day] category, 1 Thess 2:9; 3:10; 2 Tim 1:3). One would also think that every single person in the surrounding regions had heard of the faith and obedience of the budding churches (Rom 1:8; 16:19; 1 Thess 1:8). A literal interpretation of universal language statements raises difficult questions, such as, does circumcision really count for *nothing* (1 Cor 7:19)? This seems contrary to Rom 3:1–2. Or, was Paul really oppressed *every hour* (1 Cor 15:30)? Did he die *every day* (1 Cor 15:31)? Did *every person* in Asia turn away from Paul (2 Tim 1:15)? This use of universal language seems to have been very common for Paul.

Another stock expression for Paul is the use of "full of, filled" to describe a state of being. While these expressions sound very natural to our ears, accustomed as we are to their modern usage, they are nonetheless hyperbolic. A human being cannot be *full of* something.

Similar to universal language, Paul makes general statements without qualification. These statements may or may not use universal language ("all things work together for good"), but there is less of a quantitative thrust to them. Paul's citation of Prov 25:21–22 in Rom 12:20 is an example. Another is the exhortation in Rom 13 to obey the governing authorities, to which there are exceptions, as demonstrated in Acts 5:29.

Paul's most sublime language is understandably hyperbolic as well.[18] Witness Paul's comparison of himself with the Corinthians in this extended hyperbole (1 Cor 4:8–13):

> Already you have all you want! Already you have become rich! Without us you have become kings! And would that you did reign, so that we might share the rule with you! For I think that God has exhibited us apostles as last of all, like men sentenced to death, because we have become a spectacle to the world, to angels, and to men. We are fools for Christ's sake, but you are wise in Christ. We are weak, but you are strong. You are held in honor, but we in disrepute. To the present hour we hunger and thirst, we are poorly dressed and buffeted and homeless, and we labor, working with our own hands. When reviled, we bless; when persecuted, we endure; when slandered, we entreat. We have become, and are still, like the scum of the world, the refuse of all things.

Paul also transcends literality when he speaks of handing over believers to Satan for discipline (1 Cor 5:5; 1 Tim 1:20) or when he speaks metaphorically of believers' prior state: "you were darkness" (Eph 5:8).

Self-deprecation seems to come naturally to Paul. He speaks of himself as "nothing" (2 Cor 12:11) or, as in the quote above, as "the scum of the world, the refuse of all things" (1 Cor 4:13). He is "the least of the apostles"

---

18. See the interesting study of Paul's use of the hyperbolic sublime in Schoeni, "Hyperbolic Sublime," 171–92.

(1 Cor 15:9), "one untimely born" (1 Cor 15:8), "the very least of all the saints" (Eph 3:8), and the foremost of sinners (1 Tim 1:15).

A favorite metaphorical hyperbole for Paul is to describe a person's spiritual state using the metaphors of life and death. Death can describe a person living under sin and the law, whereas life signifies freedom from these (Rom 7:9–11; 8:13; 2 Cor 3:6; Eph 2:1; Col 2:13). Death is also a powerful picture of the eschewing of the pre-Christian identity when a person is baptized into Christ (Rom 6:2–4; Col 3:3).

Lastly, Paul exhibits a penchant for the use of invective. Here it is difficult to render judgment as to whether a particular instance of invective is hyperbolic. Such judgments must be rendered on a case by case basis. Certain cases are relatively clear: portraying one's opponents as having their belly as a god (Phil 3:19) or castigating the Jews as those who "displease God and oppose all mankind" (1 Thess 2:14–16) clearly crosses the line into hyperbolic territory.[19] However, does it strain the truth simply to call one's opponents "false apostles," (2 Cor 11:13), "liars whose consciences are seared" (1 Tim 4:2), or "empty talkers and deceivers" (Titus 1:10)? Such statements use generalized language and are typical of the loci of invective (see chapter 5), which was well documented in ancient times to be an exercise in hyperbole. For these reasons they may be hyperbolic.

THE FUNCTION OF HYPERBOLE IN THE PAULINE WRITINGS

Why does Paul use hyperbole? Perhaps some of his usage (full of, filled) could be classified as habitual, mere colloquialisms. Universal language (all, every, whole, always, none) is a different story. Paul uses it often in the exordia of his letters to exemplify his thankfulness and care for his fledgling congregations. Such is part of the ethos of establishing trustworthiness at the beginning of a letter. The universal language statements concerning Paul's constant prayer and the fame of the congregations have unmistakable implicatures (see chapter 4) conveying parental love and pride.

As with the rest of the NT, Paul's use of hyperbole is a servant to the larger task of defining and instructing/warning the community of faith. His general statements are like those of Jesus—they are meant to awaken interest and stir pathos (it is no accident that the hyperbole of Rom 8:28 occurs within a block of verses where Paul is rhapsodizing on God's sovereign care and the Spirit's work). His regard for the Macedonian congregations giving

---

19. For a treatment of 1 Thess 2:14–16 as hyperbole, see Schlueter, *Filling Up the Measure*.

beyond their means is Paul's version of the Pharisees swallowing a camel. Both are exaggerated and intended to convey pragmatic effects (see chapter 4), in Paul's case the encouragement by example to be generous.

Paul uses negative language to reinforce community definition and to instruct (warn) his audiences to be wary of outsiders. He uses the metaphor of death to picture the sinful pre-Christian practices as abolished and not to be returned to. He uses invective both to raise his own stature in the eyes of the community and to humiliate his opponents, who threaten to redefine the community in their own terms.

CASE STUDY: BEWARE OF THE DOGS (PHIL 3:2)

Before ending this chapter, it will be beneficial to take an in-depth examination of two possible instances of Pauline hyperbole, the first being Phil 3:2. Doing so will give us a chance to become more intimately acquainted with the form and function of Pauline hyperbole. My investigation will proceed according to the Hyperbole Scorecard.

Logical Aspects

In what ways does Paul appear to be flouting the quality maxim in Phil 3:2? In this verse there is a comparison being made between a certain group of people and "dogs ... evildoers ... mutilators."[20] It is difficult, given the relative lack of information, to know much about this group of people. However, we may assume from the context (and from Paul's use of κατατομή) that they are Jewish Christians who believe that Gentile believers must Judaize, that is, be circumcised and obey certain precepts of the Jewish law, in order to be regarded as the true Israel.[21]

In an ironic twist, Paul turns the tables on these visitors, referring to them with colorful epithets that they (the Jewish Christians) had likely used against people outside the covenant community.[22] I will take each term in the order of its occurrence.

To begin with, "dog" was known to be a term of insult: "A culture that spends millions of dollars on dogs as pets can scarcely appreciate the basic contempt that ancient society had for dogs, who were both scavengers

---

20. Most modern commentators view these three epithets as directed toward the same group.

21. Fee, *Philippians*, 293; O'Brien, *Philippians*, 355; Reumann, *Philippians*, 470.

22. In keeping with Hawthorne and Martin, *Philippians*, 172, I will use "visitors" to designate the Jewish Christians who are referred to in Phil 3:2.

(eating whatever street garbage they could find) and vicious (attacking the weak and helpless)."[23] The biblical view of dogs is extremely negative. The OT suggests that violence towards dogs was deemed acceptable (1 Sam 17:43; Prov 26:17). Being compared to a dog was a serious affront, implying that a person was of very low status (2 Kgs 8:13; Deut 23:18; 1 Sam 24:14; 2 Sam 3:8; 9:8; Prov 26:11).[24] In the NT dogs are a Jewish epithet for Gentiles (Matt 7:6; 15:26; Mark 7:27) and pictures those excluded from the kingdom of God: "Outside are the dogs and sorcerers and the sexually immoral and murderers and idolaters, and everyone who loves and practices falsehood" (Rev 22:15). Paul's use of the term, in this way, may represent a reversal—it is the Jewish Christians who find themselves outside the kingdom: "Now Paul turns the tables on them and calls them by the same derisive names that they have used for those whom they have excluded. In this satirical twist, Paul gives them a bitter taste of their own poisonous prejudice."[25]

But the question remains, "Was Paul telling the (literal) truth?" Were the visitors actual dogs? Of course not. Were they *metaphorical* dogs? This is a tougher question, since it forces us to distinguish between simple metaphor and metaphorical hyperbole. With respect to the former, if someone were to conclude that by "dogs" we mean simply people who were outside the covenant community, then Paul may well have been telling the truth—if we assume, of course, that persuading other Christians to Judaize was an damnable sin. This is an issue we will be forced to confront again in chapter 9. In this case, however, there is more to consider—namely, that "dogs" is such a strong term. How can a mature Christian like Paul compare fellow human beings, saved or unsaved, to "zoological 'low life'" and *not* be speaking hyperbolically?[26] The NT is consistent, from Jesus's prohibition against insults (Matt 5:22; 12:36–37) to James's (Jas 3:5–12; 4:11) exhortations on taming the tongue, that Christians are held to a high standard regarding how they speak about others.

I propose, then, that Paul is speaking hyperbolically, leveraging the multifaceted negativity bound up in the image of dogs to deliver a powerful punch against those who were endangering the Philippians. The visitors were not quite as worthless, vicious, and menacing as real dogs, but their

---

23. Fee, *Philippians*, 295n44; cf. Koester, "Purpose of a Polemic," 320, "dog" was "one of the strongest invective terms possible. This means that the deliberate aim of the polemic here is not to describe opponents, but to insult them." There may also be an implication of religious impurity in the use of the term, as with Vincent, *Philippians*, 92, and Silva, *Philippians*, 147.

24. Otto Michel, "κύων," *TDNT* 3:1101–4.

25. Hansen, *Philippians*, 217.

26. This description of "dogs" is from Fee, *Philippians*, 295.

efforts to counter Paul's gospel put them somewhere along the continuum (see Figure 8.3).

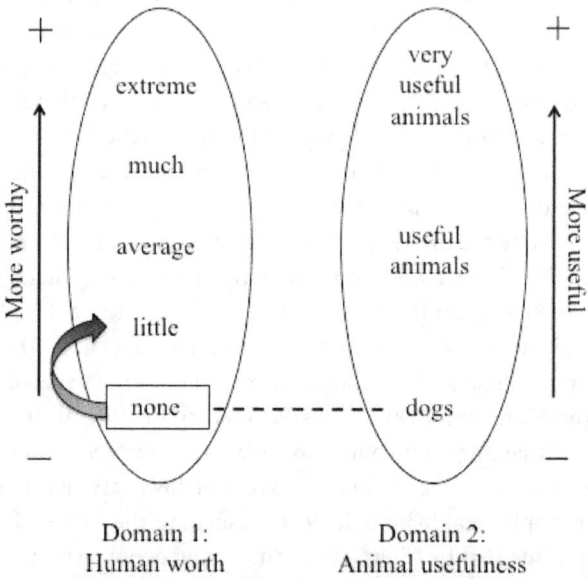

Figure 8.3. Metaphorical (Cross-Domain) Hyperbole Using "Dogs" (Phil 3:2). Vertically, "dogs" are pictured as the least useful of animals. Horizontally, "dogs" equates to worthlessness in humans. Upon mitigation, the addressee corrects the hyperbolic meaning to "little" worth.

The second term, "evildoers," is hyperbolic as well.[27] Like "dogs," there appears to be an aspect of reversal here—the Jewish Christians probably had used this epithet against Gentiles.[28] Now Paul is implicating them (the Jewish Christians) in doing evil. What was the evil of which they were guilty? Were they drawing people away from faith in Christ?[29] That seems to be a stretch—for all that we know the visitors could have been advocating the same synthesis of faith and works by which Paul and many of his messianic Jewish contemporaries lived out. Is not "evildoers" a bit strong, then, for opponents in an internecine dispute? When read through the lens of hyperbole, however, it makes sense. The visitors are not really doing evil, but what they are doing is introducing things Paul considers to be unnecessary to Gentile faith in Christ. That may not be evil *per se*, but it is harmful to Paul's

---

27. O'Brien, *Philippians*, 355, suggests that the term echoes the phrase "workers of iniquity" from the Psalter (Ps 5:5; 6:8; 14:4; 36:12, etc.).

28. Fee, *Philippians*, 295–96.

29. Proposed by Hansen, *Philippians*, 219.

agenda and potentially destructive to Jew-Gentile relationships. What's more, there is delicious irony here, since the visitors likely feel that they are doing *good works* in prescribing obedience to Torah.

The third and final noun, "mutilation," denotes "cutting in pieces" (BDAG, κατατομή). Again, the reversal aspect is present—the Jewish Christians considered themselves the circumcision (περιτομή), and Paul is stripping them of that basis for glory. "For we are the circumcision, who worship by the Spirit of God and glory in Christ Jesus and put no confidence in the flesh," Paul claims in the next verse. But the mere aspects of reversal do not entirely explain Paul's word choice here. If he wanted to convey something like "uncircumcision" he could have used ἀκροβυστία. But instead Paul chooses an outlandish term, κατατομή, to caricature the one thing that seems to be of primary importance to the visitors. It is the art of exaggeration, and it is carefully and deftly accomplished.

Literary Aspects

Βλέπετε τοὺς κύνας, βλέπετε τοὺς κακοὺς ἐργάτας, βλέπετε τὴν κατατομήν.

Philippians 3:2 contains a number of literary aspects suggestive for hyperbole. Extreme language (κύνας ... κατατομήν) and metaphor have already been mentioned. There are several other figures of speech neatly packed into the space of ten words.[30] Such creativity no doubt betrays a deliberateness on Paul's part to produce just the right rhetorical effect on his audience. First, there is anaphora in the repetition of βλέπετε in three successive clauses. Each clause is a colon of approximately equal length consisting of an imperative followed by an articular noun phrase. Second, there is no conjunction separating the clauses (asyndeton). Third, the repetition of κ-terms results in alliteration. The repeated aspirated velar sounds imbue the sentence with a harshness, as if Paul is scoffing or spitting out the words (cf. embodied pragmatic effects, i.e., those based on the structure and pronunciation of words; see chapter 4). And fourth, Paul employs paronomasia by substituting the similarly sounding κατατομή for περιτομή, providing a dramatic ending for the verse. Taken together, these features produce a heightening effect as the verse moves from beginning to end, exemplifying what Quintilian calls amplification by accumulation (see chapter 5).

---

30. For more on these figures of speech, see Hawthorne and Martin, *Philippians*, 172.

Rhetorical Aspects

The rhetorical situation in Phil 3:2 is clear: Paul senses a subversive influence on the part of a group of people apparently campaigning for circumcision among the Philippian converts. He desires to warn the Philippians against such influence. Pathos and shock are evident as well. Paul is angry at this threat to his labor among the Philippians, so his words drip with disdain.

Philippians 3:2 also contains telltale marks of invective. In chapter 5 several points were established regarding invective in the Hellenistic period:

- Invective, like its counterpart, praise, tended to be hyperbolic
- Invective was used to define a community: to build up the speaker in the eyes of the audience and to denigrate the victim, resulting in ostracism
- Invective was accompanied by pathos
- Invective centered around certain conventional loci regarding, for example, an individual's tainted origins, eccentric appearance, questionable morality, hypocrisy, cowardice, and danger to others

These qualities find clear parallels in Phil 3:2. The triple βλέπετε serves as a warning designed to isolate the visitors from the Philippian believers.[31] The pathos of the statement is evident: "That Paul's emotions are running high can be seen ... in the vivid and even abusive language he uses to describe his opponents ('dogs,' 'evildoers,' 'mutilators') ..."[32] And, the fact that Paul describes the visitors' immorality (evildoers) and danger to the Philippians (mutilation) follows the conventional loci of Hellenistic invective.

Conclusion

In this brief case study I have sought to establish that in Phil 3:2 Paul uses hyperbole for rhetorical effect (see Figure 8.4). First, it was demonstrated that, by the use of the terms "dogs," "evildoers," and "mutilators," Paul is flouting the quality maxim, a key indicator of hyperbole. Second, the numerous figures of speech in Phil 3:2 were shown to contribute to amplification (of which hyperbole is a species). Third, in addition to a clear rhetorical

---

31. Fee, *Philippians*, 293, "What Paul is about to repeat for their 'safety' begins with the threefold warning, 'look out for,' expressed with powerful rhetoric, full of invective."

32. Hawthorne and Martin, *Philippians*, 171–72.

situation, pathos, and shock, the connection between Phil 3:2 and Hellenistic invective was established.³³

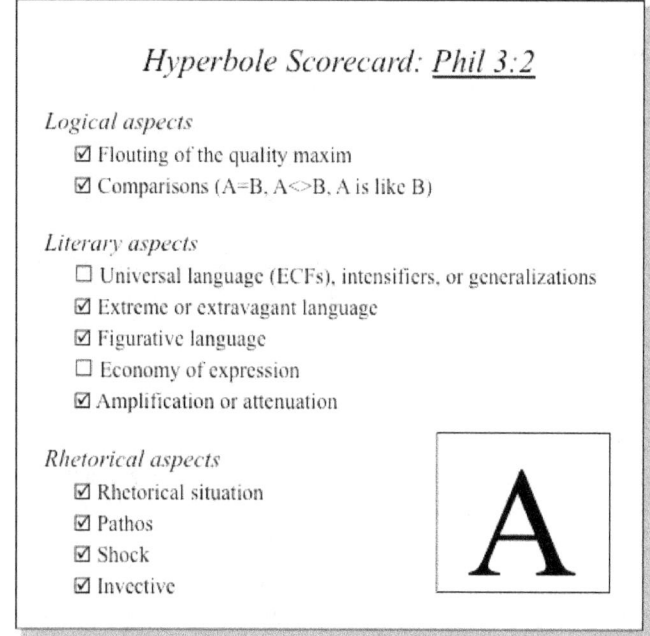

Figure 8.4. Hyperbole Scorecard for Phil 3:2.

CASE STUDY: THE PREACHING OF ANGELS (GAL 1:8)

In this final case study I will focus on the phrase ἀλλὰ καὶ ἐὰν ἡμεῖς ἢ ἄγγελος ἐξ οὐρανοῦ εὐαγγελίζηται ὑμῖν παρ' ὃ εὐηγγελισάμεθα ὑμῖν ("But even if we or an angel from heaven should preach to you a gospel other than what we preached to you . . .").³⁴ I will examine it using the criteria from the Hyperbole Scorecard to determine the likelihood that it is hyperbolic.

---

33. Note also the continuation of this line of hyperbolic invective in Phil 3:19.

34. I will not be examining the entirety of Gal 1:8–9, including the so-called double anathema. The two verses together will be taken up in chapter 9 in dealing with the Paul's attitude toward his opponents.

Logical Aspects

The first thing to examine is whether Paul could be flouting the quality maxim. A number of commentators draw attention to the fact that Gal 1:8a is structured as a third-class conditional statement, beginning with an intensive καί followed by ἐάν. According to Longenecker, "Here the subjunctive mood is used because Paul is making a statement that is somewhat doubtful, though theoretically possible, about the preaching of heresy by either himself or a heavenly being."[35] To Lightfoot the clause represents a "highly improbable supposition."[36] Martyn says it represents a "distant and theoretical" consideration.[37] It marks, in Burton's view, "the extreme nature of the supposition."[38] And De Boer puts it even more strongly: "Paul regards it as impossible that either 'we' . . . or 'an angel from heaven,' . . . would now be preaching a gospel 'different' from the one 'we' did in fact preach in Galatia. The concessive clause posits an entirely theoretical possibility for the sake of argument."[39]

Let us consider both subject phrases—"we" and "an angel from heaven" in turn (they are both linked to εὐαγγελίζηται, even though "angel" governs the person and number of the verb). Regarding the first subject, "we" could be an editorial "we" meaning "I, Paul," or it could designate Paul and his coworkers, such as Timothy and Silas.[40] Thus, Paul is either speaking of his own preaching or his own plus that of his missionary team. Is it a reasonable possibility to raise that Paul or his coworkers might deviate from their gospel message? Hardly. If there is one thing that can be said about Paul, it is that he was stubbornly persistent in his message, even in the face of life-threatening hardships.

What about an ἄγγελος ἐξ οὐρανοῦ? It is irrelevant for our purposes whether Paul's opposition had cited angelic revelation for their message.[41] Nor do we need, in order to understand this phrase, to explore the apocalyptic literature and its treatment of angels.[42] The angels in view are simply

---

35. Longenecker, *Galatians*, 16.
36. Lightfoot, *Galatians*, 77.
37. Martyn, *Galatians*, 113.
38. Burton, *Galatians*, 25.
39. De Boer, *Galatians*, 47.
40. Moo, *Galatians*, 80; Martyn, *Galatians*, 113; and De Boer, *Galatians*, 47, argue for an editorial "we." Dunn, *Galatians*, 44; Lightfoot, *Galatians*, 77; and Fung, *Galatians*, 47, view ἡμεῖς as referring to Paul's missionary team.
41. Martyn, *Galatians*, 113, "Apparently, the Teachers are telling the Galatians that their gospel is uttered to the whole of the world by an angel who speaks through them."
42. Betz, *Galatians*, 53, and Dunn, *Galatians*, 45, cite the apocalyptic references as

God's messengers.⁴³ They are "from heaven," so they carry a presumption of telling the truth.⁴⁴ Thus, it is even less believable that angels would pervert the true gospel: "It is for Paul simply impossible for an angel from heaven even to proclaim the 'different gospel' of the other missionaries."⁴⁵ We have here a clear flout of the quality maxim.

Literary Aspects

Moving to the literary aspects of Gal 1:8a, we find that Paul uses extreme language. While the curse is not a subject of this case study, it is worth noting that in the context of the mention of angels preaching there is a double anathema. The Greek word ἀνάθεμα, which translates חרם in the OT, is a strong term rarely used elsewhere by Paul (Rom 9:3; 1 Cor 12:3; 16:22).⁴⁶ It is akin to saying "May the divine curse rest on him."⁴⁷ Paul, in effect, is wishing the complete alienation from God of anyone who might preach a different gospel message.

There is amplification as well. Paul uses assonance—ἄγγελος . . . εὐαγγελίζηται . . . εὐηγγελισάμεθα—to heighten the drama of the sentence. He uses amplification via accumulation by moving from "we" (a credible witness to the gospel) to "an angel from heaven" (an *extremely* credible witness). Thurén calls this an "escalating structure" in the service of "rhetorical effectiveness."⁴⁸

Rhetorical Aspects

The exigence that drives the rhetorical situation in Galatians is nothing less than the nature of the gospel: "It is the message, not the messenger, that

---

pertinent. Moo, *Galatians*, 81, believes that such comments are unnecessary to Paul's reference.

43. In keeping with NT usage: "ἄγγελος," *NIDNTTE* 1:122.

44. Thurén, *Derhetorizing Paul*, 47, believes that Paul is using "angel from heaven" as a circumvention for God's name. He notes that in Gal 4:14, "God's angel" is parallel to "Christ Jesus." Thus, "Paul is so certain about his Gospel, that not even God Himself can change it."

45. De Boer, *Galatians*, 48.

46. Burton, *Galatians*, 25, calls this "strong language"; Thurén, *Derhetorizing Paul*, 61, labels it "a strong, extreme expression."

47. Bruce, *Galatians*, 83.

48. Thurén, *Derhetorizing Paul*, 47.

ultimately matters."[49] That message was under threat from opponents who were seeking to introduce circumcision and other Jewish observances into the Gentile congregation. Galatians 1:8, then, functions in a clearly rhetorical capacity: Paul is attempting to persuade the Galatians not to listen to anyone who would change the gospel message that Paul (and his fellow missionaries) had delivered to them.

In addition to a clear rhetorical situation, there is strong pathos in Gal 1:8: "Here Paul is breathing fire. His zeal is so fervent that he almost begins to curse the angels themselves."[50] As Nanos puts it, "[Paul] is not engaged in a level-handed descriptive task, but with the expression of parental-style disappointment and instruction.... He goes so far as to wish upon those influencing them a curse (1:8–9).... This is no exercise in systematic theology or generalized info to attach to his other more contingent letters. The Galatian discourse is hot."[51]

There is also shock value in Paul's words. Who would ever picture Paul or an angel preaching a perversion of the gospel, much less coming under divine judgment?

And, finally, invective is in play as well. Galatians, as will be discussed in chapter 9, is heavy with invective throughout: "Almost every device presented in du Toit's article on vilification can be found in Galatians."[52] Here in 1:8 there is a threat with eschatological judgment (once again, though the curse is not a focus of the case study, it is relevant to the context surrounding the mention of the preaching of the angels).

Conclusion

The reference to the preaching of angels in Gal 1:8a, then, is best viewed as an instance of hyperbole.[53] According to the Hyperbole Scorecard (Figure 8.5), it manifests a flouting of the quality maxim, extreme language, amplification, a rhetorical situation, pathos, shock, and invective. The summary "grade" for this passage is an A (high likelihood of hyperbole).

---

49. Bruce, *Galatians*, 83.
50. Luther et al., *LW*, 26:55.
51. Nanos, *Irony of Galatians*, 27.
52. Thurén, *Derhetorizing Paul*, 66.
53. Moo, *Galatians*, 80, agrees, as does Porter, *Apostle Paul*, 202.

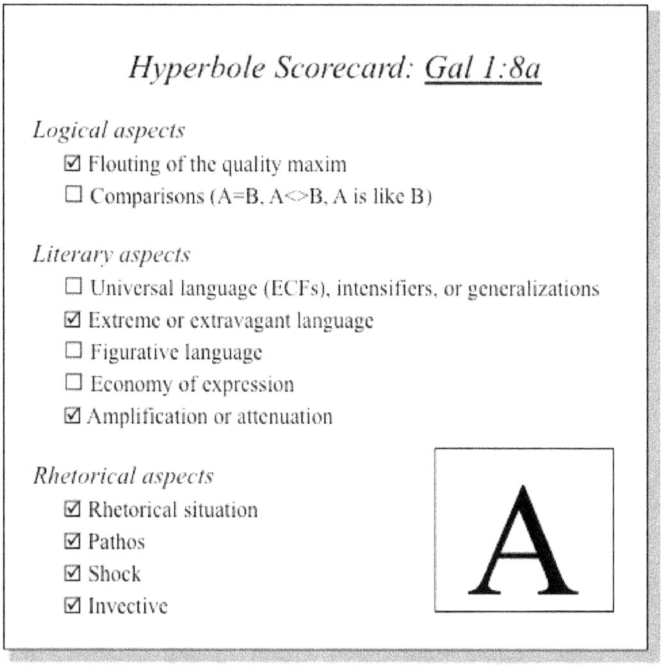

> *Hyperbole Scorecard:* <u>*Gal 1:8a*</u>
>
> *Logical aspects*
> - ☑ Flouting of the quality maxim
> - ☐ Comparisons (A=B, A<>B, A is like B)
>
> *Literary aspects*
> - ☐ Universal language (ECFs), intensifiers, or generalizations
> - ☑ Extreme or extravagant language
> - ☐ Figurative language
> - ☐ Economy of expression
> - ☑ Amplification or attenuation
>
> *Rhetorical aspects*
> - ☑ Rhetorical situation
> - ☑ Pathos
> - ☑ Shock
> - ☑ Invective

Figure 8.5. Hyperbole Scorecard for Gal 1:8a.

When we mitigate the hyperbole of Gal 1:8a (Figure 8.6) and take a fresh look at the meaning of the clause, Paul is not taking seriously the possibility that he, his team, or an angel from heaven would ever pervert the gospel. The non-hyperbolic meaning may be arrived at by placing the terms for messengers from 1:7–9 along a vertical scalar axis and moving one notch away from the extreme. In this case we land on the generic τις from 1:9, which, due to the parallelism between 1:8 and 1:9, reasonably appears to be Paul's non-hyperbolic focus. Galatians 1:8a, then, is meant rhetorically to underline the importance of the gospel message and to disassociate the Galatian believers from "anyone" who would dare to introduce new aspects.

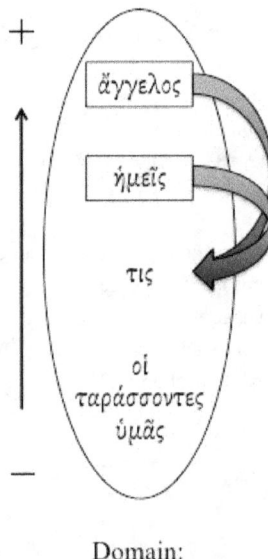

Domain:
Trustworthiness

Figure 8.6. Levels of Trustworthiness. An angel (ἄγγελος) from heaven is the most trustworthy, followed by Paul and his companions (ἡμεῖς). The "ones troubling you" (οἱ ταράσσοντες ὑμᾶς of 1:7) are the least trustworthy. The generic "anyone" (τις) from 1:9 is the non-hyperbolic focus of the saying.

CONCLUSION

In this chapter, I have threshed the NT to expose the grains of hyperbole. I am quite sure I have missed many, however, and have mistakenly included some "chaff." Such an undertaking is necessarily subjective to a certain degree. However, I have also applied the methodology developed in chapter 6 to three NT passages, one non-Pauline and two Pauline. In the next few chapters I will apply this hyperbole detection mechanism to Galatians.

PART IV

Hyperbole in Galatians

9

Paul's Vilification of His Opponents

In this chapter...

Question(s) to be answered:
- How did Paul use hyperbole when describing his opponents?

Trajectory:
- Chapters 10 and 11 will continue our focus on Galatians, examining hyperbole in Paul's attitude toward the law and the consequences of not following his recommendations.

IN THIS CHAPTER I will put the methodology developed in chapter 6 to work in examining passages in Galatians which pertain to Paul's opponents. The issue of the opposition to Paul can be approached from a couple of different angles. On the one hand, this study could identify hyperbole as a purely descriptive task—"Here is hyperbole in passages x and y and z. This proves that Paul used hyperbole." On the other hand, hyperbole could be looked at in terms of the larger interpretive problems surrounding Galatians—"Here is hyperbole in passages x and y and z. Now, how does our view of Paul's opponents change as a result?"

I plan to proceed along the latter of the two routes; therefore, it would be helpful to lay out a consensus view about Paul's opponents so that we might have a baseline against which to measure results. Unfortunately, no such consensus view exists in the literature. In fact, the identification of Paul's opponents in Galatians is a highly contentious issue. The past two centuries have not seen anything near a consensus regarding the identity of Paul's opponents (or, for that matter, on what to call them: opponents, agitators, teachers, influencers, etc.).[1] Numerous questions remain:

- Are the opponents sanctioned by the Jerusalem leadership (Baur) or not (Lightfoot; Schoeps; Munck)?[2]
- Do the opponents, in their own view, actually oppose Paul (most interpreters) or not (Howard; Munck; Jewett)?[3]
- Do the opponents represent two fronts—a legalistic and a libertine (Lütgert; Ropes)—or one (most interpreters)?[4]
- Are the opponents Jewish (Nanos), Jewish-Christian (Baur; Jewett; Howard), or Gentile (Munck, Ropes)? Are they gnostic (Schmithals)? Syncretistic (Crownfield)?[5]
- Are the opponents indigenous to the Galatian congregations or synagogues (Nanos), or are they from elsewhere (e.g., Jerusalem; most interpreters)?
- Are the opponents mostly Torah-observant (most interpreters) or lax (Crownfield; Schmithals)?

Coming to conclusions regarding Paul's opponents is also difficult because in Galatians it is not just that we are reading someone else's mail, but that we are attempting to glean information indirectly about a third party,

---

1. For treatments of the history of interpretation of the Galatian opponents, see Sumney, "Studying Paul's Opponents," 7–58; Ellis, "Paul and His Opponents," 264–98; Longenecker, *Galatians*, lxxxix–xcvi; Howard, *Paul*, 1–19.

2. As discussed in chapter 3, Baur (*Paul the Apostle*; "Die Christuspartei") purports that there were two competing factions, a Petrine and a Pauline, the former of which controlled the Jerusalem leadership. Lightfoot, *Galatians*, however, holds that Paul remained in good relations with James, Peter, and John (see especially his article "St. Paul and the Three," 292–374, of his commentary). Schoeps, *Paul*, 66, casts Peter and James as part of a moderate group at the Jerusalem conference. According to Munck, *Paul and the Salvation of Mankind*, the so-called opponents were really a group of Gentile believers who had read the OT and concluded that they needed to be circumcised.

3. Howard, *Paul*, believes that the "judaizers" misunderstood Paul's gospel message to be one of adherence to circumcision and the law. In the opinion of Jewett, "Agitators and the Galatian Congregation," 206, a group of nomistic Christians from Judea attempted to offer "completion" to Paul's work by introducing circumcision and calendrical observance in hopes of avoiding zealot reprisals.

4. Lütgert, *Gesetz und Geist*; Ropes, *Singular Problem*.

5. Nanos, *Irony of Galatians*; Schmithals, "Heretics in Galatia," 13–64; Crownfield, "Singular Problem of the Dual Galatians," 491–500.

one mentioned in only a handful of statements. The pitfalls of such mirror reading are numerous, as John Barclay discusses in a 1987 article.[6]

Most germane to our purposes are Barclay's comments concerning Galatians as a polemical letter. The polemical nature, according to Barclay, distorts the picture Paul paints of his opponents: "Paul is likely to caricature his opponents, especially in describing their motivation: were they really compelling the Galatians to be circumcised? And was it really only in order to avoid persecution for the cross of Christ (6.12)?"[7] Such distorting effects, Barclay says, means that the reader of Galatians should not take Paul's descriptions of his opponents too seriously. Instead, the reader should recognize that there may be extensive areas of agreement between Paul and the opponents which are "submerged by the polarizing effect of his polemic."[8] Likewise, the disagreements themselves may be exaggerated.

Others have echoed Barclay's sentiments. Michael Cosby describes Paul as an "erupting volcano" when he dictated Galatians, in which case:

> We should not expect a polished, logical explanation of theological concepts from a man in this frame of mind. We should expect to see fiery hyperbole directed against his opponents and their beliefs.... When [people] go looking for theological precision, however, most either miss or dilute the significance of Paul's use of hyperbole. In so doing they not only misread Paul's theology but also err in their reconstructions of the identity of his opponents.[9]

Lauri Thurén also believes that the polemics of Galatians should be taken as hyperbolic: "Classical forms of vilification are found throughout the letter.... In fact, the technique was so well known to both partners in communication, that no one took them at their face value."[10] Thurén is skeptical of obtaining historical data from the vilifying labels: "We can conclude that these stereotypical devices do not provide us with much reliable historical information about the antagonists."[11] Andre du Toit sees the situation similarly with regard to vilificatory writings such as Galatians:

---

6. Barclay, "Mirror-Reading," 79–81, lists the pitfalls as undue selectivity (in selecting passages), overinterpretation, mishandling polemics, and latching onto particular words or phrases.
7. Barclay, "Mirror-Reading," 75.
8. Barclay, "Mirror-Reading," 78.
9. Cosby, "Galatians," 296.
10. Thurén, "Was Paul Angry?," 312.
11. Thurén, "Was Paul Angry?," 314.

> From a methodological perspective it would certainly be naïve to accept a one to one relationship between the depiction of the encoded adversaries in our documents and their real-life counterparts. An element of distortion must certainly be accepted. Ideological literature works with contrasts; it does not seek the neutral middle-field. It creates heroes and villains.[12]

As du Toit explains, vilificatory utterances were part of the communication game played between speaker and addressees. The addressees knew how to recognize them and to interpret them as hyperbolic. "Everyone knew that these utterances were basically intended to convey the thrust of the author's negative feeling and convictions regarding his adversaries, and to induce his addressees to share them."[13] Like Thurén, du Toit pleads for caution in approaching vilificatory texts: "To use these texts naïvely on the informational level is to abuse them."[14]

The arguments of these scholars help to lay bare the rationale for this chapter—to achieve a clearer picture of Paul's opponents by disentangling the hyperbolic content embedded in the descriptions of them, thus removing the distorting effects. The following passages typically cited in connection with Paul's opponents will be taken into account in this chapter:

- 1:6–7   The opponents preach a false gospel
- 1:8b–9   Let the opponents be cursed
- 2:4   The opponents in the fourteen-year visit are false brothers
- 4:17   The opponents want to alienate the Galatians from Paul
- 5:12   Let the opponents emasculate themselves
- 6:12b   The opponents compel circumcision only to avoid persecution
- 6:13a   The opponents do not obey Torah

Each of these passages will be examined according to the criteria from the Hyperbole Scorecard (see chapter 6), with logical aspects, literary aspects, and rhetorical aspects of hyperbole being sought. If hyperbole is deemed to be present, the resulting impact on our interpretation will be discussed. The chapter will conclude with a reimagined description of Paul's opponents.

---

12. Du Toit, "Vilification," 411.
13. Du Toit, "Vilification," 411.
14. Du Toit, "Vilification," 412.

THE OPPONENTS PREACH A FALSE GOSPEL (1:6–7)

For this passage I will attempt to demonstrate that, whereas most commentators take it at face value that Paul is accusing the opponents of preaching a false gospel—a perversion of the gospel of Christ—there are good reasons to moderate our interpretation of Paul's words. The opponents' gospel may not have been true or beneficial in every respect, but to categorize it as *false* would be misleading.

Logical Aspects

Recall that one of the ways to demonstrate a flouting of the quality maxim is to show that a statement conflicts with the teachings of the speaker elsewhere. In this case Paul's assertion that the opponents are preaching another gospel (ἕτερον εὐαγγέλιον) which is not really another (ὃ οὐκ ἔστιν ἄλλο) needs to be unpacked and challenged in light of his statement in 2:7. To begin the unpacking, ἕτερος and ἄλλος should be treated as semantically equivalent; Paul likely uses them interchangeably for stylistic variation.[15] In the middle of his sentence, then, Paul is simply correcting himself in the heat of the moment: "you are turning to a different gospel—not that there exists a different gospel." In other words, the gospel which the opponents preach cannot even be called a gospel.[16]

But what shall we say about 2:7, where, at the outcome of the meeting in Jerusalem, it is agreed that Paul was entrusted with the τὸ εὐαγγέλιον τῆς ἀκροβυστίας while Peter was entrusted with the gospel τῆς περιτομῆς? Are these not two separate forms of the gospel? Many are hesitant to go that far.[17] For them, there is one and only one gospel; the genitive here is one of

---

15. With BDF §306; Tichy, "'Gospel' in Gal 1:6–7 Revisited," 362–63; Moo, *Galatians*, 78; Bruce, *Galatians*, 81; Lightfoot, *Galatians*, 76; Martyn, *Galatians*, 110; Fung, *Galatians*, 45. Others, such as Longenecker, *Galatians*, 15, De Boer, *Galatians*, 41, and Burton, *Galatians*, 422, prefer to uphold the classical distinction between ἕτερος (another of a different kind) and ἄλλος (another of the same kind).

16. Much has been written on the term τὸ εὐαγγέλιον. Its background is likely in Isa 40–66 and the imperial cult (so Bruce, *Galatians*, 81). Paul's usage of it to describe the opponents' message indicates that the opponents themselves used this term (so Dunn, *Galatians*, 41; Martyn, *Galatians*, 109). As Burton, *Galatians*, 422, suggests, εὐαγγέλιον "is more frequently used in a doctrinal sense, signifying the great body of teaching concerning salvation which constituted the apostle's message."

17. Fung, *Galatians*, 99, "Every indication is given in the context that the gospel preached by Paul (and Barnabas) was in all essentials the same as that which Peter, James, and John understood the gospel to be"; Longenecker, *Galatians*, 55, "The point here is not with regard to content but audience and type of outreach"; see also Lightfoot, *Galatians*, 109; Martyn, *Galatians*, 202.

sphere. Others, however, are more qualified in their approach to this issue.[18] But whether it rises to the status of a central issue—and thus a material difference—*the role of circumcision and Torah observance was clearly a distinguishing feature between the two gospel presentations*:

> The decisive difference in their content certainly lay in the way circumcision was evaluated in terms of salvation history and the extent of Torah observance to be inferred from this. Circumcision was by no means to be considered an adiaphoron (matter of indifference), for it was the entrance gate to the whole law. It documents Israel's special status among the nations, was a guarantee of this identity, and at the same time separated Israel from all other peoples. For strict Jewish Christians, there was a natural connection between faith in the Messiah Jesus of Nazareth, circumcision as a mark of belonging to God's chosen people, and, of course, observance of the Torah. For them, baptism did not take the place of circumcision, and salvation did not occur as something that transcended the law.[19]

So in Paul's mind there were two contextualized gospel presentations: one to the Gentiles and one to the Jews. Both emphasized God's grace, the lordship and resurrection of Jesus, the forgiveness of sins, repentance, and baptism.[20] The latter, however, also included circumcision and Torah observance. (We have no record of Jews of that time being taught to forsake circumcision or Torah when coming to believe in Christ. On the contrary, that is exactly what Paul was charged with teaching in Acts 21:21.)

---

18. De Boer, *Galatians*, 119, "There is but *one* gospel in view, even if this gospel can receive different formulations in different contexts"; Moo, *Galatians*, 134, "Proclaiming the same gospel to different audiences means inevitably that different emphases will rise to the surface"; Dunn, *Galatians*, 106, "[I]t was one and the same gospel . . . but as preached in the different contexts of the mission among Gentiles and that among Jews, its emphases were bound to differ"; and Burton, *Galatians*, 91, "That Paul regarded the distinction . . . as fundamentally not one of content but of the persons to whom it was addressed is plain. . . . At the same time it is evident that Paul, contending for the right to preach this one gospel to the Gentiles without demanding that they should accept circumcision, and so to make it in content also a gospel of uncircumcision, expected that Peter also would preach it to the circumcised Jews without demanding that they should abandon circumcision. Thus even in content there was an important and far-reaching difference between the gospel that Paul preached and that which Peter preached."

19. Schnelle, *Apostle Paul*, 127; others who hold to essential differences between the two gospels are Elmer, *Paul, Jerusalem and the Judaisers*, 99; and Becker, *Paul*, 90–92.

20. One need look no further than Peter's early sermons in Acts 2 and 3 for corroboration that the gospel to the circumcision included these elements.

How different was the opponents' preaching, then, from that of the gospel to the circumcision? From the text of Galatians it can be shown that the opponents were preaching the necessity of circumcision (6:12) and observance of holy days (4:10), perhaps as a way of perfecting or completing what the Galatians had heard to that point (Gal 3:3; ἐπιτελέω).[21] What about Christ? Paul never charges them with not preaching Christ. Nor does he himself write an apologetic for the death and resurrection to reorient the Galatians to basic truths about Christ. In fact, in everything he writes he assumes that the Galatians continue to love and want to serve Christ. The problem, ostensibly, is that the Galatians desire Christ *and* circumcision (5:2).

In the end, then, we are left to draw the following conclusion: *Paul is discontented, not because the gospel of the opponents is false, but because it has been falsely applied to Gentiles.* The same arguments as presented at the Jerusalem Conference undoubtedly apply in Paul's thinking: the ingathering of the Gentiles has arrived, and they have received the Holy Spirit, demonstrating that God has accepted them without being circumcised. Why should they receive the yoke of the Torah around their necks?

Paul is intentionally flouting the maxim of quality, then, in acting as if his (the gospel for the uncircumcised) is the only valid version of the gospel. To say that anything else is not a gospel or is a perversion of the gospel of Christ is hyperbole.

Literary Aspects

There are also several literary indications that Paul is speaking hyperbolically in Gal 1:6–7. Perhaps the key indication is Paul's use of the word θαυμάζω. Its use in this passage has been written about extensively. Suffice it to say that it seems to be a customary expression of perplexity in the opening of an ancient letter.[22] At issue is whether Paul's perplexity here is real or feigned (i.e., he is speaking ironically). Many believe that "Paul is genuinely surprised and chagrined."[23] J. H. Roberts, for instance, examined instances

---

21. Betz, *Galatians*, 7, "Except for the demand of obedience to the Torah and acceptance of circumcision, their 'gospel' must have been the same as Paul's. Otherwise it would be difficult to understand why Paul is so eager to demonstrate that they are so radically different from him."

22. See White, "Introductory Formulae," 91–97.

23. Moo, *Galatians*, 76; Dunn, *Galatians*, 39.

of θαυμάζω in papyri letters and concluded that in only a small percentage was it used ironically.[24]

On the opposite side is Terence Mullins, who observes that when an ancient writer uses θαυμάζω, "The whole point is that the writer is rebuking, even scolding, the addressee. And he is not using θαυμάζω in its common meaning; he is using it ironically, often sarcastically. He is not really astonished; he is irritated. This ironical use is an essential element in the form."[25] Betz concurs that θαυμάζω in Gal 1:6 implies "ironic astonishment" and is used rhetorically as "a device of indignant rebuttal and attack of things the opposition party has done and is about to do."[26] Nanos is perhaps the most ardent supporter of the view that in Gal 1:6 θαυμάζω expresses ironic rebuke.[27] He cites two factors in support: (a) Paul had already warned the Galatians (1:9) of such behavior, so they were not ignorant (and thus they were deserving of rebuke); and (b) the expression occurs within the context of a rebuke. The way Nanos sees it, Paul was speaking paternally, leveraging the highly potent weapon of shame, but doing so indirectly as to soften the blow. Paul's words, then, should not be taken literally:

> Although the parent (i.e., any authority figure) may appear to declare ignorance at the literal level, seemingly expressing a lack of knowledge or lack of appropriate anticipation in the declaration, for example, "I am surprised that you . . .," the recipient knows if it is a feigned (Socratic) expression of irony or at least should know. Indeed, the writer may have feared this development, instructed against it, provided personal examples that might help dissuade the recipient from it, all the while praying that the recipient would not succumb. And the recipient knows this only too well. That is how the ironic edge cuts its victim.[28]

---

24. Roberts, "ΘΑΥΜΑΖΩ," 109–22; Roberts, "Paul's Expression of Perplexity," 329–38, here 334, "It should be very clear that Paul is in no way feigning perplexity. He truly cannot understand their conduct." However, Roberts also admits that Gal 1:6 carries "implicatures of dissatisfaction, disappointment, reproach, rebuke, and emotional response" (335). Cf. Longenecker, *Galatians*, 14, who classifies θαυμάζω ὅτι as an "astonishment-rebuke" formula but concludes that "the note of astonishment in his rebuke seems more prominent than the note of irony." De Boer, *Galatians*, 39, agrees that "the verb functions to introduce a rebuke" but "an element of genuine astonishment on Paul's part is probably not to be excluded here."

25. Mullins, "Formulas in the New Testament Epistles," 385.

26. Betz, *Galatians*, 47; so also Martin, "Syntax of Surprise," 82.

27. Nanos, *Irony of Galatians*, 32–61.

28. Nanos, *Irony of Galatians*, 45.

In agreement with Mullins, Betz, and Nanos, then, we have figurative language (irony) as a literary aspect in support of hyperbole in Gal 1:6-7.

A second literary aspect occurs immediately after θαυμάζω ὅτι in the form of two contiguous adverbs, οὕτως ταχέως, which are generally translated as "so quickly." The first adverb, οὕτως, functions as an intensifier (BDAG calls it a "marker of a relatively high degree"). Rather than denoting a short period of time from the Galatians' evangelization to their apparent apostasy, the phrase is probably rhetorical, used to magnify the sense of Paul's disappointment.[29]

A third literary aspect in Gal 1:6-7 is extreme language, characterized by the phrase μετατίθεσθε ἀπὸ τοῦ καλέσαντος ὑμᾶς ἐν χάριτι Χριστοῦ.[30] The term μετατίθημι denotes having "a change of mind in one's allegiance" (BDAG). Several modern translations read "deserting" (ESV, NRSV, NAS, NIV). In 2 Macc 7:24 it is used to signify the possibility of a Jew turning ἀπὸ τῶν πατρίων. The Galatians are pictured, in this case, as turning from the τοῦ καλέσαντος, which no doubt refers to God (cf. Gal 1:15; 5:8; 1 Thess 2:12; 5:24; Rom 9:11).[31] Whether or not their actions warrant a charge of apostasy, the Galatians likely had no idea they were engaged in such a process, nor were they inclined toward doing so. They accepted the opponents' message because they wanted to insure that they were indeed children of Abraham (the nuances of which Paul will argue in Gal 3). Moreover, Paul writes as if he is confident of their remaining allegiance toward God. He argues from Scripture because he knows that the Galatians have come to value the Scriptures. He threatens them with alienation from Christ because he trusts that they will fear such consequences. In short, the language of apostasy here is harsh and extreme whether or not it is warranted.[32]

Rhetorical Aspects

There is no need to look far for a rhetorical situation in these verses. Paul himself supplies the rationale: the Galatians are apostatizing from God under the influence of τινές [who] εἰσιν οἱ ταράσσοντες ὑμᾶς καὶ θέλοντες

---

29. With Betz, *Galatians*, 47. Cf. Longenecker, *Galatians*, 14, who suggests that Paul may be echoing Exod 32:8 LXX and Judg 2:17 LXX, both of which use the word ταχύς in discussing Israel's apostasy, but such allusions would have likely been expecting too much knowledge on the part of the addressees.

30. Χριστοῦ has weak textual support.

31. Martyn, *Galatians*, 108.

32. Cosby, "Galatians," 304, labels this passage "an exaggerated assessment of the Galatians' apostasy from God."

μεταστρέψαι τὸ εὐαγγέλιον τοῦ Χριστοῦ. The entire letter is Paul's attempt to dissuade them against this step, and 1:6-7 constitutes his opening remarks.

The pathos of Paul's words is inescapable, as the discussion of θαυμάζω has already shown. Paul is angry, disgusted, and disappointed. He has omitted his customary thanksgiving section in favor of an ironic rebuke. He is prone to use extreme language, charging the Galatians with nothing less than desertion from the living God.

But Paul's anger is also directed at the troublemakers who have tempted the Galatian believers along this destructive path. He refers to them as τινές, an indication of his disdain and an attempt to minimize them in the eyes of the Galatians.[33] Their activity is characterized not as διδάσκοντες but rather ταράσσοντες (BDAG: to cause inward turmoil, stir up, disturb, unsettle, throw into confusion; cf. Acts 15:24). He cites their motives: they want (θέλοντες) to pervert the gospel of Christ, an insightful comment coming from someone who seems not to have known (or to have remembered) their names. The invective in this passage is palpable.

Conclusion

Figure 9.1 summarizes the findings for Gal 1:6-7. Paul flouts the quality maxim by momentarily portraying the gospel to the uncircumcised as the *only* valid gospel. In fact, the Galatians are being drawn to another valid expression of the gospel—one that includes circumcision and observance of Torah—but which is reserved for Jews. Included in the literary aspects are intensifiers, extreme language, and figurative language (in this case, irony). There is a clear rhetorical situation, and Paul uses modes of persuasion that express pathos and invective. There is a high likelihood, then, of hyperbole in Paul's contention that the gospel of the opponents is false and that, in fact, the opponents' gospel message was valid but simply misapplied in some of its aspects to Gentiles.

---

33. De Boer, *Galatians*, 42; Martyn, *Galatians*, 110, "If he knows the Teachers' names, he avoids mentioning them in order to indicate disdain. When we come to his account of the meeting in Jerusalem, we will note similarly that he does not mention the names of any of the 'False Brethren' (2:4), while readily naming James, Cephas, and John (2:9)"; Du Toit, "Vilification," 406, "The indefinite pronoun may carry a derisive connotation, especially discernible in spoken language by a certain tone of voice. In this case the identity of the referents is intentionally suppressed and the pronoun is used pejoratively.... It may be a *deliberate belittling* of the number of people comprising the opposition.... But it may also be aimed at a *deliberate blurring* of the faces of opponents in order to portray them as negative, shadowy characters" (emphasis original).

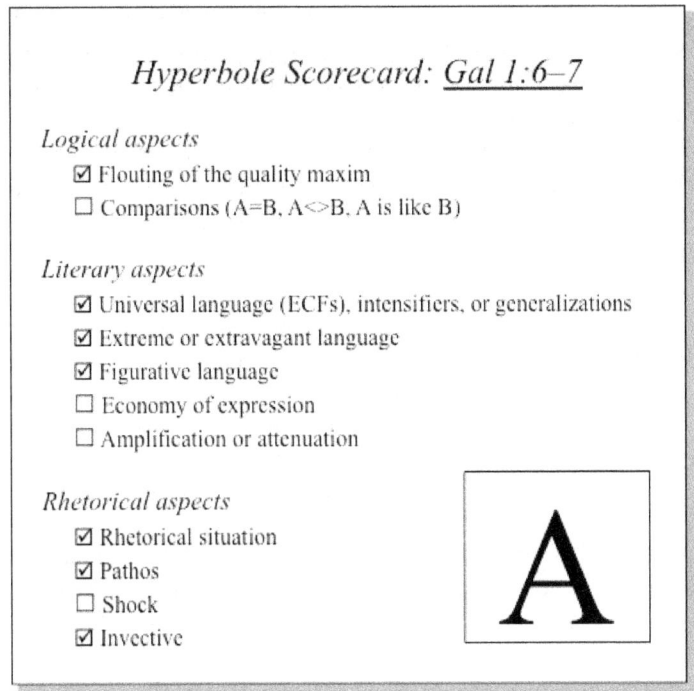

Figure 9.1. Hyperbole Scorecard for Gal 1:6-7.

What do we learn additionally about the opponents once this hyperbole is mitigated? The opponents "may not be so terrible as [Paul's] words indicate."[34] Likewise, as Betz concludes, "There is no real reason to believe that these anti-Paulinists were morally dishonest or theologically deficient. Their message must have made good sense to the Galatians and to others, and they must have been quite serious about the salvation of the Galatians."[35]

LET THE OPPONENTS BE CURSED (1:8B-9)

In this section I will deal with the double-anathema of 1:8-9 and attempt to discern whether, as Paul pronounces a curse on his opponents, he is speaking hyperbolically. Is it the case that he does not really wish eternal condemnation upon them, but rather strongly expresses his anger and dismay at their misguided enterprise among the Galatians?

---

34. Cosby, "Galatians," 304.
35. Betz, *Galatians*, 7.

The passage is structured around two conditional clauses. One, a concessive (third-class) conditional clause using ἐάν expresses the hypothetical condition that Paul (and his coworkers) or an angel might preach a gospel other than the one that Paul had already preached. Paul's wish is expressed in a third person singular imperative: ἀνάθεμα ἔστω. The other clause is a first-class condition (assumed true for argument's sake) which "invites the Galatians into active engagement with what Paul writes."[36] It too ends with the phrase ἀνάθεμα ἔστω.

Since the protasis of 1:8 was already studied in chapter 6, I will focus on the imperatival phrases here. Most commentators agree that with ἀνάθεμα Paul is calling down the eschatological wrath of God upon his opponents.[37] He is not simply relegating them to church discipline or excommunication.

Logical Aspects

It is questionable whether Paul is flouting the quality maxim in issuing the double anathema. Granted, in pronouncing ἀνάθεμα upon his opponents, Paul may be contradicting his own teaching (Rom 12:14; 1 Cor 4:12b) that one should bless one's enemies rather than curse them.[38] But one could also muster a few arguments *against* the proposition that Paul is speaking hyperbolically. First, he employs the third person singular ("let *him* be accursed"). This is less direct and intense than cursing someone in the second person singular or plural. Second, and in that same vein, he includes himself and the angels of heaven, which "demonstrates that his rebuke is rooted not in selfish ambition but in concern for the Galatians."[39] Third, Paul seems to be referring to a general rule of thumb that he has given in the past (v. 9, "as we have said before, so now I say again..").[40] As Betz observes, "[W]hat

---

36. Armitage, "Conditional Clause Exegesis," 392; cf. Wallace, *Greek Grammar*, 692; BDF §372.

37. Betz, *Galatians*, 53, "The Greek term ἀνάθεμα (in classical Greek ἀνάθηα, in Hebrew חרם) signifies something which has been withdrawn from profane use and consecrated to the deity, either as a votive offering or for its destruction. Paul means it in the latter sense of the term"; cf. Martyn, *Galatians*, 114; Moo, *Galatians*, 80; Longenecker, *Galatians*, 17; Dunn, *Galatians*, 46; Lightfoot, *Galatians*, 77; Fung, *Galatians*, 47; Bruce, *Galatians*, 83; BDAG 63; *NIDNTTE* 1:281–84.

38. Schlueter, *Filling Up the Measure*, 127, considers the double anathema of Galatians to be hyperbolic because it appears "to go beyond the ideal that Paul set for himself."

39. Armitage, "Exploration of Conditional Clause Exegesis," 392.

40. Bruce, *Galatians*, 84, takes this to be a reference back to verse 8, against the majority of commentators, who envision a prior occasion of speaking or writing (e.g., Burton, *Galatians*, 29; Longenecker, *Galatians*, 17)

appears now as a double curse is really the reissuing of a previous curse." We do not, however, know the context of his former utterance and whether it might have been hyperbolic as well.

Literary Aspects

There are a variety of literary aspects present in this passage. First, Paul speaks in generalized terms in verse 9: "if *anyone* (τις) preaches to you a gospel contrary to the one you received. . ." This is an extremely wide net (so to speak) which would ensnare a plethora of preachers who disagreed with Paul on some point or other. Second, the pronouncement of ἀνάθεμα constitutes extreme language—Paul is consigning individuals to an eternity in hell. Third, figurative language is present, as we have already noted in chapter 6, since the mention of angels from heaven preaching a false gospel is hyperbole. And fourth, amplification is present as well. Paul structures his statement in the form of two conditional statements in which he repeats the anathema word for word. The statements build upon one another—moving from Paul and his contemporaries as the subject, to the angels, and finally to anyone (the opponents included). The double anathema is a fitting example of what Quintilian calls "reiterating that which cannot be surpassed"; recall his example: "You beat your mother. What more can I say? You beat your mother."[41] Now compare Paul's version: "Let him be accursed. As we have said before, I say again: Let him be accursed."

Rhetorical Aspects

All four rhetorical aspects are present. The rhetorical situation is that Paul is attempting to persuade his addressees not to listen to the opponents. At the same time, he is likely speaking to the opponents as well, knowing that they will hear of his message (therefore he gives prominence to the anathema by repeating it in no uncertain terms).[42]

There is obvious pathos as well. The discourse is "hot" with emotion.[43] As Dunn puts it, "The depth of Paul's feeling, already evident in his talk of 'deserting' God and 'perverting the gospel,' now comes to full expression."[44]

---

41. Quintilian, *Inst.*, 8.4.7.
42. De Boer, *Galatians*, 46, "Paul appears to be speaking over the heads of the Galatians to the new preachers."
43. Nanos, *Irony of Galatians*, 27.
44. Dunn, *Galatians*, 44.

As for shock, it may be that, in some ways, Paul's cursing shocks the modern reader more than the ancient one: "The fierceness of Paul's language strikes a discord with modern sensibilities; though it is somewhat rhetorical (and therefore hyperbolic) in character, the polemic of those days was much more robust than we would think fitting."[45] But given the rhetorical aims of Paul here, it is reasonable to assume that he chose the words for their shock value. The ancient Galatians would have taken the notion of curse quite seriously.

The invective qualities of Paul's language here are fairly obvious. Paul's suggestion that his opponents fall under the judgment of God is a stock feature of Hellenistic invective, as suggested by du Toit.[46]

Conclusion

The qualities of hyperbole are easily recognized in this passage.[47] However, as discussed above, it may not necessarily be a violation of the quality maxim for Paul simply to wish that those who pervert the gospel would be consigned to a position outside the covenant community. Given the number of literary and rhetorical features (Figure 9.2) present in the double anathema of Gal 1:8–9, however, there is a moderate likelihood that Paul is speaking hyperbolically. The mitigated sense of the passage is that Paul wishes that the opponents would fail in their objective of reaching the Galatians with their version of the gospel.

---

45. Dunn, *Galatians*, 46.
46. Du Toit, "Vilification," 410.
47. Thurén, "Was Paul Angry?," 71, "The confrontation is depicted by the use of hyperbole, at its best or worst."

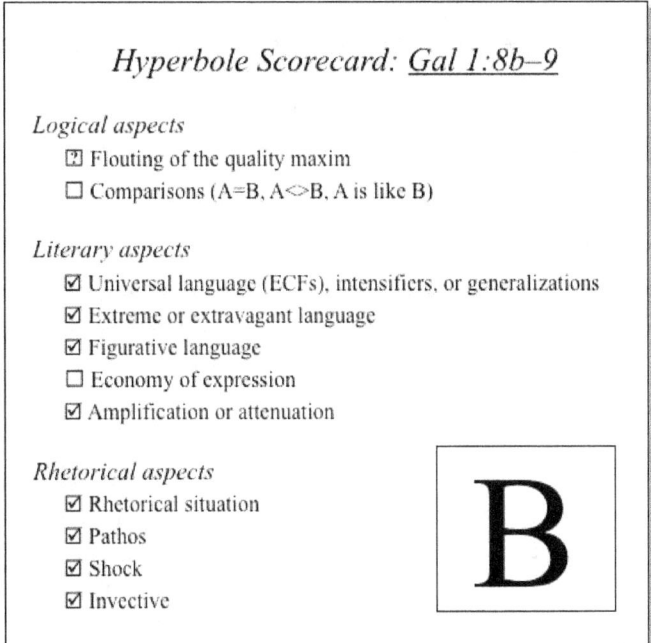

Figure 9.2. Hyperbole Scorecard for Gal 1:8b–9.

THE OPPONENTS IN THE FOURTEEN-YEAR VISIT ARE FALSE BROTHERS (2:4)

The "opponents" in view in this section are not necessarily the same ones who had been troubling the Galatians (1:7). Paul mentions this group in his account of the meeting with the Jerusalem pillars (2:1–10), commonly referred to as the "fourteen-year visit." Their precise relationship with the troublers in Galatia is unknown. Perhaps the most one can say is that "their aims and actions were the same."[48] For both groups, circumcision and the observance of Torah for Gentiles was a central concern. The groups thus seemed to have shared a "theological kinship.... We cannot be sure that the False Brothers functioned as sponsors of the Teachers, but some relationship between the two groups seems highly probable."[49]

---

48. Longenecker, *Galatians*, 51.

49. Martyn, *Galatians*, 218. It is also possible that the false brothers of 2:4 are the same as, or similar to, the visitors from Jerusalem to Antioch mentioned in Acts 15:1.

In any event, Paul levels a harsh charge against this group of opponents: they are "false brothers" (ψευδαδέλφοι). By most accounts this term means that they portrayed themselves as believers in Christ but were not actually so.[50] Paul is therefore declaring them to be excluded from membership in the church.

Does that charge, however, pass the truth test? I argue that it does not. Rather, the so-called ψευδαδέλφοι were probably Jewish believers in Christ who simply held to the essentiality of circumcision and Torah observance for all believers. For Paul to disqualify their faith in Christ simply for misapplying this theological and practical principle to Gentiles is either grossly unfair or, as is more likely the case, hyperbole.

Logical Aspects

How is Paul flouting the quality maxim? My reasoning has two principal lines. First, I will endeavor to show that other mature Christians held these opponents to be brothers in the faith. Second, I will point out that their nomism does not necessarily equate to legalism.

To the first point, it is evident that the opponents of 2:4 had a relatively positive relationship with the Jerusalem apostles. As Carol Schlueter observes:

> They were present in Jerusalem and had access to a meeting of the highest ranking officials. There is no evidence that the "pillars" threw these "deceitful ones" out of the meeting. Further, it is noteworthy that the meeting was with "those who were of repute, the pillars" (Gal. 2.2, 6, 9). It was not a public meeting of Christians which false Christians might infiltrate. Thus, the "false brethren" were known to the "pillars." That Paul made accusations against them for opposing his own view that Gentiles need not be circumcised is no proof that he did not consider them to be Christians.[51]

---

50. BDAG 1097: "one who pretends to be a fellow-believer, but whose claim is belied by conduct toward fellow-believers." Also see Burton, *Galatians*, 78; Dunn, *Galatians*, 97; Lightfoot, *Galatians*, 106; Moo, *Galatians*, 127; Fung, *Galatians*, 93; De Boer, *Galatians*, 112; Ridderbos, *Epistle of Paul*, 84, "In designating those persons the false brethren, Paul challenges their right to belong to the church." Could they be Jewish "brothers"? Betz, *Galatians*, 90n302, points out that Paul refers to non-Christian Jews as "brothers according to the flesh" (Rom 9:3). However, Nanos, "Intruding 'Spies,'" *passim*, argues that they were not Christians.

51. Schlueter, *Filling Up the Measure*, 144; cf. Longenecker, *Galatians*, 51, "They may have been regarded by the apostles ... as legitimate members of the Jerusalem congregation"; Burton, *Galatians*, 78, regarding the label of ψευδαδέλφοι, "That they

Schlueter concludes that the charge of being ψευδαδέλφοι is polemical hyperbole because "the persons accused seem to hold similar views to some of the Jerusalem apostles and are therefore Christian."[52] A further piece of evidence of their close, positive relationship with the pillars was that they attempted to compel the circumcision of Titus. Could they have done so without the acquiescence of the Jerusalem apostles, at least at the beginning? Gerd Luedemann thinks not:

> We must assume that the "false brethren" had considerable support within the Jerusalem congregation for their demand that Titus be circumcised and at the beginning probably had the "pillars" on their side. "How could they, in Jerusalem, under the very eyes of the most respected apostles, have possibly thought that they could compel the circumcision of Titus, unless the original apostles and the Jerusalem church already supported this view?" At least a majority of the congregation must have supported the "false brethren," for otherwise they could never have made the demand for circumcision so effectively.[53]

If Luedemann is correct, then we should have to lump some of the Jerusalem apostles, at least at one time, in with the false brothers.

Regarding the second point, it does not necessarily follow that if Paul's opponents believed in circumcision of Gentile converts that they therefore believed in salvation by works outside of the grace of God in Christ.[54] This conclusion may be a uniquely Lutheran importation to the traditional interpretation of Galatians. The New Perspective on Paul, though, the precursors of which may be found in George Foot Moore's *Judaism* and E. P. Sanders' *Paul and Palestinian Judaism*, has done much to dispel the notion that Second Temple Judaism was legalistic.[55] Instead, it appears that in much of Judaism acts of obedience such as circumcision and Torah observance were done in the spirit of "staying in" rather than "getting in" the covenant.[56]

---

were so looked upon by the other apostles at the time of the events here referred to does not necessarily follow."

52. Schlueter, *Filling Up the Measure*, 146.

53. Luedemann, *Opposition to Paul*, 36.

54. Nor does the fact that Paul chooses to frame the debate in terms of works versus faith necessarily imply that the opponents were preaching legalism. We must view Paul's discussion through the lens of his rhetorical genius. More will be said on this in the next chapter.

55. Moore, *Judaism*; Sanders, *Paul and Palestinian Judaism*.

56. Although, in fairness to the traditional perspective, the brothers who came from Jerusalem to Antioch in Acts 15:1 appeared to be teaching circumcision as a condition for salvation. Jews held a range of views on proselyte circumcision; see the discussion

Literary Aspects

Notwithstanding the awkward syntax (anacoluthon) in Gal 2:4, the verse shows signs of careful literary construction. Paul here builds a military metaphor, a picture of undercover spies who smuggled themselves into a camp to spy it out. It is primarily based upon four terms (definitions are from BDAG):

- παρείσακτος—pertaining to coming into a group in a surreptitious manner, secretly brought in, smuggled in, sneaked in[57]
- ψευδάδελφος—one who pretends to be a fellow-believer[58]
- παρεισέρχομαι—to come in beside, slip in[59]
- κατασκοπέω—spy out, lie in wait for[60]

Paul's use of ψευδάδελφος serves the purpose of maintaining the figurative construction and emphasizing the aspect of deceit. It may be, therefore, primarily functioning as a literary-rhetorical device.

The steady drumbeat of inflammatory terms in this verse also contributes to the likelihood that Paul is speaking hyperbolically. Here we have an instance of amplification (in this case, building words upon words). "Paul piles up words to characterise the false brothers in as negative a light as possible."[61] "The piling up of such [military] language . . . indicates Paul's total lack of sympathy towards this group . . . it is the language of polemic, which should not be regarded as an objective account."[62]

Rhetorical Aspects

Due to the awkward syntax, it is unclear to what exactly διὰ δὲ τοὺς παρεισάκτους ψευδαδέλφους refers. Paul is likely continuing his thought from verse 3 (NIV adds "This matter arose"), in which case the rhetorical

---

in Keener, *Acts*, 2212–22. Moreover, although covenantal nomism may have been characteristic of much of Judaism, there were certainly legalistic strains to be found; see Carson, O'Brien, and Seifrid, *Justification and Variegated Nomism*.

57. Cf. the use of the verbal cognate in 2 Pet 2:1.

58. Cf. 2 Cor 11:26.

59. Cf. Rom 5:19, "the 'law intruded,' i.e. came on to the main highway of salvation-history by a side road" (Bruce, *Galatians*, 112).

60. Cf. 2 Sam 10:3; 1 Chr 19:3.

61. Moo, *Galatians*, 129.

62. Dunn, *Galatians*, 99.

Paul's Vilification of His Opponents

situation in Gal 2:4 is that Paul is attempting to bolster his standing in the eyes of the Galatians by showing how he stood up to the false brothers (and the Jerusalem apostles) in the matter of the circumcision of Titus. This is all, of course, in the context of dissuading them from acceding to circumcision themselves.

The pathos of the verse is evident; as Burton suggests, "some allowance must necessarily be made for the heat of controversy" in coming to conclusions about these men from the statements of Paul.[63] In addition to the military figure, Paul brings in the twin ideas of slavery and freedom, which would have been felt viscerally by first century citizens of the Roman empire.[64] "The false brothers," he writes, "snuck in to spy out our freedom we have in Christ so that they might make us slaves."[65]

Paul's use of invective here has been noted by others. Dunn refers to 2:4 as "polemical exaggeration" by the "master of political propaganda."[66] Du Toit cites the verse as an example of vilification using the *topos* of "obscure, shadowy characters."[67] And Thurén refers to the military terms as "standard labels" and "stereotypical devices" used "to dramatize the situation and to alienate the antagonists from the addressees."[68]

Conclusion

As Figure 9.3 shows, the number of logical, literary, and rhetorical aspects combined in Gal 2:4 yield a moderate likelihood that Paul is speaking hyperbolically when he refers to his opponents as ψευδαδέλφοι. The strongest evidence, notwithstanding the over-the-top military language, is the fact that the opponents were evidently in good graces with the Jerusalem church and therefore not perceived in any way as ψευδαδέλφοι. However, there is

---

63. Burton, *Galatians*, 84.

64. Dunn, *Galatians*, 100, "For a Greek readership this was a most emotive chord to strike, since the distinction between slave and free was fundamental in Greek thought and the idealization of freedom was axiomatic in Hellenistic self-perception."

65. Interestingly, Martyn, *Galatians*, 219, speculates that Paul may have been turning the teaching of the opponents on its head: "It is likely that the Teachers offered the Galatians impressive discourses on the matter of slavery and freedom. In 5:16 we find a strong indication that they informed the Galatians both of the Impulsive Desire of the Flesh and of the Law as its antidote. Thus emphasizing that Gentile life is the perfect showplace of the effects of enslavement to the Impulsive Desire of the Flesh, the Teachers also proclaimed a message of freedom: In his Law God has provided liberation from that enslaving monster."

66. Dunn, *Galatians*, 97.

67. Du Toit, "Vilification," 406.

68. Thurén, "Was Paul Angry?," 67.

also a (in my view, small) chance that these individuals propagated a legalistic view of the same sort for which Jesus condemned the Pharisees and that Paul really did consider them outside the bounds of Christian faith.

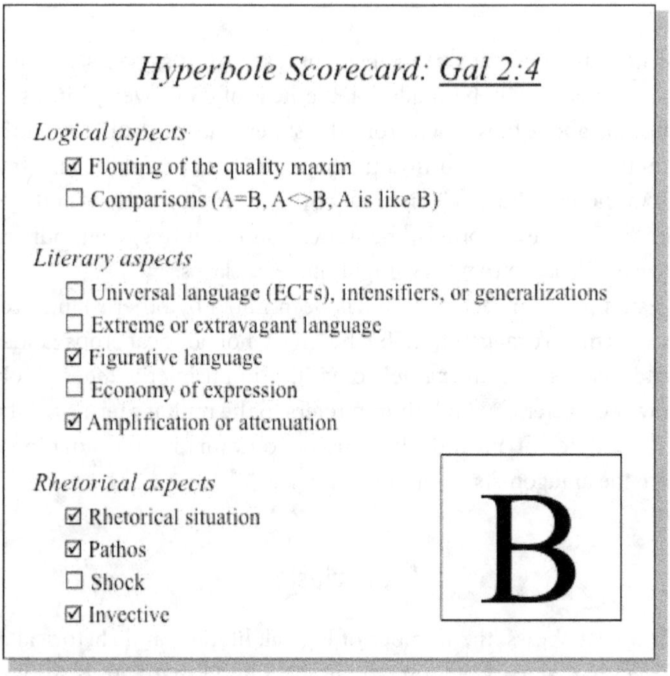

Hyperbole Scorecard: *Gal 2:4*

Logical aspects
- ☑ Flouting of the quality maxim
- ☐ Comparisons (A=B, A<>B, A is like B)

Literary aspects
- ☐ Universal language (ECFs), intensifiers, or generalizations
- ☐ Extreme or extravagant language
- ☑ Figurative language
- ☐ Economy of expression
- ☑ Amplification or attenuation

Rhetorical aspects
- ☑ Rhetorical situation
- ☑ Pathos
- ☐ Shock
- ☑ Invective

B

Figure 9.3. Hyperbole Scorecard for Gal 2:4.

Let us consider what a mitigated (non-hyperbolic) view of the opponents of 2:4 would look like. In their own eyes, at least, "they were orthodox and conscientious Jewish Christians, who were concerned both for the purity of the Christian message amongst Gentiles and for the welfare of Jewish believers amidst the rising tide of Jewish nationalism."[69] Might this have been how Paul perceived them as well, but for the heat of anger and the rhetorical need to be consummately persuasive in this situation? These individuals were likely brothers indeed, just brothers "gone wrong on some point."[70]

---

69. Longenecker, *Galatians*, 51, concerning the self-perception of the false brothers.
70. Schlueter, *Filling Up the Measure*, 144.

THE OPPONENTS WANT TO ALIENATE THE GALATIANS FROM PAUL (4:17)

In this section I will apply the criteria for hyperbole to Gal 4:17. This brief passage is puzzling for a couple of reasons. For one, Paul appears to abruptly turn from his personal aside to the Galatians to a comment about the motive of the opponents, whom he does not mention by name or even pronoun (although the context and the third person plural forms of the verbs indicate that he has them in view).[71] The more important puzzle in this verse is what Paul is referring to with ἐκκλεῖσαι ὑμᾶς θέλουσιν. Against what entity do the opponents wish to shut out the Galatians, Paul (and company) or the kingdom of Christ?

In favor of the former option is the personal nature of the larger passage. It speaks of close friendship between Paul and the Galatians. Paul does not want anything or anybody to come in the way of that. Second, the verb ζηλόω (BDAG: with a personal object, to court someone's favor) has a strong interpersonal connotation in this context: "[T]he purpose clause that depends on this statement, ἵνα αὐτοὺς ζηλοῦτε, suggests . . . that the issue is more focused on gaining disciples: the agitators want to exclude the Galatians from the orbit of Paul's ministry and gospel so that the Galatians might 'have zeal for,' attach themselves to, the agitators."[72] Third, the logic of the passage does not work as well if the kingdom of Christ is in view. Why would the opponents wish to shut the Galatians *out of* the kingdom? Perhaps they are pictured as some sort of gatekeepers of the kingdom (like the Pharisees in Matt 23:13), with the power to apply entrance criteria (presumably, circumcision and some level of Torah obedience). But their wish would then be to *admit* the Galatians into the kingdom, not to shut them out (unless Paul is speaking ironically or unless he means that the *net result* of the opponents' missionary work is to shut the Galatians out of the kingdom). The former interpretation is to be preferred, therefore, and Longenecker offers a logically sustainable reading in that vein: "[Those people] earnestly court you, but for no good. What they desire is to exclude you [from us], so that you would earnestly court them."[73]

---

71. Moo, *Galatians*, 287, "A neat logical sequence is difficult to find."

72. Moo, *Galatians*, 287.

73. Longenecker, *Galatians*, 193, brackets are his. This interpretation is also favored by BDAG 303; Moo, *Galatians*, 287; Betz, *Galatians*, 230; Ridderbos, *Epistle of Paul*, 168; Fung, *Galatians*, 200; and Bruce, *Galatians*, 211. Interpreters who view ἐκκλείω as pertaining to fellowship with Christ include De Boer, *Galatians*, 283; Burton, *Galatians*, 246; Lightfoot, *Galatians*, 177; and Martyn, *Galatians*, 422-23.

The question next becomes, "Is Paul exaggerating?" Are the opponents really attempting to steal away the loyalties and affections of the Galatian believers? Let us apply the criteria for hyperbole.

Logical Aspects

In searching for obvious signs that Paul is flouting the quality maxim, there are no contradictions to be found between Gal 4:17 and his own statements elsewhere. What we do have is a simple declaration concerning the motives of his opponents. But the telling thing is that this declaration comes from Paul's own lips. How does Paul know what someone else's motives are? Who/what are his sources? We have no information indicating that Paul knew these people personally or that he had conversations with them. It appears, then, that Paul is engaged in mindreading of sorts, which is just what one would expect from invective, which as the reader will recall, tends toward exaggeration.

Literary Aspects

Paul uses a couple of literary devices which may signal that he is speaking figuratively. First, he uses word repetition, with the verb ζηλόω occurring three times (taking vv. 17 and 18 together as a sentence). Second, the arrangement of terms in v. 17 suggests a chiasm (see below, with the relevant parts translated):

- A   ζηλοῦσιν ὑμᾶς οὐ καλῶς   They are zealous for you . . .
- B   ἀλλ' ἐκκλεῖσαι ὑμᾶς θέλουσιν . . .
- A' ἵνα αὐτοὺς ζηλοῦτε   That for them you may be zealous

Rhetorical Aspects

The rhetorical situation is relatively apparent. In a passage of direct personal appeal, Paul intrudes upon his topic to warn the Galatians against the influence of the opponents. The Galatians' relationship with Paul is at stake. There is evident pathos here as well. As Longenecker observes, "4:12–20 is a passionate and emotionally charged section."[74]

---

74. Longenecker, *Galatians*, 188.

The strongest aspect pointing to hyperbole, as noted above, is invective. How much stock should we take in the words of a man with a clear rhetorical agenda, one who may have never met the people whose motives he maligns, and one who lived in a time and culture where making exaggerations of one's opponents was common? Betz finds here nothing more than "rhetorical topoi and devices to discredit his opponents emotionally rather than 'theologically.'"[75] Paul "portrays them as nothing but shallow, hollow, and grabby 'flatterers.' This caricature, of course, should not be taken uncritically as reality itself; it means next to nothing in regard to the question as to who the opponents really were and what they really had in mind."[76]

Conclusion

As can be seen from Figure 9.4, Gal 4:17 is "somewhat likely" for hyperbole. Besides a hint of figurative language, the verse manifests pathos and invective. Such indications invite the reader to presume that Paul is temporarily laying aside truthfulness (i.e., flouting the quality maxim) in order to comment on a matter (the opponents' motives) about which he cannot have possibly known for certain. However, even without knowing for sure, it may have been reasonable for Paul to assume that the opponents wanted not just the temporary obedience of the Galatians but desired to be their permanent teachers, in essence diverting their allegiance from Paul.

---

75. Betz, *Galatians*, 231.
76. Betz, *Galatians*, 230.

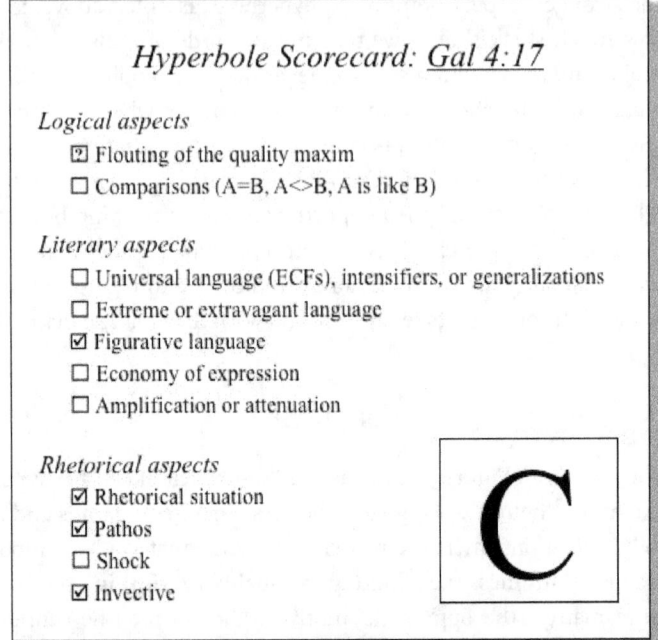

Figure 9.4. Hyperbole Scorecard for Gal 4:17.

LET THE OPPONENTS EMASCULATE THEMSELVES (5:12)

The next passage under study is composed of a mere six words in the Greek, yet these words appear to contain such irreverent and disdainful force (it has been called "the crudest and rudest of all Paul's extant statements") that some theologians have rushed to Paul's side in an attempt to exonerate him from his seemingly unchristian attitude:

> I doubt whether ... [Paul] would have yielded so completely to pure ill-temper as to say what this favored interpretation attributes to him. It is true that the ancient peoples, and many of the modern peoples in the same regions, resort to foul language when they express anger.... There would be nothing suitable, nothing characteristic, nothing that adds to the force of the passage, in the act which, on the ordinary interpretation, Paul desires that this grave Jew of high standing should perform on himself. It was expressly forbidden by the law of Moses. The

scornful expression would be a pure insult, as irrational as it is disgusting.⁷⁷

Ramsay, quoted here, prefers the reading of the AV ("I would they were even cut off which trouble you"), which takes Paul's words figuratively. Most commentators since Chrysostom, however, are persuaded that Paul speaks of emasculation because of (a) the context (circumcision is the issue) and (b) the well-known use of the term ἀποκόπτω for such action (BDAG notes that "private parts" is implied by the absolute usage).⁷⁸ What we are left with, then, is a picture of the Apostle Paul not just violating, but going far beyond his own principles—unless, of course, he is speaking hyperbolically.

Logical Aspects

Paul signals that he is speaking hyperbolically by flouting the quality maxim, in this case appearing to contradict his expressed ethical principles of love toward enemies (see the section above on Gal 1:7-8) and refraining from crude joking (Eph 5:4). Paul does not seem to hedge his statement in any obvious way; the use of ὄφελον with ἀποκόψονται in the future indicative expresses an attainable wish.⁷⁹ He gives every appearance, at least, that he would like the emasculation of the opponents to happen.

Literary Aspects

There are other clues for hyperbole here. Paul uses extreme language with the ascensive καί followed by ἀποκόπτω.⁸⁰ The topic itself is extreme. (The Galatians might have been familiar with the idea of castration, however, as one of the chief towns in North Galatia, Pessinus, was home to a temple to the goddess Cybele, whose priests would castrate themselves.)⁸¹

Paul also uses figurative language. His use of ὄφελον, for instance, could signal the use of irony (saying something he does not mean), as it

---

77. The first (shorter) quote is from Longenecker, *Galatians*, 234. The second (longer) is from Ramsay, *Historical Commentary on Galations*, 163.

78. Among modern interpreters who hold that Paul is referring to emasculation are Lightfoot, *Galatians*, 207; Martyn, *Galatians*, 478; Bruce, *Galatians*, 238; Betz, *Galatians*, 270; Moo, *Galatians*, 338; Longenecker, *Galatians*, 234; Burton, *Galatians*, 288; Dunn, *Galatians*, 283; Ridderbos, *Epistle of Paul*, 195; Fung, *Galatians*, 242.

79. BDF §359.1, §384.

80. The καί "obviously points to a climax as compared with what has gone before" (*TDNT* 3:854).

81. This observation is more significant if the North Galatian theory is true.

does in the two other places where it occurs (1 Cor 4:8; 2 Cor 11:1). It is worth noting, however, that Paul is *not* using sarcasm, despite this being a favorite term among commentators describing this verse.[82] Sarcasm pretends to be serious while intending to cause pain to the addressee;[83] that is, it uses neutral or pleasant sounding words to make a harsh statement (Paul, for instance, might have sarcastically said, "I wish nothing but the best for those troublemakers"). In Gal 5:12, however, there is nothing neutral or pleasant about Paul's words. He is employing hyperbole—possibly also irony—but not sarcasm.

Rhetorical Aspects

The rhetorical situation is that Paul is attempting to dissuade the Galatians from fellowship with his opponents. He wishes that "the knife might slip in the hand of those who count circumcision indispensable to participation in the assembly of the Lord, so that they might find the same rules excluding themselves."[84]

There is undeniable pathos and shock in Gal 5:12. Commentators are unanimous in noting the disgust, disparagement, and fierceness in Paul's otherwise simple sentence. Dunn is typical: "There is something shocking about the vehemence of Paul's language and of the wish itself."[85]

It is a relatively straightforward decision, then, to classify Paul's statement as invective. His crude remark directed towards οἱ ἀναστατοῦντες (Betz: rabble-rousers; cf. Acts 17:6; 21:38), is nothing more than an attempt to caricature and discredit them in the eyes of the Galatians. Paul obviously does not believe his wish will come to fruition.

Conclusion

As can be seen in Figure 9.5, the evidence for hyperbole is quite strong, given the extremes of speech Paul reaches in Gal 5:12. Paul's flouting of the quality maxim (contradiction of his own teachings and those of the NT) is

---

82. Paul's words have been characterized as a "sarcastic blast" (Moo, *Galatians*, 337), a "sarcastic and indeed 'bloody' joke" (Betz, *Galatians*, 270), a "touch of sarcasm" (Fung, *Galatians*, 241), and a "final sarcastic and dismissive snort" (Dunn, *Galatians*, 282); also see Longenecker, *Galatians*, 234.

83. Clark, *Using Language*, 373–74.

84. Dunn, *Galatians*, 283.

85. Dunn, *Galatians*, 283. Cf. *TDNT* 3:855, "Paul's cry is one of biting scorn and is obviously not meant to be taken literally."

unmistakable. Attempts to rehabilitate Paul from sounding crude and boorish in Gal 5:12 have either taken ἀποκόπτω figuratively or sarcastically. Neither one is appropriate, for the reasons given above. Paul is speaking in hyperbole. He does not *really* wish for the opponents to emasculate themselves, but something short of that goal—for their influence with the Galatians to be severed.

> *Hyperbole Scorecard: Gal 5:12*
>
> *Logical aspects*
> ☑ Flouting of the quality maxim
> ☐ Comparisons (A=B, A<>B, A is like B)
>
> *Literary aspects*
> ☐ Universal language (ECFs), intensifiers, or generalizations
> ☑ Extreme or extravagant language
> ☑ Figurative language
> ☐ Economy of expression
> ☐ Amplification or attenuation
>
> *Rhetorical aspects*
> ☑ Rhetorical situation
> ☑ Pathos
> ☑ Shock
> ☑ Invective
>
> **A**

Figure 9.5. Hyperbole Scorecard for Gal 5:12.

THE OPPONENTS COMPEL CIRCUMCISION ONLY TO AVOID PERSECUTION (6:12B)

In Gal 6:12b Paul accuses the opponents of trying to compel (conative present tense, ἀναγκάζουσιν) the circumcision of the Galatians *only that they might not be persecuted for the cross of Christ*. The latter clause begins with μόνον (only), which will be significant in our analysis, followed by τῷ σταυρῷ, a dative of cause which, by metonymy, likely refers to the entire doctrine of salvation through by faith in Christ (i.e., the gospel to the uncircumcised). It appears, then, that although the opponents themselves preached Christ, they combined it with circumcision so that they would not be persecuted, perhaps by zealot-minded Jews in Jerusalem who tolerated messianism as long as it did not undermine Torah:

> Paul does not mean that these Jewish-Christian missionaries were persecuted (by other Jews) simply because they preached a crucified Jesus as Messiah; that message was clearly at the heart of the gospel for the Christian Jews in Palestine also, and they remained relatively undisturbed. Nor can we infer that the "different gospel" of i.6 denied the cross in any direct or overt manner. Paul must mean rather that the policy of insisting on circumcision was a way of removing that which in the common preaching of a crucified Messiah constituted an offence to most other Jews (v. 11). And that must refer to the claim of Paul (and others) that the cross was a sufficient basis for acceptance into the inheritance of Israel—that is, the cross alone.[86]

But was avoidance of persecution the *only* reason for the opponents' preaching? In this section I will argue "no," that Paul is speaking hyperbolically.

Logical Aspects

Paul offers, not just one, but three motives for the opponents in 6:12–13:

- They wish to make a good showing in the flesh (6:12a)
- They wish to boast in the Galatians' flesh (6:13b)
- They wish to avoid persecution for the cross of Christ (6:12b)

To say that avoidance of persecution is the *only* (μόνος) motivation, then, appears to be flouting the maxim of quality. This is recognized as such by

---

86. Dunn, *Galatians*, 337; Moo, *Galatians*, 394, "It was not, then, simply for proclaiming the cross of Christ that persecution might come; it was for preaching the cross of Christ *as Paul understood it*, as the sole basis for acceptance with God, that would have sparked the resistance" (emphasis mine). Moo, Longenecker, *Galatians*, and Bruce, *Galatians*, 269, adopt the viewpoint of Jewett, "Agitators and the Galatian Congregation," who hypothesizes (205) that "Jewish Christians in Judea were stimulated by Zealotic pressure into a nomistic campaign among their fellow Christians in the late forties and early fifties. Their goal was to avert the suspicion that they were in communion with lawless Gentiles. It appears that the Judean Christians convinced themselves that circumcision of Gentile Christians would thwart Zealot reprisals." In line with these commentators, Barclay, "Mirror-Reading," 80, warns against misconstruing Paul's polemic to the point of believing that the opponents played down the message of the cross: "They may have been entirely happy to talk about the cross, even emphasize its saving significance, only failing, *in Paul's view*, to see its message as excluding obedience to the law" (emphasis original).

commentators. As Fung writes, "In view of the other two motives, the expression 'their sole object' or 'the only reason' (NIV) clearly cannot be taken literally."[87] Dunn and de Boer both refer to μόνον as polemical exaggeration.[88]

Even without appealing to the other two motives above, it is reasonable to assume that the opponents had more than one motive for acting the way they did. Let us take for granted that they wanted to avoid persecution. Why not simply cease and desist all evangelistic operations? They must have had other motives (some positive) in carrying out their activities. Perhaps, as I have suggested earlier, they were sincere believers in Christ who wanted to make him known among the nations.

Literary Aspects

The term μόνος plays the role of an intensifier. Recall from chapter 4 that intensifiers frequently signal hyperbolic constructions.

The only other literary aspect to this brief passage is the metonymy ἵνα τῷ σταυρῷ τοῦ Χριστοῦ. This phrase functions for economy of expression.

Rhetorical Aspects

The rhetorical situation in this passage is that, once again, Paul is dissuading the Galatians from contact with the opponents. His tactic here is to impugn their motives.

The pathos of the passage is evident in the content of Paul's obviously angry complaint. It is enhanced by the use of pronoun οὗτοι, which is in the emphatic position and "indicates Paul's anger at their motivation" that he expresses in the previous clause.[89]

Also evident in this passage is the use of invective. Du Toit categorizes 6:12 under the vilification *topos* of moral depravity.[90] Paul here "follows a practice common in debates of every age. He claims to be able to enter the Teachers' minds, characterizing . . . what he takes to be their reprehensible motives."[91] The fact that it is unverifiable makes such mindreading so effective as invective: Who knows whether the opponents really are or are not

---

87. Fung, *Galatians*, 305.
88. Dunn, *Galatians*, 336; De Boer, *Galatians*, 398.
89. De Boer, *Galatians*, 396.
90. Du Toit, "Vilification," 408.
91. Martyn, *Galatians*, 560–61.

motivated purely by selfish concerns?[92] There is a mixture here of "objective facts and subjective judgments," and who can separate them?[93] The ring of plausibility gives Paul's invective its effective inroad as rhetoric.

Conclusion

Figure 9.6 shows the results of the analysis of Gal 6:12b. It is highly likely that Paul is using hyperbole in characterizing the motives of the opponents as *only* being oriented toward avoiding persecution. A mitigated (non-hyperbolic) impression of the opponents would be that, although avoidance of persecution may have been *one particular* motive, the opponents were likely sincere in their Jewish Christian faith, and from such faith sprang their fervor for outreach.

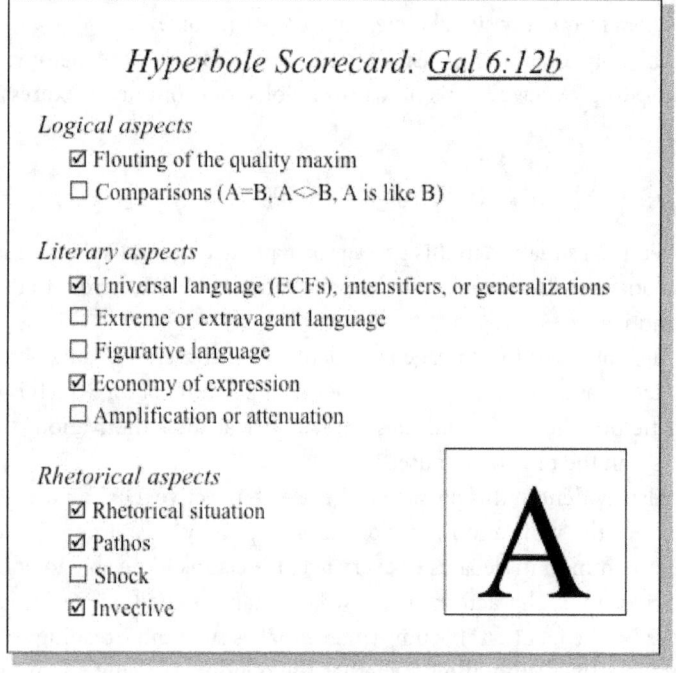

Figure 9.6. Hyperbole Scorecard for Gal 6:12b.

---

92. De Boer, *Galatians*, 397, "These accusations are not subject to proof, either by the Galatians who will receive this letter or by interpreters today."

93. Betz, *Galatians*, 314.

THE OPPONENTS DO NOT OBEY TORAH (6:13A)

Another harsh word of accusation follows in 6:13a: οὐδὲ γὰρ οἱ περιτεμνόμενοι αὐτοὶ νόμον φυλάσσουσιν. The majority of modern commentators take the present participle to have some sort of middle sense, referring, therefore, to Paul's opponents ("those who belong to the circumcision" or "those who cause circumcision").[94] This interpretation is confirmed by the context, as verse 13 most naturally continues the thought of verse 12 in which the opponents are being discussed.

But why would Jewish Christian missionaries not keep the law themselves? A definitive answer to this question has eluded investigators. Walter Schmithals leveraged doubts about this verse into a theory that the opponents were gnostics.[95] However, even if we accept that the subject of Paul's statement is, indeed, his Jewish Christian opponents, we are left with no evidence of their disobedience of which to speak within the letter. Perhaps the missionaries could not fulfill all of their ritual obligations (e.g., sacrificing of the paschal lamb) outside of Jerusalem. Or maybe Paul merely speaks in generalities here, as he does in Rom 2, regarding Jews who have the law but do not uphold it. Or, in keeping with the most popular theory of commentators, it is possible that Paul was aware of specific ways in which the opponents did not rigorously keep the law.[96] A final option also needs to be considered: Paul is using hyperbole.

---

94. A few take it to be a passive, i.e., "those who are being circumcised," in which case Gentiles may be in view (Burton, *Galatians*, 353; Munck, *Paul and the Salvation*, 87–90).

95. Schmithals, "Heretics in Galatia," 33–34, "These false teachers can hardly have been Judaizers." But others think that Schmithals has made too much of this verse: Fung, *Galatians*, 302, "But Schmithals has surely over-capitalized on this text. The expression 'do not keep' is in fact ill-fitted to indicate 'a renunciation of the law in principle'; the sense of categorical denial would have been much better conveyed by some other word"; Barclay, "Mirror-Reading," 76, "I am pretty sure that Schmithals has been far too gullible in taking at face value Paul's accusation in 6.13 that the opponents (or those who get circumcised) do not themselves keep the law."

96. Ridderbos, *Epistle of Paul*, 223, Paul is referring to the "hypocrisy and practical expediencies to which precisely these foremost proponents of the law sometimes took recourse"; Longenecker, *Galatians*, 292, "Despite the loftiness of their assertions and their rigid theology, the Judaizers, at least in Paul's eyes, fell short of keeping all the law scrupulously themselves"; cf. Dunn, *Galatians*, 338; Lightfoot, *Galatians*, 222; Fung, *Galatians*, 302; Howard, *Paul*, 15.

Logical Aspects

As with our other analyses, the first thing to be decided is whether Paul has flouted the quality maxim. Often that takes the form of Paul appearing to contradict his own teachings or some other part of the NT. Here, however, we have no other statements from Paul that might indicate that he is contradicting anything in accusing the opponents of not keeping the law. The problem is, of course, that we have no evidence *in favor of* Paul's accusation either. This leaves us with the possibility that he is simply using invective.

We do know that accusing one's opponent of immorality was a stock topic in ancient invective (see, again, du Toit).[97] Such an accusation did not necessarily have to be true in order to be persuasive. That is not to say, of course, that Paul is engaged in deception. As with hyperbole, a flout of the quality maxim involves a game of communication—including a signal to the addressee that one is speaking in a non-literal fashion. As long as the addressee is accustomed to the rules of communication—and it is reasonable to assume that the Galatians knew the "game" of ancient invective—then the message is accurately received and transposed to the intended meaning: in the case of the opponents, "These people are unhelpful for you. Stay away from them. Reject their message."

Literary Aspects

Paul speaks in *generalized* terms regarding the opponents. He does not cite particular instances of their disobedience, only that they do not "keep the law." "To 'keep [*phylassō*] the law' (cf. Rom 2:26; Acts 7:53; 21:24) is merely another way of saying to 'observe [*poieō*] the law' (5:3). Both expressions are traditional."[98] Thus, Paul is speaking in vague generalities concerning their Torah observance, which may be suggestive for hyperbole.

Rhetorical Aspects

The rhetorical situation is the same as in the last section: Paul is casting aspersions on his opponents to win the Galatians' allegiance away from them and back to himself. While the pathos inherent in the particular phrase under study may not be particularly strong, it is felt through the larger context of 6:12–13 amid the repetition of accusations.

---

97. Du Toit, "Vilification," 408.
98. De Boer, *Galatians*, 399.

Paul's Vilification of His Opponents

The most obvious rhetorical aspect is Paul's use of invective. As mentioned above, 6:13a plainly involves a stock vilification technique.

Conclusion

Given that Paul's charge against the opponents is a general one couched in a context that suggests he is speaking in anger, Gal 6:13a is "somewhat" suggestive for hyperbole (Figure 9.7). The fact that Paul's vague charge is unprovable, however, cuts both ways. Paul may have had evidence that he chose not bring to light. Or, he may not have had evidence and was purely using invective:

> This accusation is beyond proof, for we do not know what would constitute evidence for such a charge. That is, we do not know on what grounds, if any, the Galatians will be able to say, "That's right—they don't," when they hear the letter. . . . The charge may be true in one way or another. But we cannot know that it was.[99]

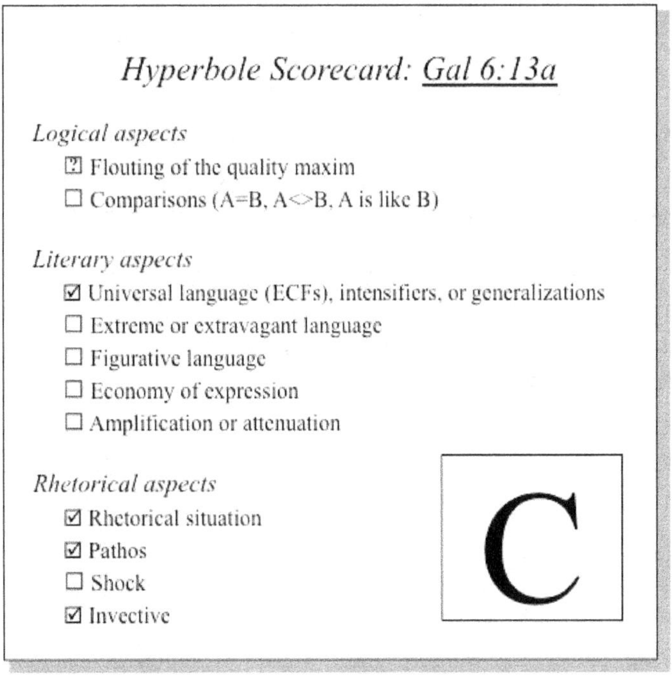

Hyperbole Scorecard: Gal 6:13a

Logical aspects
- ☒ Flouting of the quality maxim
- ☐ Comparisons (A=B, A<>B, A is like B)

Literary aspects
- ☒ Universal language (ECFs), intensifiers, or generalizations
- ☐ Extreme or extravagant language
- ☐ Figurative language
- ☐ Economy of expression
- ☐ Amplification or attenuation

Rhetorical aspects
- ☒ Rhetorical situation
- ☒ Pathos
- ☐ Shock
- ☒ Invective

C

Figure 9.7. Hyperbole Scorecard for Gal 6:13a.

99. De Boer, *Galatians*, 399.

A REIMAGINING OF PAUL'S OPPONENTS

Table 9.1 summarizes the findings from this chapter. Four passages were found to have a high likelihood (A) of being hyperbolic, while one has a moderate likelihood (B), and two are somewhat likely (C) to be hyperbolic.

Table 9.1. Hyperbole in Paul's Vilification of His Opponents

Passage		Grade
1:6–7	The opponents preach a false gospel	A
1:8b–9	Let the opponents be cursed	B
2:4	The opponents in the fourteen-year visit are false brothers	B
4:17	The opponents want to alienate the Galatians from Paul	C
5:12	Let the opponents emasculate themselves	A
6:12b	The opponents compel circumcision only to avoid persecution	A
6:13a	The opponents do not obey Torah	C

Note: A=highly likely, B=moderately likely, C=somewhat likely, D=not likely

How do these findings inform our interpretation of Paul's opponents? We are in a position now to render several tentative conclusions:

- The opponents were Jewish-Christian brothers in the Lord
- They were sincere in their belief in the gracious gospel of Jesus Christ
- Like the Jerusalem apostles, they believed that circumcision and Torah observance were essential for Jewish believers in Christ
- They also, however, applied this rule to Gentile converts
- They offered a "completion" to Paul's gospel to his Gentile converts, partly out of sincere wish to serve God and partly out of fear of persecution by zealot forces
- They may have been antagonistic to Paul (witness his defensiveness in the first part of the letter) and wished to win the Galatians' allegiance away from him

In this chapter we have encountered a skilled writer, Paul, using the rhetorical and literary conventions of his day to effect his missionary objective of keeping the Galatian believers true to the gospel which he preached to them initially. He uses hyperbole to make his opponents appear worse than they are—more crafty, more insidious, more manipulative, more threatening—all the while assuming that his rhetorical gamesmanship will be perceived for what it is. On the cognitive level, the Galatians would have mitigated the content of Paul's statements—just as simply as people today render "I'm starving" into "I'm hungry" without giving it a second thought. But on the emotional level his audience would have felt a white-hot blast of parental anger, disappointment, and stern warning—the urgency of hyperbole bearing an exceptionally potent payload, the force of the carefully chosen words hitting their mark with precision.

10

Paul's Denigration of the Law

> *In this chapter...*
>
> *Question(s) to be answered:*
> - How did Paul use hyperbole in describing the law?
>
> *Trajectory:*
> - Chapters 10 and 11 attempt to provide a solution for the Paul-of-Galatians versus Paul-of-Romans/Acts problem elucidated in the first three chapters.

IN THE FIRST CHAPTER, I attempted to show how Paul's statements regarding the law in Galatians are uniformly negative. I went on to hypothesize that these statements are hyperbolic—that Paul had, rather, a positive opinion of the law as demonstrated in Romans and Acts. In this chapter and the next I will present for analysis the same passages from chapter 1. These passages will be studied according to the methodology of chapter 6 to determine whether they represent hyperbole on Paul's part. The passages are as follows:

- The law's tainted origins (3:19d–20)
- The law's insidious purpose, part 1: To provoke transgressions (3:19b)
- The law's insidious purpose, part 2: To imprison all things under sin (3:22–24)
- The law's limited duration (3:19c, 23b, 25)

Since these passages were already exegeted in chapter 1, the reader is referred to that chapter for a fuller account of them. This chapter will focus on the aspects associated with hyperbole.

THE LAW'S TAINTED ORIGINS (3:19D)

Paul's point in this passage is that the law is inferior to the Abrahamic promise because it (the law) was ordained by angels through a mediator (Moses), as opposed to the promise, which came directly from God. There is much controversy surrounding this passage, and the interpretive ramifications are enormous. Paul seems to be distancing the law from God, ascribing its ordination to angelic beings. As Burton writes, "The intent of the whole phrase is to depreciate the law as not given directly by God."[1] Longenecker quotes Burton's statement, insisting that it is "impossible to read 'ordained through angels' in any other way."[2] Martyn goes further, demonstrating how Paul's language points to actual angelic authorship of the law.[3]

Paul's distancing of the law from God leaves interpreters in a bind. For one, we are forced to wrestle with the idea of an inconsistent Paul, as presented in chapters 1 and 2:

> According to some commentators, Paul speaks of angels here because he did not think of the law as a work of God but as a counterenterprise set up by angels against the promise of God. This notion is to be rejected in consideration of Paul's attitude towards the Old Testament in general and the giving of the law in particular.... Paul is not setting up a front against the law as such, whose holiness and divine origin he roundly acknowledges.[4]

And, what about the apparent anti-Judaic sentiment in the message of a god-less Torah? Martyn, who champions the angelic authorship view, sees this ramification as a potential "abyss."[5] Martyn attempts to sidestep the conflict by redefining the "Law." It is more than the Sinaitic law; it also encompasses the Abrahamic promise. Thus, Paul only separates the former part from God, not the latter part. It can still be said, then, that the "Law" is from God.[6]

The above interpretive attempts—on the one hand to avoid the plain sense of Paul's words ("the natural literal understanding of 3.19-20,

---

1. Burton, *Galatians*, 189; cf. Hübner, *Law in Paul's Thought*, 26, "It is practically uncontested that the intention of this pronouncement is to emphasize the inferiority of the Law."

2. Longenecker, *Galatians*, 140.

3. Martyn, *Galatians*, 366, "Moses, the mediator, did not speak for God, but rather for the angels. God had no role of any kind in the genesis of the Law."

4. Ridderbos, *Epistle of Paul*, 139.

5. Martyn, *Galatians*, 368.

6. Martyn, *Galatians*, 368-70.

according to which the law was given by the angels alone"), and on the other hand, to rescue Paul from anti-Judaic tendencies—are unnecessary.[7] There is, of course, another possibility—that Paul is speaking in hyperbole, overstating the role of angels in the giving of the law in order to amplify the impact of his rhetoric against the influence of the opponents. In this section I will examine the logical, literary, and rhetorical aspects of this passage which contribute to my interpretation.

Logical Aspects

To prove that Paul is flouting the quality maxim, I will demonstrate that (a) he is contradicting the received tradition of his day regarding angelic involvement in the law and (b) he is contradicting his own words elsewhere. To begin with, the scriptural evidence for angelic intervention is slight, as there is nothing in the MT that directly states angels were present at Mount Sinai.[8] What Paul likely had was the LXX of Deut 33:2 (see chapter 1) and possibly the rabbinic tradition of Ps 68:18 (LXX 67:18), which understood the myriads of chariots to be angels.[9] In these sources, however, the activity of the angels is peripheral at best, far short of Paul's assertion that they "ordained" the law. Josephus *Ant*. 15.136 ("We have learned from God the most excellent of our doctrines, and the most holy part of our law, by angels or ambassadors") and Acts 7:53, where Stephen says that the Jews received the law εἰς διαταγὰς ἀγγέλων, are more suggestive.[10]

> It was such an understanding of angels as being present at the giving of the Mosaic law that seems to have been the dominant tradition in Paul's day. . . . Such a mediatorial role for angels in the giving of the law seems to have been part of the widespread attempt in early Judaism to assign a role for angels in all the major revelatory and redemptive events of Scripture.[11]

However, in the above sources, the intervention of angels is always presented positively, as a way of bringing glory to the law. Paul's disparaging view of angelic mediation was unique: "We do not find Jewish parallels to

---

7. Quote is from Räisänen, *Paul and the Law*, 132.

8. Longenecker, *Galatians*, 139, "The MT has no explicit reference to angels being present in the giving of the law at Mt. Sinai."

9. Callan, "Pauline Midrash," 551.

10. Callan, "Pauline Midrash," 552, regarding *Ant*. 15.136, "It is disputed whether *aggelōs* refers to angels or to prophets or priests."

11. Longenecker, *Galatians*, 140; cf. Callan, "Pauline Midrash," 549–67.

Paul's Denigration of the Law

his negative view of angelic mediation of the law."[12] A closer parallel to Paul's view would be the later gnostic writings that see the angels as giving the law in order to enslave human beings.[13]

Second, Paul appears elsewhere to have a rather positive outlook on the law, both in his theology and in his way of life (see chapter 2; also see Gal 5:14; 6:2).[14] Galatians 3:19d presents us, then, with "what must be regarded as a violent contrast between Paul's estimate of the law here (even when due allowance is made for the polemical context of the passage) and that in Romans (cf. in particular Rom. 2:17f.; 7:12)."[15] In Romans, the law is not the law ordained by angels but is the νόμος τοῦ θεοῦ (7:22, 25; 8:7; cf. 3:1; 7:14).

To summarize, Paul goes beyond the traditions of his day and beyond even his own words elsewhere in order to portray the law in a negative light as ordained by angels in Gal 3:19:

> We are apparently once more faced with an internal contradiction in Paul. Once more we find him in the course of a polemical discussion suggesting something radical about the law.... We have seen that Paul could seize on various traditions and reinterpret them for his own use.... In Gal 3.19f. he has taken up the Jewish tradition about the presence of angels on Sinai. The radical application seems to be an *ad hoc*-adaptation of that tradition. In the light of the context and the fact that Paul never returns to this suggestion of the origin of the law it looks as if he were simply toying with an idea which, however, seemed rather too daring even to him—at least later on.... The statement in Gal 3.19f. would seem to be steeped in emotion. Paul dictates his letter in anger. He has "overreacted."[16]

Literary Aspects

There is nothing particularly suggestive of hyperbole among the literary aspects of this passage.

---

12. Callan, "Pauline Midrash," 553.

13. See Callan, "Pauline Midrash," 554, for a discussion.

14. See chapter 6 for my discussion of 5:14 and 6:2. In essence, these texts provide a base from within the letter itself from which Paul's more negative statements may be indicated as hyperbole. Galatians 5:14 and 6:2 suggest that Paul viewed the law positively as a norm for human behavior.

15. Fung, *Galatians*, 160; for this reason, Fung rejects the reading "ordained by angels."

16. Räisänen, *Paul and the Law*, 133.

Rhetorical Aspects

In 3:19d–20 Paul is making the argument that the law is inferior to the promise because it (the law) was ordained by angels and delivered through the agency of a mediator, Moses. The promise, by contrast, came directly from God, who needs no mediator. The larger rhetorical situation, of course, is that Paul is attempting to dissuade the Galatians from consenting to circumcision.

As for pathos, Räisänen, above, characterizes this verse as "steeped in emotion."[17] Paul is feeling "the heat of debate," speaking in radical new ways about the law, the foundation and treasure of the Judaism to which he still belonged (to speak of Christianity as a separate religion this early is anachronistic).[18] It is not difficult to imagine, behind the words, the depth of anger he had at the instigation of the opponents who were troubling his converts. That anger spurred him to create an ideological separation between himself and the opponents. What they were for, he was against, including even the law itself.

Martyn twice uses the term "shocking" to describe Paul's account of the genesis of the law.[19] Surely any Jew reading Paul's letter would have considered it shocking (Martyn remarks that Paul would have never written such a letter to his fellow Jews).[20] Even the Galatian addressees, though, after hearing of the law's holiness from the opponents, would have been shocked at Paul's intensely negative outlook.

Regarding invective, Longenecker detects a polemical thrust to this verse. "It was probably the case that the Judaizers were citing the angels' presence at Sinai as evidence of the law's glory and God's approval. Paul, however, turns this tradition in *ad hominem* fashion against them."[21]

Conclusion

The probability that Paul is flouting the quality maxim is strong. He is working mostly from traditional material, but he is extreme even by those standards. While Jewish Christians would have been offended at Paul's sentiments, the Galatians, having likely been taught the OT by Paul and the opponents, would see through Paul's over-the-top characterization of the

---

17. Räisänen, *Paul and the Law*, 133.
18. Quoted words are from Sanders, *Paul, the Law*, 68.
19. Martyn, *Galatians*, 369–70.
20. Martyn, *Galatians*, 368.
21. Longenecker, *Galatians*, 140.

law in light of the rhetorical exigency that caused him to write. These were tough times, which called for tough words.

The lack of literary aspects is understandable when dealing with such a small number of words. Verses 19 and 20 are something of a parenthesis in Paul's argument anyway.

Given the flouting of the quality maxim and the presence of all four rhetorical aspects, then, the likelihood of hyperbole in this passage is rated as "B—moderate" (Figure 10.1).

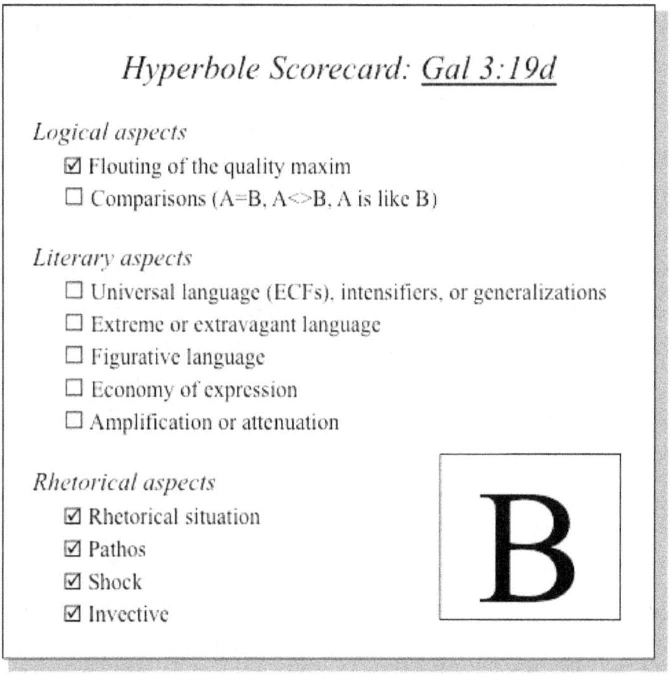

Hyperbole Scorecard: Gal 3:19d

Logical aspects
- ☑ Flouting of the quality maxim
- ☐ Comparisons (A=B, A<>B, A is like B)

Literary aspects
- ☐ Universal language (ECFs), intensifiers, or generalizations
- ☐ Extreme or extravagant language
- ☐ Figurative language
- ☐ Economy of expression
- ☐ Amplification or attenuation

Rhetorical aspects
- ☑ Rhetorical situation
- ☑ Pathos
- ☑ Shock
- ☑ Invective

B

Figure 10.1. Hyperbole Scorecard for Gal 3:19d.

THE LAW'S INSIDIOUS PURPOSE, PART 1: TO PROVOKE TRANSGRESSIONS (3:19B)

What would an observant first-century Jew say if asked the question, "Why was the law given to Israel?" Perhaps something along the lines of, "Because we are God's chosen people, and he loves us." Or, "To keep us from sinning against him." Or maybe, "Because it is his perfection and wisdom encoded in words." Such a Jew most certainly would not reply, "To provoke us to sin against him." Words like that would be scandalous, out of keeping with typical Jewish thought. But such in fact are Paul's words: τῶν παραβάσεων χάριν προσετέθη.²²

> It must be clear that Paul's whole argument about the purpose of the Law sounds blasphemous to Jewish ears, that it must inevitably have had a shocking effect on Jews and not merely on the Pharisaic element among them. To suppose for one moment that the Law was intended to provoke sins! By contrast in Ab 1.1 we read: "make a hedge around the Torah!" Like this demand, the Pharisaic view tended towards further specifying the stipulations of the Torah for the very purpose of ensuring that no transgression of it should take place. Moreover to Jewish ears it was offensive to suggest that the Torah should merely have been "*added to*" (προσετέθη) the promises. This must have had a particularly offensive note about it if as may be supposed there was already in the first century A.D. a belief in the pre-existence of the Torah.²³

"How did Paul, a former Pharisaic Jew, reach such a radically un-Jewish position with regard to the Torah?"²⁴ What was he thinking? Mindreading is a risky venture, of course. It is safer to conclude, given a relatively clear rhetorical situation and other signals, that we can tell what Paul was *doing*. His primary objective was to persuade his addressees, and in service to that objective he used hyperbole.

Logical Aspects

Logically, Paul's view lies outside of the mainstream Jewish thought of his age. The popular consensus would have been that the law was certainly not *added*.²⁵ On the contrary, it has always been (and always will remain, as I will discuss in a future section). Moore describes this belief thusly:

---

22. See chapter 1 for the exegesis behind this reading. The majority of modern commentators agree that Paul here is speaking in terms of a telic function for the law, i.e., that it is for the sake of producing and increasing sins.

23. Hübner, *Law in Paul's Thought*, 32.

24. The question is posed by Betz, *Galatians*, 165.

25. Bruce, *Galatians*, 176, "Several Western witnesses to the text exhibit the simple verb ἐτέθη ('was laid down') in place of προσετέθη, but this variant is usually combined with an alteration of παραβάσεων designed to remove what a scribe or editor felt to be the scandalous statement that the purpose of the law was the production of transgressions."

> Religion was not an afterthought of God; it was impossible to conceive a world like this without religion. Since the two are thus indissolubly connected, the world must be made, we might say, on a religious plan. And since religion was in Jewish apprehension a complete system of divinely revealed beliefs and duties, obligatory, not discretionary—a law—this system in its integrity must have existed before the world, and the world must have been made to correspond to it.[26]

Moreover the rabbinical view of the law was that it was given by God as a gift to enable the Jews to remain within the covenant; it even included a system of atonement in the case of wrongdoing.[27]

For the purposes of this study, however, it is not enough to show that Paul contradicted his contemporaries. It must be shown that he contradicted himself, Jesus, or other biblical writers (see chapter 6 for the criteria for flouting of the quality maxim). I will take each of those one by one.

To begin with, Paul contradicts his own, more positive, words elsewhere. For instance, further on in Galatians (5:14; 6:2), he implies that the law continues as a norm for human behavior. Likewise, in Romans, the law is "holy," the commandment "holy, righteous, and good" (7:12). The law stimulates, not sin itself, but the consciousness of sin (3:20).[28]

Second, Paul contradicts Jesus regarding the law. There is no evidence in the Sermon on the Mount that the law has a negative function or that it provokes sin. Rather, Jesus looks upon the law positively (Matt 5:17–20): (a) he has come to fulfill it, (b) it will not pass away, (c) one should do the commandments and teach them, and (d) a certain level of righteousness according to the law is necessary for entrance to the kingdom of heaven.

Third, Paul is at variance with the Jewish Scriptures regarding the law. According to the Pentateuch the law was given to cement the relationship between God and Israel: she was to be his "treasured possession among all peoples. . . . a kingdom of priests and a holy nation" (Exod 19:5-6). The law was to be Israel's wisdom and understanding in the sight of the nations (Deut 4:6). In it she would find forgiveness and restoration in relation to her God. The psalmists celebrate the law. Compare, for instance, Ps 1 and the blessed man whose delight is in the law of the Lord. Compare also Ps 119 and its extended meditation on the law. And then there is Ps 19, about which Peter Craigie comments:

---

26. Moore, *Judaism*, 268.
27. Sanders, *Paul and Palestinian Judaism*, 180.
28. See chapter 2 for my treatment of Rom 5:20 and 7:5.

In every sense and dimension, the Lord's *Torah* is good: it is "perfect," "sure," "upright," "pure," "radiant," and "true." And each of these six characteristics of *Torah* is illustrated by reference to its role with respect to human beings:

(i) "reviving the life"

(ii) "making wise the simple"

(iii) "making the heart rejoice"

(iv) "enlightening the eyes"

(v) "enduring forever"

(vi) "they are entirely righteous"[29]

In fact, the portrait that Paul paints of God is of a wholly different perspective from that of the OT. The lawgiver of Gal 3:19 is a malicious one: "[A]n interim measure which went on provoking transgressions for more than a millennium, without providing remedy for all that time, would imply a remarkably heartless picture of the God who so failed to provide."[30] In view of all of the above evidence, it would seem highly likely, then, that in Gal 3:19b Paul is flouting the quality maxim.

Literary Aspects

The passage under study in this section is brief (four words). There are no apparent literary aspects for hyperbole.

Rhetorical Aspects

The rhetorical situation for Gal 3:19b is that Paul is attempting to persuade the Galatians that the law is inferior to the promissory covenant made with Abraham.

As for pathos, Paul's negative view of the law here has both cognitive *and* emotive dimensions: it is, in other words, an expression of "the heat of the argument," versus the relatively more sober reflections of Paul in Romans.[31]

---

29. Craigie, *Psalms 1–50*, 181–82.

30. Dunn, *Galatians*, 190, who rejects the telic interpretation for that reason; cf. Longenecker, *Galatians*, 138, "For why should God want an increase of sin building up to the coming of Christ?"

31. Sanders, *Paul and Palestinian Judaism*, 550; cf. Sanders, *Paul, the Law*, 68.

Moreover, the statement that the law was added is shocking. Paul's use of προστίθημι, which recalls ἐπιδιατάσσομαι of verse 15, where Paul claimed that no one may add to a previously ratified covenant, implies that "[s]uch tampering [that is, the addition of the law] has no legal status, since only the testator himself can annul or change his own will. . . . Verse 19b, therefore, can only mean that the law 'was added' to God's promise by actors other than God himself."[32] Martyn calls this feature of v. 19 "shocking."[33]

Conclusion

As with the previous passage (Gal 3:19d), the evidence for flouting of the quality maxim is sufficiently strong—Paul's words are so out of keeping with biblical and traditional teaching—that hyperbole is indicated even in the absence of literary aspects. There is also a clear rhetorical situation, and Paul's words are designed to produce pathos and shock in the addressees (Figure 10.2).

---

32. De Boer, *Galatians*, 228.

33. Martyn, *Galatians*, 354; cf. Hübner, *Law in Paul's Thought*, 32, that Paul's words "must inevitably have had a shocking effect on Jews."

> **Hyperbole Scorecard: *Gal 3:19b***
>
> *Logical aspects*
> ☒ Flouting of the quality maxim
> ☐ Comparisons (A=B, A⇔B, A is like B)
>
> *Literary aspects*
> ☐ Universal language (ECFs), intensifiers, or generalizations
> ☐ Extreme or extravagant language
> ☐ Figurative language
> ☐ Economy of expression
> ☐ Amplification or attenuation
>
> *Rhetorical aspects*
> ☒ Rhetorical situation
> ☒ Pathos
> ☒ Shock
> ☐ Invective
>
> **B**

Figure 10.2. Hyperbole Scorecard for Gal 3:19b.

THE LAW'S INSIDIOUS PURPOSE, PART 2: TO IMPRISON ALL THINGS UNDER SIN (3:22-24)

In Gal 3:21 Paul asks a crucial question: Is the law against the promise of God? He answers strongly in the negative (μὴ γένοιτο). He then proceeds to show how the two operate independent of each other to produce what God wills to happen. The promise, for its part, is the one that gives life. It awaits fulfillment in the age of faith in Christ. Meanwhile, the law acts like a jailor, temporarily imprisoning all things under sin until Christ comes.[34] Or, in a similar analogy, the law acts like a παιδαγωγός, a slave whose job it is to closely supervise a young boy in a patrician household. When the boy reaches maturity, he is free, no longer under a παιδαγωγός.

Paul's assertions raise several questions in relation to the theology of the Bible: (1) Does the biblical witness (outside of Paul, that is) bifurcate law

---

34. Dunn, *Galatians*, 195, "God confined a whole epoch of universal history 'under the power of sin' simply to bring out the fact that the power of the promise only comes to effect within the human condition 'from faith'"; in the words of Moo, *Galatians*, 242, it was a "servitude to sin from which the law was unable to provide a release."

and promise? (2) Does it teach a negative purpose for the institution of the law? (3) Does it view the Messiah's coming as the fulfillment of the Abrahamic promises only? Addressing each of the questions adequately would require far more space than I have here, but I will attempt to render here a condensed biblical theology of the law.

First, the Bible makes no rigid distinction between the Abrahamic promises and the Sinaitic law. They were both given out of the grace of God. Both have unconditional and conditional aspects. To expand a bit, the promises to Abraham were conditioned, in some respects, on his continued obedience (Gen 17:1, 10; 18:19; 22:16–18; 26:5). And, the Sinaitic law contained unconditional elements—clearly teaching (e.g., Deut 30:1–10) that God would one day, even after they had disobeyed him, circumcise the hearts of the Israelites so that they might live.

Second, as discussed in the previous section, the Bible tends to view the institution of the Sinaitic law quite positively. The Israelites were chosen and given a choice of "two ways" (Deut 30:15)—life or death—with the way of life to result from obedience to the law. And they often reaped the blessings of the covenant; the Deuteronomic history is not all negative. The Israelites succeeded in capturing portions of the promised land, they won numerous battles against their enemies, they built a flourishing capital city and temple, and they expanded the kingdom to its height under Solomon. The wisdom writings are replete with praise for the law and the blessed life that comes from following it. And, although Abraham is held to be the paradigm of faith for Paul, numerous figures of the OT are mentioned in Heb 11 for their faithfulness to the Sinaitic law.[35]

Third, in regard to the Messiah's coming, the Bible views it as the fulfillment of the entire OT—the law and the prophets.[36] Jesus said as much (Matt 5:17; Luke 24:44). He is not just the true Abraham but he is the new Moses (Deut 18:15–18; Matt 5–7). He is the true Israel, the perfect temple, and even the sacrifices and festivals find their fulfillment in him.[37]

So where does Paul's negative view of the law's purpose come from? It could possibly be viewed as a retrojection upon the OT, a solution in search of a plight. In other words, Christ has come, so the old way *must* be weak and inferior. Better, however, is to view it as a rhetorical strategy.

---

35. People are also commended for their righteousness, including Noah, Lot, Job, David, Hezekiah, Josiah, Enoch, Joseph (Mary's husband), Simeon, and the parents of John the Baptist.

36. I.e., without distinction between Abraham and Sinai.

37. For extensive treatments on these subjects see Goldsworthy, "Gospel and Kingdom," 1–148; Beale, *Temple and the Church's Mission*; Wright, *Paul and the Faithfulness of God*, 774–1042; Goppelt, *Typos*; Seitz, *Figured Out*.

The Galatians want to become children of Abraham, and the opponents no doubt have taught the necessity of circumcision via Gen 17. Paul ignores chapter 17, emphasizing Gen 15 instead, and hives off circumcision into the realm of the law, which he exaggerates to be some sort of prison warden.

Now, it is true that the OT is *largely* (that word is key here) a story of the failure of the Israelites to live up to God's requirements. They looked forward to the promise of a new and better covenant where their hearts would be circumcised (Jer 31:31–34; Ezek 36:27). But to bifurcate the two ages (pre- and post-messianic) in such a way as to suggest that humanity was *imprisoned* by the law under sin—that is, they were not free to do anything other than sin—is an overgeneralization.

Of course, one might retort, "The Bible is a progressive revelation. Paul is inspired to interpret the OT. Therefore, Galatians trumps the OT evidence." But to reach that conclusion one must also ignore the testimony of the other NT writers who expressed no such negativity toward the law. The most coherent way to view the situation, then, is that Paul is speaking in hyperbole.

Logical Aspects

In the preceding paragraphs I have attempted to establish that, in Gal 3:22–24, Paul is speaking in contradiction to the biblical witness in terms of the purpose of the law. It is also noteworthy that he contradicts his own, softer, rhetoric from Romans. Martyn summarizes the situation thusly:

> Two observations can serve to emphasize the shocking character of this affirmation. (1) We have already noted that Paul's insistence on the Law's impotence to make alive is without parallel in Jewish thought. How much more so is his view of the Law as enslaver! There is nothing truly like it in ancient Hebraic thought, in Judaism, and in Christian Judaism. (2) The shock is also underlined when we note that later, writing to the Roman church, Paul softens the motif of enslavement under the Law's power (Rom 6:14–15). It is as though the different setting, or something that happened in the interim between the writing of the two letters, or some new concern on Paul's part, or a combination of these factors led Paul to avoid referring in Romans 7 to the Law itself as an enslaver, speaking rather of Sin's *use* of the Law (Rom 7:11).[38]

---

38. Martyn, *Galatians*, 371–72.

Paul's Denigration of the Law

Paul is also constructing metaphorical hyperbole by using comparisons. The first compares the law to a prison warden: "The written law is the official who locks the law-breaker up in the prison-house of which sin is the jailor."[39] The second one likens the law to a παιδαγωγός. This second comparison, it should be noted, is also negative, meant as a "radical devaluation of the law."[40] It is not a picture of a benevolent schoolmaster but rather a harsh governing/restraining force in the life of a young boy (set in opposition to the freedom which a mature man enjoys).[41]

Literary Aspects

I have already argued that Paul is generalizing, broad brushing the scope of salvation history with the law playing a negative role. Another literary aspect in that same category is universal language, which arises in dealing with the term τὰ πάντα. The meaning of this term is debated: is it "all Jews," "all people," or "all things"? Paul is likely referring to "all things," the more natural meaning of the neuter plural, presenting a sweeping cosmic picture of imprisonment under sin.

The use of comparisons (imprisonment, παιδαγωγός) are examples of figurative language. These comparisons indicate that Paul is not just using simple hyperbole, but metaphorical hyperbole.

Rhetorical Aspects

As with the previous passage, the rhetorical situation is that Paul is attempting to persuade the Galatians against circumcision by demonstrating the inferiority of the law vis-à-vis the Abrahamic promise.

By comparing the law to an imprisoning force or a παιδαγωγός, Paul is inviting pathos and shock (see Martyn's extended quote under Logical Aspects). He paints a picture of an "objectively desperate situation" created by the law.[42] The figures of imprisonment and domination by a παιδαγωγός are demeaning, viscerally repulsive, and intended to cause the addressees to want to distance themselves from the law.

---

39. Bruce, *Galatians*, 180.

40. Betz, *Galatians*, 178.

41. The emphasis in this comparison is on the supervisory role of the pedagogue, the inferior status of the one under supervision, and the temporary nature of the relationship (Longenecker, *Galatians*, 148).

42. Fung, *Galatians*, 24.

Conclusion

Figure 10.3 displays the results of the analysis of Gal 3:22–24. Besides flouting the quality maxim, Paul utilizes comparisons (of the A=B variety). Under the category of literary aspects, Paul uses universal language, generalizations, and figurative language. The rhetorical situation, pathos, and shock are all listed as rhetorical aspects. Due to the degree of exaggeration coupled with the number of aspects, this passage rates an A (high likelihood of being a hyperbole).

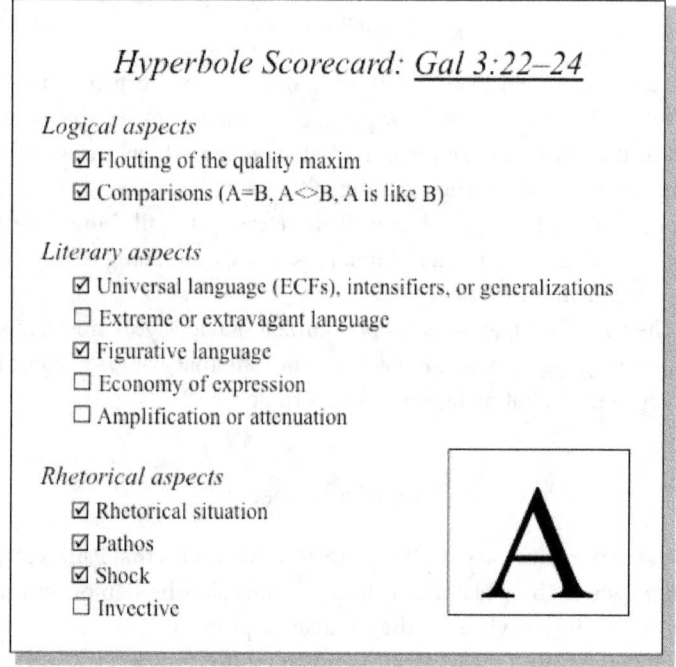

Figure 10.3. Hyperbole Scorecard for Gal 3:22–24.

THE LAW'S LIMITED DURATION (3:19C, 23B, 25)

"The era of the law has ended with the coming of Christ. Humanity is no longer imprisoned under its brutal dictatorship. Paul himself has died to the law and now lives for Christ (Gal 2:19)." So goes Paul's logic in Galatians. I will focus in this section on the following three verses, since they are within the scope of the analyzed verses so far (3:19–25):

- [The law was added] until the seed could come to whom the promise was made (3:19c)
- [We were] imprisoned until the coming faith was revealed (3:23b)[43]
- Now that faith has come, we are no longer under a guardian (3:25)

However, the theme of the temporariness of the law is found not just in the above verses; it is a thread that runs throughout Galatians (cf. 2:18; 4:4–5, 9).

There is nothing particularly controversial about the wording of the above three phrases; they are typically the least commented on parts of the passage. Taken together, however, they represent quite a controversial idea—the *terminus ad quem* of the law in salvation history. As Longenecker remarks, "Paul's view here, of course, deviates widely from that of Judaism."[44] Jewish writings instead speak of the eternality of the law (see chapter 1). "It would, in fact, be difficult to find any Jew who thought otherwise."[45] Paul appears to be speaking, once again, in the style of hyperbole.

Logical Aspects

In this section I will suggest that there are several logical difficulties with Paul's assertions in Galatians regarding the ending of the law:

- The OT affirms the eternality of the law
- Jesus teaches that the law is still in force in Matt 5:18
- Paul behaves as if the law in still in force in Acts
- Paul views the law as still in force in Romans
- Paul views the law as still in force in Gal 5:14

The OT Affirms the Eternality of the Law

In chapter 1 I briefly touched on the conclusions of W. D. Davies's book *Torah in the Messianic Age and/or the Age to Come* that there was no expectation of any abolition of the old Torah in the messianic age. At this point I shall review some of the evidence he presents from the OT.

---

43. Reading εἰς as temporal.
44. Longenecker, *Galatians*, 139.
45. Longenecker, *Galatians*, 139.

Jer 31:31–34 refers to the coming of a new covenant in which Yahweh promises, "I will put my law within them, and I will write it on their hearts." Davies argues from this passage that the law here is none other than the existing law: "No new kind of Torah is mentioned in the passage, but merely a new covenant, formulated, it is implied, on the basis of the existing Torah. Under the new covenant contemplated, it is the demands of the old Torah, both moral and ceremonial, that are to be obeyed."[46] Indeed, other scriptures speak of the written Torah as being "in the heart" (Ps 37:31; 40:8; Deut 30:14).

Next, Davies turns to the Servant of Yahweh in Isaiah. Noting that "there is . . . impressive support for the Messianic interpretation of the Servant," Davies highlights the role of the Servant in bringing מִשְׁפָּט (Isa 42:2) and תּוֹרָה (Isa 42:4) to the nations of the world. "The imparting of Torah is a central function of the Servant of Yahweh: this Torah will be directed to the world."[47]

Finally, Davies covers Isa 2:1–4, where the law is said to go out from Zion in the last days. The term תּוֹרָה in verse 4 may include a more general meaning of "instruction," but, as Davies notes, should not be emptied of its connotation as law.[48]

Jesus Teaches that the Law Is Still in Force in Matt 5:18

In Matt 5:18, Jesus, speaking of the written law (as is evident from ἰῶτα ἓν ἢ μία κεραία), announces that it will not pass away until ἕως ἂν παρέλθῃ ὁ οὐρανὸς καὶ ἡ γῆ. The end of world history is in view.[49] Even though the phrase ἕως ἂν πάντα γένηται could denote eschatological fulfillment—the coming of Jesus—the context argues in favor of the permanence of the law: "In light of Jesus' claim not to be abolishing the law (verse 17) and of the insistence in v. 19 that even the least of the commandments remains important, v. 18 can hardly be stating the 'jots and tittles' have in fact been invalidated by the coming of fulfillment in Jesus."[50]

---

46. Davies, *Torah in the Messianic Age*, 13–14.
47. Davies, *Torah in the Messianic Age*, 34.
48. Davies, *Torah in the Messianic Age*, 37.
49. So Betz, *Sermon on the Mount*, 184.
50. France, *Matthew*, 185–86; in considering this same objection (i.e., eschatological fulfillment), Davies and Allison, *Matthew 1–7*, 494, likewise conclude that "'until heaven and earth pass away' (so 18a) most naturally suggests that there is still a long period of time to elapse before the law passes away."

Paul Behaves as if the Law Is Still in Force in Acts

As discussed in chapter 2, there are several instances of Paul behaving in a Torah-observant way in Acts. He circumcises Timothy (16:3), he takes a vow (18:18), he keeps the feasts (20:6, 16), and he joins in the purification rites of four men who had taken a vow (21:23–24, 26). The last exercise in this list was done to disprove the rumors that he was *not* Torah-observant.[51] Then there are the defense speeches, in which Paul asserts at several points that he keeps the law (23:1, 6; 24:14, 16; 25:8; 26:5). In summary, "Acts portrays the Gentile missionary Paul as a Jewish Christian who is utterly loyal to the law."[52]

Paul Views the Law as Still in Force in Romans

Galatians and Romans share much in common. It is too simplistic to say that one is anti-law and the other pro-law. In Romans, for instance, Paul writes: "[Y]ou have died to the law through the body of Christ" (7:4) and "Now, we are released from the law, having died to that which held us, so that we might serve in newness of spirit and not in the oldness of the letter [i.e., the written code]." There is, then, in Romans a sense that people are called to escape the condemnation of the law—the code that defines transgressions against God—by fleeing to the grace of Christ and the power of the Spirit.

Is the law, then, abolished in Romans? Has it reached its *terminus ad quem*? Only in a manner of speaking, and certainly not as explicitly as described in Galatians. Yes, the Christ-less law, the law as a source of ethnic pride and religious status, gives way to a universalized ethical system with Christ as king (Rom 12:9–21; 13:8–14; 14:8). So Paul can say elsewhere, "You are all one in Christ Jesus" (Gal 3:28). And yes, the Spirit-less law, the law empowered by frail human will gives way to one divinely energized (Rom 8:2f.; Ezek 36:27). But Paul still talks about the law in the present tense (e.g., Rom 7:12, 14). He nevertheless recognizes that Jewish Christians will continue to circumcise their infant boys. They will still keep the feasts and honor the Sabbath. Under what pretext? In a work as thickly theological as Romans, Paul leaves us wanting for more explanation. But the reader must acknowledge that Romans is, like Galatians, a rhetorical work. Paul's purpose was not to justify the Jewish Christian lifestyle.

---

51. "Thus all will know that there is nothing in what they have been told about you, but that you yourself also live in observance of the law" (Acts 21:24, ESV).

52. Vielhauer, "On the 'Paulinism' in Acts," 38.

This brings us to the passage that is, for many, determinative in viewing the law as abolished in Romans: "τέλος γὰρ νόμου Χριστός" (10:4). I argue the teleological viewpoint in chapter 2: The law leads us to Christ. It *points forward* to him. This verse does not imply that the law ends at the arrival of Christ.

Paul Views the Law as Still in Force in Gal 5:14

Paul exhorts the Galatians to serve one another through love, for (γάρ) the whole law is fulfilled in one word: "you shall love your neighbor as yourself." Here he connects his exhortation to its rationale, the Sinaitic law, which presents a contradiction.[53] Räisänen accepts it as such: "Paul states in unambiguous terms that the law has been abolished.... The abolition notwithstanding, Paul also makes positive statements which imply that the law is still valid."[54] Essentially, Paul is addressing the recipients on what he perceives to be common ground: respect for the law and desire to fulfill it.[55] One would expect for consistency's sake that Paul would refrain from mentioning the law at all, but he not only mentions it, he engages in a bit of rabbinic wordplay, summarizing the law into one commandment. This does not appear to be a careless, offhanded comment. Rather, Paul wants his readers to be right from the standpoint of the law, at least as much as uncircumcised Gentiles can be (cf. Sanders's covenantal nomism and the concept of "staying in" the covenant).

Other Logical Aspects

Verse 23b and 25 occur within comparisons of the law to an imprisoning force and a παιδαγωγός, respectively.

Literary Aspects

As noted in previous analyses, Paul uses figurative language (metaphor) to draw his comparisons. There is also economy of expression in 3:23 and 3:25,

---

53. See chapter 2 for additional interpretations of Gal 5:14.

54. Räisänen, *Paul and the Law*, 199.

55. I do not think we can let Paul off the hook (so to speak) by emphasizing the difference between ποιέω and πληρόω, as does Westerholm, *Israel's Law*, 203–5 and interpreting Paul as if he is not advocating "doing" the law. Paul is here (5:13 and 5:14) clearly connecting the two ideas.

where Paul uses ἡ πίστις to refer to the age of faith in Christ. This expression serves to oversimplify the division of ages, as if to suggest that law and faith are mutually exclusive.

Rhetorical Aspects

The rhetorical situation for these verses, as stated previously, is the need to persuade the Galatians against circumcision by emphasizing the inferiority of the law in contrast to the Abrahamic promise.

As for pathos and shock, these passages retain these qualities from their larger context, which has already been reviewed above. There is here an additional resounding of shock in Paul's words concerning the law coming to an end.

Conclusion

As shown in Figure 10.4, the likelihood of Gal 3:19c, 23b, and 25 being hyperbolic is high. Paul is clearly flouting the quality maxim in picturing the law's demise. He uses vibrant metaphors to undergird his presentation, which are pathos-laden and shocking.

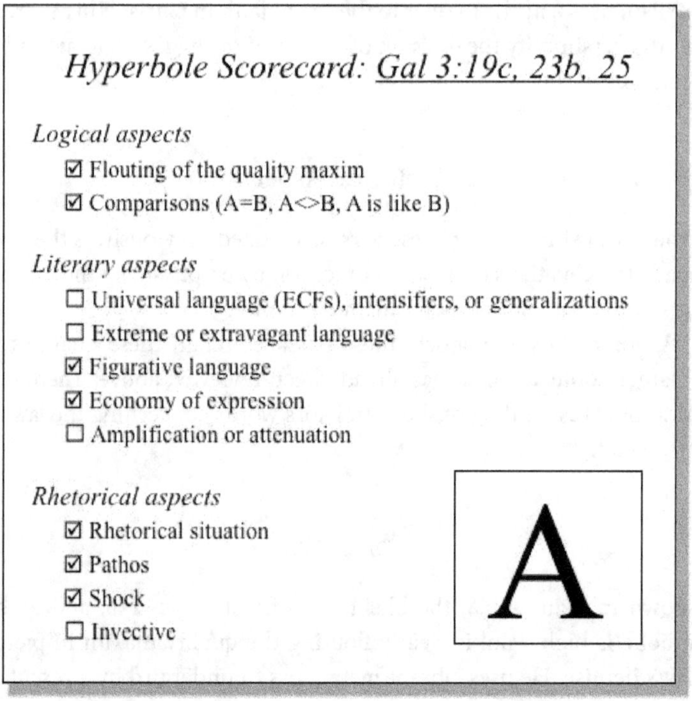

> **Hyperbole Scorecard: _Gal 3:19c, 23b, 25_**
>
> *Logical aspects*
> ☑ Flouting of the quality maxim
> ☑ Comparisons (A=B, A<>B, A is like B)
>
> *Literary aspects*
> ☐ Universal language (ECFs), intensifiers, or generalizations
> ☐ Extreme or extravagant language
> ☑ Figurative language
> ☑ Economy of expression
> ☐ Amplification or attenuation
>
> *Rhetorical aspects*
> ☑ Rhetorical situation
> ☑ Pathos
> ☑ Shock
> ☐ Invective
>
> **A**

Figure 10.4. Hyperbole Scorecard for Gal 3:19c, 23b, 25.

A REIMAGINING OF THE LAW

Table 10.1 summarizes the findings from this chapter. Two passages were found to have a moderate likelihood (B) of being hyperbolic, while two have a high likelihood (A).

Table 10.1. Hyperbole in Paul's Denigration of the Law

Passage		Grade
3:19d–20	The law's tainted origins	B
3:19b	The law's insidious purpose, part 1: To provoke transgressions	B
3:22–24	The law's insidious purpose, part 2: To imprison all things under sin	A
3:19c, 23b, 25	The law's limited duration	A

Note: A=highly likely, B=moderately likely, C=somewhat likely, D=not likely

How do these findings inform our interpretation of Paul's view of the law? Once the hyperbole of Paul's statements is mitigated we can render the following conclusions:

- The law originated from God, who may have been accompanied by angels
- The law is holy and good but its demands were difficult for Israel to keep; viewed from a certain perspective, then, Israel's experience with the law was negative:
    o Israel's sin multiplied before God
    o Why would Gentiles, then, wish to recapitulate Israel's experience with the law by taking its yoke upon themselves?
- Viewed from another perspective, however, Israel's experience with the law was positive:
    o The law was not strictly bifurcated from the promises; in both, God took to himself a people, rewarded their faithfulness, punished their unfaithfulness, forgave their sins, and promised a future glory
    o Participation in the law was, generally speaking, the delight of the Jew
    o The law and promises were a shadow of the kingdom age that the messiah was to bring
    o Once the messiah arrived, Jewish Christians continued to serve God through the law
- By omitting the positive perspective, Paul overstated his case in order to most effectively dissuade the Galatians from becoming full (circumcised) Jewish proselytes, since such was not needed in order to receive the Holy Spirit

11

Paul's Magnification of the Consequences of Circumcision

> *In this chapter...*
>
> *Question(s) to be answered:*
> - How did Paul use hyperbole in describing the consequences of becoming circumcised?
>
> *Trajectory:*
> - This chapter is the last in a series of three main chapters discussing hyperbole in Galatians.

THE FINAL QUESTION TO be answered regarding Galatians is how Paul views the consequences of taking the law upon oneself. The Galatians are at a moment of decision: accept or reject Paul's admonishment. Paul paints a bleak picture of what life will be like for them if they choose to reject his words. The following three passages will be studied in this chapter:

- The law brings a curse upon anything less than perfect obedience (3:10)
- The law enslaves (4:3, 9)
- The law severs fellowship with Christ (5:2-4)

THE LAW BRINGS A CURSE UPON ANYTHING LESS THAN PERFECT OBEDIENCE (3:10)

A substantial amount of literature is devoted to Gal 3:10, as it is regarded as one of the most difficult passages in Galatians. One difficulty is that it appears at first glance to be a non sequitur. The verse's tortured logic appears to run thusly: "Those who *do* the works of the law are cursed because Deuteronomy says that those who *do not do* the works of the law are cursed!"[1] The most common solution to this problem is for interpreters to insert a premise as part of the logical syllogism as follows:

1. Cursed is everyone who does not keep the whole law (3:10b)
2. (Implied premise) No one keeps the whole law
3. Therefore, cursed is everyone who is ἐξ ἔργων νόμου (3:10a)[2]

With the implied premise intact, the verse is traditionally taken to be a statement of human inability to fulfill the law:

> [The traditional reading] views Paul as addressing legalistic impulses within Judaism driven by an anthropological optimism whereby humans are thought to be able to earn salvation before God on the basis of their good works. Paul's argument, on such a view, articulates an intense anthropological skepticism, so that he is claiming in Gal 3.10 that anyone who attempts to earn salvation before God on the basis of doing good works is doomed to failure, since all such efforts inevitably fall short of the Law's perfect demand because of human sinfulness.[3]

Another difficulty is that, in adapting Deut 27:26, Paul modifies the language of the MT in a couple of ways (see Table 11.1). The first is that he twice employs πᾶς ("everyone," "all the things written . . ."), which intensifies the sense of the MT. This is, however, a rather benign change for a few reasons. To begin with, "everyone" is not a significant departure from the MT's אֲשֶׁר (which can roughly be translated "the one who" or "anyone"). Moreover, the equivalent of the second πᾶς occurs in the Samaritan Pentateuch and a few medieval Hebrew manuscripts, which supply כֹּל before דִּבְרֵי הַתּוֹרָה־הַזֹּאת (or Paul may have been influenced by the כָּל־מִצְוֺתָיו in the next

---

1. Silva, "Galatians," 799.
2. The phrase ἐξ ἔργων νόμου is variously paraphrased as those who "rely on works of the law" (ESV, NRSV, NIV), "men of the Torah" (Betz, *Sermon on the Mount*, 144), *nomosmenschen* (i.e., all "die ihre religiöse Existenz auf die Werke des Gesetzes aufbauen" [Mussner, *Der Galaterbrief*, 225]). Gombis, "Arguing with Scripture," 83, and Silva, "Galatians," 799, regard the phrase as referring to the Galatian opponents.
3. Gombis, "'Transgressor' and the 'Curse of the Law,'" 82n3.

verse). And, Paul's version tracks closely in this regard with the LXX, which contains both instances of πᾶς.⁴

Table 11.1. Paul's Citation in Gal 3:10 Compared with the Source Text

Gal 3:10b (NA28)	Deut 27:26 (MT)	Deut 27:26 (LXX)
ἐπικατάρατος πᾶς	אָר֕וּר אֲשֶׁ֧ר	Ἐπικατάρατος πᾶς ἄνθρωπος,
ὃς οὐκ ἐμμένει	לֹא־יָקִ֛ים	ὅστις οὐκ ἐμμενεῖ
<u>πᾶσιν τοῖς γεγραμμένοις ἐν τῷ</u>	אֶת־דִּבְרֵ֥י	ἐν πᾶσιν τοῖς λόγοις
<u>βιβλίῳ τοῦ νόμου</u>	הַתּוֹרָֽה־הַזֹּ֖את	τοῦ νόμου τούτου
τοῦ ποιῆσαι αὐτά.	לַעֲשׂ֣וֹת אוֹתָ֑ם	ποιῆσαι αὐτούς.
	וְאָמַ֥ר כָּל־הָעָ֖ם	καὶ ἐροῦσιν πᾶς ὁ λαός
	אָמֵֽן׃	Γένοιτο.
Cursed is everyone	Cursed is anyone	Cursed is every man
who does not abide by	who does not confirm	who does not abide by
<u>all the things written in the</u>	the words	all the words
<u>book of the law,</u>	of this law,	of this law,
to do them.	to do them.	to do them.
	And all the people shall say,	And all the people shall say,
	"Amen."	"So be it."

The literal English translation beneath each version is my own.

LXX text is from the Göttingen critical edition, which differs from Rahlfs in using ὅστις for ὅς and in omitting τοῦ before ποιῆσαι.

The second and more significant change (underlined in Table 11.1) is that Paul refers to τοῖς γεγραμμένοις ἐν τῷ βιβλίῳ τοῦ νόμου, which enlarges the set of commandments under the purview of the curse. In its original context Deut 27:26 is the last part of the Shechemite dodecalogue, a series of twelve curses which Moses instructs the Levites to speak on Mount Ebal when they cross the Jordan. The curses are for specific sins, such as illicit sexual relations or the movement of a neighbor's boundary stone. As the twelfth and final curse, Deut 27:26 looks backward at "this law" (the

---

4. Also unremarkable are the change of ἄνθρωπος to ὅς, the lack of ἐν before πᾶσιν, and the omission of the ending oath formula. The LXX's translation of the hiph'il קוּם (BDB: cause to stand, establish; ESV: confirm) as ἐμμένω (on which, see Bruce, *Galatians*, 159) is intriguing, but again Paul simply follows the LXX here. For an exhaustive discussion of Paul's wording as compared to the LXX in Gal 3:10, see Stanley, *Paul and the Language*, 238–43.

dodecalogue). Paul's reinterpreted version, however, has as its scope the entirety of the Torah.[5]

What are we to make, then, of Gal 3:10, in which the use of Deut 27:26 by Paul introduces both difficult theology (everyone under the law is cursed because no one obeys it perfectly) and questionable handling of the source text regarding its original scope? These problems are ameliorated when we see that Paul is speaking hyperbolically.

Logical Aspects

Paul is flouting the quality maxim by broad-brushing OT Judaism as a religion that curses its adherents for anything less than perfect obedience.[6] Such an idea, however, is foreign to the OT, with its regard for God's mercy and allowances for repentance and the sacrificial system.[7] Nor is there any "hint in Rabbinic literature of a view such as that of Paul in Gal. 3.10 . . . that one must achieve legal perfection."[8] Even with regard to Deut 27:26, the later rabbis emphasized the Hebrew יָקִים such that what was required was *confirmation* of the law, not keeping it without error.[9] Based on a literal reading, then, it seems that in Gal 3:10 Paul is painting a caricature of Judaism, one that "would never have been conceded by a Jewish opponent."[10]

---

5. Mussner, *Der Galaterbrief*, 224n55, "Paulus hat die Tora in ihrer Totalität mit all ihren Geboten und Verboten im Auge"; see also Silva, "Galatians," 797; Bruce, *Galatians*, 158; Fung, *Galatians*, 141. Bachmann, "Zur Argumentation von Galater 3.10–12," 527, suggests that Paul was thinking of Deut 28:58 when he modified Deut 27:26.

6. Cranford, "Possibility of Perfect Obedience," 242, "That Paul's argument as a whole . . . rests on his belief that the law demanded perfect obedience is an assumption under the traditional view of such importance that it cannot be overstated."

7. Moore, *Judaism*, 3:151, "How a Jew of Paul's antecedents could ignore, and by implication deny, the great prophetic doctrine of repentance, which, individualized and interiorized, was a cardinal doctrine of Judaism, namely that God, out of love, freely forgives the sincerely penitent sinner and restores him to his favor—that seems from the Jewish point of view inexplicable"; Nock, *St. Paul*, 29, "The observance of the Law did not for a Jew involve the pitiless antithesis of complete success and complete failure which Paul here portrays, since in Jewish belief no idea was more stressed than the infinite and unceasing willingness of God to forgive the penitent sinner."

8. Sanders, *Paul and Palestinian Judaism*, 137; Gutbrod, "νόμος," *TDNT* 4:1058, writes regarding the rabbinic writings, "In the main it is asserted in principle that the Law can be fulfilled."

9. Bruce, *Galatians*, 159; Sanders, *Paul and Palestinian Judaism*, 137. For the view that Paul was a Shammaite Pharisee who believed that God required perfect obedience to the law, see Hübner, "Gal 3,10 und die Herkunft des Paulus," 215–31; W. Grundmann, "μέγας," *TDNT* 4:529–44; Bruce, *Galatians*, 159.

10. Moore, *Judaism*, 1:494.

Literary Aspects

As noted above, Paul adds text to his citation of Deut 27:26 that, in effect, generalizes (with an ECF) the scope to include "all the things written in the book of the law." This change occurs on top of Paul's having selected a verse that already contains (in the LXX version) two ECFs: "everyone," and "all the things [written]."

Paul also uses extreme language in this passage. The language of being "under a curse" would have been serious, even shocking, to the former pagans of Galatia.

Rhetorical Aspects

The rhetorical situation of Gal 3:10 is best seen from the perspective of the entire chapter. The following is an outline of Paul's argument:

- 3:1–5 God's Spirit and miraculous work among you came as a result of faith, not observing the law. . .
- 3:6–9 So be children of Abraham:
    They have faith
    They are blessed along with Abraham
- 3:10–14 Do not be those who are ἐξ ἔργων νόμου:
    They must live by the law (yet they cannot)
    They are cursed
- 3:15–23 The way of faith/promise is superior to the law

Throughout this chapter Paul is constructing numerous dichotomies: (a) the promise versus the law, (b) the way of Abraham/faith versus the way of Moses/works, (c) blessing versus curse.[11] These dichotomies revolve around a single main dichotomous choice: circumcision or faith in Christ. Even here Paul is engaged in hyperbole, in this case what is called the "false dilemma." Known in antiquity, this rhetorical trick was a "ploy whereby Cicero tells a jury that it has to choose between only two possibilities, allegedly mutually exclusive, when in fact those possibilities may not be mutually exclusive at all and there may also be others available, at least one of which is more plausible than either of those that Cicero puts on offer."[12] The attractiveness of the false dilemma was that "[i]t was simple, symmetrical and economical,

---

11. Paul will develop other dichotomies in the coming verses, such as freedom versus slavery (3:26—4:31) and spirit versus flesh (5:16—6:10).

12. Seager, "Cicero and the 'False Dilemma,'" 99.

easy for a jury to understand, perhaps welcome to a jury not reluctant to be saved from the effort of excessive thought. More than that, it left no loose ends."[13] But in keeping it simple Paul is guilty of oversimplification. There is a broad gray area between the poles of submitting to circumcision and having faith in Christ. In fact, Paul and other Jewish Christians occupied that gray area.[14] Why could not the Galatians have both, as Paul himself had? For whatever reasons Paul felt that such a situation was unsatisfactory.

Both pathos and shock are present in abundance in this passage. Paul's words are designed to incite fear—fear of being accursed and fear of being burdened by the entirety of the law.

Conclusion

In Gal 3:10 Paul exaggerates the requirement of law keeping while understating the aspects of mercy and forgiveness which every Jew held to be central. He also exaggerates the extent to which his cited text applies to the rest of Scripture. For those reasons, and the inherent pathos and shock evident in this passage, there is a high likelihood that Paul is using hyperbole to further his rhetorical aims (see Figure 11.1).

13. Seager, "Cicero and the 'False Dilemma,'" 107.

14. Luedemann, *Opposition to Paul*, 61, "At the time of Paul's last trip to Jerusalem the church there stood completely within Judaism and had tolerated no abrogation of the law."

> **Hyperbole Scorecard: <u>Gal 3:10</u>**
>
> *Logical aspects*
> - ☒ Flouting of the quality maxim
> - ☐ Comparisons (A=B, A<>B, A is like B)
>
> *Literary aspects*
> - ☒ Universal language (ECFs), intensifiers, or generalizations
> - ☒ Extreme or extravagant language
> - ☐ Figurative language
> - ☐ Economy of expression
> - ☐ Amplification or attenuation
>
> *Rhetorical aspects*
> - ☒ Rhetorical situation
> - ☒ Pathos
> - ☒ Shock
> - ☐ Invective
>
> **A**

Figure 11.1. Hyperbole Scorecard for Gal 3:10.

THE LAW ENSLAVES (4:3, 9)

Paul's point in Gal 4:1–11 can be summarized with the imperative: "Grow up!" The Galatians, in their flirtation with circumcision and Jewish calendrical observances, are behaving like slave children, not like the heirs they are, heirs who have been adopted as sons. Just like Jews, who, in the time before Christ, were enslaved to the law, as if to the elementary substances of the cosmos (τὰ στοιχεῖα τοῦ κόσμου), the Galatians demonstrate that they are now wishing to return to a more primitive state of being, to paganism, to the slavery of those same elementary substances.[15]

It is remarkable that Paul lumps paganism and Judaism under the same umbrella concept—τὰ στοιχεῖα—and in doing so portrays the Sinaitic

---

15. See chapter 1 for a discussion of this phrase. "Elementary substances" was the dominant meaning for τὰ στοιχεῖα in the first century. See Gerhard Delling, "στοιχεῖον," *TDNT* 7:684, "A man of NT days would take στοιχεῖα τοῦ κόσμου to refer to the 'basic materials' of which everything in the cosmos, including man, is composed"; Moo, *Galatians*, 262; Martyn, *Galatians*, 394–95; De Boer, *Galatians*, 252–56.

law as an enslaving force. Such a comparison presents interpreters with the difficulty of trying once again to defend Paul's extremely harsh statements. Hübner calls it a "monstrous" saying.[16] In Longenecker's words it is "radical in the extreme."[17] Of course, this difficulty is alleviated when we see that Paul is simply speaking hyperbolically.

Logical Aspects

Paul's flouting of the quality maxim may be seen when the evidence previously presented is taken into account: (a) his statements elsewhere, especially in Romans, where the law is seen as a special, beneficial part of the relationship established between God and Israel (Rom 3:1–2; 7:12–13; 9:4–5); (b) his actions elsewhere, especially in Acts, where Paul lives out his own commitment to the law (Acts 16:3; 18:18; 19:21; 20:16; 21:20–24); and (c) the OT view of the law (see especially Ps 19:7–11; 119). The assertion that the law is slavery is nowhere to be found outside of Galatians. Indeed, in the prologue to the Ten Commandments (Exod 20:2) God has led the Israelites *out of* slavery into service to him through his law.

Paul's statements in Gal 4:3, 9 are not just hyperbole, but *metaphorical* hyperbole. He establishes a comparison (of the A=B variety) that following the law is akin to being enslaved to the elementary substances of the cosmos. This comparison is made more certain by verse 10, in which he references the Galatians' observance of the Jewish calendar.

Literary Aspects

That Paul calls the elementary substances ἀσθενῆ καὶ πτωχὰ (ESV: weak and worthless) may be seen as an intensification. There is no grammatical need for these terms. Rather, they fulfill the literary role of intensifying the hyperbole: The Galatians are not only wishing to be enslaved to their former masters, but masters who are *weaklings* and *good for nothing*!

Another instance of intensification is the combined use of πάλιν and ἄνωθεν. BDAG regards it as a strengthening of the sense of ἄνωθεν. In Lightfoot's estimation it is "a strong expression to describe the completeness of their *relapse*."[18]

---

16. Hübner, *Law in Paul's Thought*, 33.
17. Longenecker, *Galatians*, 181.
18. Lightfoot, *Galatians*, 171, emphasis original.

Paul's language in this passage is far from ordinary. On the contrary, the extreme (and figurative) language of slavery, the motif of impotence regarding the slave master, and the "sarcastic mockery" of Paul's diatribe style all emphasize the hyperbolic character of this utterance.[19]

Rhetorical Aspects

The rhetorical situation in these verses is that Paul is attempting to disparage the law in order to make it unattractive to the Galatian converts. Paul is hoping that they will be dissuaded from accepting circumcision.

The pathos is undeniable, especially in verse 9 where Paul poses "the emotionally loaded rhetorical question" about how the Galatians could turn away from the God who had made himself known to them (emphasizing God's initiative in the process) back to that which had formerly enslaved them.[20] He uses conversion language (ἐπιστρέφω) to state that the Galatians are basically re-converting to another religion altogether.

Several commentators note the shock value of Paul's comparison of the law with the elementary substances in verse 9. Barrett calls it "as extraordinary a statement as is to be found anywhere in [Paul's] letters. . . . Here in Galatians he virtually equates Judaism with heathenism. To go forward into Judaism is to go backward into heathenism."[21] Hübner, alluded to above, proclaims, "Something monstrous is being said: the function of the Torah is identical with that of the pagan deities."[22] For Bruce, "This is an astonishing statement for a former Pharisee to make."[23] And Martyn writes, "Shocking is the fact that Paul uses the motif of impotence to characterize observance of the Law on the part of Gentiles."[24]

---

19. Quoted words are from Martyn, *Galatians*, 412. On the rhetorical use of the image of slavery, see Joshel, *Slavery in the Roman World*, 10, "Because slavery was considered a degrading condition, Roman satirists, poets, philosophers, and historians could label an individual or a behavior servile when they wanted to denigrate someone or some act. In short, slavery shaped the Roman mentality."

20. De Boer, *Galatians*, 274.

21. Barrett, *Freedom and Obligation*, 61.

22. Hübner, "Gal 3,10 und die Herkunft des Paulus," 33.

23. Bruce, *Galatians*, 202–3.

24. Martyn, *Galatians*, 411–12.

Conclusion

Figure 11.2 depicts the results of our study into Gal 4:3, 9. Paul flouts the quality maxim by comparing Judaism to an enslaving force in the face of much evidence to the contrary. In light of this and the other logical, literary, and rhetorical aspects, there is a high likelihood that he is using hyperbole.

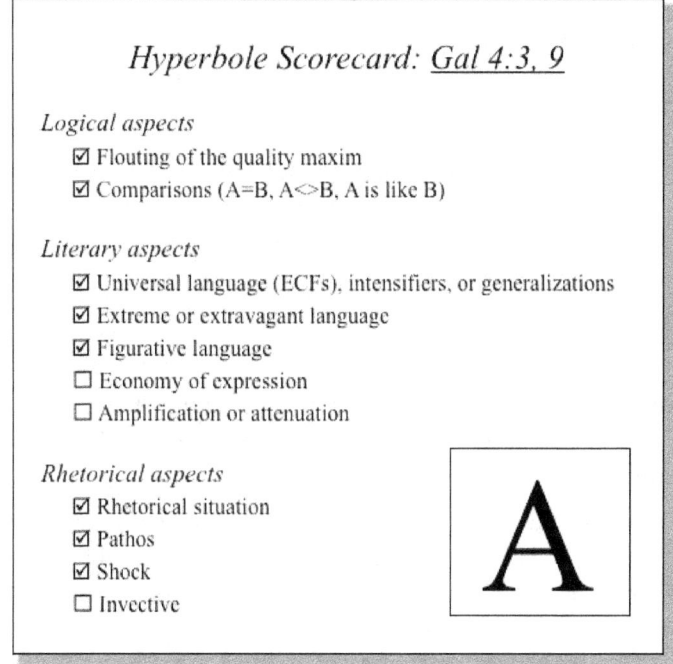

Figure 11.2. Hyperbole Scorecard for Gal 4:3, 9.

THE LAW SEVERS FELLOWSHIP WITH CHRIST (5:2-4)

There is a sequential thought process in Gal 5:2-4, as for the first time in the letter Paul explicitly indicates that the Galatians are being pressured to accept circumcision.[25] Circumcision inevitably leads to being encumbered by

---

25. The three verses are highly interconnected, which is why they are treated as a unit here. Verses 2 and 4 share the theme of alienation from Christ, while verse 3 conveys that theme indirectly. Verse 3 is linked to verse 2 by (a) the connective δέ, (b) the phrase μαρτύρομαι... πάλιν ("I tell you again"), which implies a reiteration of what was just said (cf. 1:8-9), and (c) the wordplay ὠφελήσει (verse 2)... ὀφειλέτης (verse 3).

the entire law and seeking one's righteousness from it. Hence, one is severed from Christ. It is a domino effect of the gravest proportions.

This is likely a very different picture than what the opponents had painted for the Galatians. Undoubtedly the consequences were presented in a positive way: Become circumcised, and you will be true children of Abraham and believers in the Messiah Jesus. It was a *both-and* scenario. Paul, however, untethers the two facets: "In a stark portrayal of the options typical of Paul's rhetoric in this letter, he insists that circumcision and Christ cannot mix. One cannot choose circumcision *and* Christ: it is circumcision *or* Christ."[26]

But why not? Why can a Gentile not enter the gray area of Torah-Christianity in which the Jewish Christians lived? Such a question is out of bounds as regards Paul's argument. He does not in any way appear to perceive a middle ground, but rather strict bipolar positions. Paul assumes that the reader will simply go along with his creation of a straw man. He constructs it along three points:

1. (Verse 2) If you are circumcised, Christ will benefit you nothing. In other words, salvation comes from Christ, not from the law. Therefore, *if you trust in the law for your salvation*, then Christ will not be able to save you.

2. (Verse 3) And, you will have to keep the entire law. In other words, circumcision is a gateway into the Jewish way of life. This idea would not be utterly foreign to the Galatians, since the opponents likely had already told them as much. What is new from Paul is the idea that taking the law upon yourself—specifically in a way in which *you search for righteousness* ἐξ ἔργων νόμου—brings you under a curse, since no one can do the whole law (3:10).

3. (Verse 4) So, then, any attempt to *justify yourself through the law* will result in a severing of your relationship with Christ.

Note how in each of Paul's three points (especially the parts I have italicized above) there is an assumption of incipient legalism—not that Paul is necessarily charging the Galatians with legalism but that he is painting a picture of what would be entailed if they choose that path.[27] Paul's legalistic straw

---

26. Moo, *Galatians*, 322.

27. Modern translations tend to give a conative force to δικαιοῦσθε in verse 4, rendering it as "trying/attempting to be justified," but do so in a way that makes it appear as if Paul is accusing the Galatians of already being legalistic (e.g., NIV: "You who are trying to be justified by the law"). While that is possible, an element of conditionality in the translation is preferable, as with the NJB: "once you seek to be reckoned as upright

man seeks his righteousness through the law and so has alienated himself from Christ.

What is the problem, then, if the Galatians have not yet gone down the road of legalism (ἐὰν plus the subjunctive περιτέμνησθε of v. 2 seems to indicate that they had not yet been circumcised)? How is there anything wrong with Paul saying that legalism deals a catastrophic blow to one's spiritual health? After all, this is a true enough statement in principle. The problem, exegetically, is that it is a straw man argument and should be seen as such. For all Paul knows, some of the Galatians, perhaps most, believed wholeheartedly in God's gracious forgiveness of sins through Christ and were persuaded through Scripture that circumcision was a way to honor that gift. Paul knew that the Galatians had received the Spirit (3:2). Did he think that the Spirit would depart from them if they were circumcised?[28] Better is to acknowledge that Paul is once again using hyperbole by constructing extreme positions (faith in Christ with no involvement in the law versus complete legalism) and presupposing the absence of any middle ground.[29] Paul's straw man is a person who is doomed to failure, but he is not representative of the Galatians as such. The rhetorical message is, "Do not be that person."

Logical Aspects

Paul flouts the quality maxim in that he exaggerates the mindset of the Galatians in constructing a straw man seeking righteousness through the law. Could it be that Paul is not exaggerating at all, and they *are* very legalistic? Perhaps so. But we have a situation where Jewish Christians are reaching out to Gentile Christians to supplement the latter's faith in Christ with law keeping (see chapter 9), presumably in the same way that Jewish Christians like Paul are able to synthesize the two.[30] Giving the Galatian converts the benefit of the doubt, we might assume that they are entering into dialogue with the Jewish Christians with open minds and a clear conscience, wanting simply to do the right thing.

---

through the Law, then you have separated yourself from Christ, you have fallen away from grace."

28. I must avoid debate here on Paul's view of eternal security.

29. Burton, *Galatians*, 272, "The possibility of any compromise between the two conceptions of religion he does not consider."

30. Longenecker, *Galatians*, 228, "The Judaizers must have assured the Galatians that in accepting supervision for their lives from the prescriptions of the Mosaic law they were not forsaking Christ or renouncing grace, but rather were completing their commitment to both."

As for verse 3, it carries with it the same flout of the quality maxim entailed with 3:10 (see above section). Implied is that taking the whole law upon oneself is a risky proposition, presumably because of the impossibility of fulfilling it. But a curse does not necessarily fall upon every adherent to the law due to the smallest amount of disobedience. The system of sacrifices and holy days were designed to cleanse God's people of sin.[31] Moreover, Jewish Christians could continue to observe the law and yet find their ultimate forgiveness in Christ, the fulfillment of the sacrifices and holy days.

Literary Aspects

There are several literary aspects that are indicative of hyperbole. First, Paul's use of ὅλον τὸν νόμον in verse 3 is an extreme case formulation. Though "a doctrine of the necessity of doing all the law was not absent in early or formative Judaism," Paul's allusion to doing the whole law here is not simply a matter-of-fact statement.[32] It is meant to discourage (threaten) the Galatians from wanting to enter into the law, as if it were too cumbersome and carried with it a threat of curse for disobedience.

Second, the phrases κατηργήθητε ἀπὸ Χριστοῦ and τῆς χάριτος ἐξεπέσατε constitute extreme/extravagant language. Within Gal 5:2–4 these are the "most damning statements of all."[33] The term καταργέω means "to remove from the sphere of activity."[34] Applied to one's relationship with Christ it connotes estrangement. Likewise, "fallen from grace" speaks of alienation from God himself. Whereas once the person had been secure in God's gracious care, now there is only emptiness and wrath.

Third, the phrase τῆς χάριτος ἐξεπέσατε also constitutes figurative language. "God's grace in Christ is like the stem which supports the flower and through which the life-sustaining sustenance flows."[35] In this case, the believer's fall from grace is suggestive of "a withered flower falling off from its stem to the ground."[36]

---

31. Dunn, *Galatians*, 266–67, "No Jew that we know of thought of the Jewish way of life as a perfect life, that is, without any sin or failure. Rather, it was a *total* way of life which, through the cult, its sacrifices and atonement, provided a means of dealing with sin and failure."
32. Longenecker, *Galatians*, 227.
33. Longenecker, *Galatians*, 228.
34. Gerhard Delling, *TDNT* 1:452; cf. BDAG, "be discharged, be released."
35. Dunn, *Galatians*, 268.
36. Dunn, *Galatians*, 268.

Fourth, the three verses taken together are parallel and constitute amplification by accumulation.[37] Longenecker calls them the "litany of dire consequences."[38] Paul begins verse 2 with the rather demonstrative phrase, Ἴδε ἐγὼ Παῦλος. Then, he starts verse 3 likewise in dramatic fashion with μαρτύρομαι δὲ πάλιν, reinforcing what has already been said in verse 2.[39] Finally, he concludes the trio of verses with the starkest words yet: κατηργήθητε ἀπὸ Χριστοῦ . . . τῆς χάριτος ἐξεπέσατε.

Rhetorical Aspects

The rhetorical situation has already been discussed. The Galatians have begun to observe the Jewish ritual calendar and are considering circumcision. Paul attempts to dissuade them from being the legalistic straw man who ends up estranged from Christ.

Pathos and shock are evident in the dreadful consequences Paul expounds. Also, by introducing the passage with Ἴδε ἐγὼ Παῦλος, he intends to "bring the relationship into play."[40] Paul wants to make sure he has the full attention of his addressees so that he can implore them from his heart to change course.

Conclusion

Figure 11.3 summarizes the results. Several logical, literary, and rhetorical aspects are noted that contribute toward a high probability of hyperbole in Gal 5:2–4. Essentially, in this passage Paul is constructing a straw man, a caricature of the Galatian believers, one who is bent on circumcision for legalistic reasons.

---

37. Moo, *Galatians*, 325, notes the "parallelism that is evident among verses 2, 3, and 4."
38. Longenecker, *Galatians*, 228.
39. Longenecker, *Galatians*, 226; De Boer, *Galatians*, 313.
40. Moo, *Galatians*, 321.

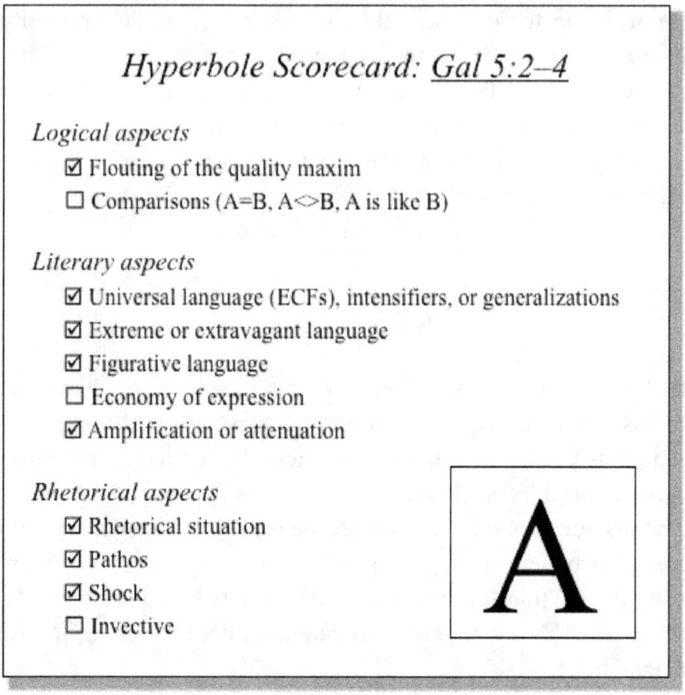

> **Hyperbole Scorecard: Gal 5:2–4**
>
> *Logical aspects*
> ☑ Flouting of the quality maxim
> ☐ Comparisons (A=B, A<>B, A is like B)
>
> *Literary aspects*
> ☑ Universal language (ECFs), intensifiers, or generalizations
> ☑ Extreme or extravagant language
> ☑ Figurative language
> ☐ Economy of expression
> ☑ Amplification or attenuation
>
> *Rhetorical aspects*
> ☑ Rhetorical situation
> ☑ Pathos
> ☑ Shock
> ☐ Invective
>
> **A**

Figure 11.3. Hyperbole Scorecard for Gal 5:2–4.

REIMAGINING THE CONSEQUENCES OF CIRCUMCISION

Table 11.2 summarizes the analyses presented in this chapter. All three passages rate "A" (high likelihood for hyperbole) due to the extent to which Paul is flouting the quality maxim in each, combined with other aspects.

Table 11.2. Hyperbole in Paul's Magnification of the Consequences of Circumcision

Passage		Grade
3:10	The law brings a curse upon anything less than perfect obedience	A
4:3, 9	The law enslaves	A
5:2–4	The law severs fellowship with Christ	A

Note: A=highly likely, B=moderately likely, C=somewhat likely, D=not likely

To summarize Paul's reasoning:

- His goal is to present a dire picture of taking on circumcision
- He uses hyperbole, a means of persuasion available to him and common to ancient speakers
    - o He exaggerates the impact of taking on the law
    - o He constructs a straw man—a hyper-legalistic version (caricature) of the Galatian believers
    - o This hyper-legalistic person risks being enslaved to the law, cursed, and severed from fellowship with Christ
- Paul's rhetorical imperative is, "Do not be like that person!"

12

A Fresh Perspective on Galatians

In this chapter...

Question(s) to be answered:
- How can Paul's letter to the Galatians be perceived in the light of all that has been demonstrated in this study?

Trajectory:
- This chapter summarizes the results of the study.

AT SOME POINT IN his missionary travels Paul received word that the Galatians had a developing situation in their church. They were being taught by Jewish Christians that they needed to take another step in order to become full sons of Abraham. They needed to be circumcised and submit to the Sinaitic law (or at least to a subset of strictures). The Galatians were already beginning to take part in some of the calendrical observances.

Paul also learned that these Jewish Christian teachers were maligning his character, questioning his apostolic credentials, and disparaging his faith-only gospel to be that of a man-pleaser. In the honor-shame culture of that era, Paul took this as a challenge to defend his honor. He needed to respond in full force and discredit the teachers who had now become his opponents.

Paul was utterly confident in his own law-free version of the gospel to the Gentiles. After all, God had demonstrated his gracious election of the Gentiles by granting them the Holy Spirit (Acts 15:8), a phenomenon Paul himself had witnessed on numerous occasions. The apostles in Jerusalem had agreed, given that the promise of God had been extended to the

Gentiles outside of a nomistic context, that nothing more would be required than abstaining from what had been sacrificed to idols, from blood, from what had been strangled, and from sexual immorality (Acts 15:19–29).

Paul then set to laying out his case. Using the style of invective common to his era, Paul branded the "gospel" of his opponents as false and placed them under a curse for preaching it. He openly questioned their motives, charging that they were only interested in winning the Galatians over to avoid persecution, perhaps from zealot-minded Jews in Jerusalem; the Galatians were nothing more than a notch on the missionary belts of the opponents, Paul alleged. And, in a fit of pique, he wished upon them complete emasculation.

But the Galatians would have seen through Paul's angry screed. They had come to know the Jewish Christian teachers as brothers in the Lord, sincere in their belief in the gospel of Jesus Christ. They had been persuaded by many hours of careful reasoning in the scriptures, no doubt Gen 17 and possibly also Deut 27:26. They were accustomed to the use of invective and knew how to process it as hyperbole. To them the whole argument amounted to an intense competition between prize fighters, with words substituting for fists. They observed with eager anticipation.

Paul continued his case by framing the issue, like an expert lawyer in front of a jury. He wanted the choice to be crystal clear between the two alternatives, so he spoke in black-and-white terms. Faith in Christ was antithetical to works of the law. If you choose the former, you will be blessed as a child of Abraham. If you choose the latter, you will be cursed. No matter that many thousands of Jewish believers in Jesus had found a synthesis between the two and did not believe they were under a curse—that fact was not to be entered into evidence. Paul's speech needed to be hyperbolic in the interest of being highly persuasive.

Salvation history was also on Paul's mind. The giving of the promise was not like the giving of the law. While the former was established directly between God and Abraham, the latter was ordained through angels and mediated through Moses—a muddy and inferior situation. The purpose of the law was to increase sins and imprison all people under sin until Christ could come. No matter that Paul himself remained obedient to this same law. Left unsaid were the many scriptural and traditional voices in praise of the law as perfect, holy, and everlasting. In the business of hyperbolic speech, reality gets distorted, as if gazing into a fun house mirror.

So Galatians is not systematic theology. It does not purport to be, nor should we allow it to be, given its strongly situational nature and hyperbolic character. The argument of Galatians is clearly not one that Paul would make to fellow Jews, for instance. Can we, then, effectively harmonize Galatians with Romans or any other book of the NT? Can we discover the core of Paul's beliefs concerning the law within its pages? Such exercises risk assigning importance to overly simplistic dichotomies that cannot bear the weight of the rest of Scripture thrust upon them. We should rather allow Galatians to speak to us hyperbolically, with all of its loudness and bipolarities, its effusiveness and color, its caricatures and straw men, this magnificent exercise in arm twisting on the part of a beloved apostle to his dear flock.

Bibliography

Anthony, C. V. "The Hebrew Hyperbole." *Methodist Review* 87 (1905) 742-47.
Arena, Valentina. "Roman Oratorical Invective." In *A Companion to Roman Rhetoric*, edited by William Dominik and Jon Hall, 149-59. Malden, MA: Wiley-Blackwell, 2010.
Aristotle. *Art of Rhetoric*. Translated by J. H. Freese. LCL 193. Cambridge: Harvard University Press, 1926.
———. *On Rhetoric*. Translated by George Kennedy. 2nd ed. New York: Oxford University Press, 2007.
Armitage, David J. "An Exploration of Conditional Clause Exegesis with Reference to Galatians 1,8-9." *Biblica* 88 (2007) 365-92.
Austin, J. L. *How to Do Things with Words*. 2nd ed. Cambridge: Harvard University Press, 1975.
Bach, Kent, and Robert M. Harnish. *Linguistic Communication and Speech Acts*. Cambridge, MA: MIT Press, 1979.
Bachmann, Michael. "Zur Argumentation von Galater 3.10-12." *NTS* 53 (2007) 524-44.
Badenas, Robert. *Christ the End of the Law: Romans 10.4 in Pauline Perspective*. JSNTSup 10. Sheffield, England: JSOT Press, 1985.
Barclay, John M. G. "Mirror-Reading a Polemical Letter: Galatians as a Test Case." *JSNT* 31 (1987) 73-93.
Barrett, C. K. *The Acts of the Apostles*. 2 vols. ICC. New York: T. & T. Clark, 1998.
———. *A Commentary on the First Epistle to the Corinthians*. New York: Harper & Row, 1968.
———. *Freedom and Obligation: A Study of the Epistle to the Galatians*. Philadelphia: Westminster, 1985.
Baur, Ferdinand Christian. *The Church History of the First Three Centuries*. 3rd ed. London: Williams and Norgate, 1878.
———. "Die Christuspartei in der korinthischen Gemeinde, der Gegensatz des paulinischen und petrinischen Christentums in der ältesten Kirche, der Apostel Petrus in Rom." *Tübinger Zeitschrift für Theologie* 4 (1831) 61-206.

———. *Paul the Apostle of Jesus Christ: His Life and Works, His Epistles and Teachings.* 2 vols. London: Williams & Norgate, 1873–75. Repr., Peabody, MA: Hendrickson, 2003.

Beale, G. K. *The Temple and the Church's Mission: A Biblical Theology of the Dwelling Place of God.* Edited by D. A. Carson. New Studies in Biblical Theology. Downers Grove, IL: InterVarsity, 2004.

Becker, Jürgen. *Paul: Apostle to the Gentiles.* Louisville: Westminster John Knox, 1993.

Betz, Hans Dieter. *Galatians: A Commentary on Paul's Letter to the Churches in Galatia.* Philadelphia: Fortress, 1979.

———. *The Sermon on the Mount.* Minneapolis: Augsburg Fortress, 1995.

Bitzer, Lloyd F. "The Rhetorical Situation." *Philosophy and Rhetoric* 1 (1968) 1–14.

Blass, Friedrich, et al. *A Greek Grammar of the New Testament and Other Early Christian Literature.* Chicago: University of Chicago Press, 1961.

Bock, Darrell L. *Acts.* BECNT. Grand Rapids: Baker, 2007.

Bonilla, Plutarco. "Jesus, What an Exaggerator." *Journal of Latin American Theology* 8 (2013) 77–85.

Borgen, Peder. "From Paul to Luke: Observations toward Clarification of the Theology of Luke-Acts." *CBQ* 31 (1969) 168–82.

Bornkamm, Günther. "The Missionary Stance of Paul in I Corinthians 9 and in Acts." In *Studies in Luke-Acts*, edited by Leander E. Keck and J. Louis Martyn, 194–207. Nashville: Abingdon, 1966.

Botha, Pieter J. J. "The Verbal Art of the Pauline Letters: Rhetoric, Performance and Presence." In *Rhetoric and the New Testament: Essays from the 1992 Heidelberg Conference*, edited by Stanley E. Porter, 409–28. JSNTSup 90. Sheffield, England: Sheffield, 1993.

Bruce, F. F. *The Acts of the Apostles: The Greek Text with Introduction and Commentary.* 3rd ed. Grand Rapids: Eerdmans, 1990.

———. *The Epistle to the Galatians: A Commentary on the Greek Text.* NIGTC. Grand Rapids: Eerdmans, 1982.

———. "Is the Paul of Acts the Real Paul?" *BJRL* 58 (1976) 282–305.

Bullinger, E. W. *Figures of Speech Used in the Bible.* 1898. Repr., New York: Cosimo Classics, 2012.

Burton, Ernest DeWitt. *A Critical and Exegetical Commentary on the Epistle to the Galatians.* ICC. Edinburgh: T. & T. Clark, 1921. Repr., Greenwood, SC: Attic, 1980.

Butarbutar, Robinson. *Paul and Conflict Resolution: An Exegetical Study of Paul's Apostolic Paradigm in 1 Corinthians 9.* Waynesboro, GA: Paternoster, 2007.

Callan, Terrance. "Pauline Midrash: The Exegetical Background of Gal 3:19b." *JBL* 99 (1980) 549–67.

Carson, D. A. "Paul's Inconsistency: Reflections on I Corinthians 9.19–23 and Galatians 2.11–14." *Churchman* 100 (1986) 7–45.

Carson, D. A., Peter T. O'Brien, and Mark A. Seifrid, eds. *Justification and Variegated Nomism.* Vol. 1, *The Complexities of Second Temple Judaism.* Grand Rapids: Baker, 2001.

Chadwick, Henry. "All Things to All Men." *NTS* 1 (1955) 261–75.

Christensen, Duane L. *Deuteronomy 1:1—21:9.* WBC 6A. Nashville: Thomas Nelson, 2001.

Cicero. *Divisions of Oratory.* Translated by H. Rackham. LCL 349. Cambridge: Harvard University Press, 1942.

———. *In Pisonem*. Translated by N. H. Watts. LCL 252. Cambridge: Harvard University Press, 1931.
———. *On Invention*. Translated by H. M. Hubbell. LCL 386. Cambridge: Harvard University Press, 1949.
———. *On the Orator (De Oratore)*. Translated by E. W. Sutton and H. Rackham. LCL 348, 349. Cambridge: Harvard University Press, 1942.
———. *Rhetorica ad Herennium*. LCL 403. Cambridge: Harvard University Press, 1954.
Claridge, Claudia. *Hyperbole in English: A Corpus-Based Study of Exaggeration*. New York: Cambridge University Press, 2011.
Clark, Herbert H. *Using Language*. Cambridge: Cambridge University Press, 1996.
Classen, Carl Joachim. "Can the Theory of Rhetoric Help Us to Understand the New Testament, and in Particular the Letters of Paul?" In *Paul and Ancient Rhetoric: Theory and Practice in the Hellenistic Context*, edited by Stanley E. Porter and Bryan R. Dyer, 13–39. New York: Cambridge University Press, 2016.
———. *Rhetorical Criticism of the New Testament*. Boston: Brill, 2002.
———. "St. Paul's Epistles and Ancient Greek and Roman Rhetoric." In *Rhetoric and the New Testament: Essays from the 1992 Heidelberg Conference*, edited by Stanley E. Porter and Thomas H. Olbricht, 265–91. JSNTSup 90. Sheffield, England: Sheffield Academic, 1993.
Colston, Herbert L. *Using Figurative Language*. New York: Cambridge University Press, 2015.
Conzelmann, Hanz. *Acts of the Apostles*. Translated by James Limburg, Thomas Kraabel, and Donald H. Juel. Philadelphia: Fortress, 1987.
———. *First Corinthians*. Philadelphia: Fortress, 1975.
Corbeill, Anthony. "Ciceronian Invective." In *Brill's Companion to Cicero: Oratory and Rhetoric*, edited by James M. May, 197–218. Boston: Brill, 2002.
Cosby, Michael R. "Galatians: Red-Hot Rhetoric." In *Rhetorical Argumentation in Biblical Texts: Essays from the Lund 2000 Conference*, edited by Anders Eriksson et al., 296–309. Harrisburg, PA: Trinity, 2002.
Craig, Christopher P. "Audience Expectations, Invective, and Proof." In *Cicero the Advocate*, edited by Jonathan G. F. Powell and Jeremy Paterson, 187–214. Oxford: Oxford University Press, 2004.
Craigie, Peter C. *Psalms 1–50*. WBC 19. Nashville: Thomas Nelson, 1983.
Cranford, Michael. "The Possibility of Perfect Obedience: Paul and an Implied Premise in Galatians 3:10 and 5:3." *NovT* 36 (1994) 242–58.
Crownfield, Frederic R. "The Singular Problem of the Dual Galatians." *JBL* 64 (1945) 491–500.
Culy, Martin M. "Would Jesus Exaggerate?: Rethinking Matthew 26.38//Mark 14.34." *The Bible Translator* 57 (2006) 105–9.
Daube, David. *New Testament and Rabbinic Judaism*. Peabody, MA: Hendrickson, 1956.
Davies, W. D. *Torah in the Messianic Age and/or the Age to Come*. JBL Monograph Series 7. Philadelphia: Society of Biblical Literature, 1952.
Davies, W. D., and Dale C. Allison. *Matthew 1–7*. ICC. New York: T. & T. Clark, 1988.
De Boer, Martinus C. *Galatians: A Commentary*. NTL. Louisville: Westminster John Knox, 2011.
Demetrius. *On Style*. Translated by Doreen C. Innes. LCL 199. Cambridge: Harvard University Press, 1995.

Douglas, Claude C. *Overstatement in the New Testament.* New York: Henry Holt, 1931.
Du Toit, Andrie B. "Vilification as a Pragmatic Device in Early Christian Epistolography." *Biblica* 75 (1994) 403–12.
Dunn, James D. G. *The Epistle to the Galatians.* Peabody, MA: Hendrickson, 1993.
———. *The New Perspective on Paul.* Rev. ed. Grand Rapids: Eerdmans, 2005.
———. *Romans 1–8.* WBC 38A. Nashville: Thomas Nelson, 1988.
———. *Romans 9–16.* WBC 38B. Nashville: Thomas Nelson, 1988.
Edwards, Derek. "Extreme Case Formulations: Softeners, Investment, and Doing Nonliteral." *Research on Language and Social Interaction* 33 (2000) 347–73.
Ellis, E. Earle. "Paul and His Opponents: Trends in Research." In *Christianity, Judaism and Other Greco-Roman Cults: Studies for Morton Smith at Sixty*, edited by Jacob Neusner, 264–98. Leiden: Brill, 1975.
Elmer, Ian J. *Paul, Jerusalem and the Judaisers: The Galatians Crisis in Its Broadest Historical Context.* WUNT 258. Tübingen: Mohr Siebeck, 2009.
Eybers, Ian Heinrich. "Some Examples of Hyperbole in Biblical Hebrew." In vol. 1 of *Semitics*, edited by Ian Heinrich Eybers and J. J. Glück, 38–49. Pretoria: University of South Africa, 1970.
Fee, Gordon. *The First Epistle to the Corinthians.* Rev. ed. NICNT. Grand Rapids: Eerdmans, 2014.
Fee, Gordon D. *Paul's Letter to the Philippians.* NICNT. Grand Rapids: Eerdmans, 1995.
Fitzmyer, Joseph A. *First Corinthians.* Anchor Yale Bible. New Haven: Yale University Press, 2008.
———. *Romans: A New Translation with Introduction and Commentary.* AB 33. New York: Doubleday, 1993.
Fogelin, Robert J. *Figuratively Speaking.* Rev. ed. New York: Oxford University Press, 2011.
Fontanier, Pierre. *Les Figures du Discours.* Paris: Gallimard, 1977.
Forbes, Christopher. "Ancient Rhetoric and Ancient Letters: Models for Reading Paul, and Their Limits." In *Paul and Rhetoric*, edited by J. Paul Sampley and Peter Lampe, 143–60. New York: T. & T. Clark, 2010.
France, R. T. *The Gospel of Matthew.* NICNT. Grand Rapids: Eerdmans, 2007.
Freyne, Sean. "Vilifying the Other and Defining the Self: Matthew's and John's Anti-Jewish Polemic in Focus." In *"To See Ourselves as Others See Us": Christians, Jews, "Others" in Late Antiquity*, edited by Jacob Neusner and Ernest S. Frerichs, 118–23. Chico, CA: Scholars, 1985.
Fung, Ronald Y. K. *The Epistle to the Galatians.* NICNT. Grand Rapids: Eerdmans, 1988.
Gager, John G. *The Origins of Anti-Semitism: Attitudes Toward Judaism in Pagan and Christian Antiquity.* New York: Oxford University Press, 1983.
———. *Reinventing Paul.* New York: Oxford University Press, 2000.
———. *Who Made Early Christianity? The Jewish Lives of the Apostle Paul.* New York: Columbia University Press, 2015.
García Cordero, Maximiliano. "Hipérboles y Paradojas en la Predicación (Ia Parte)." *Ciencia Tomista* 132 (2005) 63–110.
———. "Hipérboles y Paradojas en la Predicación (IIa Parte)." *Ciencia Tomista* 132 (2005) 237–63.
Garland, David E. *1 Corinthians.* BECNT. Grand Rapids: Baker, 2003.
Gasque, W. Ward. "The Historical Value of Acts." *TynBul* 40 (1989) 136–57.
———. "The Historical Value of the Book of Acts." *TZ* 28 (1972) 177–96.

Gaston, Lloyd. *Paul and the Torah*. Vancouver: University of British Columbia Press, 1987.
Gibbs, Raymond W. *The Poetics of Mind: Figurative Thought, Language and Understanding*. Cambridge: Cambridge University Press, 1994.
Goldsworthy, Graeme. "Gospel and Kingdom." In *The Goldsworthy Trilogy*, 1–148. Colorado Springs: Paternoster, 2000.
Gombis, Timothy G. "Arguing with Scripture in Galatia: Galatians 3:10–14 as a Series of Ad Hoc Arguments." In *Galatians and Christian Theology: Justification, the Gospel, and Ethics in Paul's Letter*, edited by Mark W. Elliott et al., 82–90. Grand Rapids: Baker, 2014.
———. "The 'Transgressor' and the 'Curse of the Law': The Logic of Paul's Argument in Galatians 2–3." *NTS* 53 (2007) 81–93.
Goppelt, Leonhard. *Typos: The Typological Interpretation of the Old Testament in the New*. Grand Rapids: Eerdmans, 1982.
Grice, Paul. *Studies in the Way of Words*. Cambridge: Harvard University Press, 1989.
Haenchen, Ernst. *The Acts of the Apostles: A Commentary*. Translated by Bernard Noble, Gerald Shinn, and R. McL. Wilson. Philadelphia: Westminster, 1971.
———. "The Book of Acts as Source Material for the History of Early Christianity." In *Studies in Luke-Acts*, edited by Leander E. Keck and J. Louis Martyn, 258–78. Nashville: Abingdon, 1966.
Hansen, G. Walter. *The Letter to the Philippians*. The Pillar New Testament Commentary. Grand Rapids: Eerdmans, 2009.
Hausrath, Adolf. *A History of New Testament Times*. Translated by L. Huxley. 4 vols. London: Williams and Norgate, 1895.
Hawthorne, Gerald F., and Ralph P. Martin. *Philippians*. Rev. ed. WBC 43. Nashville: Thomas Nelson, 2004.
Hemer, Colin J. *The Book of Acts in the Setting of Hellenistic History*. WUNT 49. Tübingen: J. C. B. Mohr, 1989. Repr., Winona Lake, IN: Eisenbrauns, 1990.
Herrick, James A. *The History and Theory of Rhetoric*. 3rd ed. New York: Allyn and Bacon, 2005.
Hilbert, Benjamin D. H. "185,000 Slain Maccabean Enemies (Times Two): Hyperbole in the Books of Maccabees." *ZAW* 122 (2010) 102–6.
Horn, Laurence R. "On the Semantic Properties of Logical Operators in English." PhD diss., University of California at Los Angeles, 1972.
Howard, George. *Paul: Crisis in Galatia*. Vol. SNTSMS 35. New York: Cambridge University Press, 1979.
Huang, Yan. *Pragmatics*. 2nd ed. New York: Oxford University Press, 2014.
Hübner, Hans. "Gal 3,10 und die Herkunft des Paulus." *KD* 19 (1973) 215–31.
———. *Law in Paul's Thought*. Translated by James C. G. Greig. Edinburgh: T. & T. Clark, 1984.
Hughes, Frank W. "Paul and Traditions of Greco-Roman Rhetoric." In *Paul and Ancient Rhetoric: Theory and Practice in the Hellenistic Context*, edited by Stanley E. Porter and Bryan R. Dyer, 86–95. New York: Cambridge University Press, 2016.
Hvalvik, Reidar. "Paul as a Jewish Believer—According to the Book of Acts." In *Jewish Believers in Jesus: The Early Centuries*, edited by Oskar Skarsaune and Reidar Hvalvik, 121–53. Peabody, MA: Hendrickson, 2007.

Jenni, Ernst. "Sprachliche Übertreibungen im Alten Testament." In *Sprache—Bilder—Klänge: Dimensionen der Theologie im Alten Testament und in seinem Umfeld*, edited by Christiane Karrer-Grube et al., 75–88. Münster: Ugarit-Verlag, 2009.

Jervell, Jacob. *Luke and the People of God: A New Look at Luke-Acts*. Minneapolis: Augsburg, 1972.

———. *The Theology of the Acts of the Apostles*. Cambridge: Cambridge University Press, 1996.

Jewett, Robert. "The Agitators and the Galatian Congregation." *NTS* 17 (1971) 198–212.

———. *Romans*. Minneapolis: Fortress, 2007.

Jipp, Joshua W. *Christ Is King: Paul's Royal Ideology*. Minneapolis: Fortress, 2015.

Johnson, Luke Timothy. *The Acts of the Apostles*. Sacra Pagina 5. Collegeville, MN: Liturgical Press, 1992.

———. "The New Testament's Anti-Jewish Slander and the Conventions of Ancient Polemic." *JBL* 108 (1989) 419–41.

Josephus, Flavius. *Josephus: The Complete Works*. Translated by William Whiston. Nashville: Thomas Nelson, 1998.

Joshel, Sandra R. *Slavery in the Roman World*. New York: Cambridge University Press, 2010.

Keener, Craig S. *Acts: An Exegetical Commentary*. 4 vols. Grand Rapids: Baker, 2012–15.

Kennedy, George A. *Comparative Rhetoric: An Historical and Cross-Cultural Introduction*. New York: Oxford, 1998.

———. "Historical Survey of Rhetoric." In *Handbook of Classical Rhetoric in the Hellenistic Period 330 B.C.–A.D. 400*, edited by Stanley Porter, 3–42. New York: Brill, 1997.

———. *New Testament Interpretation through Rhetorical Criticism*. Chapel Hill: University of North Carolina Press, 1984.

———. *Progymnasmata: Greek Textbooks of Prose Composition and Rhetoric*. Translated by George A. Kennedy. Atlanta: Society of Biblical Literature, 2003.

Kern, Philip H. *Rhetoric and Galatians: Assessing an Approach to Paul's Epistle*. Cambridge: Cambridge University Press, 1998.

Kingsbury, Jack Dean. *Matthew as Story*. 2nd ed. Philadelphia: Fortress, 1988.

Kissling, Paul J. "Self-Defense and Identity Formation in the Depiction of Battles in Joshua and Esther." In *Interested Readers: Essays on the Hebrew Bible in Honor of David J. A. Clines*, edited by James K. Aitken et al., 105–19. Atlanta: Society of Biblical Literature, 2013.

Kittel, Gerhard, and Gerhard Friedrich, eds. *Theological Dictionary of the New Testament*. Translated by Geoffrey W. Bromiley. 10 vols. Grand Rapids: Eerdmans, 1964–76.

Knox, Wilfred L. *St. Paul and the Church of Jerusalem*. Cambridge: Cambridge University Press, 1925.

Koester, Helmut. "The Purpose of a Polemic of a Pauline Fragment (Philippians III)." *NTS* 8 (1962) 317–32.

Kremmydas, Christos. "Hellenistic Rhetorical Education and Paul's Letters." In *Paul and Ancient Rhetoric: Theory and Practice in the Hellenistic Context*, edited by Stanley E. Porter and Bryan R. Dyer, 68–85. New York: Cambridge University Press, 2016.

Lampe, Peter. "Can Words Be Violent or Do They Only Sound That Way? Second Corinthians: Verbal Warfare from Afar as a Complement to a Placid Personal

Presence." In *Paul and Rhetoric*, edited by J. Paul Sampley and Peter Lampe, 223–40. New York: T. & T. Clark, 2010.

———. "Rhetorical Analysis of Pauline Texts—Quo Vadit?: Methodological Reflections." In *Paul and Rhetoric*, edited by J. Paul Sampley and Peter Lampe, 3–24. New York: T. & T. Clark, 2010.

Lausberg, Heinrich. *Handbook of Literary Rhetoric: A Foundation for Literary Study*. Edited by David E. Orton and R. Dan Anderson. Translated by Matthew T. Bliss, Annemie Jansen, and David E. Orton. Boston: Brill, 1998.

Lavoie, Jean-Jacques. "Ironie et ambiguïtés en Qohélet 10, 16–20." *Studies in Religion/Sciences Religieuses* 37 (2008) 183–209.

Lentz, John Clayton, Jr. *Luke's Portrait of Paul*. SNTSMS 77. Cambridge: Cambridge University Press, 1993.

Levinson, Stephen C. *Presumptive Meanings: The Theory of Generalized Conversational Implicature*. Cambridge, MA: MIT Press, 2000.

Lightfoot, J. B. *The Epistle of St. Paul to the Galatians: With Introductions, Notes and Dissertations*. 1865. Repr., Grand Rapids: Zondervan, 1969.

Livesey, Nina E. *Galatians and the Rhetoric of Crisis*. Salem, OR: Polebridge, 2016.

Loftus, Elizabeth E., and John C. Palmer. "Reconstruction of Automobile Destruction: An Example of the Interaction Between Language and Memory." *Journal of Verbal Learning and Verbal Behavior* 13 (1974) 585–89.

Longenecker, Richard N. *The Epistle to the Romans: A Commentary on the Greek Text*. NIGTC. Grand Rapids: Eerdmans, 2016.

———. *Galatians*. WBC. Dallas: Word Books, 1990.

———. *Paul: Apostle of Liberty*. New York: Harper & Row, 1964.

Longinus. *On the Sublime*. Translated by W. H. Fyfe and revised by Donald Russell. LCL 199. Cambridge: Harvard University Press, 1995.

Luedemann, Gerd. *Opposition to Paul in Jewish Christianity*. Translated by M. Eugene Boring. Minneapolis: Fortress, 1989.

Lütgert, Wilhelm. *Gesetz und Geist: Eine Untersuchung zur Vorgeschichte des Galaterbriefes*. Gütersloh: Druck und Verlag von Bertelsmann, 1919.

Luther, Martin, Jaroslav Pelikan, Hilton C. Oswald, Helmut T. Lehmann, and Christopher Boyd Brown. *Luther's Works*. 55 vols. St. Louis: Concordia, 1955.

Luz, Ulrich. *Matthew*. Hermeneia. Minneapolis: Fortress, 2007.

Mac Cormac, Earl R. *A Cognitive Theory of Metaphor*. Cambridge: MIT Press, 1985.

Manuwald, Gesine. "The Function of Praise and Blame in Cicero's *Philippics*." In *Praise and Blame in Roman Republican Rhetoric*, edited by Christopher Smith and Ralph Covino, 199–214. Wales: The Classical Press of Wales, 2011.

Mariaselvam, Abraham. *The Song of Songs and Ancient Tamil Love Poems*. Rome: Editrice Pontificio Istituto Biblico, 1988.

Marshall, I. Howard. *The Acts of the Apostles: An Introduction and Commentary*. Grand Rapids: Eerdmans, 1980.

———. *Luke: Historian and Theologian*. Downers Grove, IL: InterVarsity, 1970.

Marshall, Peter. *Enmity in Corinth: Social Conventions in Paul's Relations with the Corinthians*. WUNT 23. Tübingen: J. C. B. Mohr, 1987.

Martin, Josef. *Antike Rhetorik: Technik und Methode*. München: C. H. Beck'sche Verlagsbuchhandlung, 1974.

Martin, Troy W. "The Syntax of Surprise, Irony, or Shifting of Blame in Gal 1:6–7." *Biblical Research* 54 (2009) 79–98.

Martyn, J. Louis. *Galatians*. AB. New York: Doubleday, 1997.

———. *Theological Issues in the Letters of Paul*. Nashville: Abingdon, 1997.

Matlock, R. Barry. "Saving Faith: The Rhetoric and Semantics of πίστις in Paul." In *The Faith of Jesus Christ: Exegetical, Biblical, and Theological Studies*, edited by Michael F. Bird and Preston M. Sprinkle, 73–90. Peabody, MA: Hendrickson, 2009.

Mattill, A. J. "The Value of Acts as a Source for the Study of Paul." In *Perspectives on Luke-Acts*, edited by Charles H. Talbert, 76–98. Danville, VA: Association of Baptist Professors of Religion, 1978.

McCarthy, Michael, and Ronald Carter. "'There's Millions of Them': Hyperbole in Everyday Conversation." *Journal of Pragmatics* 36 (2004) 149–84.

McFadden, K. "Hyperbole." In *The New Princeton Encyclopedia of Poetry and Poetics*, edited by Alex Preminger and T. V. F. Brogan, 648. Princeton: Princeton University Press, 1993.

Moo, Douglas J. *The Epistle to the Romans*. NICNT. Grand Rapids: Eerdmans, 1996.

———. *Galatians*. BECNT. Grand Rapids: Baker, 2013.

———. "'Law,' 'Works of the Law,' and Legalism in Paul." *WTJ* 45 (1983) 73–100.

Moore, George Foot. *Judaism in the First Centuries of the Christian Era: The Age of Tannaim*. 3 vols. Cambridge: Harvard University Press, 1927. Repr., Peabody, MA: Hendrickson, 1997.

Morris, Leon. *The Epistle to the Romans*. Grand Rapids: Eerdmans, 1988.

Mullins, Terence Y. "Formulas in the New Testament Epistles." *JBL* 91 (1972) 380–90.

Munck, Johannes. *The Acts of the Apostles*. Garden City, NY: Doubleday, 1967.

———. *Paul and the Salvation of Mankind*. Richmond: John Knox, 1959.

Mussner, Franz. *Der Galaterbrief*. Freiburg im Breisgau: Herder, 1977.

Nanos, Mark D. "Intruding 'Spies' and 'Pseudo-Brethren': The Jewish Intra-Group Politics of Paul's Jerusalem Meeting (Gal 2:1–10)." In *Paul and His Opponents*, edited by Stanley E. Porter, 59–98. Atlanta: Society of Biblical Literature, 2005.

———. *The Irony of Galatians: Paul's Letter in First-Century Context*. Minneapolis: Fortress, 2002.

———. "Paul's Relationship to Torah in Light of His Strategy 'to Become Everything to Everyone' (1 Corinthians 9.19–23)." In *Paul and Judaism: Crosscurrents in Pauline Exegesis and the Study of Jewish-Christian Relations*, edited by Reimund Bieringer and Didier Pollefeyt, 106–40. LNTS 463. New York: T. & T. Clark, 2012.

Nanos, Mark D., and Magnus Zetterholm, eds. *Paul within Judaism: Restoring the First-Century Context to the Apostle*. Minneapolis: Fortress, 2015.

Neill, Stephen, and Tom Wright. *The Interpretation of the New Testament 1861–1986*. 2nd ed. New York: Oxford University Press, 1988.

Neusner, Jacob, ed. *The Babylonian Talmud: A Translation and Commentary*. Translated by Jacob Neusner. 22 vols. Peabody, MA: Hendrickson, 2011.

Nisbet, Robin G. M., ed. *M. Tulli Ciceronis in L. Calpurnium Pisonem Oratio*. Oxford: Clarendon, 1961.

Nock, Arthur Darby. *St. Paul*. New York: Harper & Brothers, 1938.

Norrick, Neal R. "Hyperbole." In *The Pragmatics Encyclopedia*, edited by Louise Cummings, 201–3. New York: Routledge, 2010.

———. "Hyperbole, Extreme Case Formulation." *Journal of Pragmatics* 36 (2004) 1727–39.

———. "On the Semantics of Overstatement." In *Sprache Erkennen und Verstehen*, edited by K. Detering, 168–76. Tübingen: Niemeyer, 1982.

O'Brien, Peter T. *The Epistle to the Philippians*. NIGTC. Grand Rapids: Eerdmans, 1991.
Padilla, Osvaldo. *The Acts of the Apostles: Interpretation, History and Theology*. Downers Grove, IL: InterVarsity, 2016.
Perrin, Laurent. "La Vérité dans l'Exagération: Comment les Rhétoriciens Voyaient les Dessous de l'Hyperbole." *Etudes de Lettres: Revue de la Faculté des Lettres, Université de Lausanne* (1991) 23–44.
Pervo, Richard I. *Acts*. Minneapolis: Fortress, 2009.
Philo. *The Works of Philo*. Translated by Charles Duke Yonge. Peabody, MA: Hendrickson, 1993.
Pitts, Andrew W. "Paul in Tarsus: Historical Factors in Assessing Paul's Early Education." In *Paul and Ancient Rhetoric: Theory and Practice in the Hellenistic Context*, edited by Stanley E. Porter and Bryan R. Dyer, 43–67. New York: Cambridge University Press, 2016.
Plato. *Gorgias*. Translated by W. R. M. Lamb. LCL 166. Cambridge: Harvard University Press, 1925.
Plutarch. *Essay on the Life and Poetry of Homer*. Edited by J. J. Keaney and Robert Lamberton. Atlanta: Scholars, 1996.
Polhill, John B. *Acts*. NAC 26. Nashville: Broadman, 2001.
Pomerantz, Anita. "Extreme Case Formulations: A Way of Legitimizing Claims." *Human Studies* 9 (1986) 219–29.
Porter, Stanley E. *The Apostle Paul: His Life, Thought, and Letters*. Grand Rapids: Eerdmans, 2016.
———. "Hellenistic Oratory and Paul of Tarsus." In *Hellenistic Oratory: Continuity and Change*, edited by Christos Kremmydas and Kathryn Tempest, 319–60. Oxford: Oxford University Press, 2013.
———. "Paul as Epistolographer *and* Rhetorician?" In *The Rhetorical Interpretation of Scripture: Essays from the 1996 Malibu Conference*, edited by Stanley E. Porter and Dennis L. Stamps, 222–48. JSNTSup 180. Sheffield, England: Sheffield, 1999.
———. *Paul in Acts*. Peabody, MA: Hendrickson, 2001.
———. "Paul of Tarsus and His Letters." In *Handbook of Classical Rhetoric in the Hellenistic Period, 330 B.C.–A.D. 400*, edited by Stanley E. Porter, 553–86. New York: Brill, 1997.
———. "The Theoretical Justification for Application of Rhetorical Categories to Pauline Epistolary Literature." In *Rhetoric and the New Testament: Essays from the 1992 Heidelberg Conference*, edited by Stanley E. Porter and Thomas H. Olbricht, 100–122. JSNTSup 90. Sheffield, England: Sheffield, 1993.
Porter, Stanley E., and Bryan R. Dyer. "Paul and Ancient Rhetoric: An Introduction to a Continuing Discussion." In *Paul and Ancient Rhetoric: Theory and Practice in the Hellenistic Context*, edited by Stanley E. Porter and Bryan R. Dyer, 1–10. New York: Cambridge University Press, 2016.
Quintilian. *The Orator's Education*. Translated by Donald A. Russell. LCL 124–28, 494. Cambridge: Harvard University Press, 2001.
Räisänen, Heikki. *Paul and the Law*. 2nd ed. WUNT 29. Tübingen: Mohr Siebeck, 1983. Repr., Eugene, OR: Wipf & Stock, 2010.
Ramsay, William M. *The Bearing of Recent Discoveries on the Trustworthiness of the New Testament*. London: Hodder & Stoughton, 1915. Repr., Grand Rapids: Baker, 1953.
———. *The Cities of St. Paul: Their Influence on His Life and Thought*. London: Hodder and Stoughton, 1907. Repr., Grand Rapids: Baker, 1949.

———. *Historical Commentary on Galations*. Edited by Mark Wilson. Grand Rapids: Kegel, 1997.

———. *St. Paul the Traveller and the Roman Citizen*. London: Hodder and Stoughton, 1897. Repr., Grand Rapids: Baker, 1962.

Reumann, John. *Philippians*. The Anchor Yale Bible 33B. New Haven: Yale University Press, 2008.

Rhoads, David, Joanna Dewey, and Donald Michie. *Mark as Story: An Introduction to the Narrative of a Gospel*. 2nd ed. Minneapolis: Fortress, 1999.

Richardson, Peter. "Pauline Inconsistency: 1 Corinthians 9:19–23 and Galatians 2:11–14." *NTS* 26 (1980) 347–62.

Richardson, Peter, and Paul W. Gooch. "Accommodation Ethics." *TynBul* 29 (1978) 89–142.

Ridderbos, Herman. *The Epistle of Paul to the Churches of Galatia*. NICNT. Grand Rapids: Eerdmans, 1953.

Roberts, J. H. "Paul's Expression of Perplexity in Galatians 1:6: The Force of Emotive Argumentation." *Neot* 26 (1992) 329–38.

———. "ΘΑΥΜΑΖΩ: An Expression of Perplexity in Some Examples from Papyri Letters." *Neot* 25 (1991) 109–22.

Robertson, Archibald, and Alfred Plummer. *A Critical and Exegetical Commentary on the First Epistle of St. Paul to the Corinthians*. 2nd ed. ICC. Edinburgh: T. & T. Clark, 1914.

Rodriguez, Rafael, and Matthew Thiessen, eds. *The So-Called Jew in Paul's Letter to the Romans*. Minneapolis: Fortress, 2016.

Ropes, James Hardy. *The Singular Problem of the Epistle to the Galatians*. Cambridge: Harvard University Press, 1929.

Rowe, Galen O. "Style." In *Handbook of Classical Rhetoric in the Hellenistic Period 330 B.C.–A.D. 400*, edited by Stanley E. Porter, 121–58. New York: Brill, 1997.

Rudolph, David J. *A Jew to the Jews: Jewish Contours of Pauline Flexibility in 1 Corinthians 9:19–23*. WUNT 304. Tübingen: Mohr Siebeck, 2011.

Ruiz, Javier Herrero. *Understanding Tropes: At the Crossroads between Pragmatics and Cognition*. New York: Peter Lang, 2009.

Ryken, Leland. *How to Read the Bible as Literature and Get More Out of It*. Grand Rapids: Zondervan, 1984.

Sanders, E. P. *Paul and Palestinian Judaism*. Minneapolis: Fortress, 1977.

———. *Paul, the Law and the Jewish People*. Philadelphia: Fortress, 1983.

Sandy, D. Brent. *Plowshares and Pruning Hooks: Rethinking the Language of Biblical Prophecy and Apocalyptic*. Downers Grove, IL: InterVarsity, 2002.

Schlier, Heinrich. *Der Brief an die Galater*. 6th ed. Göttingen: Vandenhoeck & Ruprecht, 1989.

———. *Der Römerbrief*. Herders theologischer Kommentar zum Neuen Testament. Freiburg: Herder, 1979.

Schlosser, S. E. "Babe the Blue Ox: Minnesota Tall Tales." http://americanfolklore.net/folklore/2010/07/babe_the_blue_ox.html.

Schlueter, Carol J. *Filling Up the Measure: Polemical Hyperbole in 1 Thessalonians 2:14–16*. Sheffield, England: Sheffield Academic, 1994.

Schmithals, Walter. *Der Römerbrief: Ein Kommentar*. Gütersloh: Gütersloher, 1988.

———. "The Heretics in Galatia." In *Paul and the Gnostics*, 13–64. New York: Abingdon, 1972.

Schnabel, Eckhard J. *Acts*. Zondervan Exegetical Commentary on the New Testament. Grand Rapids: Zondervan, 2012.

Schneckenburger, Mathias. *Ueber den Zweck der Apostelgeschichte*. Bern: Fischer, 1841.

Schnelle, Udo. *Apostle Paul: His Life and Theology*. Translated by M. Eugene Boring. Grand Rapids: Baker, 2005.

Schoeni, Marc. "The Hyperbolic Sublime as a Master Trope in Romans." In *Rhetoric and the New Testament: Essays from the 1992 Heidelberg Conference*, edited by Stanley E. Porter and Thomas H. Olbricht, 171–92. JSNTSup 90. Sheffield, England: Sheffield Academic, 1993.

Schoeps, H. J. *Paul: The Theology of the Apostle in the Light of Jewish Religious History*. Translated by Harold Knight. Philadelphia: Westminster, 1959.

Schökel, Luis Alonso. *A Manual of Hebrew Poetics*. Rome: Editrice Pontificio Istituto Biblico, 1988.

Schreiner, Thomas R. *The Law and Its Fulfillment: A Pauline Theology of the Law*. Grand Rapids: Baker, 1993.

———. *Romans*. BECNT. Grand Rapids: Baker, 1998.

Seager, Robin. "Cicero and the 'False Dilemma.'" In *Praise and Blame in Roman Republican Rhetoric*, edited by Christopher Smith and Ralph Covino, 99–110. Wales: The Classical Press of Wales, 2011.

Searle, John R. *Expression and Meaning: Studies in the Theory of Speech Acts*. New York: Cambridge University Press, 1979.

Seibert, Eric A. "Harder than Flint, Faster than Eagles: Intensified Comparatives in the Latter Prophets." In *Inspired Speech: Prophecy in the Ancient Near East; Essays in Honor of Herbert B. Huffmon*, edited by John Kaltner and Louis Stulman, 286–301. New York: T. & T. Clark, 2004.

Seitz, Christopher R. *Figured Out: Typology and Providence in Christian Scripture*. Louisville: Westminster John Knox, 2001.

Seltzer, Claudia. "Does Paul Need to Be Saved?" *Biblical Interpretation* 13 (2005) 289–97.

Sheets, Herchel H. *When Jesus Exaggerated: The Master's Hyperboles*. Lima, OH: C.S.S., 1977.

Silva, Moisés. "Galatians." In *Commentary on the New Testament Use of the Old Testament*, edited by D. A. Carson and G. K. Beale, 785–812. Grand Rapids: Baker, 2007.

———. *Philippians*. BECNT. Grand Rapids: Baker, 2005.

———, ed. *New International Dictionary of New Testament Theology and Exegesis*. 2nd ed. 5 vols. Grand Rapids: Zondervan, 2014.

Sperber, Dan, and Deirdre Wilson. *Relevance: Communication and Cognition*. 2nd ed. Malden, MA: Blackwell, 1995.

Spitzbardt, Harry. "Overstatement and Understatement in British and American English." *Philologica Pragensia* 6 (1963) 277–86.

Stanley, Christopher D. *Paul and the Language of Scripture: Citation Technique in the Pauline Epistles and Contemporary Literature*. New York: Cambridge University Press, 1992.

Stein, Robert H. *A Basic Guide to Interpreting the Bible: Playing by the Rules*. 2nd ed. Grand Rapids: Baker, 2011.

———. *Difficult Sayings in the Gospels: Jesus' Use of Overstatement and Hyperbole*. Grand Rapids: Baker, 1985.

———. *The Method and Message of Jesus' Teachings*. Rev. ed. Louisville: Westminster John Knox, 1994.
Stendahl, Krister. *Paul Among Jews and Gentiles*. Minneapolis: Fortress, 1976.
Stevenson, Tom. "Tyrants, Kings and Fathers in the *Philippics*." In *Cicero's Philippics*, edited by Tom Stevenson and Marcus Wilson, 95–113. Auckland, New Zealand: Polygraphia, 2008.
Stowers, Stanley K. *A Rereading of Romans: Justice, Jews, and Gentiles*. New Haven: Yale University Press, 1994.
Stuckenbruck, Loren. "Theology, Exegesis and Paul's Thought: Reflections on *Paul and the Torah* by Lloyd Gaston." *Koinonia* 11 (1990) 130–53.
Sumney, Jerry L. "Studying Paul's Opponents: Advances and Challenges." In *Paul and His Opponents*, edited by Stanley Porter, 7–58. Atlanta: Society of Biblical Literature, 2005.
Süss, Wilhelm. *Ethos: Studien zur Älteren Griechischen Rhetorik*. Leipzig and Berlin: Teubner, 1910.
Syme, Ronald. *The Roman Revolution*. Oxford: Clarendon, 1939. Repr., Oxford: Oxford University Press, 1960.
Tatum, W. Jeffrey. "Invective Identities in *Pro Caelio*." In *Praise and Blame in Roman Republican Rhetoric*, edited by Christopher Smith and Ralph Covino, 165–80. Wales: The Classical Press of Wales, 2011.
Taylor, Mark. *1 Corinthians*. NAC 28. Nashville: B&H, 2014.
Tertullian. *Against Marcion*. Vol. 3. ANF. 1885. Repr., Peabody, MA: Hendrickson, 2004.
Theobald, Michael. "Wie die Bergpredigt gelesen werden will: Zwölf Hinweise aus der Sicht heutiger Forschung." *Theologische Quartalschrift* 192 (2012) 256–80.
Thielman, Frank. *From Plight to Solution: A Jewish Framework for Understanding Paul's View of the Law in Galatians and Romans*. New York: Brill, 1989.
Thiessen, Matthew. *Paul and the Gentile Problem*. New York: Oxford University Press, 2016.
Thiselton, Anthony. *The First Epistle to the Corinthians: A Commentary on the Greek Text*. NIGTC. Grand Rapids: Eerdmans, 2000.
Thurén, Lauri. "'By Means of Hyperbole' (1 Cor 12:13b)." In *Paul and Pathos*, edited by Thomas H. Olbricht and Jerry L. Sumney, 97–114. Atlanta: Society of Biblical Literature, 2001.
———. *Derhetorizing Paul: A Dynamic Perspective on Pauline Theology and the Law*. Harrisburg, PA: Trinity Press International, 2002.
———. "Epistolography and Rhetoric: Case Not Closed." In *Paul and Ancient Rhetoric: Theory and Practice in the Hellenistic Context*, edited by Stanley E. Porter and Bryan R. Dyer, 141–59. New York: Cambridge University Press, 2016.
———. "Was Paul Angry? Derhetorizing Galatians." In *The Rhetorical Interpretation of Scripture: Essays from the 1996 Malibu Conference*, edited by Stanley E. Porter and Dennis L. Stamps, 302–21. JSNTSup 180. Sheffield, England: Sheffield Academic, 1999.
Tichy, Ladislav. "The 'Gospel' in Gal 1:6–7 Revisited." *NovT* 56 (2014) 359–72.
Towner, Philip H. *The Letters to Timothy and Titus*. NICNT. Grand Rapids: Eerdmans, 2006.
Tryphonis. "Περὶ Τρόπων." In *Rhetores Graeci*, edited by Leonhard von Spengel, 191–206. Vol. 3. Leipzig, 1856.

Tyson, Joseph B. "Wrestling With and For Paul: Efforts to Obtain Pauline Support by Marcion and the Author of Acts." In *Contemporary Studies in Acts*, edited by Thomas E. Phillips, 13–28. Macon, GA: Mercy University Press, 2009.

Uría, Javier. "The Semantics and Pragmatics of Ciceronian Invective." In *Cicero on the Attack: Invective and Subversion in the Orations and Beyond*, edited by Joan Booth, 47–70. Wales: The Classical Press of Wales, 2007.

Van Unnik, W. C. *Tarsus or Jerusalem: The City of Paul's Youth*. Translated by George Ogg. London: Epworth, 1962.

Vielhauer, Philipp. "On the 'Paulinism' in Acts." In *Studies in Luke-Acts*, edited by Leander E. Keck and J. Louis Martyn, 33–50. Philadelphia: Fortress, 1966.

Vincent, Marvin R. *A Critical and Exegetical Commentary on the Epistles to the Philippians and to Philemon*. ICC. Edinburgh, Scotland: T. & T. Clark, 1897.

Wallace, Daniel B. *Greek Grammar Beyond the Basics: An Exegetical Syntax of the New Testament*. Grand Rapids: Zondervan, 1996.

Watson, Duane F. "The Influence of George Kennedy on Rhetorical Criticism of the New Testament." In *Words Well Spoken: George Kennedy's Rhetoric of the New Testament*, edited by C. Clifton Black and Duane F. Watson, 41–62. Waco: Baylor University Press, 2008.

———. "The Three Species of Rhetoric and the Study of the Pauline Epistles." In *Paul and Rhetoric*, edited by J. Paul Sampley and Peter Lampe, 25–47. New York: T. & T. Clark, 2010.

Watson, Francis. *Paul, Judaism and the Gentiles*. SNTSMS 56. New York: Cambridge University Press, 1986.

Watson, L. C. "Invective." *OCD*: 740.

Watson, Wilfred G. E. *Classical Hebrew Poetry*. JSOTSup 26. Sheffield, England: JSOT, 1984.

———. "Hebrew Poetry." In *Text in Context: Essays by Members of the Society for Old Testament Study*, edited by A. D. H. Mayes, 253–88. New York: Oxford University Press, 2000.

———. *Traditional Techniques in Classical Hebrew Verse*. JSOTSup 170. Sheffield, England: Sheffield, 1994.

Weaver, Dorothy Jean. "Transforming Nonresistance: From *Lex Talionis* to 'Do Not Resist the Evil One.'" In *The Love of Enemy and Nonretaliation in the New Testament*, edited by Willard M. Swartley, 32–61. Louisville: Westminster John Knox, 1992.

Weiss, Johannes. *The History of Primitive Christianity*. New York: Wilson-Erickson, 1937.

Westerholm, Stephen. *Israel's Law and the Church's Faith: Paul and His Recent Interpreters*. Grand Rapids: Eerdmans, 1988.

White, John L. "Introductory Formulae in the Body of the Pauline Letter." *JBL* 90 (1971) 91–97.

Whitekettle, Richard. "When More Leads to Less: Overstatement, *Incrementum*, and the Question in Job 4:17a." *JBL* 129 (2010) 445–48.

Witherington, Ben. *New Testament Rhetoric: An Introductory Guide to the Art of Persuasion in and of the New Testament*. Eugene, OR: Cascade, 2009.

Wright, N. T. *Paul and the Faithfulness of God*. 2 vols. Minneapolis: Fortress, 2013.

Zetterholm, Karin Hedner. "The Question of Assumptions: Torah Observance in the First Century." In *Paul within Judaism: Restoring the First-Century Context to the*

Apostle, edited by Mark D. Nanos and Magnus Zetterholm, 32–61. Minneapolis: Fortress, 2015.

Ziesler, John. *Paul's Letter to the Romans*. TPINTC. Philadelphia: SCM, 1989.

Zuck, Roy B. *Basic Bible Interpretation*. Wheaton, IL: Victor, 1991.

———. *Teaching as Jesus Taught*. Eugene, OR: Wipf and Stock, 2002.

Scripture Index

GENESIS

4:24	133
6:5	134
6:9	135
11:4	135
13:16	134
15	222
15:5	134
17	60, 222, 249
17:1	135, 221
17:10	221
18:3	135
18:5	135
18:19	221
18:27	135
20:3	135
22:16–18	221
22:17	134
25:32	135
26:4	134
26:5	221
28:14	134
29:31	135
29:33	135
31:7	133
31:41	133
32:12	134
41:49	134
42:10	135
42:11	135
42:13	135
42:28	136

EXODUS

3:8	135
12:33	135
16:3	136
18:21	135
19:5–6	217
20:2	239
20:5	135
22:26–27	154
32:8	183
32:13	134

LEVITICUS

26:26	133

NUMBERS

6:1–21	28
6:18	27
11:6	135
11:29	135
13:33	135, 142
14:22	133
23:10	134

DEUTERONOMY

1:10	134
1:21	134
1:28	135, 141–43
4:6	217
7:14	135
8:7–9	135

DEUTERONOMY (cont.)

9:1	135
10:22	134
18:15–18	221
20:8	142
21:15–17	135
23:18	163
24:3	135
24:12–13	154
27–28	56
27:26	11, 56, 59, 233–36, 249
28:62	134
28:67	136
30:1–10	221
30:11–14	28
30:12–14	23
30:14	226
30:15	221
32:21	24
33:2	4, 6, 212

JOSHUA

2:11	136, 142
5:1	136, 142
7:5	136, 142
11:4	134
11:23	134
20:16	136
21:44–45	134

JUDGES

2:17	183
4:16	134
5:20	137
7:12	134
15:2	135

RUTH

2:13	135
4:15	133

1 SAMUEL

1:8	133
1:11	135
2:5	133
13:5	134
17:43	135, 163
18:7	134
21:11	134
24:14	163
24:15	135
25:28	135
26:20	135
29:5	134
29:6	135
29:9	135

2 SAMUEL

1:23	124, 135
3:8	135, 163
5:6	136
9:8	135, 163
10:3	192
14:17–20	135
16:9	135
17:11	134
17:12	134
19:1	136
19:28	135
22:43	135
24:3	134

1 KINGS

1:31	133
1:40	135, 136
4:20	134
4:29	134
10:5	136
10:27	132, 134
12:10	135
14:23	134
19:4	136
19:10	134
20:10	134
20:27	134

2 KINGS

6:17	134
8:13	163
16:4	134
17:10	134
18:32	135
19:23–24	136
21:16	134

Scripture Index

1 CHRONICLES

19:3	192
27:23	134
29:15	136

2 CHRONICLES

1:9	134
28:4	134
36:23	134

NEHEMIAH

2:3	133
4:3	136
4:12	133
9:23	134

JOB

1:1	135
3:4–9	133
3:15	134
4:17	137
6:3	134
14:2	136
14:13	135
16:11–16	133
19:3	133
20:17	135
22:6	136
24:7	136
24:10	136
27:16	131, 134
29:18	134
30:19	136
37:1	131

PSALMS

1	217
3:6	134
5:5	164
5:10	131
6:6	136
6:8	164
14:4	164
18:42	135
19	217
19:4	24
19:7–11	239
21:4	133
21:22	125
22:14	134, 136
22:16–18	133
23:1	124
32:3	136
36:12	164
37:31	226
40:2	136
40:8	226
42:3	xi
61:7	133
68:18	212
69:2–3	133
69:4	134
69:14–15	133
72:5	133
74:1	133
74:3	133
78:27	134
79:3	134
102:11	136
103:15	136
109:23	136
119	217, 239
119:136	136
119:164	133
139:18	134
141:7	131
144:4	136

PROVERBS

1:22	135
3:9–10	135
10:3	135
13:21	135
15:1	135
17:10	134
19:4	136
24:16	133
25:21–22	160
26:11	163
26:15	136
26:17	163

ECCLESIASTES

6:3	133
6:6	133, 134

ECCLESIASTES (cont.)

6:12	136
7:19	133
8:12	134
10:20	137

SONG

2:2	135
2:5	135
2:8	136
5:8	135
5:10	134
6:4	135
6:5	135
8:6	135
8:7	135

ISAIAH

1:21	136
2:1–4	226
2:7	134
4:1	133
5:10	133
5:11	136
5:22	136
5:27	135
10:14	136
10:22	134
13:7	142
13:10	136
13:12	132
14:13–14	136
19:1	142
20:2–4	136
28:8	134
34:10	133, 135
37:24–25	136
40:2	133
40:6	136
40:22	135
41:15	135
42:2	226
42:4	226
47:8	136
48:19	131, 134
52:17	24
53:1	24
56:5	132
58:7	136
60:4–7	140
65:1	24
65:2	24

JEREMIAH

4:13	132
4:23–26	136
5:3	131
5:16–17	133
7:26	132
8:16	135
9:1	136
9:21	134
9:22	131
13:13	134
15:7–9	133
15:8	131, 134
15:14	133
16:12	132
17:27	133
18:16	133
31:29	137
31:31–34	222, 226
33:22	134
46:23	131
51:9	135

LAMENTATIONS

2:13	134

EZEKIEL

3:9	132
5:6–7	132
6:13	134
11:6	134
16:47	132
16:51–52	132
18:2	137
18:7	136
18:16	136
23:11	132
28:2	136
28:3	132
28:9	136
30:11	134

Scripture Index

36:27	222, 227
37:1	134

DANIEL

1:20	133
2:4	133
3:9	133
5:10	133
6:6	133
6:21	133
11:36	136

HOSEA

1:10	134
2:11	136

JOEL

2	133
4:18	135

AMOS

2:9	135
2:16	136
4:1	136
5:3	133
6:9	133
9:2–4	133

OBADIAH

4	135

JONAH

2:6	133

MICAH

5:5	133
5:7	134
6:6–7	133
6:7	134

NAHUM

3:15b–17	133
3:16	131, 134

HABAKKUK

1:8	132
1:9	134

ZEPHANIAH

3:3	136

HAGGAI

2:16	133

ZECHARIAH

8:5	134
9:3	131, 134

MALACHI

1:3	135

MATTHEW

2:3	146
2:10	148, 149
3:5	146
3:11	147
4:23	146
4:24	146
5–7	221
5:3–10	147
5:16	147
5:17–48	155
5:17–20	153, 217
5:17	15, 221, 226
5:18	16, 226
5:19	147, 226
5:20	147
5:21–26	150
5:22	147, 163
5:27–30	150
5:28–30	147
5:29–30	147
5:30	xi
5:31–32	150
5:32	147
5:33–37	147, 150
5:34	147
5:38–41	153–58
5:39–41	147
5:42	125, 147, 150

MATTHEW (cont.)

5:48	147
6:3	147
6:4	147
6:24	147
7:1	123
7:3	147
7:6	163
7:7	147
8:8	147
8:20	148
8:34	146
9:24	145, 148
9:35	146
10:30	146
11:11	147
12:15	146
12:25	146
12:30	147
12:36–37	163
14:35	146
15:26	163
16:19	148
16:23	148, 151
17:2	145, 146
17:20	147
17:23	148
18:19	148
19:24	147
20:1–16	147
21:10	146, 149
21:22	147
22:40	15
23:6–7	152
23:13–35	148
23:13	151, 195
23:15	146, 151, 152, 153
23:16	151
23:17	151
23:23	151, 153
23:24	147, 151
23:25	146, 151
23:27–28	146
23:27	151
23:29	151
23:33	151, 153
24:2	123
26:22	148
26:38	148
26:52	147
26:63–64	150
26:63b	147
27:25	146
27:54	148

MARK

1:7	147
1:28	146, 149
1:33	146
1:37	146
1:45	146
4:34	147
5:5	146
5:20	146
5:26	148
5:42	148
6:4	147
6:33	146, 149
7:27	163
7:37	148
8:36	146
9:15	146, 148, 149
9:23	147
9:40	147
10:26	148
10:30	146
11:18	148
12:44	148
13:1–2	148
13:24–25	148
14:33–34	148
14:53	146
16:18	148

LUKE

1:6	147
1:65	146
2:25	147
2:37	146
2:40	146
2:47	146
3:3	146
3:15	146
3:21	146
4:15	146
4:22	146

4:24	147	**JOHN**	
4:28	146	2:10	146
4:37	146	3:26	146
4:40	146	3:32	146
5:17	146	6:53	147
5:26	148, 149	6:70	148, 151
5:39	147	7:7	147
6:19	146, 149	7:38	147
6:20	126	8:33	146
6:37	147	8:44	148, 151
7:17	146	9:33	146
7:29	146	9:39–41	145, 148
8:37	146, 148	11:11	145, 148
9:25	146	11:49	146
9:58	148	12:19	146
10:4	146	12:25	147
10:19	148	14:26	146
11:23	147	16:6	146
12:46	147	18:22–23	154
13:17	146	21:25	146
13:32	148		
13:34	42	**ACTS**	
14:16–24	147		
14:26	147	1:1–11	42
15:1–7	147	1:67	43
15:32	148	2–3	180
16:10	147	2:5	146
16:13	147	2:47	146
16:17	16	3:19–21	43
17:6	147	3:25–26	42
17:10	147	5:3	146
18:43	146	5:28	146
19:7	146	5:29	160
19:40	147	6:15	146
21:38	146	7:38	4, 6
22:4	146	7:51	146, 147, 148
22:44	145, 148	7:52–53	42
22:70	146	7:53	4, 6, 206, 212
23:5	146	7:58—8:3	42
23:33–49	42	9:1	42
23:48	146	9:13	42
23:49	146	9:20	39
23:50–56	42	10:22	146
24:1–11	42	10:42	43
24:12–53	42	13	43
24:44	221	13:10	148
		13:13–43	38
		15:1–2	26
		15:1	189, 191

ACTS *(cont.)*

15:8	248
15:19–29	249
15:24	184
16:3	25–26, 34, 43, 45, 49, 227, 239
16:9–10	27
17:6	146, 200
17:13–16	39
17:18	148
17:21	146
17:24–27	42
17:31	43
18:1	42
18:18	27, 30, 34, 45, 227, 239
19:21	28, 239
20	28
20:6	28, 30, 227
20:16	28–29, 34, 227, 239
20:31	146
21	18, 29–31, 37
21:13	148
21:17–26	34, 43, 47, 49
21:17	29
21:20–24	239
21:20	29
21:21	29, 180
21:23–26	45
21:23–24a	29, 227
21:24	206
21:24b	29
21:26	30, 227
21:28	146
21:31	146
21:38	200
21:39	48
22:3	31, 48, 116
23	3
23:1	31, 34, 227
23:2–5	154
23:3	31
23:5	30, 31
23:6	31, 32, 34, 227
24:5	148
24:11–21	32
24:14	31, 32, 34, 227
24:16	32, 34, 227
24:21	31
25:8	33, 34, 227
26:4–5	31
26:5	33, 34, 227
26:6–8	31
26:22–23	38
26:22	31
28:22	146
28:26	42

ROMANS

1:8	158, 159
1:9–10	158, 159
1:9	147, 150
1:19–23	42
1:19	38
1:29	158
2	205
2:7	21
2:8–9	21
2:10	21
2:14–15	21
2:17	213
2:26	206
3:1–2	160, 239
3:1	19, 213
3:9–20	21
3:20	19, 22, 217
3:21	22
3:27–31	28
4	63
4:6	115
4:9	115
4:12	63
4:15	8, 21
4:17	63
4:18	63
4:19–22	63
5:13	8
5:19	192
5:20	8, 20, 217
6:2–4	159, 161
6:14–15	222
6:21	23
6:22	23
7:4	227
7:5	20, 217
7:7	8
7:9–11	159, 161
7:9	21

7:10	19	16:19	158, 159
7:11–13	19		
7:11	222	**1 CORINTHIANS**	
7:12–16	28	1:4–5	158
7:12–13	239	1:7	158
7:12	19, 213, 217, 227	1:8	23
7:13	8, 21	1:17	117
7:14	19, 159, 213, 227	1:22	48
7:22	19, 213	1:24	48
7:25	19, 213	1:25	159
8:2	227	2:1–5	117
8:7	19, 213	2:2	158
8:13	159, 161	2:4	115
8:28	125, 158, 161	3:2	159
9–11	42	3:7	158
9:3	169	3:21	158
9:4–5	22, 239	4:6	115
9:6	24	4:8–13	125, 159, 160
9:11	183	4:8	200
9:13	159	4:11	159
9:28	115	4:12	186
9:30—10:21	23	4:13	159, 160
9:30	24	5:3	123
9:31	24	5:5	159, 160
9:33	24	6:1–6	123
10:1–4	23	6:12	158
10:2–3	24	6:15	159
10:4	22–24, 228	7:17–24	51
10:5–21	23	7:17	51
10:6–8	28	7:18–19	26, 28
11:3	42	7:19	49, 51, 158, 160
11:7–8	42	7:29–31	158
11:11	43	8–10	45
11:13	48	8:1—11:1	45, 48–50
12:9–21	227	8:1	48
12:14	186	9:19–23	43, 44–51, 123
12:20	154, 158, 160	9:19	43
13	160	9:20	30, 43, 45, 47
13:1	158	9:21	50
13:7	23	9:22	158
13:8–14	227	9:27	45
13:9	115	10:11	23
14–15	45	10:19–20	50
14	44	10:23	158
14:8	227	10:32–33	45, 50
15	42	10:32	48, 49
15:7–13	42	10:33	158
15:14	158	11:1	50

1 CORINTHIANS *(cont.)*

11:2	158
12:3	169
12:13	48
13:1–3	125, 159
13:2	158
13:7	158
14:3	115
15	42
15:1–11	42
15:8	161
15:9	159, 161
15:24	23
15:30–31	158
15:30	160
15:31	xi, 160
16:22	169

2 CORINTHIANS

1:13	23
1:23	147, 150
3:6	159, 161
3:13	23
4:4	159
4:8	158
6:8	115
6:10	159
7:4	158
8:3	158
8:7	158
10:10	117
11:1	200
11:6	117
11:13	159, 161
11:15	23
11:17	117
11:24	48
11:26	192
12:11	159, 160

GALATIANS

1:1	64
1:6–7	179–85
1:6	202
1:7–9	171
1:7–8	199
1:7	172, 189
1:8–9	64, 167, 185–89
1:8	4, 167–72
1:9	172, 182
1:10	44
1:13	55
1:15–24	39
1:15	183
1:20	147, 150
1:23	55
2:1–10	189
2:1	25
2:2	190
2:3–5	26
2:3	25, 26, 48
2:4	184, 189–94
2:6	190
2:7	179
2:9	184, 190
2:10–14	55
2:11–15	55
2:11–14	47
2:12	30, 48
2:13	26
2:14	48
2:15–21	54, 60
2:15–19	52
2:15	55
2:16	55
2:18	14, 55, 225
2:19	3, 15, 55–56, 224
3	63, 65–66
3:1–5	236
3:1–2	21
3:2	8, 243
3:3	181
3:5	8
3:6–9	236
3:8	58
3:10–14	52, 56, 58, 60, 236
3:10	10, 11, 27, 233–38, 242, 244
3:13–14	59
3:13	11
3:14	58–59
3:15–23	236
3:16	5
3:17	4, 5
3:18	5
3:19–25	10
3:19	14, 20
3:19b	7–10, 215–20

Scripture Index

3:19c	224–30	5:4	199
3:19d–20	4–7	5:8	159, 160
3:19d	211–15	5:18	158
3:21	9, 220	6:18	158
3:22–25	9–10		
3:22–24	220–24	### PHILIPPIANS	
3:22–23	11	1:3	158, 159
3:23	14	1:7	115
3:23b	224–30	1:8	147
3:24	9, 57	1:11	158
3:25	15, 224–30	1:13	158
3:26—4:31	236	1:27	31
3:28	49, 227	2:1	115
4:1–11	238	2:21	158
4:3	11, 12, 27, 57, 238–41	3:2	127, 159, 162–67
4:4–5	15, 225	3:5	51
4:4	57	3:19	23, 159, 161, 167
4:5	57	3:20	31
4:9	12, 15, 57, 225, 238–41	4:4	158
4:10	13, 181, 239	4:13	158
4:12–20	196		
4:14	169	### COLOSSIANS	
4:15	115	1:9	158, 159
4:17	195–98	1:15–20	52
4:21–31	57, 59, 60	2:13	159, 161
4:24	115	3:3	159, 161
4:25	59	3:5	159
5:2–4	11–13, 241–46	4:10–11	48
5:2	26, 181		
5:3	16, 27, 60, 206	### 1 THESSALONIANS	
5:6	28, 49	1:2	158, 159
5:8	183	1:8	158, 159
5:11	26	2:7	158
5:12	198–201	2:9	158, 159
5:14	4, 15–16, 123, 213, 217, 228	2:12	115, 183
5:16—6:10	236	2:14–16	159, 161
6:2	123, 213, 217	2:16	23
6:12	177, 181	3:2	39
6:12b	201–4	3:10	158, 159
6:13	60, 202	4:13–15	145, 159
6:13a	205–7	5:16–17	158
6:15	28, 49	5:24	183
### EPHESIANS		### 2 THESSALONIANS	
2:1	159, 161	1:3	158, 159
2:11	48	3:10	150
3:8	159, 161		
3:19	158		

1 TIMOTHY

1:5	23
1:15	159, 161
1:20	159, 160
4:2	159, 161
4:4	158
5:6	159
6:4	158
6:10	158

2 TIMOTHY

1:3	158, 159
1:4	158
1:15	158, 160
2:7	158
2:17	158
2:26	159
3:12	158
4:17	125, 159

TITUS

1:10	159, 161
1:12	158
1:15	158
3:2	158
3:3	159

PHILEMON

4	158, 159

HEBREWS

2:2	4, 6
2:15	148
2:17	146
4:15	146
5:12	12, 148
6:6b	147
7:3	146
11	221
11:4	147
11:12	146, 149

JAMES

1:5	147
1:8	146, 149
2:10	146, 149
3:2	147
3:5–12	163
3:6	148
3:7	146, 150
3:8	146
3:16	146, 150
4:11	163
4:14	148
5:1–6	148

1 PETER

1:24	148
2:2	148
2:13–14	147
5:8	145, 146

2 PETER

1:9	145, 148
2:1	152, 192
2:15	148, 153
3:4	145, 148

1 JOHN

2:11	145, 148
2:15	147
3:8	147
3:15	146
3:22	147
5:15	147

JUDE

11	148
23	148

REVELATION

1:10	145, 146
3:17	145. 148
6:1	146
9:7–10	146
18:5	146
22:15	163

Subject Index

extreme case formulations, 77–78, 124

Gricean theory, 81–82, 122

hyperbole
   amplification, 96–97, 126
   basic, 76
   categories, 75–80
   characteristics, 72–75
   comparisons, 124
   composite, 76, 131
   criteria, 87–90, 121–29
   definition, 71–72
   discrepancy, 75
   economy of expression, 125
   extreme case formulations (see Extreme case formulations)
   figurative language, 125
   gradability, 74
   intentionality, 73
   invective (see Invective)
   metaphorical, 76, 124, 131
   mitigation, 85–86
   modulation, 74
   nature, 69–90
   nonveridicality, 72–73
   pathos, 127
   rhetoric (see rhetoric of hyperbole)
   rhetorical situation, 126–27
   shock, 127
   subjectivity, 73–74

taxonomies, 78–80
universal language (see Extreme case formulations)

invective (vilification)
   against Paul's opponents, 175–209
   audience, 106–7
   criterion for hyperbole, 128
   definition, 104
   in the New Testament, 109–12, 152–53
   practice, 104–6
   truth, 107–9
   used by Jesus, 151

law
   consequences, 11–14, 21–22, 233–47
   duration, 14–16, 22–24, 224–30
   origin, 4–7, 19, 211–15
   purpose, 7–10, 19–21, 215–24

metaphors, primary, 85

New Perspective on Paul, xiii, 65–66, 191

Paul
   birth, 116
   circumcision of Timothy, 25–27
   defense speeches, 31–33
   education, 116–17

Paul *(cont.)*
    opponents, 175–78
    rhetorician, 112–18
    vow at Cenchrea, 27–28
Paul within Judaism, xiii, 51–61,
    65–66
pragmatic effects, 84–85

quality maxim, 81–82

relevance theory, 82–84
rhetoric (of hyperbole)
    Ad Herennium, 94–95

Aristotle, 93–94
Cicero, 95
Demetrius, 100
Lausberg, 100
Longinus, 99
Martin, 101–2
Porter, 102
Quintilian, 95–98

speech act theory, 80–81

Tübingen school, 36–38, 40–41

www.ingramcontent.com/pod-product-compliance
Lightning Source LLC
Chambersburg PA
CBHW071239230426
43668CB00011B/1513